William Sims, Richard Frewin

The rates of merchandize, as settled by the acts of 12 Car. II. cap. 4.

11 Geo. I. cap. 7.

And subsequent acts of Parliment; with the duties and drawbacks payable on all goods imported, exported, and carried coastwise

William Sims, Richard Frewin

The rates of merchandize, as settled by the acts of 12 Car. II. cap. 4. 11 Geo. I. cap. 7.

And subsequent acts of Parliment; with the duties and drawbacks payable on all goods imported, exported, and carried coastwise

ISBN/EAN: 9783337713294

Printed in Europe, USA, Canada, Australia, Japan

Cover: Foto ©ninafisch / pixelio.de

More available books at **www.hansebooks.com**

RATES OF MERCHANDIZE,

As settled by the ACTS of

12 CAR. II. cap. 4.   11 GEO. I. cap. 7.

AND

Subsequent ACTS OF PARLIAMENT.

WITH THE

DUTIES AND DRAWBACKS

PAYABLE ON ALL GOODS

IMPORTED, EXPORTED, AND CARRIED COASTWISE.

TOGETHER WITH THE

BOUNTIES, PREMIUMS, AND ALLOWANCES,

ON

IMPORTATION AND EXPORTATION.

AND ALSO

A LIST OF GOODS

PROHIBITED TO BE

IMPORTED INTO, OR EXPORTED FROM,

GREAT BRITAIN.

COMPILED,

By Order of the COMMISSIONERS of His Majesty's CUSTOMS,

By WILLIAM SIMS and RICHARD FREWIN,

Of the LONG ROOM, CUSTOM-HOUSE, LONDON.

LONDON:

Printed by T. HARRISON and S. BROOKE, Warwick-Lane.
M.DCC.LXXXII.

CONTENTS.

	Page
Table of Reference - - - - - - -	vi
List of Branches - - - - - - - - -	vii
The One per Cent. Duty - - - - - - -	ix
Goods Inwards, the Net Duties and Drawbacks, with the Rates thereon - - - - - - - - - - -	3
Duties and Drawbacks on Wine - - - - - -	303
London Duty on Wine - - - - - - - -	314
Duty and Drawbacks on Unrated East India Goods - - -	316
Goods Outwards, the Net Duties, with the Rates thereon - -	322
Goods Coastwise Inwards - - - - - - -	357
Goods Coastwise Outwards - - - - - - -	358
Bounties, Premiums, and Allowances - - - - -	359
List of Goods prohibited to be imported or exported - - - -	371

A TABLE

Whereby the REFERRING LETTERS in the Column between the DUTIES and DRAWBACKS explain the particular Branches to which any Article of Goods is liable by correspondent Numbers, distinguishing those Branches as they stand in the LIST on the opposite Side.

Referring Letters	Corresponding Numbers distinguishing the several Branches.	Referring Letters	Corresponding Numbers distinguishing the several Branches.	Referring Letters	Corresponding Numbers distinguishing the several Branches.
A	1 2 3 4 5 44	F u	1 2 3 4 5 11 16 22 23 44	U a	1 2 3 44
A a	1 2 3 5 44	F w	1 III 2 3 4 5 6 11 44	O b	1 2 3 4 5 32 44
A b	1 2 3 5 10 44	F y	10 44	O c	1 2 3 4 5 6 10 11 22 23 44
A c	1 2 3 5 12 44	F z	1 2 3 44		17 44
A d	1 5 10 44		1 2 3 4 8 11 12 14 15 16 43 44 45	P b	1 2 3 44
A e	6 44	G	1 2 3 4 5 10 11 14 15 16 43 44 45	P c	1 2 3 4 44
A f	1 2 3 4 5 6 44	G a	1 2 3 4 5 10 11 44	P d	38
A g	1 2 3 4 5 10 44	G b	1 2 3 5 10 28 29 44		1 III 2 3 4 5 10 11 37 44
B	1 44	G c	1 2 3 5 6 10 28 29 44	Q	19 44
B a	1 5 44	G d	1 2 3 4 6 10 11 44	Q a	1 2 3 4 5 11 24 25 44
B b	1 2 3 4 5 32 44	G e	20 2 3 6 10 39 44	Q c	1 2 3 4 5 24 25 44
B c	1 2 5 11 44	H	20 27 44 5 9 44 48		40 44
B d	1 2 3 4 5 6 10 44	H a	1 2 3 4 5 8 12 14 15 43 44 45	R b	1 2 3 5 6 10 32 44
B e	1 2 3 4 5 11 44	H c	1 2 3 4 5 12 44	R c	22 44
C	1 III 2 3 5 6 10 44	H d	30 44 51	R e	1 2 3 5 6 11 16 37 44
C a	1 2 3 5 6 11 44	I a	1 2 3 4 5 12 44	R f	1 III 2 3 5 6 11 44
C b	1 III 2 3 5 6 10 43 44	I e	22 44	R h	1 2 3 5 6 11 30 44
C c	1 2 3 5 10 44		14 15 16 43 44 45	R i	38
C d	1 2 3 5 6 10 43 44	K	1 2 3 4 5 10 19 44	S	44 51 52 53 54
C e	1 2 3 4 5 10 44	K a	1 2 3 4 5 10 11 19 44	S a	1 2 3 4 5 11 23 44
C f	10 44	K b	1 III 2 3 4 5 12 44	S b	10 11 44
C g	5 7 13 44	K c	1 2 3 4 5 6 10 19 44	S c	1 2 3 5 6 10 44
D a	3 9 7 13 44	K d	1 2 3 4 5 6 10 19 44	S e	1 2 3 4 5 11 44
D b	33 44	K e	1 2 3 4 5 7 10 18 44	S h	1 2 3 4 5 12 23 25 44 46
D c	3 4 5 6 11 19 44	K h	1 III 1 2 3 4 5 6 10 17 44	T a	44 51
D d	44 49	L	1 2 3 5 11 19 44	T c	1 2 3 4 5 11 16 23 25 44 46
E a	11 44	L b	1 2 3 5 44	V b	1 2 3 5 6 9 44 46
E b	24 25 44	L c	1 2 3 6 13 22 44	V e	44 50
E c	1 2 3 4 5 11 12 44	L d	1 III 2 3 4 5 6 13 19 44	V f	30
E d	44 50	M	1 2 3 4 5 10 33 44	W a	1 2 3 4 5 6 10 24 25 44
E e	1 2 3 4 5 11 12 16 44	M a	4 44	W b	1 2 3 4 5 6 11 16 44
E f	1 2 3 5 10 44	M c	1 2 3 5 6 9 44	W c	1 2 3 4 5 10 24 44
F a	1 2 3 5 6 10 16 44	M d	16	W d	1 2 3 4 5 11 31 44
F b	11 10 44	M f	14	Z a	1 2 3 5 11 31 44
F c	1 2 3 4 5 6 10 16 44	N a	1 2 3 5 6 9 47 48	Z b	1 2 3 4 5 8 12 15 43 44 45
F f	25 44	N b	47	Z c	1 2 3 4 8 12 14 15 43 44 45
F g	1 2 3 4 5 11 16 19 44	N c	1 2 3 4 5 6 22 48	Z d	1 III 2 3 4 8 14 15 43 44 45
F h	20 44	N d	1 2 3 6 44 48	Z e	44 44
F m	1 2 3 5 6 11 16 44	N e	1 2 3 5 11 44 48	Z f	1 2 3 4 8 14 15 43 44 45
F n	1 2 3 4 5 6 44 48	N f	1 III 2 3 5 11 44 48	Z g	6 10 44
F o	1 2 3 4 5 11 10 44	O	1 2 3 4 5 11 22 23 44		
F p	1 III 2 3 4 5 11 10 44				
F q	1 2 3 4 5 10 44				

A LIST

OF THE

Several BRANCHES of the Revenue of CUSTOMS,

Referred to in the preceding TABLE.

I. OLD Subfidy.
II. Petty Cuftom.
III. Additional Duty.
IV. One per Cent. Inwards.
2. New Subfidy.
3. One Third Subfidy.
4. Two Thirds Subfidy.
5. Subfidy 1747.
6. Subfidy 1759.
7. Subfidies on Spirits.
8. Impoft on Wines and Vinegar.
9. Impoft on Tobacco.
10. Impoft 1690.
11. Impoft 1692.
12. Coinage on Wine and Beer, &c.
13. Coinage on Spirits.
14. Duty on Wine 1745.
15. Duty on Wine 1763.
16. Second 25 per Cent. on French goods.
17. Duty of 15 per Cent. on Muflins.
18. Duty on Spices, Pictures, &c.
19. Additional Duty on Spice, Pictures, &c.
20. Duty 1709 on Pepper, Raifins, &c.
21. Duty on Whalefins.
22. Duty on Hides, Skins, &c.
23. Additional Duty on ditto.
24. Duty on Sope, Paper, &c.
25. Additional Duty on ditto.
26. Duty on Coals imported and brought coaftwife.
27. Additional Duty on ditto.
28. Duty on Candles.
29. Additional Duty on Candles.
30. Duty on Sailcloth.
31. Duty on Wrought Plate.
32. Duty on Apples.
33. Duty on Hops.
34. Duty on Linen-yarn.
35. Duty on Gum Senega.
36. Additional Duty on ditto.
37. Duty on Crapes and Tiffanies.
38. Duty on India Wrought Silks, &c.
39. Additional Duty on Drillings and Broad Linen.
40. Additional Duty on Canvas and Lawns.
41. Duty on Coals and Culm for building Churches, &c.
42. Duty on Glafs.
43. Duty on Wine 1778.
44. Additional Impoft 1779.
45. Duty on Wine 1780.
46. Duty on Starch 1780.
47. Duty on Britifh Plantation Tobacco imported not directly from the place of its growth.
48. Duty on Sugar and Tobacco 1781.
49. Duty on Cotton Wool 1781.
50. Duty on Verdigreafe 1781.
51. Subfidy and One per Cent. Outwards.
52. Duty on Coals exported 1714.
53. Duty on Coals exported 1757.
54. Duty on Coals exported 1765.
55. Duty on Beaver-fkins exported 1764.
56. Duty on Cambricks exported 1766.

A TABLE of the DUTIES and DRAWBACKS on FRENCH GOODS, except those Articles that are particularly charged as such in their Alphabetical Course; and also except DRUGS, for which see Page 104 to 106.

Article	DUTIES to be paid on IMPORTATION.		Reference to the several Branches, see Page xvi.	DRAWBACKS to be repaid on EXPORTATION.*	
	By BRITISH.	By ALIENS.		If exported to any legal place, except as mentioned in the following column.	If the produce of Europe or the East Indies, and exported to the British Colonies in America.
	L. s. d. 20ths	*L. s. d.* 20ths		*L. s. d.* 20ths	*L. s. d.* 20ths
For every 20 s. of the Rate, or if not rated, for every 20 s. of the value upon oath:	0 14 8 8	0 14 11 11	F	0 9 2 8	0 8 8 8
On all goods of the produce of France, not for Dyers use, — if of the produce of France for Dyers use, as by 3 and 4 Ann. cap. 4. and not exempt from duty by 8 Geo. I. cap. 15.	0 12 7 4	0 12 10 7	F a	0 7 1 4	0 6 7 4
On all goods of the produce of any other French dominions, not for Dyers use	0 9 5 8	0 9 8 11	C	0 8 11 8	0 8 5 8
— if of the produce of any other French dominions, for Dyers use, as by 3 and 4 Ann. cap. 4. and not exempt from duty by 8 Geo. I. cap. 15.	0 7 4 4	0 7 7 7	Bd	0 6 10 4	0 6 4 4

* If imported by Aliens Drawback more, 1 s. 3 d. for every 1 col. of the Rate or Value.

The ONE PER CENT. DUTY,

Granted by 14 CAR. II. cap. 11. continued by several subsequent Acts, and by 7 ANN. cap. 14. & 1 GEO. I. cap. 12. made perpetual.

INWARDS.

THIS duty is payable, *over and above all other duties*, upon all goods and merchandizes (liable to Customs) imported from any port or place of the Mediterranean sea beyond the port of Malaga into any port of Great Britain, in any ship or vessel that hath not two decks, and doth carry less than 16 pieces of ordnance mounted, together with two men for each gun, and other ammunition proportionable; but British ships exporting from any of his Majesty's dominions fish (taken and cured by his Majesty's subjects only) so that one moiety of their full lading be fish only, in that case the goods or merchandizes imported in the same ship for that voyage are not liable to this duty.

The amount of this duty is as follows:

	For every Twenty Shillings of the Rate or Value.	
	DUTY.	DRAWBACK.
	£. s. d. 20ths	£. s. d. 20ths
On Earthen ware of the manufacture of Europe	0 0 5 5 2/4	0 0 5 5 2/4
Glass manufactures not rated by 12 Car. II. cap. 4.	0 0 3 15	0 0 3 3
Linen	0 0 3 15	0 0 3 3
Wrought Silks (being Crapes or Tiffanies)	0 0 3 15	0 0 3 3
Toys	0 0 3 7	0 0 3 3
Wine. *See the Table of duties, &c. on Wine, at the end of the Rates Inwards.*		
All other goods *liable to * Customs*	0 0 2 10 2/5	0 0 2 4/5

Except Pearl, Pot, Weed and Wood Ashes, Bound Books, Pictures, Raw Silk, and Succus Liquoritiæ, which being charged with a certain positive sum under every circumstance of importation, are therefore not affected by this duty.

* On Raisins —————————————— out of this duty in lieu of damage. See pag. 153 and 137.

OUTWARDS.

	DUTY.	
L.	s.	d. 20ths
0	0	2.10 ⅔

This duty is payable, *over and above all other duties*, upon all goods and merchandizes liable to the Subsidy Outwards, exported from any port of Great Britain, capable of a ship or vessel of 200 tons upon an ordinary full sea, to any part or place of the Mediterranean sea beyond the port of Malaga, in any ship or vessel that hath not two decks and doth carry less than 16 pieces of ordnance mounted, together with two men for each gun, and other ammunition proportionable.

The amount of this duty is as follows:

or every twenty shillings of the rate or value of all goods liable to the Subsidy Outwards ———

The One per Cent. duty being payable over and above all other duties under the particular circumstances of importation and exportation before mentioned, could not, consistent with the size of the page, be explained in the course of the Rates; it was therefore thought necessary, that the account of this duty should precede the general work.

RATES of GOODS and MERCHANDIZE

INWARDS,

As settled by the ACTS of

12 Car. II. cap. 4. and 11 Geo. I. cap. 7. &c.

INWARDS.

A.

INWARDS	DUTIES to be paid on IMPORTATION.		Reference to the several Branches, see Page vi.	DRAWBACKS to be repaid on EXPORTATION.*		RATES, or supposed value, by 12 Car. II. cap. 4. 11 Geo. I. cap. 7. from whence the foregoing Duties are computed.
	By BRITISH. £. s. d. 20ths	By ALIENS. £. s. d. 20ths		If exported to any legal place, except as mentioned in the following column. £. s. d. 20ths	If the produce of Europe or the East Indies, and exported to the British Colonies in America. £. s. d. 20ths	£. s. d.
ADZES for Coopers, the dozen	0 2 6 4/5	0 2 8 2 3/5	A			0 12 0
And besides for every Cwt. of Iron containing 112 lb.	0 5 3	0 5 3	D			
Aggets, small as a bean, the 100 dozen	0 2 9 12	0 2 11 14 3/5	A	0 2 5 12	0 2 1 12	0 13 0
— large, the piece	0 0 1 5 1/5	0 0 1 6 3 3/5/4		0 0 1 2 3/5	0 0 0 19 1/5	0 0 0
Ale. *Vide Beer.*						
Almonds. *Vide in Grocery.*						
Almonds bitter. *Vide in Drugs.*	0 0 12	0 0 17 3 3/4	A	0 0 11	0 0 9 12	0 5 0
Alphabets, the set containing twenty-four	0 15 9	0 16 8 3/4		0 13 10 10	0 12 0	3 15 0
Alpifti, or Canary feed, the Cwt.						2 0 0
Alum, the Cwt. for Dyers ufe, as by 3 & 4 Ann. cap. 4. Vide in Drugs for Ronifh or Roch Alum, and for Alumen Plume.	0 6 9 18	0 7 4 4	A d	0 5 9 18	0 4 9 18	
Amber, the pound						0 3 8
— the maft, containing 2 1/2 lb.	0 1 1 17	0 1 2 8 3/5	C	0 1 0 11	0 0 11 13 1/5	0 8 4
— beads, the pound	0 2 7 10	0 2 8 16 3 3/4	C	0 2 5 10	0 2 2 10 8	0 10 0
— oil. *Vide in Drugs.*						
Anchor-ftocks. *Vide in Wood.*						
Anchovies, the little barrel, not exceeding 16 lb. of fifth, as by 4 & 5 W. & M. cap. 5.	0 1 11 12 1/2	0 2 0 16 1/8	C	0 1 9 7 1/2	0 1 7 2 3/4	0 7 6

* But if imported by Aliens Drawback more, 1s. 3d. for every 100l. of the Rate or Value.

INWARDS.

	Duties to be paid on Importation. By British. £.	s.	d.	20ths	Duties to be paid on Importation. By Aliens. £.	s.	d.	20ths	Reference to the several Branches, see Page vi.	Drawbacks to be repaid on Exportation.* If exported to any legal place, except as mentioned in the following column. £.	s.	d.	20ths	Drawbacks to be repaid on Exportation.* If the produce of Europe or the East Indies, and exported to the British Colonies in America. £.	s.	d.	20ths	Rates, or supposed value, by 12 Car. II. cap. 4. & 11 Geo. I. cap. 7. from whence the foregoing Duties are computed. £.	s.	d.
Andirons or Creepers of Latten, the pound	0	0	3	3	0	0	3	6 3/20	C	0	0	2	17	0	0	2	11	0	1	0
——— Iron, the pair	0	2	1	4	0	2	2	15 1/2	A	0	1	10	4	—	—	—	—	0	10	0
And besides for every Cwt. of Iron	0	5	3		0	5	3		D	0	5	3		—	—	—	—			
Andlets, or Mayles, the pound ‖	0	0	7	11 1/5	0	0	8	0 13/20	A	0	0	6	13 1/5	0	0	5	15 1/5	0	3	0
And besides, if of Iron, *the Cwt.*	0	5	3		0	5	3		D	0	5	3		—	—	—	—			
Aneil of Barbary, the pound	0	0	3	15 3/5	0	0	4	0 13/40	A	0	0	3	6 3/5	0	0	3	6 3/5	0	1	6
Anniseeds. *Vide in* Grocery.																				
Annotto, the pound, for Dyers use, *as by* 3 & 4 *Ann. cap.* 4.	—	—	—	—	—	—	—	—		—	—	—	—	—	—	—	—	0	1	0
But by 8 *Geo. I. cap.* 15. § 10. *if regularly imported, entered, and landed,* duty free.																				
But on failure thereof, then to pay	0	0	1	5 1/5	0	0	1	8 7/25	Bb	0	0	0	19 1/5	0	0	0	13 1/5			
Anvils, the Cwt.	0	12	10	7	0	13	0	14 1/4	B	0	12	5	17	—	—	—	—	0	15	0
Apples, the bushel	0	2	2	0 4/5	0	2	2	1 17/25		0	0	1	18 4/5	0	0	1	16 4/5	0	0	4
——— the Barrel, containing 3 bushels	0	6	6	2 2/5	0	6	6	5 11/20	Bc	0	0	5	16 2/5	0	0	5	10 2/5	0	1	0
——— *vocat.* Pippins or Runnets, the barrel	0	6	11	3 1/5	0	6	11	12 13/20		0	0	10	5 1/5	0	0	9	7 1/5	0	3	0
But if of France, then more, Apples, the barrel	0	0	6	6	0	0	6	6	Fb	0	0	3	6	0	0	3	6			
But if of France, then more, Pippins, or Runnets, the barrel	0	1	6	18	0	1	6	18		0	0	9	18	0	0	9	18			
——— dried. *Vide* Pears.																				
Aqua fortis. *Vide in* Drugs.																				

‖ If Iron no Drawback to the British Colonies in America.

* But if imported by Aliens Drawback more, 1s. 3d. for every 100l. of the Rate or Value.

INWARDS.

	DUTIES to be paid on IMPORTATION.		DRAWBACKS to be repaid on EXPORTATION.*		RATES, or supposed value, by 12 Car. II. cap. 4. 11 Geo. I. cap. 7. from whence the foregoing Duties are computed.
	By BRITISH.	By ALIENS.	Reference to the several Branches, see Page vii. If exported to any legal place, except as mentioned in the following column.	If the produce of Europe or the East Indies, and exported to the British Colonies in America.	
	£. s. d. 20ths	£. s. d. 20ths	£. s. d. 20ths	£. s. d. 20ths	£. s. d.
Aqua vitæ, the barrel, containing 42 gallons, the hogshead	0 17 6	0 18 2 8	Db 0 16 2	0 14 10	2 13 4
	1 6 3	1 7 3 12	1 4 3	1 2 3	4 0 0
Subject also to the Excise duties.					
—— from Guernsey, Jersey, Sark or Alderney. See Spirits.					
Note, *That all Spirits called Brandy wine, or Aqua vitæ, imported in ships not belonging to Great-Britain or Ireland, or in foreign-built ships, pay duty as if imported by aliens,* 12 Car. II. cap. 18. § 9.					
Archella, or Spanish weed, for Dyers use, as by 3 & 4 Ann. cap. 4. the Cwt. But by 8 Geo. I. cap. 15. § 10. Archella, or Orchella, *if regularly imported, entered, and landed,* is duty free.	Bd 0 2 10 13	0 3 1 10 ¾	0 2 5 3	0 1 11 13	† 0 18 4
But on failure thereof, then to pay					
Argol, white and red, or powder, the Cwt. for Dyers use, as by 3 and 4 Ann. cap. 4. But by 8 Geo. I. c. 15. § 10. *if regularly imported, entered, and landed,* is duty free.	Bb 0 2 5 8	0 2 9 1 ¼	0 1 10 8	0 1 3 8	1 3 4
But on failure thereof, then to pay					

* But if imported by Aliens Drawback more, 1s. 5d. for every 100l. of the Rate or Value.

INWARDS.

	DUTIES to be paid on IMPORTATION.		Reference to the several Branches, see Page vi.	DRAWBACKS to be repaid on EXPORTATION.*		RATES, or supposed value, by 12 Car. II. cap. 4. †11 Geo. I. cap. 7. from whence the foregoing Duties are computed.
	By BRITISH.	By ALIENS.		If exported to any legal place, except as mentioned in the following column.	If the produce of Europe or the East Indies, and exported to the British Colonies in America.	
	£ s. d. 20ths	£ s. d. 20ths		£ s. d. 20ths	£ s. d. 20ths	£ s. d.
Armour old, the Cwt.	0 9 5 8	0 9 8 11				1 0 0
Arrack. For the duty, *vide* Spirits.						
Arrows for trunks, the groce, 12 dozen						
Ashes — Pot-ashes, the barrel, 220 weight	0 1 4 16	0 1 5 17	A	0 1 2 16	0 1 0 16	0 6 8
Note, that all Pot-ashes, &c. imported in ships not belonging to Great-Britain or Ireland, or imported in ships foreign-built, pay duty as if imported by Aliens, 12 Car. II. cap. 18. §9.						
Pearl-ashes of the produce of Germany may be imported from thence, paying the customs and duties as Pot-ashes, by 10 and 11 W. III. cap. 21. but of and from all other countries (America excepted, when accompanied with a proper certificate) they pay duty at value.						1 5 0
Wood or Sope-ashes, the last, 12 barrels	0 2 1 4	0 2 1 4	B			0 10 0
Pot-ashes of any country, the Cwt. —— But by 20 Geo. III. cap. 25. from May 31, 1780, until May 31, 1783.						0 6 0

* But if imported by Aliens Drawback more, 1s. 3d. for every 100l. of the Rate or Value.

INWARDS

	DUTIES to be paid on IMPORTATION.		Reference to the several Branches, see Page vi.	DRAWBACKS to be repaid on EXPORTATION*.		RATES, or supposed value, by 12 Car. II. cap. 4. 11 Geo. I. cap. 7. from whence the foregoing Duties are computed.
	By BRITISH.	By ALIENS.		If exported to any legal place, except as mentioned in the following column.	If the produce of Europe or the East Indies, and exported to the British Colonies in America.	
	£ s. d. 20ths	£ s. d. 20ths		£ s. d. 20ths	£ s. d. 20ths	£ s. d.
Ashes — Pearl-ashes of and from Germany, the Cwt.	0 2 1 4	0 2 1 4	B			
— of any other country, the Cwt.	0 2 1 4	0 2 1 4	C			
Burt Pc-ashes *and* Pearl-ashes *made in and imported from the British Plantations in America (if regularly imported, entered, and landed, and accompanied with proper certificates)* duty-free.						
Weed-ashes of any country, the Cwt.	0 0 0 6 6	0 0 0 6 6	C			
Wood-ashes of any country, the Cwt.	0 0 0 6 6	0 0 0 6 6	C			
Awl Blades, the thousand	0 0 2 9 12	0 0 2 11 14	A	0 0 2 5 12		0 13 4
And besides for every Cwt. of Iron			D			
Augers for Carpenters, the groce	0 0 5 3 8	0 0 5 3 11	A	0 0 5 3 8		1 0 0
And besides for every Cwt. of Iron			D			
Axes or Hatchets, the dozen	0 0 4 2 8	0 0 4 5 3	A	0 0 5 1 2 16		0 6 8
And besides for every Cwt. of Iron	0 0 1 4 16	0 0 1 5 17	D			
	0 0 5 3	0 0 5 3	D	0 0 5 3		

* But if imported by Aliens Drawback more, 1s. 3d. for every 100l. of the Rate or Value.

INWARDS.
B.

	DUTIES to be paid on IMPORTATION.		Reference to the several Branches, see Page vi.	DRAWBACKS to be repaid on EXPORTATION.*		RATES, or supposed value, by 12 Car. II. cap. 4. 11 Geo. I. cap. 7. from whence the foregoing Duties are computed.
	By BRITISH.	By ALIENS.		If exported to any legal place, except as mentioned in the following column.	If the produce of Europe or the East Indies, and exported to the British Colonies in America.	
	£. s. d. 20ths	£. s. d. 20ths		£. s. d. 20ths	£. s. d. 20ths	£. s. d.
BABIES or Puppets, for children, the groce, containing 12 dozen	0 3 8 18 4/5	0 3 11 14 39/40	A	0 3 3 11 4/5	0 2 10 4/5	0 17 10
Babies heads of earth, the dozen	0 2 9 12	0 2 11 14		0 2 5 12	0 2 1 12	0 13 4
All other Toys for children, for every 20 shillings value on oath:						
French	0 15 9	0 16 0 3	F	0 10 1	0 0 9 5	‡ 2 0 0
not French	0 6 3 12	0 6 6 45	C	0 5 7 12	0 4 11 12	‡ 2 0 0
Babies jointed, the dozen { not French	0 11 2 7 4	0 13 1 10	C	0 11 3 4	0 9 11 4	
French	1 11 6	1 12 0 6	F	1 2 2	0 18 10	
Backs for chimnies. Vide Iron.						
Bacon, of Ireland. Free.						
of Westphalia, Hambro', or the like, the Cwt.	2 4 9 12	2 5 1.16	C	2 4 1 12	0 5 12	1 6 8
And besides, if of France, the Cwt.	0 7 0	0 7 0	Fx	0 0 4 4/5	0 3 4/5	
Bags, with locks, the dozen	0 10 0 19 1/3	0 10 8 10 4/5	A	0 8 10 11 1/5	0 7 3	2 8 0
And besides for every Cwt. of Iron in the locks	0 5 3	0 5 3	D	0 5 3		
with steel rings without locks, the dozen	0 6 8 12 4/5	0 7 1 13 3/5	A	0 5 11 0 4/5	0 5 1 8 4/5	1 12 0
And besides for every Cwt. of Steel in the rings	0 5 9 6	0 5 9 6	D	0 5 9 6		

* But if imported by Aliens Drawback more, 1s. 3d. for every 100L. of the Rate or Value.

[9] B

INWARDS.

	DUTIES to be paid on IMPORTATION.		Reference to the several Branches, see Page vi.	DRAWBACKS to be repaid on EXPORTATION.*		RATES, or supposed value, by 12 Car. II. cap. 4. ‡ 11 Geo. I. cap. 7. from whence the foregoing Duties are computed.
	By BRITISH.	By ALIENS.		If exported to any legal place, except as mentioned in the following column.	If the produce of Europe or the East Indies, and exported to the British Colonies in America.	
	£. s. d. 20ths	£. s. d. 20ths		£. s. d. 20ths	£. s. d. 20ths	£. s. d.
And if the Leather be the most valuable part of the bags, for every 20s. of their real value upon oath	0 6 3 12	0 6 3 12	D	0 0 3 12	0 0 3 12	
called Runnet-bags, the dozen	0 1 0 12	0 1 1 4 3/5	c	0 0 11 8	0 0 10 4	‡ 0 4 0
Balances, vocat. Gold balances, the grocc, containing 12 dozen pair ||	1 2 4 16	1 3 9 12	A	0 19 8 16	0 17 0 16	5 6 8
──── Ounce balances, the grocc, containing 12 dozen pair	0 11 2 8	0 11 10 16	A	0 9 10 8	0 8 6 8	2 13 4
And besides for such ⎫ Iron, for every Cwt. the said Balances as ⎬ Brass, for every 20s. are made of ──── ⎭ of the rate	0 14 11 6 4/5 0 5 3	0 15 10 3 9/10 0 5 3	A D	0 13 1 19 4/5 0 5 3	0 11 4 12 4/5	3 11 2
Balks great, the hundred, containing 120 —— But note, all Timber in Balks of eight inches square, or upwards, is rated according to the measure of Timber, the foot square 3d. which is for every load, containing 50 such feet, a rate of 0l. 12s. 6d.	0 1 0 12	0 1 0 12	E	0 1 0 12	0 1 0 12	12 0 0
──── of and directly from any part of America, if regularly entered and landed, free. On failure thereof. See in Wood.						

* But if imported by Aliens Drawback more, 2 s. 3 d. for every 100 l. of the Rate or Value.

\|\| If Iron the Drawback to the British Colonies in America.

C

INWARDS.

	DUTIES to be paid on IMPORTATION.		Reference to the several Branches, see Page vi.	DRAWBACKS to be repaid on EXPORTATION.*		RATES or supposed value, by 12 Car. II. cap. 4. † 11 Geo. I. cap. 7. from whence the foregoing Duties are computed.
	By BRITISH.	By ALIENS.		If exported to any legal place, except as mentioned in the following column.	If the produce of Europe or the East Indies, and exported to the British Colonies in America.	
	£. s. d. 20ths	£. s. d. 20ths		£. s. d. 20ths	£. s. d. 20ths	£. s. d.
Balks great, of or from any part of Europe, except Ireland or France	0 3 11 5	0 4 1 4	B	0 3 7 10	0 3 3 15	5 0 0
—— of Ireland, Africa, or Asia. *See in Wood.*	0 2 7 10	0 2 9 9 ⅜	A	0 2 3 15	0 2 0	
Balks middle, the hundred, containing 120 of, and directly from, any part of America, if regularly entered and landed, free. *On failure thereof. See in Wood.* —— of or from any part of Europe, except Ireland or France	1 11 6	1 12 9 15	B	1 9 0	1 6 6	
—— of Ireland, Africa, or Asia. *See in France.*	1 1 0	1 2 3 15	A	0 18 6	0 16 0	
Balks small, the hundred, containing 120 of, and directly from, any part of America, if regularly entered and landed, free. *On failure thereof. See in Wood.* —— of or from any part of Europe, except Ireland or France	0 12 7 4	0 13 1 10	B	0 11 7 4	0 10 7 4	2 0 0
—— of Ireland, Africa, or Asia.	0 8 4 16	0 8 11 2	A	0 7 4 16	0 6 4 16	

* But if imported by Aliens Drawback more, 1s. 3d. for every 100 L. of the Rate or Value.

B [11] B

INWARDS	Duties to be paid on IMPORTATION. By BRITISH. £ s. d./20ths	By ALIENS. £ s. d./20ths	Reference to the several Branches, see Page vi.	DRAWBACKS to be repaid on EXPORTATION.* If exported to any legal place, except as mentioned in the following column. £ s. d./20ths	If the produce of Europe or the East Indies, and exported to the British Colonies in America. £ s. d./20ths	RATES, or supposed value, by 12 Car.II.cap.4. †11 Geo.I.cap.7. ‡from whence the foregoing Duties are computed. £ s. d.
—— of France. *See in Wood.*						
Note, *Balks imported in foreign ships pay duty as Aliens.*						
Balls, vocat. Tennis balls, the thousand	0 8 4.16	0 8 11 2	A	0 7 4.16	0 6 4.16	2 0 0
—— Washing balls, the grocc	0 8 4.16	0 8 11 2	A			2 0 0
And besides for every lb. weight of Soap contained therein	0 0 3	0 0 3 3	E a			
—— for children, the small groce	0 6 3.12	0 6 15 2	C	0 5 7.12	0 4 11.12	‡ 1 0 0
—— if French	0 15 9	0 16 0 3	F	0 10 1 1	0 9 5	
Bandeliers; the hundred, containing five score	0 3 6	0 3 8.12	A	0 3 1	0 2 8	0 16 8
And besides, if the Leather be the most valuable part, for every 20s. of the real value thereof upon oath						
—— if French	0 6 3.12	0 6 3.12	D c	0 3 3	0 3 12	
Band, vocat. Flanders bands of Bonelace, the band	2 2 0	2 4 7.10	A	1 17 0	1 12 0	10 0 0
—— Cut work of Flanders, or any other country						20 0 0
—— for Kettles. *Vide in Iron.*						
Band-strings, the dozen knots						0 10 0
Twist for Band-strings. *See in T.*						
Bankers of Verdure, the dozen pieces	1 5 2 8	1 6 3	C	1 3 2 8	1 1 2 8	4 0 0

* But if imported b. Aliens Drawback more, 1 s. 3 d. for every 100 l. of the Rate or Value.

INWARDS.

	DUTIES to be paid on IMPORTATION.								Reference to the several Branches, see Page vi.	DRAWBACKS to be repaid on EXPORTATION.*								RATES, or supposed value, by 12 Car. II. cap. 4. 11 Gen 1. cap. 7. from whence the foregoing Duties are computed.		
	By BRITISH.				By ALIENS.					If exported to any legal place, except as mentioned in the following column.				If the produce of Europe or the East Indies, and exported to the British Colonies in America.						
	L.	s.	d.	20ths	L.	s.	d.	20ths		L.	s.	d.	20ths	L.	s.	d.	20ths	L.	s.	d.
Barbers aprons, or checks, the piece, not above 10 yards	0	3	6		0	3	8	2	C	0	3	6		0	2	10		0	13	4
And besides, for every 20s. of the real value upon oath																				
Barillia, or Saphora, to make glass, the barrel, containing 200 weight	0	6	3	12	0	6	3	12	E a	0	6	3	12	0	6	3	12	1	0	0
And besides, for every Cwt.	0	4	2	8	0	4	5	11	A	0	3	8	8	0	3	2	8			
Bark of oak, the Cwt.	0	2	7	10	0	2	7	10	D	0	2	7	10	0	2	7	10	0	10	0
But by 12 Geo. III. cap. 50. the duties payable upon this rate are repealed, and from and after the 25th of June, 1772, for the term of five years, and from thence to the end of the then next session of parliament, is imposed, in lieu thereof, a duty upon every Cwt. imported, of ___ to be raised and collected according to the directions of that law, whenever the prices fixed by it will admit its importation. Which law is, by 17 Geo. III. cap. 44. continued from the expiration thereof to the further term of five years, and from	0	1	1		0	1	1		P a	0	0	0								

* But if imported by Aliens Drawback more, 1s. 3d. for every 100l. of the Rate or Value.

††

B [13] B

INWARDS.

	DUTIES to be paid on IMPORTATION.		Reference to the several Branches, see Page vi.	DRAWBACKS to be repaid on EXPORTATION.*		RATES, or supposed value, by 12 Car. II. cap. 4. 11 Geo. I. cap. 7. from whence the foregoing Duties are computed.
	By BRITISH.	By ALIENS.		If exported to any legal place, except as mentioned in the following column.	If the produce of Europe or the East Indies, and exported to the British Colonies in America.	
	£. s. d. 20ths	£. s. d. 20ths		£. s. d. 20ths	£. s. d. 20ths	£. s. d.
thence to the end of the then next sessions of parliament.						
Barley. *Vide* Corn.						
Barley hulled. *Vide in* Drugs.						
Barlings the hundred, containing 120 —— of, and directly from, any part of America, if regularly entered and landed, free.	0 10 6	0 10 11 5	B	0 0 9 8	0 0 8 10 4	1 13 4
On failure thereof. *See in* Wood. —— of or from any part of Europe, except Ireland or France —— of Ireland, Africa, or Asia —— of France. *See in* Wood.	0 7 0	0 7 5 5	A	0 0 6 2	0 0 5 4	
Note, Balks imported in foreign ships pay duty as Aliens.						
Burmillians. *Vide* Fustians.						
Basket rods, the bundle	0 1 4 16	0 1 5 17 ½	A	0 0 2 16	0 1 0 16	0 6 8
Baskets, vocat. Hand-baskets, or Sports,	0 0 8 8	0 0 8 18 ⅓	A	0 0 7 8	0 0 6 8	0 3 4
the dozen ——						
Basons of Latten, the pound	0 0 4 4	0 0 4 8	C	0 0 3 16	0 0 3 8	0 1 4

* But if imported by Aliens Drawback more, 1s. 3d. for every 100l. of the Rate or Value.

INWARDS.

	Rated (l. s. d.)	Duties to be paid on Importation. By British. (£. s. d. 20ths)	Duties to be paid on Importation. By Aliens. (£. s. d. 20ths)	Reference to the several Branches, see Page vi.	Drawbacks to be repaid on Exportation.* If exported to any legal place, except as mentioned in the following column. (£. s. d. 20ths)	Drawbacks to be repaid on Exportation.* If the produce of Europe or the East Indies, and exported to the British Colonies in America. (£. s. d. 20ths)	Rates, or supposed value, by 12 Car. II. cap. 4. & 11 Geo. I. cap. 7. from whence the foregoing Duties are computed. (£. s. d.)
Bast or Straw Hats and Bonnets, *rated by* 10 *Geo. III. cap.* 43.							
each Hat or Bonnet not exceeding 22 inches in diameter, the dozen	0 12 6	0 2 7 10	0 2 9 9 3/8	A	0 2 3 15	0 2 0	
each Hat or Bonnet exceeding 22 inches in diameter, the dozen	1 5 0	0 5 3	0 5 6 18 1/4	A	0 4 7 10	0 4 0	
Chip, Cane, and Horse-hair Hats and Bonnets, *rated by* 10 *Geo. III. cap.* 43.							
each Hat or Bonnet not exceeding 22 inches in diameter, the dozen	0 12 6	0 3 3 7 1/2	0 3 5 6 7/8	C	0 2 11 12 1/2	0 2 7 17 1/2	
each Hat or Bonnet exceeding 22 inches in diameter, the dozen	1 5 0	0 6 6 15	0 6 10 13 3/4	C	0 5 11 5	0 5 3 15	
Bast-ropes, the rope		0 0 1 5 1/3	0 0 1 6 31/40	A	0 0 1 2 1/3	0 0 0 19 1/5	0 0 6
—— the bundle, containing 10 ropes		0 1 0 12	0 1 1 7 3/4	A	0 0 11 2	0 0 9 12	0 5 0
—— the Cwt.		0 1 8 3 1/3	0 1 9 8 2/3	A	0 1 5 15 1/3	0 1 3 7 1/5	0 8 0
Battens. *Vide* Wood.							
Battery, Bathroons, or Kettles, the Cwt.		2 3 0 12	2 5 4 19	C	1 18 6 12	1 14 0 12	9 0 0

* But if imported by Aliens Drawback more, 1s. 3d. for every 100l. of the Rate or Value.

[15]

INWARDS.

	DUTIES to be paid on IMPORTATION.		DRAWBACKS to be repaid on EXPORTATION.*		RATES, or supposed value, by 12 Car. II. cap. 4. ‡ 11 Geo. I. cap. 7. from whence the foregoing Duties are computed.
	By BRITISH.	By ALIENS.	Reference to the several Branches, see Page vi.	If exported to any legal place, except as mentioned in the following column.	If the produce of Europe or the East Indies, and exported to the British Colonies in America.	
	£. s. d. 20ths	£. s. d. 20ths		£. s. d. 20ths	£. s. d. 20ths	£. s. d.
Bays of Florence, per yard	0 5 3 8	0 5 6 18	A	0 4 7 10	0 4 0 8	1 5 0
Beads of Amber, the pound	0 4 2	0 4 3 19	C	0 3 11 8	0 3 8	0 10 0
12 small groce { Bone, the great groce containing }	0 6 3 12	0 6 8 6	A	0 5 6 12	0 4 9 12	1 10 0
Box, the great groce	0 6 3 12	0 6 8 6	A	0 5 6 12	0 4 9 12	1 10 0
Christal, the thousand	0 12 7 4	0 13 4 13	A	0 11 1 4	0 9 7 8	3 0 0
Coral, the pound	0 4 2 8	0 4 3 19	C	0 3 11 8	0 3 8 8	0 10 0
Glass of all sorts, the great groce. But, by 17 Geo. II. cap. 31. § 1. Glass Beads of all sorts are to pay the same duties, and be intitled to the same drawback on exportation, as Great Eugle. Vide Bugle.						
Jasper square, the hundred stones	0 8 4 16	0 8 11 2	A	0 7 4 16	0 6 4 16	2 0 0 ‡
Jet, the pound	0 1 3 15	0 1 4 10 3/4	C	0 1 2 5	0 1 0 15	0 5 0
Horn, the small groce, containing 12 dozen	0 1 3 15	0 1 4 10 1/2	C	0 1 2 5	0 1 0 15	0 5 0 ‡
Wood of all sorts, the great groce	0 2 1 4	0 2 2 15 1/2	A	0 1 10 4	0 1 7 4	0 10 0
Beads. *Vide* Corn.						
Bezupers, the piece containing 24 or 25 yards	0 7 10 10	0 8 2 8 3/4	C	0 7 3	0 6 7 10	1 5 0

* But if imported by Aliens Drawback more, 1s. 3d. for every 100l. of the Rate or Value.

INWARDS.

	Duties to be paid on Importation. By British. £.	s.	d.	20ths	By Aliens. £.	s.	d.	20ths	Reference to the several Branches, see Page vi.	Drawbacks to be repaid on Exportation.* If exported to any legal place, except as mentioned in the following column. £.	s.	d.	20ths	If the produce of Europe or the East Indies, and exported to the British Colonies in America. £.	s.	d.	20ths	Rates, or supposed value, by 12 Car. II. cap. 4. ‡ 11 Geo. I. cap. 7. from whence the foregoing Duties are computed. £.	s.	d.
Beef of Ireland or Scotland, free.																				
—— or Pork of Ireland or Scotland, free.																				
Beer, called Spruce beer, the barrel, containing 42 gallons	0	14	10	10	0	15	6	7 ½	E b	0	13	7	10	0	12	4	10	‡ 2	10	0
—— of all other sorts, or Ale: For every 20s. of the value upon oath	0	5	3		0	5	6	3	C	0	4	9		0	4	3				
—— of all other sorts, or Ale: For every ton	0	10	6		0	10	6		I b	0	10	6		0	10	6				
Subject also to the Excise duties.																				
But of and from Guernsey, Jersey, Alderney, Sark, and Man, may be imported without payment of any other duty, than such Excise as is chargeable for the time being on the like liquors made in this kingdom.																				
Bell metal, the Cwt.	0	7	0		0	7	5	5	A	0	6	2		0	5	4		1	13	4
Bellows, the pair	0	0	8	8	0	0	8	18 ½	A	0	0	7	8	0	0	6	8	0	3	4
And if the leather be the most valuable part of the Bellows, for every 20s. of their real value upon oath	0	6	3	12	0	6	3	12	D c	0	0	3	12	0	0	3	12			
Bells vocat. Clapper bells, the pound	0	0	2	10 ⅔	0	0	2	13 11/20	A	0	0	2	4 ⅖	0	0	1	18 ⅔	0	1	0
—— Dog bells, the small groce	0	0	3	7 ⅓	0	0	3	11 ⅖	A	0	0	2	19 ⅕	0	0	2	11 ⅓	0	1	4

* But if imported by Aliens Drawback more, 1s. 3d. for every 100l. of the Rate or Value.

[17]

INWARDS.

	DUTIES to be paid on IMPORTATION.		Reference to the several Branches, see Page vi.	DRAWBACKS to be repaid on EXPORTATION.*		RATES, or supposed value, by 12 Car. II. cap. 4. †11 Geo. I. cap. 7. from whence the foregoing Duties are computed.
	By BRITISH.	By ALIENS.		If exported to any legal place, except as mentioned in the following column.	If the produce of Europe or the East Indies, and exported to the British Colonies in America.	
	£. s. d. 20ths	£. s. d. 20ths		£. s. d. 20ths	£. s. d. 20ths	£. s. d.
Hawks bells, French making, the dozen pair	0 3 8 2	0 3 8 17 ¾	F	0 2 3 12	0 2 2 4⅘	0 5 0
Hawks bells, Norembourgh making, the dozen pair	0 0 5 0	0 0 5 7 1/15	A	0 0 4 8 ⅘	0 0 3 16 4/5	0 2 0
Horse bells, the small groce	0 2 1 4	0 2 2 15 1/2	A	0 1 10 4	0 1 7 4	0 10 0
Morrice bells, the small groce	0 1 0 12	0 1 1 7 ¼	A	0 0 11 2	0 0 9 12	0 5 0
And besides for such of the aforesaid bells (except French Hawks bells,) as are made of brass, for every 20s. of their respective rates	0 1 0 12	0 1 0 12	E	0 1 0 12	0 1 0 12	
Berries British, from the Plantations, for Dyers use, as by 3 and 4 Ann. cap. 4 for every 20s. of their value upon oath	0 3 1 16	0 3 4 19	Bd	0 2 7 16	0 2 7 16	
French, for Dyers use, as by 3 & 4 Ann. cap. 4. for every 20s. of their value upon oath	0 12 7 4	0 12 10 7	Fa	0 7 1 4	0 6 7 4	
Bestials, of and from the Isle of Man, may be imported under proper certificates duty free, by 5 Geo. III. cap. 43. § 11.						
Binding for brooms, the Cwt.	0 4 4 10	0 4 7 2 ½	C	0 3 11 10	0 3 6 10	† 0 16 8
Birds of stone. Vide Whistles.						

* But if imported by Aliens Drawback more, 1s. 3d. for every 100l. of the Rate or Value.

[18]

INWARDS.

	DUTIES to be paid on IMPORTATION.			DRAWBACKS to be repaid on EXPORTATION.*		RATES, or suppofed value, by 12 Car. II. cap. 4. 11 Geo. I cap.7. from whence the foregoing Duties are computed.
	By BRITISH.	By ALIENS.	Reference to the feveral Branches, fee Page vi.	If exported to any legal place, except as mentioned in the following column.	If of the produce of Europe or the Eaſt Indies, and exported to the Britiſh Colonies in America.	
	£. s. d. 20ths	£. s. d. 20ths		£. s. d. 20ths	£. s. d. 20ths	£. s. d.
Birds, *vocat.* Singing birds, the dozen — of all ſorts, *not rated by* 12 Car. II. cap. 4. the dozen	0 2 4 7	0 2 5 15 7/10	C	0 2 1 13	0 1 10 19	⅓ 0 9 0
Vide Pheaſants and Quails.						
Biſket. *Vide* Bread.	0 3 1 16	0 3 3 13 4/5	C	0 2 10 4	0 2 6 12	⅓ 0 12 0
Bits for Bridles, the dozen —	0 4 2 8	0 4 5 11	A	0 3 8 8	—	1 0 0
And beſides for every Cwt. *of* Iron	0 5 3	0 5 3	D	0 14 5 3	—	—
Blacking or Lamp-black, the Cwt.	0 16 9 12	0 17 10 4	A	0 14 9 12	0 12 9 12	4 0 0
And beſides if Lamp-black, *the* Cwt.	0 16 9 12	0 16 9 12	E	0 16 9 12	0 16 9 12	—
Bladders, the dozen —	0 0 1 1	0 1 2 1/10	C	0 0 0 19	0 0 0 17	⅓ 0 0 4
Blankets, *vocat.* Paris Mantles coloured, the Mantle	0 5 7 4	0 5 11 8	A	0 4 11 4	0 4 3 4	1 6 8
And beſides if of the manufacture of France						
——— Paris Mantles or others uncoloured, the Mantle	0 14 0	0 14 0	F b	0 7 4	0 7 4	—
And beſides if of the manufacture of France	0 4 2 8	0 4 5 11	A	0 3 8 8	0 3 2 8	1 0 0
Blubber. *Vide* Oil.			F b	0 5 6	0 5 6	—
Boards of Beech. *Vide* Wood.	0 10 6	0 10 6				

* But if imported by Aliens Drawback more, 1s. 3d. for every 100l. of the Rate or Value.

INWARDS.

Boards, vocat.	Duties to be paid on IMPORTATION. By BRITISH. (L. s. d./20ths)	By ALIENS. (L. s. d./20ths)	Reference to the several Branches, see Page vi.	DRAWBACKS to be repaid on EXPORTATION.* If exported to any legal place, except as mentioned in the following column. (L. s. d./20ths)	If the produce of Europe or the East Indies, and exported to the British Colonies in America. (L. s. d./20ths)	RATES, or supposed value, by 12 Car. II. cap. 4. ‡11 Geo. I. cap. 7. from whence the foregoing Duties are computed. (L. s. d.)
Barrel-boards, the hundred containing 120 — of, and directly from, any part of America, if regularly entered and landed, free.						
On failure thereof. See in Wood.						
— of or from any part of Europe, except Ireland or France	0 1 6 18	0 1 7 13 3/4	B	0 1 5 8	0 1 3 18	0 5 0
— of Ireland, Africa, or Asia. See in Wood.	0 1 0 12	0 1 1 7 3/4	A	0 0 11 2	0 0 9 12	
— of France. See in Wood.						
Clap-boards, the hundred containing 120 — of, and directly from, any part of America, if regularly entered and landed, free.						
On failure thereof. See in Wood.						
— of or from any part of Europe, except Ireland and France	0 4 8 14	0 4 11 1 1/4	B	0 4 4 4	0 3 11 14	0 15 0
— of Ireland, Africa, or Asia	0 3 1 16	0 3 4 3 1/4	A	0 2 9 6	0 2 4 16	
— of France. See in Wood.						

* But if imported by Aliens Drawback more, 1s. 3d. for every 100l. of the Rate or Value.

INWARDS.

Boards, viz.

		DUTIES to be paid on IMPORTATION.		DRAWBACKS to be repaid on EXPORTATION.*		RATES, or supposed value, by 12 Car. II. cap. 4. 11 Geo. I. cap. 7. from whence the foregoing Duties are computed.
	Reference to the several Branches, see Page vi.	By BRITISH.	By ALIENS.	If exported to any legal place, except as mentioned in the following column.	If the produce of Europe or the East Indies, and exported to the British Colonies in America.	
		£. s. d. 20ths	£. s. d. 20ths	£. s. d. 20ths	£. s. d. 20ths	£. s. d.
Pipe Boards or Pipe Holt the hundred containing 120 —— of, and directly from, any part of America, if regularly entered and landed, free. *On failure thereof. See in Wood.*						
—— of or from any part of Europe, except Ireland or France	B	0 6 3 12	0 6 15	0 5 9 12	0 5 3 12	1 0 0
—— of Ireland, —— of France.	A	0 4 2 8	0 4 5 11	0 3 8 8	0 3 2 8	
Africa, or Asia ——						
See in Wood.						
White Boards for Shoemakers, the board —— of, and directly from, any part of America, if regularly entered and landed, free. *On failure thereof. See in Wood.*						
—— of or from any part of Europe, except Ireland or France	B	0 0 3 15 ¾	0 0 3 18 ¼	0 0 3 9 ⅗	0 0 3 3 ⅗	0 1 0

* But if imported by Aliens Drawback more, 1 s. 3 d. for every 100 l. of the Rate or Value.

INWARDS.

	DUTIES to be paid on IMPORTATION.		DRAWBACKS to be repaid on EXPORTATION.*		RATES or supposed value, by 12 Car. II. cap. 4. 11 Geo. I. cap. 7. from whence the foregoing Duties are computed.
	By BRITISH.	By ALIENS.	Reference to the several Branches, see Page vi.	If exported to any legal place, except as mentioned in the following column.	If the produce of Europe or the East Indies, and exported to the British Colonies in America.
	£. s. d. 20ths	£. s. d. 20ths		£. s. d. 20ths	£. s. d. 20ths	£. s. d.
———— of Ireland, Africa, or Asia ———— of France. *See in* Wood. ‡	0 2 10 ⅖	0 2 13 11/20	A	0 0 2 4 ⅔	0 0 1 18 ⅖	0 13 4
Paste Boards for Books, the thousand——						
And besides for every Cwt. *of Paste Boards or* Milled Boards	0 2 9 12	0 2 11 14	A	0 2 5 12	0 2 1 12	
	0 7 10 10	0 7 10 10	E a	0 7 10 10	0 7 10 0	
Bodkins, the small groce	0 1 4 16	0 1 5 17	A	0 1 2 16	0 1 0 16	0 6 8
But if made of { brass	0 1 9	0 1 10 1	C	0 1 7	0 1 5	
{ Iron	0 1 4 16	0 1 5 17	A	0 1 2 16		
And besides for every Cwt. *of such* Iron ————	0 5 3	0 5 3	D	0 5 3		1 13 4
Boom Spars, the hundred containing 120 of, and directly from, any part of America, if regularly entered and landed, free.						
On failure thereof. See in Wood.						
———— of or from any part of Europe, except Ireland or France	0 10 6	0 10 11 5	B	0 9 8	0 8 10 0	
———— of Ireland, Africa, or Asia ———— of France. *See in* Wood. †	0 7 0	0 7 5 5	A	0 6 2	0 5 4	
Borntoes, or Bombavines, narrow, the single piece, not above 15 yards	1 5 2 8	1 6 9 6	A	1 2 2 8	0 19 2 8	6 0 0

* But if imported by Aliens Drawback more, 1s. 3d. for every 100l. of the Rate or Value.

† If imported in foreign ships to pay duty as Aliens.

B [22] B

INWARDS

	DUTIES to be paid on IMPORTATION.		Reference to the several Branches, see Page vi.	DRAWBACKS to be repaid on EXPORTATION.*		RATES, or supposed value, by 12 Car. II. cap. 4. 11 Geo. I. cap. 7. from whence the foregoing Duties are computed.
	By BRITISH.	By ALIENS.		If exported to any legal place, except as mentioned in the following column.	If the produce of Europe or the East Indies, and exported to the British Colonies in America.	
	£. s. d. 20ths	£. s. d. 20ths		£. s. d. 20ths	£. s. d. 20ths	£. s. d.
Boratoes, or Bombazines, broad, the single piece, not above 15 yards ——— of silk. *Vide* Silk wrought.	1 9 4 16	1 11 2 17	A	1 5 10 16	1 2 4 16	7 0 0
Books bound, the Cwt. *by 9 Geo. I. cap. 19.* ——— French	0 18 4 10	0 18 4 10	F	—	—	
——— not French	0 18 4 10	0 18 4 10	C	—	—	
Books unbound, the basket or maund, containing 8 bales or 2 fats ——— the fat, containing half a maund						
Note, *The Table of Tares having deemed this basket or maund to contain 8 C. wt. it is therefore usual to enter unbound books by the Cwt. at the rate of* ——— £.1 0 0						8 0 0
Bosses for bridles, the small grosse { French	0 14 11 11	0 14 11 11	F	0 9 2 8	0 8 8 8	
{ not French	0 8 7 19	0 8 7 19	C	0 7 10 16	0 7 4 16	4 0 0
And besides, if made of { Brass, the small grosse	0 4 5 11	0 4 5 11	A	0 3 8 8	0 3 2 8	
{ Iron, the Cwt.	0 1 0 12	0 1 0 12	E	0 1 0 12	0 1 0 12	1 0 0
	0 5 3	0 5 3	D	0 5 3	—	
Botanoes, per piece	0 2 1 4	0 2 15 ½	A	0 1 10 4	0 1 7 4	0 10 0

* But if imported by Aliens Drawback more, 1 s. 3 d. for every 100 l. of the Rate or Value.

‖ If Iron no Drawback to the British Colonies in America.

INWARDS

	DUTIES to be paid on IMPORTATION.		Reference to the several Branches, see Page vi.	DRAWBACKS to be repaid on EXPORTATION. *		RATES, or supposed value, by 12 Car.II.cap.4. 11 Geo.I.cap.7. from whence the foregoing Duties are computed.
	By BRITISH.	By ALIENS.		If exported to any legal place, except as mentioned in the following column.	If the produce of Europe or the East Indies, and exported to the British Colonies in America.	
	£. s. d. 20ths	£. s. d. 20ths		£. s. d. 20ths	£. s. d. 20ths	£. s. d.
Botargo, the pound	0 0 3 3	0 0 3 6 2/10	C	0 0 2 17	0 0 2 11	0 1 0
Bottles of Earth or Stone, the dozen	0 1 0 12	0 1 1 7	A	0 0 11 2	0 0 9 12	0 5 0
Glass covered with wicker, the dozen	0 7 4	0 7 7	B	0 6 10 4	0 6 4 4	1 0 0
Glass with vices, covered with leather, the dozen	1 13 0 18	1 14 3 1 1/2	B	1 10 9 18	1 8 6 18	4 10 0
Glass uncovered, the dozen	0 1 7 16 9/10	0 1 8 11 1/2	B	0 1 6 9 9/10	0 1 5 2 7/10	0 4 6
And besides if Glass, for every dozen quarts which they contain — of Wood, vocat. Sucking bottles, the groce	0 4 2 8	0 4 2 8	B	0 0 2 8	0 0 2 8	
Bottoms for laces. Vide Hair bottoms.						
Boultel Rains, the piece	0 2 1 4	0 2 2 15 4/5	Zc	0 1 10 4	0 1 7 4	0 10 0
— the bale, containing 20 pieces	2 10 4 16 4/5	2 12 6	A	2 3 16	2 1 8	8 0 0
Bowls or Buckets of wood, the dozen	0 0 10 10	0 0 11 1/2	C	0 0 9 10	0 0 8 10	0 3 4
Bows, vocat. Stone bows of steel, the piece	0 1 4 6	0 2 15 6	C	1 1 10 4	2 4 16	0 10 0
And besides for every Cwt. of Steel			A			
Bow staves, the hundred, containing 120 staves			D			

* But if imported by Aliens Drawback more, 1s. 3d. for every 100l. of the Rate or Value.

INWARDS.

Description	Reference to the several Branches, see Page vi.	Duties to be paid on Importation — By British £. s. d. 20ths	Duties to be paid on Importation — By Aliens £. s. d. 20ths	Drawbacks to be repaid on Exportation* — If exported to any legal place, except as mentioned in the following column £. s. d. 20ths	Drawbacks to be repaid on Exportation* — If the produce of Europe or the East Indies, and exported to the British Colonies in America £. s. d. 20ths	Rates, or supposed value, by 12 Car.II.cap.4. 11 Geo.I.cap.7. from whence the foregoing Duties are computed £. s. d.
Bow staves of, and directly from, any part of America, if regularly entered and landed, free.						
On failure thereof. See in Wood. — of or from any part of Europe, except Ireland and France — of Ireland, Africa, or Asia — of France. See in Wood. †						
Boxes, viz. Fire, or Tinder-boxes, containing 12 dozen boxes	B	1 5 2 8	1 6 3	1 3 2 8	1 1 2 8	1 0 0
Money-boxes of wood, the small groce	A	0 16 9 12	0 17 10 4	0 14 9 2	0 12 9 12	0 15 0
Nest-boxes, the groce, containing 12 dozen nests	A	0 4 2 8	0 4 5 11	0 3 8 8	0 3 2 8	3 0 0
Pepper-boxes, the groce, containing 12 dozen boxes	C	0 3 11 5	0 4 1 12 ¼	0 3 6 15	0 3 2 5	
Pill-boxes, or Boxes entered as such, of wood, the small groce, containing 12 dozen nests, each nest containing 4 boxes	A	0 12 7 4	0 13 4 13	0 11 1 4	0 9 7 4	1 2 6
	A	0 4 8 14	0 5 0 4 ⅔	0 4 1 19	0 3 7 4	
	C	0 1 3 15	0 1 4 10 ¼	0 1 2 5	0 1 0 15	0 5 0

* But if imported by Aliens Drawback more, 1 s. 3 d. for every 100 l. of the Rate or Value.

† If imported in foreign ships to pay duty as Aliens.

B [25] B

INWARDS.	DUTIES to be paid on IMPORTATION.		DRAWBACKS to be repaid on EXPORTATION.*		Reference to the several Branches, see Page vi.	RATES, or supposed value, by 12 Car.II. cap.4. ‡11 Geo.I. cap.7. from whence the foregoing Duties are computed.
	By BRITISH.	By ALIENS.	If exported to any legal place, except as mentioned in the following column.	If the produce of Europe or the East Indies, and exported to the British Colonies in America.		
	£. s. d. 20ths	£. s. d. 20ths	£. s. d. 20ths	£. s. d. 20ths		£. s. d.
——— Round boxes, or French boxes, for marmalade or jelly, the dozen	0 3 3 13 4/5	0 3 4 7 19/20	0 2 0 16 4/5	0 1 11 9 4/5	F	0 4 6
Sand-boxes, the groce, containing 12 dozen	0 4 2 8	0 4 5 11	0 3 8 8	0 3 2 8	A	1 0 0
Snuff-boxes { of wood, plain, the dozen	0 2 7 10	0 2 9 1 1/2	0 2 4 10	0 2 1 10	C	‡ 0 10 0
of horn, plain, the dozen	0 5 3	0 6 3	0 4 9	0 4 3	C	‡ 1 0 0
of ivory or tortoise-shell, the dozen	0 10 6	0 11 0 6	0 9 6	0 8 6	C	‡ 2 0 0
Soap-boxes, the shock, containing three score boxes	0 8 4 16	0 8 11 2	0 7 4 16	0 6 4 16	A	2 0 0
Spice-boxes, the dozen	0 1 3 2 2/5	0 1 4 1 3/5	0 1 1 6	0 0 11 10 1/5	A	0 6 0
Tobacco-boxes, the groce, containing 12 dozen	0 6 3 12	0 6 8 6 1/2	0 5 6 12	0 4 9 12	A	1 10 0
Touch-boxes covered with Leather, the dozen	0 0 7 11 1/5	0 0 8 0 13/20	0 0 6 13 1/5	0 0 5 15 1/5	D c	0 3 0
And besides, if the Leather be the most valuable part of the boxes, for every 20 s. of the real value thereof upon oath	0 6 3 12	0 6 3 12	0 3 12	0 3 12		

* But if imported by Aliens Drawback more, 1 s. 3 d. for every 100 l. of the Rate or Value.

INWARDS.

	DUTIES to be paid on IMPORTATION.		Reference to the several Branches, see Page vi.	DRAWBACKS to be repaid on EXPORTATION.*		RATES, or supposed value, by 12 Car. II. cap. 4. † 11 Geo. I. cap. 7. from whence the foregoing Duties are computed.
	By BRITISH.	By ALIENS.		If exported to any legal place, except as mentioned in the following column.	If of the produce of Europe or the East Indies, and exported to the British Colonies in America.	
	£. s. d. /20ths	£. s. d. /20ths		£. s. d. /20ths	£. s. d. /20ths	£. s. d.
Velvet, the dozen ———— Touch-boxes covered with	0 3 1 16	0 3 4 3 ¼	A	0 2 9 6	0 2 4 16	0 15 0
———— of Iron, or other metal gilt, the dozen ‖	0 4 2 8	0 5 11	A	0 3 8 8	0 3 2 8	1 0 0
And besides, if Iron, the Cwt.	0 5 3	0 5 3	D	0 5 3		
Box-wood. Vide Wood.						
Bracelets or Necklaces, of glass, the small groce, containing 12 bundles or dickers red, the small groce, containing the same	0 4 6 3 3/5	0 4 6 4 3/5	F	0 3 4 19 3/5	0 3 3 15 3/5	0 4 0
———— if of France	0 3 5 11 3/5	0 3 6 4 3/5	C	0 3 4 7 3/5	0 3 3 3 3/5	0 4 0
———— if not of France						
Brandy. Vide Spirits.						
Brass Lamps, the dozen	0 2 7 10	0 2 9 4	C	0 2 4 10	0 2 1 10	0 10 0
———— Old. Vide Shruff.						
———— Laver cocks, the pound	0 3 4 4	0 3 3 13 ⅘	C	0 2 10 4	0 2 6 12	0 1 0
———— Pile weights, the pound	0 3 1 16 ⅗	0 3 3 13 ⅗	C	0 3 1 6	0 3 8	0 12 0
———— Trumpets, the dozen	0 4 4 ½	0 4 8 ½	C	0 3 16	0 3	† 0 1 4
———— Wrought, not rated in the Book of Rates, the pound						
———— Powder. Vide Powder.						

‖ If Iron no Drawback to the British Colonies in America.   * But if imported by Aliens Drawback more, 1s. 3d. for every 100l. of the Rate or Value.

INWARDS

	DUTIES to be paid on IMPORTATION.		Reference to the several Branches, see Page vi.	DRAWBACKS to be repaid on EXPORTATION.*		RATES, or supposed value, by 12 Car. II. cap.4. ‡ 11 Geo.I. cap.7. from whence the foregoing Duties are computed.
	By BRITISH.	By ALIENS.		If exported to any legal place, except as mentioned in the following column.	If the produce of Europe or the East Indies, and exported to the British Colonies in America.	
	£. s. d. 20ths	£. s. d. 20ths		£. s. d. 20ths	£. s. d. 20ths	£. s. d.
Bread, or Bisket, the Cwt	0 1 9	0 1 10 1	C	0 1 7	0 1 5	0 6 8
Brick-stones. *Vide* Earthen-ware.						1 0 0
Bridles, the dozen	0 5 3	0 5 6	C			1 0 0
And besides, if the Leather be the most valuable part of the Bridles, for every 20s. of the real value thereof upon oath						
Brimstone, the Cwt	0 6 3 12	0 6 3 12	Dc	0 4 9	0 4 3	0 6 8
And besides, if of France			Fx			
Bristles dressed, the dozen pound	0 0 3 12	0 0 4 13	C	0 0 3 12	0 0 3 12	
rough, or undressed, the dozen pound	0 0 3 12	0 0 4 13	C			
Brooms, called Flag brooms, or Whisk brooms, the dozen	0 0 1	0 0 1 ⁷⁄₂₀	A	0 0 1	0 0 ⁴⁄₅	0 0 4
Brouches, of copper, the groce	0 2 6 4	0 2 8 ²⁄₅	E	0 2 2 12	0 1 11 0	0 12 0
And besides, for every Cwt.	0 18 4 10	0 18 4 10	C	0 18 4 10	0 18 4 10	
Beard-brushes, *if of Latten*, the groce	0 3 1 16	0 3 3 ⁴⁄₅	A	0 2 10 4	0 2 6 12	0 12 8
of Hair, *viz:* Comb-brushes, the dozen	0 1 4 16	0 1 5 17 ⁴⁄₅	A	0 1 0 4	0 1 0 15	0 6 4
Head-brushes, the dozen	0 2 9 12	0 2 11 14 ⁴⁄₅	A	0 2 5 12	0 2 1 12	0 13 8
Rubbing-brushes, the dozen	0 1 4 16	0 1 5 17	A	0 1 0 4	0 1 0 16	0 6 8
Brushes vizt.	0 0 3 7	0 0 3 11 ¹⁄₅	A	0 0 2 19	0 0 2 11 ¹⁄₅	0 1 4

* But if imported by Aliens Drawback more, 1 s. 3 d. for every 100 l. of the Rate or Value.

INWARDS.

	Duties to be paid on Importation. By British. £.	s.	d.	20ths	Duties to be paid on Importation. By Aliens. £.	s.	d.	20ths	Reference to the several Branches, see Page vi.	Drawbacks to be repaid on Exportation.* If exported to any legal place, except as mentioned in the following column. £.	s.	d.	20ths	If the produce of Europe or the East Indies, and exported to the British Colonies in America. £.	s.	d.	20ths	Rates or supposed value by 12 Car. II, cap. 4. ‡ 11 Geo. I. cap. 7. from whence the foregoing Duties are computed. £.	s.	d.
Brushes *vocat.* of Hair, *vocat.* Weavers brushes, the dozen	0	1	0	12	0	1	1	7 3/4	A	0	0	11	2	0	0	9	12	0	5	0
Brushes of Heath, coarse, the dozen	0	0	7	11 1/3	0	0	8	0 13/20	A	0	0	6	13 1/3	0	0	5	15 1/3	0	3	0
Brushes of Heath, fine, or head-brushes, the dozen	0	1	4	16	0	1	5	17	A	0	1	2	16	0	1	0	16	0	6	8
Brushes of Heath, *vocat.* rubbing-brushes, the dozen	0	0	2	10 2/5	0	0	2	13 11/20	A	0	0	2	4 2/5	0	0	1	18 2/5	0	1	0
Buckets. *Vide* Bowls.																				
Buckles, for girdles, the small groce	0	4	2	8	0	4	5	11	A	0	3	8	8	0	3	2	8	1	0	0
And besides, if made of Brass, *the groce*	0	1	0	12	0	1	0	12	E	0	1	0	12	0	1	0	12			
Buckles, for girths, the groce ‖	0	1	6	18	0	1	8	1 5/8	A	0	1	4	13	0	1	2	8	0	7	6
And besides, if made of Brass, *the groce*	0	0	4	14 1/2	0	0	4	14 1/2	E	0	0	4	14 1/2	0	0	4	14 1/2			
And besides, if made of Iron, *the Cwt.*	0	5	3		0	5	3		D	0	5	3		—	—	—	—			
Buckrams *vocat.* Callico Buckrams. *Vide* Buggasins.																				
Buckrams *vocat.* Carrick Buckrams, the short piece	0	0	6	6	0	0	6	12 3/10	C	0	0	5	14	0	0	5	2	0	2	0
Buckrams of East country, the roll or half piece	0	1	3	15	0	1	4	10 3/4	C	0	1	2	5	0	1	0	15	0	5	0
Buckrams of French making, the dozen pieces	1	16	9		1	17	4	17 1/2	F	1	3	0		1	1	9		2	10	0
Buckrams of Germany, or fine, per piece	0	2	7	10	0	2	9	1 1/2	C	0	2	4	10	0	2	1	10	0	10	0

‖ If Iron no Drawback to the British Colonies in America.

* But if imported by Aliens Drawback more, 1s. 3d. for every 100l. of the Rate or Value.

B [29] B

INWARDS.

	DUTIES to be paid on IMPORTATION.		Reference to the several Branches, see Page vi.	DRAWBACKS to be repaid on EXPORTATION*		RATES, or supposed value, by 12 Car. II. cap. 4. ‡ 11 Geo. I. cap. 7. from whence the foregoing Duties are computed.
	By BRITISH.	By ALIENS.		If exported to any legal place, except as mentioned in the following column.	If the produce of Europe or the East Indies, and exported to the British Colonies in America.	
	£. s. d. 20ths	£. s. d. 20ths		£. s. d. 20ths	£. s. d. 20ths	£. s. d.
Buck-wheat. *Vide* Corn.						
Busins, Moccadoes, and Lile Grograms, narrow, the single piece, not above 15 yards	0 12 7 4	0 13 4 13	A	0 11 1 4	0 9 7 4	3 0 0
— broad, the single piece, not above 15 yards	0 18 10 16	1 0 0 19 ½	A	0 16 7 16	0 14 4 16	4 10 0
Buggasins, or Callico buckrams, the half piece	0 1 3 15	0 1 4 10 ¾	C	0 1 2 5	0 1 0 15	0 5 0
Bugle great, the pound	0 1 5 12 ⅘	0 1 6 5	B	0 1 4 8 ⅘	0 1 3 4 ⅘	0 4 8
— small, or Seed bugle, the pound	0 2 5 8	0 2 6 9	B	0 2 3 8	0 2 1 8	0 6 8
Note, By 5 Geo. III. cap. 30. §. 4. Bugle may, on importation, be warehoused, first paying down one half of the Old Subsidy, which is not drawn back on exportation; and if taken out, in order to be used in this kingdom, then to pay up the remainder of the duties due and payable upon the importation: under which circumstances, therefore, the duties will stand as follow:						
Bugle great, the pound	0 0 1 4	0 0 1 4	M			

* But if imported by Aliens Drawback more, 1s. 3d. for every 100l. of the Rate or Value.

B [30] B

INWARDS.

	DUTIES to be paid on IMPORTATION.		Reference to the several Branches, see Page vi.	DRAWBACKS to be repaid on EXPORTATION.*		RATES, or supposed value, by 12 Car. II. cap. 4. & 11 Geo. I. cap. 7. from whence the foregoing Duties are computed.
	By BRITISH.	By ALIENS.		If exported to any legal place, except as mentioned in the following column.	If the produce of Europe or the East Indies, and exported to the British Colonies in America.	
	£. s. d. 20ths	£. s. d. 20ths		£. s. d. 20ths	£. s. d. 20ths	£. s. d.
And if taken out to be used in this kingdom, more — small, or Seed bugle, the pound	0 1 4 8	0 1 5 1⅖	B			0 0 8
And if taken out to be used in this kingdom, more	0 0 2 0	0 0 2	M			
But if not warehoused, then are the duties and drawbacks payable as above specified, opposite to their respective rates.	0 2 3 8	0 2 4 9	B			
Bugle-laces, the pound	0 2 11 5	0 3 0 10 4/5	B	0 2 8 17 ⅔	0 2 6 9	0 10 0
Bullion, and foreign coin inwards, may be landed by any person without warrant or fee.						
Bullions for purses, the groce, containing 12 dozen	0 2 1 4	0 2 2 15 ½	A	0 1 10 4	0 1 7 4	1 0 0
Bullrushes, the load	0 4 2 8	0 4 5 11	A	0 3 8 8	0 3 2 8	2 10 0
Burs for millstones, the hundred, containing five score	0 10 6	0 11 1 17 ½	A	0 9 3	0 8 0	
And besides, if of France	1 6 3	1 6 3	Fb	0 13 9	0 13 9	
Buskins of leather, the dozen pair	1 1 0	1 2 12	C	0 19 0	0 17 0	4 0 0
And besides, for every 20s. of the real value of the Leather upon oath	0 6 3 12	0 6 3 12	Dc	0 0 3 12	0 0 3 12	

* But if imported by Aliens Drawback more, 1s. 3d. for every 100l. of the Rate or Value.

B [31] B

INWARDS.

	Duties to be paid on Importation.		Reference to the ſeveral Franches, ſee Page vi.	Drawbacks to be repaid on Exportation.*		Rates, or ſuppoſed value, by 12 Car.II. cap.4. †11 Geo.I. cap.7. from whence the foregoing Duties are computed.
	By British	By Aliens		If exported to any legal place, except as mentioned in the following column.	If the produce of Europe or the Eaſt-Indies, and exported to the British Colonies in America.	
	L. s. d./20ths	*L. s. d.*/20ths		*L. s. d.*/20ths	*L. s. d.*/20ths	*L. s. d.*
Buſtians, the ſingle piece, not above 15 yards	0 8 4 16	0 8 11 2	A	0 7 4 16	0 6 4 16	2 0 0
Butter, the barrel	0 4 2 8	0 4 5 11	A	0 3 8 8	0 3 2 8	1 0 0
— of Ireland, free.						
Buttons of braſs, the great groce, containing 12 ſmall groce, every groce 12 dozen			C			2 13 4
— of Bugle, the dozen			B			0 10 0
— of Chryſtal, the dozen			A			0 8 0
— of Copper, the great groce, containing 12 ſmall groce, every groce 12 dozen			A			2 13 4
And beſides for every Cwt.			E			
— of Fine damaſk work, the dozen			A			1 0 0
— of Glaſs, the great groce, containing 12 ſmall groce, every groce 12 dozen			B			1 6 8
— of Hair, the groce, containing 12 dozen			C			0 4 0
— for Handkerchiefs, the groce, containing 12 dozen			A			4 0 0

* But if imported by Aliens Drawback more, 1 s. 3 d. for every 100 l. of the Rate or Value.

INWARDS.

	DUTIES to be paid on IMPORTATION.			Reference to the several Branches, see Page vi.	DRAWBACKS to be repaid on EXPORTATION.		RATES, or supposed value, by 12 Car. II. cap. 4. ‡ 11 Geo. I. cap. 7. from whence the foregoing Duties are computed.
	By BRITISH.		By ALIENS.		If exported to any legal place, except as mentioned in the following column.	If the produce of Europe or the East Indies, and exported to the British Colonies in America.	
	£. s. d. 20ths		£. s. d. 20ths		£. s. d. 20ths	£. s. d. 20ths	£. s. d.
Buttons of Latten, the great groce, containing 12 small groce, every groce 12 dozen				C			2 13 4
—— of Silk, the great groce, containing 12 small groce, every groce 12 dozen				B			2 0 0
—— of Steel, the great groce, containing 12 small groce, every groce 12 dozen				A			2 13 4
And besides for every Cwt. of Steel				D			
—— of Thread, the great groce, containing 12 small groce, every groce 12 dozen				A			1 0 0

C

INWARDS	DUTIES to be paid on IMPORTATION — By BRITISH (£.s.d.20ths)	By ALIENS (£.s.d.20ths)	Reference to the several Branches, See Page vi.	DRAWBACKS to be repaid on EXPORTATION — If exported to any legal place, except as mentioned in the following column (£.s.d.20ths)	If the produce of Europe or the East Indies, and exported to the British Colonies in America (£.s.d.20ths)	RATES, or supposed value, by 12 Car. II. cap. 4. ‡11 Geo. I. cap. 7. from whence the foregoing Duties are computed (£.s.d.)
CABINETS of Amber, the piece	0.15.9	0.16.6 9	C	0.14.3	0.12.9	‡3.0.0
or Counters { small, the piece	0.8.4 16	0.8.11 2	A	0.7.4 16	0.6.4 16	2.0.0
{ large, the piece	0.16.9 12	0.17.10 4	A	0.14.9 12	0.12.9 12	4.0.0
Cables, tarred or untarred, the Cwt.	0.8.0 12	0.8.2 14	B			0.13.4
Caddas, or Cruel Ribband, the dozen pieces, every piece containing 36 yards	0.12.7 4	0.13.4 13	A	0.11.1 4	0.9.7 4	3.0.0
Callico fine or coarse. *Vide* Linen.						
Buckrams. *Vide* Buggafins.						
Cupboard cloths. *Vide* Pintadoes.						
Callivers. *Vide* Guns.						
Calpins for Fans, the dozen	0.1.11.12 1/2	0.2.0.16	C	0.1.9 7 1/2	0.1.7 2	‡0.7.6
And besides if made of Leather, and the Leather be the most valuable part of the Calpins, for every 20s. of the real value thereof, upon oath	0.6.3 12	0.6.3 12	Dc	0.0.3 12	0.0.3 12	
Calve skins in the hair, the piece. See Skins.						
—— of Ireland, raw. See Skins.	0.2.12 1/2	0.2.15	C	0.0.2 7	0.0.2 2	0.0.10

* But if imported by Aliens Drawback more, 1 s. 3 d. for every 100 l. of the Rate or Value.

But by 21 Geo. III. cap. 29. *Raw or un-dreffed Calve skins may be imported duty free from Ireland, or any of the British Colonies or Plantations in America, until*

F

INWARDS. [34]

	DUTIES to be paid on IMPORTATION.		Reference to the several branches, see Page vi.	DRAWBACKS to be repaid on EXPORTATION.*		RATES or supposed value, by 12 Car. II. cap. 4. †11 Geo. I c.p.7. from whence the foregoing Duties are computed
	By BRITISH.	By ALIENS.		If exported to any legal place, except as mentioned in the following column.	If the produce of Europe or the East Indies, and exported to the British Colonies in America.	
	£. s. d. 20ths	£. s. d. 20ths		£. s. d. 20ths	£. s. d. 20ths	£. s. d.
the 1st of June, 1786, or at any time thereafter, before the end of the then next session of parliament, under a due entry and Landing being made thereof.						
Calves velves to make rennet, the Cwt.	0 5 3	0 5 6 3	C	0 4 9	0 4 3	1 1 0 0
Cambogium. *Vide* Drugs.						
Cantleto, half silk, half hair, the yard	0 3	0 3 7	B			
Canary feeds. *Vide* Alpisti.						
Candle-plates, or Wallers of brass or latten, the pound			C			
Candles of tallow, the Cwt. { green, the pound	0 1 6 2 3	0 1 6 6 11 ½	Ga	0 2 10 16	0 2 7 16	0 1 8
of wax { white, or yellow, the pound	0 0 3 3	0 0 3 6 3/5	C	0 12 11 8	0 3 16 8	† 0 1 0
And besides, the pound	0 0 4 14 8	0 0 4 19 2/5 4/5	C H	0 9 3	0 1 2 6	† † 0 1 0
Candlesticks of brass or latten, the pound	0 0 4 16	0 0 4 8	C	0 12 11 8	0 0 11 8	0 1 4
of wire, the dozen	0 1 4 16	0 15 7 ½	A	0 15 6	0 14 8	0 6 8
Candlewick, the Cwt.	0 10 9	0 1 11 17	A	0 9 3	0 14 3	0 6 8
Canes, or Reeds, the thousand	1 15 9	1 17 17	C	0 14 6	0 13 3	3 10 0
Walking canes, the thousand	0 15 9	0 16 4 17	C	0 14 6	0 13 3	3 10 0
Rattans, the thousand	0 2 7 10	0 2 7 10	Ae	0 2 7 10	0 2 7 10	2 10 0
And besides if of East India						

* But if imported by Aliens Drawback more, 1s. 3d. for every 100l. of the Rate or Value.

[35]

INWARDS.

	DUTIES to be paid on IMPORTATION.		Reference to the several Branches, see Page vi.	DRAWBACKS to be repaid on EXPORTATION.*		RATES, or supposed value, by 12 Car. II. cap. 4. † 11 Geo. I cap. 7. from whence the foregoing Duties are computed.
	By BRITISH.	By ALIENS.		If exported to any legal place, except as mentioned in the following column.	If the produce of Europe or the East Indies, and exported to the British Colonies in America.	
	£. s. d. 20ths	£. s. d. 20ths		£. s. d. 20ths	£. s. d. 20ths	£. s. d.
Canes of Wood, the dozen	0 0 10 1 ⅓	0 0 10 14 ⅕	A	0 0 8 17 ⅓	0 0 7 13 ⅗	0 4 0
—— the ſhock, containing 60	0 4 2 8	0 4 5 11	A	0 3 8 8	0 3 2 8	1 0 0
Canes ——						
Canns of Wood, the dozen	0 0 10 10	0 0 11 0 ½	C	0 0 9 10	0 0 8 10	†0 3 4
Cant Spars, the hundred, containing 120 —— of, and directly from, any part of America, if regularly entered and landed, free.						1 13 4
On failure thereof. See in Wood.						
—— of or from any part of Europe, except Ireland and France	0 10 6	0 10 11 5	B	0 9 8	0 8 10	
—— of Ireland, Africa, or Aſia						
—— of France. *See in Wood.*	0 7 0	0 7 5 5	A	0 6 2	0 5 4	3 13 4
If imported in foreign ſhips, to pay duty as Aliens.						
Capravens, the hundred, containing 120 —— of, and directly from, any part of America, if regularly entered and landed, free. *On failure thereof. See in Wood.*						

* But if imported by Aliens Drawback more, 1s. 3d. for every 100 l. of the Rate or Value.

F 2

INWARDS.

	DUTIES to be paid on IMPORTATION.		Reference to the several Branches, see Page vi.	DRAWBACKS to be repaid on EXPORTATION.*		RATES, or supposed value, by 12 Car. II. cap. 4. 11 Geo. I. cap. 7. from whence the foregoing Duties are computed.
	By BRITISH.	By ALIENS.		If exported to any legal place, except as mentioned in the following column.	If the product of Europe or the East Indies, and exported to the British Colonies in America.	
	£. s. d./20ths	£. s. d./20ths		£. s. d./20ths	£. s. d./20ths	£. s. d.
Capravens, of or from any part of Europe, except Ireland and France ⎰ of Ireland, Africa, or Asia ⎱ of France. *See in Wood.*	1 3 4 0 15 4 16	1 4 0 15 0 16 7	B A	1 1 3 4 0 13 6 16	0 19 5 4 0 11 8 16	0 0 6 0 15 0
If imported in foreign ships, to pay duty as Aliens.						
Capers, the pound	0 0 15 1/5	0 0 1 6 3/10	A	0 0 1 2 1/5	0 0 0 19 1/5	
Cap-hooks, or Hook-ends, the gross, ⎰ containing 12 dozen ⎱ *And besides for every Cwt. of Iron*	0 3 1 16 0 5 3	0 3 4 3 1/4 0 5 3	A D	0 2 9 6 0 5 3		0 6 8
Caps, vizt. Cotton or Thread, the dozen	0 1 9	0 1 10 1	C	0 1 7	0 0 1 5	
And besides, if Cotton, for every 20s. of the value, according to the gross price at the candle			Q			
Caps, vizt. Double tufted, or Cockered ⎰ caps, the dozen ⎱ for children, the dozen ⎰ Night-caps, of sattin and ⎱ velvet, the dozen	0 3 1 16 0 10 0 19 1/5 0 4 2 8	0 3 1 16 0 10 8 10 1/5 0 4 5 11	A A	0 3 1 16 0 8 10 11 0 3 8 8	0 3 1 16 0 7 8 3 0 3 2 8	2 8 0 1 0 0 3 0 0

* But if imported by Aliens Drawback more, 1s. 3d. for every 100 of the Rate or Value.

INWARDS.

	Duties to be paid on Importation. By British. £.	s.	d.	20ths	By Aliens. £.	s.	d.	20ths	Reference to the several Branches, see Page vi.	Drawbacks to be repaid on Exportation.* If exported to any legal place, except as mentioned in the following column. £.	s.	d.	20ths	If the produce of Europe or the East Indies, and exported to the British Colonies in America. £.	s.	d.	20ths	Rates, or supposed value, by 12 Car. II. cap. 4. ‡ 11 Geo. I. cap. 7. from whence the foregoing Duties are computed. £.	s.	d.
——— of silk knit, the dozen ———	—	—	—	—	—	—	—	—		—	—	—	—	—	—	—	—	4	0	0
——— of linen, the dozen ———	0	1	8	3 1/5	0	1	9	8 2/5	A	0	1	5	15 1/5	0	1	3	7 1/5	0	8	0
——— of woollen, the dozen ———	0	4	2	8	0	4	5	11	A	0	3	8	8	0	3	2	8	1	0	0
Cards, *vocat.* Playing cards, the groce, containing 12 dozen pair ———	1	5	2	8	1	6	9	6	A	1	2	2	8	0	19	2	8	6	0	0
And besides, for every pack ———	0	0	6	6	0	0	6	6	I a	0	0	0	6	0	0	0	6			
——— Wool cards, new, the dozen pair ———	0	2	1	4	0	2	2	15 1/2	A	0	1	10	4	0	1	7	4	0	10	0
——— old, the dozen pair ———	0	1	3	2 2/5	0	1	4	1 3/10	A	0	1	1	6 2/5	0	0	11	10 2/5	0	6	0
Carpets, of Brunswick, striped and unstriped, the piece ———	0	2	7	10	0	2	9	1 1/2	C	0	2	4	10	0	2	1	10	0	10	0
——— of China, of cotton, coarse, the piece ———	0	2	1	4	0	2	1	16 3/5	G c	0	2	0		0	1	10	16	0	4	0
And besides, for every 20s. of the groce price at the candle ———	0	3	1	16	0	3	1	16	Q	0	3	1	16	0	3	1	16			
——— of Cornix, the carpet, two yards and an half long ———	0	6	6	15	0	6	10	13 3/4	C	0	5	11	5	0	5	3	15	1	5	0

* But if imported by Aliens Drawback more, 1s. 3d. for every 100l. of the Rate or Value.

INWARDS

	DUTIES to be paid on IMPORTATION.		DRAWBACKS to be repaid on EXPORTATION.*		RATES, or supposed value, by 12 Car. II. cap. 4. & 11 Geo. I. cap. 7. from whence the foregoing Duties are conjectured.
	By BRITISH.	By ALIENS.	Reference to the several Brantleys, see Page &c.	If exported to any legal place, except as mentioned in the following column.	If the produce of Europe or the East Indies, and exported to the British Colonies in America.
	£. s. d. 20ths	£. s. d. 20ths		£. s. d. 20ths	£. s. d. 20ths	£. s. d.
Carpets, Ghentish, the dozen	0 15 9	0 16 6 9	C	0 14 3	0 12 9	3 0 0
—— of Persia, the yard square, the yard	1 3 7 10	1 4 2 11 ¼	G	1 2 6	1 1 4 10	2 5 0
—— of Scotland, the piece, free.						
—— of Tonney, the piece, containing two yards and an half long	0 7 10 10	0 8 3 4 ½	C	0 7 1 10	0 6 4 10	1 10 0
—— of Turkey or Venice, short, the piece	0 7 10 10	0 8 3 4 ½	C	0 7 1 10	0 6 4 10	1 10 0
—— long, containing four yards and upwards	2 2 0	2 4 1 4	C	1 18 0	1 14 0	8 0 0
Carrels, the piece, containing 15 yards	0 5 7 4	0 5 11 8	A	0 4 11 4	0 4 3 4	1 6 8
Cases for bottles, the piece not exceeding 12 bottles	0 0 10 10	0 0 11 0 ½	C	0 0 9 10	0 0 8 10	0 3 4
—— if above 12 bottles	0 1 3 15	0 1 4 10 ¼	C	0 1 2 5	0 1 0 15	0 5 0
—— for combs, { single, the groce, containing 12 dozen	0 4 2 8	0 4 5 11	A	0 3 8 8	0 3 2 8	1 0 0
—— double, the groce, containing 12 dozen	0 8 4 16	0 8 11 2		0 7 4 16	0 6 4 16	2 0 0
—— for needles { or Pin cases, the groce, containing 12 dozen	0 2 9 12	0 2 11 14	A	0 2 5 12	0 2 1 12	0 13 4
—— French gilt, the dozen	0 3 8 2	0 3 8 17 ¼	F	0 2 3 12	0 2 2 2	0 5 0

* But if imported by Aliens Drawback more, 1s. 3d. for every 100l. of the Rate or Value.

INWARDS.

Cases for Looking-glasses

Item	Duties on Importation By British £ s. d. 20ths	Duties on Importation By Aliens £ s. d. 20ths	Ref. to branches, see Page vi.	Drawbacks on Exportation — If exported to any legal place, except as mentioned in the following column £ s. d. 20ths	Drawbacks on Exportation — If the produce of Europe or the East Indies, and exported to the British Colonies in America £ s. d. 20ths	Rates, or supposed value, by 12 Car. II. cap. 4. 11 Geo. I. cap. 7. from whence the foregoing Duties are computed £ s. d.
for spectacles, gilt, the groce, containing 12 dozen	0 5 7 4	0 5 11 8	A	0 4 11 4	0 4 3 4	1 6 8
for spectacles, ungilt, the groce, containing 12 dozen	0 2 9 12	0 2 11 14	A	0 2 5 12	0 2 1 12	0 13 4
with Ivory combs, large, garnished, the dozen	0 16 9 12	0 17 10 4	A	0 14 9 12	0 12 9 12	4 0 0
middle sort, garnished, the dozen	0 8 4 16	0 8 11 2	A	0 7 4 16	0 6 4 16	2 0 0
small, garnished, the dozen	0 5 7 4	0 5 11 8	A	0 4 11 4	0 4 3 4	1 6 8
Cases with Wooden combs, garnished the dozen	0 4 2 8	0 4 5 11	A	0 3 8 8	0 3 2 8	1 0 0
gilt, of N° 3 and 4, the dozen	0 0 10 1	0 0 10 14 1/5	A	0 0 8 17 3/5	0 0 7 13 4/5	0 4 0
N° 5 and 6, the dozen	0 1 5 12	0 1 6 14 1/2	A	0 1 3 10	0 1 1 8	0 7 0
N° 7 and 8, the dozen	0 2 1 4	0 2 2 15	A	0 1 10 4	0 1 7 4	0 10 0
N° 9 and 10, and upwards the dozen	0 7 0	0 7 5 5	A	0 6 2	0 5 0	1 13 4
ungilt, of N° 3 and 4, the dozen	0 0 5 16 3/5	0 0 5 7 1/5	A	0 0 4 8	0 0 3 16 3/5	0 2 0
N° 5 and 6, the dozen	0 0 8 16	0 0 9 7	A	0 0 7 15	0 0 6 14	0 3 6
N° 7 and 8, the dozen	0 0 1 12	0 1 1 7	A	0 0 11 2	0 0 9 12	0 5 0
N° 9 and 10, the dozen	0 3 6	0 3 8 12	A	0 3 1	0 2 8	0 16 8

* But if imported by Aliens Drawback more, 1s. 3d. for every 100l. of the Rate or Value.

INWARDS.

	Duties to be paid on Importation. By British. £.	s.	d.	20ths	Duties to be paid on Importation. By Aliens. £.	s.	d.	20ths	Reference to the several Branches, see Page vi.	Drawbacks to be repaid on Exportation.* If exported to any legal place, except as mentioned in the following column. £.	s.	d.	20ths	If the produce of Europe or the East Indies, and exported to the British Colonies in America. £.	s.	d.	20ths	Rates, or supposed value, by 12 Car. II. cap. 4. ‡ 11 Geo. I. cap. 7. from whence the foregoing Duties are computed. £.	s.	d.
Caskets of iron, large, the dozen	0	12	7	4	0	13	4	13	A	0	11	1	4	—	—	—	—	3	0	0
—— middle sort, the dozen	0	10	0	19 1/5	0	10	8	10 2/5	A	0	8	10	11 1/5	—	—	—	—	2	8	0
—— small, the dozen	0	6	3	12	0	6	8	6 1/2	A	0	5	6	12	—	—	—	—	1	10	0
And besides for every Cwt. of Iron	0	5	3		0	5	3		D	0	5	3		—	—	—	—			
Caskets of steel, the dozen	1	5	2	8	1	6	9	6	A	1	2	2	8	—	—	—	—	6	0	0
And besides for every Cwt. of Steel	0	5	9	6	0	5	9	6	D	0	5	9	6	—	—	—	—			
Casks empty, the ton	0	7	10	10	0	8	3	4 1/2	C	0	7	1	10	0	6	4	10	‡ 1	10	0
Catlings. *Vide* Harp-strings *and* Lute-strings.																				
Cattle great, imported from Ireland, free.																				
Caviare, the Cwt.	0	4	2	8	0	4	5	11	A	0	3	8	8	0	3	2	8	1	0	0
Cauls of linen for women, the dozen	0	1	8	3 1/5	0	1	9	8 2/5	A	0	1	5	15 1/5	0	1	3	7 1/5	0	8	0
Cauls of silk, the dozen	—	—	—	—	—	—	—	—		—	—	—	—	—	—	—	—	1	6	8
Chaffing-dishes, brass or latten, the pound	0	0	4	4	0	0	4	8 1/5	C	0	0	3	16	0	0	3	8	0	1	4
—— iron, the dozen	0	2	9	12	0	2	11	14	A	0	2	5	12	—	—	—	—	0	13	4
And besides for every Cwt. of Iron	0	5	3		0	5	3		D	0	5	3		—	—	—	—			
Chains for dogs, coarse, the dozen ‖	0	0	8	8	0	0	8	18 1/2	A	0	0	7	8	0	0	6	8	0	3	4
And besides, if { Brass, the dozen	0	0	2	2	0	0	2	2	E	0	0	2	2	0	0	2	2			
{ Iron, the Cwt.	0	5	3		0	5	3		D	0	5	3		—	—	—	—			
—— for keys or purses, fine, the dozen ‖	0	1	8	3 1/5	0	1	9	8 2/5	A	0	1	5	15 1/5	0	1	3	7 1/5	0	8	0

‖ If Iron no Drawback to the British Colonies in America.

* But if imported by Aliens Drawback more, 1s. 3d. for every 100l. of the Rate or Value.

C [41] C

INWARDS.	DUTIES to be paid on IMPORTATION.		Reference to the several Branches, see Page vi.	DRAWBACKS to be repaid on EXPORTATION.*		RATES, or supposed value, by 12 Car.II. cap.4. 11 Geo.I. cap.7. from whence the foregoing Duties are computed.
	By BRITISH.	By ALIENS.		If exported to any legal place, except as mentioned in the following column.	If the produce of Europe or the East Indies, and exported to the British Colonies in America.	
	£ s. d. 20ths	£ s. d. 20ths		£ s. d. 20ths	£ s. d. 20ths	£ s. d.
And besides, if { Brass, the dozen	0 5 0 4/5	0 5 3 4/5	E	0 5 3	0 5 0 4/5	2 10 0
{ Iron, the Cwt.	0 0 10	0 13 9	D	0 11 10 10	0 10 7 10	0 10 0
Chairs matted, the dozen	0 1 4	0 2 15	C	0 1 10 4	0 1 7 4	0 10 0
of walnut-tree, the piece	0 2 1 16	0 3 3 7 1/5	A	0 2 10 16	0 2 7 16	0 3 0
Chamlets, half silk, half hair, the yard	0 3 7 11 1/5	0 3 8 4/5	B	0 0 6 13	0 0 5 15 1/5	0 5 0
unwatered, or Mohairs, the yard	0 0 11	0 1 1	A	0 0 11 2	0 0 9 12	0 0 0
watered, the yard	0 1 0 12	0 1 1 7	A	0 0 11 2	0 0 9 12	0 0 0
Checks. Vide Barbers aprons.						
Cheese, the Cwt.	0 4 16	0 5 17	A	0 1 2 16	0 1 0 16	0 6 8
Cherries, the Cwt.	0 4 2 8	0 4 5 11	A	0 3 8 8	0 3 2 8	0 1 0
Chess boards, the dozen	0 4 2 8	0 4 4 11	A	0 3 8 8	0 3 2 8	0 1 0
Chests of Iron, large, the piece	0 2 6 4 4/5	0 2 8 2 2/3	A	0 2 2 12	0 2 2 8	0 12 0
men, the groce, containing 12 dozen	0 18 0	0 9 9	A	0 1 4 8	0 1 11 0	6 13 4
middle sort, or small, the piece	1 1 0	1 2 3 15	A	0 18 6		
piece						
And besides, for every Cwt,	0 5 3	0 5 3	D	0 5 3		5 0 0
of Cyprus wood, the neft, containing three chests	1 13 7 4	1 15 8 8	A	1 9 7 4	1 5 7 4	8 0 0
of Spruce, or Danske, the neit, containing three chests	0 6 3 12	0 6 8 8	A	0 5 6 12	0 4 9 12	1 10 0
painted, the dozen	0 8 4 16	0 8 11 2	A	0 7 4 16	0 6 4 16	2 0 0

* But if imported by Aliens Drawback more, 1 s. 3 d. for every 100 l. of the Rate or Value.

[42]

INWARDS.

Item	Duties by British £ s. d./20ths	Duties by Aliens £ s. d./20ths	Ref.	Drawbacks if exported to any legal place, except as mentioned in the following column £ s. d./20ths	Drawbacks if the produce of Europe, or the East Indies, and exported to the British Colonies in America £ s. d./20ths	Rates, or supposed value, by ‡ 12 Car. II. cap. 4. † 11 Geo. I. cap. 7. from whence the foregoing Duties are computed £ s. d.
Chimney-backs, large, the piece	0 5 3	0 5 2	B	0 4 11	—	‡13 4
—— small, the piece	0 2 7 10	0 2 11	B	0 2 5 10	0 0 6 8	0 6 8
China pease, the pound	0 0 8 8	0 0 8 18 1/2	A	0 0 7 8	—	0 3 4
China-ware. *Vide* Earthen-ware.						
Chizels for Joiners, the dozen	0 0 10 1 3/5	0 0 10 14 1/5	A	0 0 8 17 3/5	—	0 4 0
And bisides for every Cwt. of Iron			D	0 0 5 3	—	—
Cinnamon. *Vide in* Grocery.						
Cisterns of Latten, the pound	0 0 4 4	0 0 4 8	C	0 0 3 16	0 0 3 8	‡ 1 4
Citron waters. *Vide* Spirits.						
Citterns, the dozen	0 12 7 4	0 13 4 13	A	0 11 1 4	0 0 9 7 4	3 0 0
Clapholt, or Clapboards, the hundred, containing 120						0 15 0
America, if regularly entered and landed, of, and directly from, any part of free.						
On failure thereof. See in Wood.						
—— of or from any part of Europe, except Ireland and France	0 4 8 14	0 4 11 1 1/4	B	0 4 4 4	0 3 11 14	—
—— of Ireland, Africa, or Asia	0 3 1 16	0 3 4 3 1/4	A	0 2 9 6	0 2 4 16	—
—— of France. *See in* Wood.						

* But if imported by Aliens Drawback more, 1s. 3d. for every 100 l. of the Rate or Value.

INWARDS.

	DUTIES to be paid on IMPORTATION.		Reference to the several Branches, see Page vi.	DRAWBACKS to be repaid on EXPORTATION.*		RATES, or supposed value, by 12 Car. II. cap. 4. † 11 Geo. I. cap. 7. from whence the foregoing Duties are computed.
	By BRITISH.	By ALIENS.		If exported to any legal place, except as mentioned in the following column.	If the produce of Europe or the East Indies, and exported to the British Colonies in America.	
	£. s. d. 20ths	£. s. d. 20ths		£. s. d. 20ths	£. s. d. 20ths	£. s. d.
If imported in foreign ships, to pay duty as Aliens.						
Claricords, the pair	0 2 9 12	0 2 11 14	A	0 2 5 12	0 2 1 12	0 13 4
Cloaks of felt, the piece	0 8 4 16	0 8 11 2	A	0 7 4 16	0 6 4 16	2 0 0
Cloths, all manner of woollen cloths imported, per yard	1 15 8 8	1 17 11 3 ½	A	1 11 5 8	1 7 2 8	8 10 0
Cloth rashes. *Vide* Rashes.						
Cloves. *Vide in* Grocery.						
Coals of Scotland, the ton						
But by 5 Ann. cap. 8. subject to the Craft duties only.			C			
Coals imported. For every 20 s. of their true value upon oath	0 5 3	0 5 6 3	H a	0 4 9	0 4 3	0 6 8
	0 5 3	0 5 3		0 5 3	0 5 3	
And besides, for every { Ton, containing 20 Cwt. or Chalder, containing 36 bushels, Winchester measure }	0 7 10 10	0 7 10 10	H a	0 7 10 10	0 7 10 10	

* But if imported by Aliens Drawback more, 16 s. 3 d. for every 100 l. of the Rate or Value.

C   [44]   C

INWARDS.	Reference to the several Branches, see Page vi.	DUTIES to be paid on IMPORTATION.		DRAWBACKS to be repaid on EXPORTATION.*		RATES, or supposed value, by 12 Car. II. cap. 4. 11 Geo. I. cap. 7. from whence the foregoing Duties are computed.
		By BRITISH.	By ALIENS.	If exported to any legal place, except as mentioned in the following column.	If the produce of Europe or the East Indies, and exported to the British Colonies in America.	
		L. s. d. 20ths	*L. s. d.* 20ths	*L. s. d.* 20ths	*L. s. d.* 20ths	*L. s. d.*
And besides, for all Coals imported into the port of London, for every ⎰ Ton, containing 20 Cwt. ⎱ or ⎰ Chalder, containing 35 bushels, Winchester measure ⎱	Vb	0 3 1 1/16	0 3 1 1/16	0 0 1 1/16	0 0 1 1/16	
But 100 Chalder are annually allowed for the use of Chelsea hospital, free of this duty.	Vb	0 3 1 1/16	0 3 1 1/16	0 0 1 1/16	0 0 1 1/16	
Cobalt, by 21 Geo. III. cap. 62. may, during the present hostilities with France, Spain, and the United Provinces, or either of them, be imported by any persons, from any port or place whatsoever, in British or Irish ships legally navigated, or in any ship belonging to any state in amity with His Majesty, if regularly entered and landed, duty free. But on failure thereof, then to pay, for every 20s. of the real value upon oath						
Cochineal, for Dyers use, as by 3 and 4 Ann. cap. 4. *vicat.* Silvester, or Campechia Cochineal, the pound	L	0 6 1 1 3/5	0 6 4 4 3/5	0 5 7 1 3/5	0 5 1 1 3/5	0 1 8

* But if imported by Aliens Drawback more, 1s. 3d. for every 100l. of the Rate or Value.

INWARDS.

INWARDS	DUTIES to be paid on IMPORTATION. By BRITISH.				By ALIENS.				Reference to the several Branches, see Page vi.	DRAWBACKS to be repaid on EXPORTATION.* If exported to any legal place, except as mentioned in the following column.				If the produce of Europe or the East Indies, and exported to the British Colonies in America.				RATES, or supposed value, by 12 Car. II. cap. 4. 11 Geo. I. cap. 7. from whence the foregoing Duties are computed.		
	L.	s.	d.	20ths	L.	s.	d.	20ths		L.	s.	d.	20ths	L.	s.	d.	20ths	L.	s.	d.
— of all sorts, except Silvester and Campechia Cochineal, the pound ——	0	2	2		0	2	7	1/4										0	6	8
But by 8 Geo. I. cap. 15, if regularly imported, entered and landed, free.																				
But on failure thereof, then to pay { Silvester, or Campechia									Bb	0	0	1	12	0	0	1	2			
All other sorts	0	8	8		0	9	9		Bb	0	0	6	8	0	0	4	8			
Cocks for lavers. Vide Brass.																				
Cocks for bellows. Vide Whistles.																				
Cocoa-nuts, not being rated by act 12 Car. II. were by 10 Geo. I. cap. 10. rated by the Cwt. at l. 2. 10 0. On which said rate, the duties payable are as follow:																				
—— of any French colony or plantation	1	3	7	10	1	4	3	7 1/2	C	1	2	4	10	1	2	4	10			
—— of any British colony or plantation in America	0	13	7	10	0	13	9	7 1/2	C	0	13	1	10	0	13	1	10			
—— of any other place	0	13	1	10	0	13	9	7 1/2	C	0	11	10	10	0	11	10	10			
But by 6 Geo. III. caf. 52. § 22. Cocoa-nuts are allowed to be imported for re-																				

* But if imported by Aliens Drawback more, 1 s. 3 d. for every 100 l. of the Rate or Value.

INWARDS.

	DUTIES to be paid on IMPORTATION.		Reference to the several Branches, see Page vi.	DRAWBACKS to be repaid on EXPORTATION.*		RATES or supposed value by 12 Car. II. cap. 4. 11 Geo. I. cap. 7. from whence the foregoing Duties are computed.
	By BRITISH.	By ALIENS.		If exported to any legal place, except as mentioned in the following column.	If the produce of Europe or the East Indies, and exported to the British Colonies in America.	
	L. s. d. 20ths	L. s. d. 20ths		L. s. d. 20ths	L. s. d. 20ths	L. s. d.
——— British, the Cwt. from any of the British Dominions in America———	0 1 3	0 1 3	M			
——— foreign, the Cwt.	0 1 3	0 1 3	M	0 1 3	0 1 3	
But if taken out of the warehouse in Great Britain for home consumption, then to pay were:						
——— from any French colony, or plantation	1 2 4 10	1 3 0 7½	C			
——— from any other place	0 11 0 10	0 12 6 7½	C			

Coffee, not being rated by the act of 12 Car. II. was, by 10 Geo. I. cap. 10. §48. rated by the Cwt. at 7 l.

exportation, on paying down half the old Subsidy, and being warehoused; which duty, on such as are of the growth of any British colony or plantation in America, is (on their re-exportation as merchandize) allowed, by the 7th of Geo. III. cap. 46. §6. to be wholly drawn back: Therefore the duties and drawbacks are as follow:

* But if imported by Aliens Drawback more, 1 s. 3 d. for every 100 l. of the Rate or Value.

[47]

INWARDS.

	DUTIES to be paid on IMPORTATION.		Reference to the several Branches, see Page vi.	DRAWBACKS to be repaid on EXPORTATION.*		RATES, or supposed value, by 12 Car. II. cap. 4. 11 Geo. I. cap. 7. from whence the foregoing Duties are computed.
	By BRITISH.	By ALIENS.		If exported to any legal place, except as mentioned in the following column.	If the produce of Europe or the East Indies, and exported to the British Colonies in America.	
	£. s. d. 20ths	£. s. d. 20ths		£. s. d. 20ths	£. s. d. 20ths	£. s. d.
On which said rate, the duties payable are as follow:						
—— of any French colony or plantation	3 6 1 16	3 7 11 17	C	3 2 7 16	3 2 7 16	
—— of any British colony or plantation in America	1 16 9	1 18 7 1	C	1 16 9	1 16 9	
—— of any other place	1 16 9	1 18 7 1	C	1 13 3	1 13 3	

But by 6 Geo. III. cap. 52. §22. in order to encourage the growth of Coffee in the British dominions in America, its importation into, and exportation from Great Britain, it is allowed to be imported from thence for re-exportation, on paying down half the Old Subsidy, and being warehoused; which duty, on such as is of the growth of any British colony or plantation in America, is (on its re-exportation as merchandize) allowed, by 7 Geo. III. cap. 46. §. 6. to be wholly drawn back. Therefore,

* But if imported by Aliens Drawback more, 1 s. 3 d. for every 100 l. of the Rate or Value.

C [48] C

INWARDS.	DUTIES to be paid on IMPORTATION.		Reference to the several Branches, see Page vi.	DRAWBACKS to be repaid on EXPORTATION.*		RATES, or supposed value, by 12 Car. II. cap. 4. ⅓ 11 Geo. I. c. p. 7. from whence the foregoing Duties are computed.
	By BRITISH.	By ALIENS.		If exported to any legal place, except as mentioned in the following column.	If of the produce of Europe or the East Indies, and exported to the British Colonies in America.	
	£. s. d. 20ths	£. s. d. 20ths		£. s. d. 20ths	£. s. d. 20ths	£. s. d.
Coffee, of the growth or produce of any British colony or plantation in America, imported directly from thence ————	0 3 6	0 3 6	M	0 3 6	0 3 6	
———— foreign, which shall have been warehoused upon the continent of America, and imported directly from thence, in the manner required by 6 Geo. III. cap. 52. § 22. or any other act in force	0 3 6	0 3 6	M			
But if taken out of the warehouse in Great Britain, for home consumption, then to pay more ————	1 13 3	1 15 1 1	C			
Subject also to the Inland Duties of Excise.						
Coffers, covered with gilt leather, the dozen ————	0 8 4:16	0 8 11 2	A	0 7 4:16	0 6 4:16	2 0 0
———— covered with velvet, the dozen	0 16 9:12	0 17 10 4	A	0 14 9:12	0 12 9:12	4 0 0
———— painted, the nest, containing three coffers	0 3 4 6 ⅔	0 3 6:16 ⅘	A	0 2 11 10 ⅔	0 2 6 14 ⅔	0 16 0
———— plain, the nest, containing three coffers	0 2 9:12	0 2 11 14	A	0 2 5 12	0 2 1 12	0 13 4

* But if imported by Aliens Drawback more, 1s. 3d. for every 100l. of the Rate or Value.

C [49] C

INWARDS.		DUTIES to be paid on IMPORTATION.				Reference to the several Branches, see Page vi.	DRAWBACKS to be repaid on EXPORTATION.*						RATES, or supposed value, by 12 Car.II. cap.4. ‡ 11 Geo.I. cap.7. from whence the foregoing Duties are computed.		
		By BRITISH.					If exported to any legal place, except as mentioned in the following column.				If the produce of Europe or the East Indies, and exported to the British Colonies in America.					
		L.	*s.*	*d.*	20ths		By ALIENS.				*L.*	*s.*	*d.*	20ths	*L.*	*s.*	*d.*	20ths	*L.*	*s.*	*d.*
——— with iron bars, the neat containing three coffers		0	6	8	12 4/5		0	7	1	13 3/5	A	0	5	11	0 4/5				1	12	0
And besides for every Cwt. of Iron		0	5	3			0	5	3		D	0	5	3							
Coin. *Vide* Bullion *and* Copper.																						
Coker nuts for cane heads, or cups, the thousand		0	2	7	10		0	2	9	1 1/2	C	0	2	4	10	0	2	1	10	0	10	0
Combs of Bone, the pound		0	0	1	3/5		0	0	10	14 1/5	A	0	0	8	17 4/5	0	0	7	13 3/5	0	4	0
——— of Box, the groce, containing 12 dozen		0	2	1	4		0	2	15	1 1/2	A	0	1	10	4	0	3	16	4	0	10	0
——— of Horn, for Barbers, the pound		0	0	5	0 4/5		0	0	5	7 1/10	A	0	0	4	8 4/5	0	0	7	13 3/5	0	2	0
——— *vocat.* Horse combs, the dozen		0	0	10	1 3/5		0	0	14	5 2/5	A	0	0	8	17	0	0	1	7	4	0	4	0
——— of Ivory, the pound		0	2	1	4		0	2	15	1 1/2	A	0	1	10	4	0	0	16	4/5	0	10	0
——— *vocat.* Light-wood combs, the groce, containing 12 dozen		0	1	4	16		0	1	17	3/4	A	0	1	2	16	0	0	12		0	6	8
——— for Wool, the pair, old or new		0	1	0	12		0	1	1	7	A	0	0	11	2	0	0	9	12	0	5	0
Comashes out of Turkey, the piece		0	16	9	12		0	17	10		A	0	14	9	12	0	12	9	12	0	4	0
Comfits, the pound		0	0	5	0 4/5		0	0	5	1 1/2	C	0	0	4	8 4/5	0	0	3	16 4/5	0	2	0
Compasses of Brass, the dozen		0	1	0	12		0	1	1	4 1/2	A	0	0	11	8	0	0	10	4	0	4	0
——— of Iron for Carpenters, the dozen		0	0	5	0 4/5		0	0	5	7 1/10	D	0	0	4	8 4/5					0	2	0
And besides for every Cwt. of Iron		0	5	3			0	5	3		A	0	5	3								
——— for ships, the dozen		0	1	6	18		0	1	8	1	A	0	1	4	13	0	1	2	8	0	7	6

* But if imported by Aliens Drawback more, 1s. 3d. for every 100l. of the Rate or Value.

[50]

INWARDS.

	DUTIES to be paid on IMPORTATION.		Reference to the several Branches, see Page vi.	DRAWBACKS to be repaid on EXPORTATION.*		RATES, or supposed value, by 12 Car. II. cap. 4. 11 Geo. I. cap. 7. from whence the foregoing Duties are computed.
	By BRITISH.	By ALIENS.		If exported to any legal place, except as mentioned in the following column.	If the produce of Europe or the East Indies, and exported to the British Colonies in America.	
	£. s. d. 20ths	£. s. d. 20ths		£. s. d. 20ths	£. s. d. 20ths	£. s. d.
Copper chains, the chain	0 0 5 4	0 0 5 7 6/10	A	0 0 4 8 7/10	0 0 3 16 3/10	0 2 0
And besides for every Cwt.	0 18 4 10	0 18 4 10	E	0 18 4 10	0 18 4 10	0 6 8
— ore, the Cwt.			C			0 2 6
— purles, or plate, the mark	0 1 7 7	0 1 5 1/2	A	0 1 7 2	0 0 6 7	
And besides, for every Cwt.	0 18 4 10	0 18 4 10	E	0 18 4 10	0 18 4 10	0 10 0
— unwrought bricks or plates, round or square, or Rose copper, the Cwt.	0 2 1 4	0 2 2 15 1/2	A	0 1 10 4	0 1 7 4	
And besides, if { called ⅔, bricks, copper coin, and all cast copper, the Cwt. { plates, the Cwt.	0 7 10 10	0 7 10 10	E	0 7 10 10	0 7 10 10	6 0 0
— part wrought as bars, rods, or ingots, hammered or raised, the Cwt.	0 13 1 10	0 13 1 10	E	0 13 1 10	0 13 1 10	
— of all sorts, fully wrought, not particularly rated in the Book of Rates, the Cwt.	1 18 3 18	1 19 16 16	C	1 15 3 18	1 12 3 18	9 6 8
But Copper bars are not to be allowed a drawback, unless imported from the East Indies, or the coast of Barbary, and exported by any of his Majesty's subjects.	2 17 6 18	3 0 0 6	C	2 12 10 18	2 8 2 8	

* But if imported by Aliens Drawback more, 1s. 3d. for every 100l. of the Rate or Value.

INWARDS.

	DUTIES to be paid on IMPORTATION.		Reference to the several Branches, see Page vi.	DRAWBACKS to be repaid on EXPORTATION.*		RATES, or supposed value, by 12 Car. II. cap. 4. & 11 Geo I. cap. 7. from whence the foregoing Duties are computed.
	By BRITISH.	By ALIENS.		If exported to any legal place, except as mentioned in the following column.	If the produce of Europe or the East Indies, and exported to the British Colonies in America.	
	£. s. d. 20ths	£. s. d. 20ths		£. s. d. 20ths	£. s. d. 20ths	£. s. d.
Copperas, for Dyers use, *as by 3 and 4 Ann. cap. 4.* green, the Cwt. *Vide in Drugs.*	0 1 6 18	0 1 9 5¼	B b	0 1 2 8	0 0 9 18	0 15 0
— white or blue. *Vide in Drugs.*						
Coral. *Vide in Drugs.*						
Cordage, or Ropes tarred, or untarred, the Cwt.	0 8 0 12	0 8 2 14	B	0 3 1 8 17	0 0 2 8 ⅓	0 13 4
Cordial waters. *Vide Spirits.*						
Cork for Shoemakers, the dozen pieces	0 0 10 6	0 0 10 14	A	0 0 4 4 15	0 0 4 5	0 4 8
— of all other forts, the Cwt.	0 0 3 0	0 0 3 12	A	0 0 1 2 16		0 15 8
Corks ready made, the groce, containing 32 dozen	0 0 5 5	0 0 5 10	C	0 0 5 3		0 1 8
Cork-tacks of Iron, for every Cwt.	0 1 4 16	0 1 5 17	A	0 0 0 2		0 6 8
— And besides *for every Cwt.*	0 5 3 0	0 5 3 10	D	0 5 5 3		1 13 4
— of Steel, the thousand	0 7 0 0	0 7 5 5	A			
— And besides, *for every Cwt.*	0 5 9 6	0 5 9 6	D	0 5 9 6		1 6 8
Corn and Grain, *vocat.* Barley and Malt, not exceeding the price of 3s. 6d. the bushel, or 28s. per quarter, at the place of importation, by the bushel 3s. 4d. which is by the quarter, containing 8 bushels						

* But if imported by Aliens Drawback more, 1s. 3d. for every 100 l. of the Rate or Value.

C [52] C

INWARDS.

	DUTIES to be paid on IMPORTATION.		Reference to the several Branches, fee Page vi.	DRAWBACKS to be repaid on EXPORTATION.*		RATES, or supposed value, by 12 Car. II. cap. 4. 11 Geo. I cap. 7. from whence the foregoing Duties are computed.
	By BRITISH.	By ALIENS.		If exported to any legal place, except as mentioned in the following column.	If the produce of Europe or the East Indies, and exported to the British Colonies in America.	
	£. s. d. 20ths	£. s. d. 20ths		£. s. d. 20ths	£. s. d. 20ths	£. s. d.
						0 5 0

Corn and Grain, *vocat*. Barley and Malt: when it shall exceed that rate by the quarter

And by 22 *Car.* II. *cap.* 13. when not exceeding 32s. per quarter, the sum to b: paid for Cu*ft*oms, in*ft*ead of Poundage, on the rates above-mentioned, is per quarter, containing 8 bu*ft*hels, and each bu*ft*hel 8 gallons —

Old *fub*.   *l. s. d.*
            0 16 0

But by 13 *Geo.* III. *cap.* 43; whenever the price of middling Briti*ft*h Barley *ft*hall appear to be at, or above, 24s. per quarter, at the place of importation, according to the methods directed for a*ft*certaining the prices of Corn and Grain imported, then the duty on the above rates cea*ft*es, and in lieu thereof, a duty of two pence per quarter is laid on; *ft*o that the net duties payable thereon, under th: following circumstances, will be thus:

* But if imported by Aliens Drawback more, 1s. 3d. for every 100l. of the Rate or Value.

INWARDS.

	DUTIES to be paid on IMPORTATION.		DRAWBACKS to be repaid on EXPORTATION.*		RATES, or supposed value, by 12 Car. II. cap. 4. † 11 Geo. I. cap. 7. from whence the foregoing Duties are computed.
	By BRITISH.	By ALIENS.	If exported to any legal place, except as mentioned in the following column.	If the produce of Europe or the East Indies, and exported to the British Colonies in America.	
	Reference to the several Branches, see Page vi.				
	£. s. d. 20ths	£. s. d. 20ths	£. s. d. 20ths	£. s. d. 20ths	£. s. d.
——— not exceeding the price of 28s. per quarter, and yet under 24s. the quarter	1 1 0	1 1 0	0 13 0		
But at, or above, 24s. the quarter ———	0 0 2 2	0 0 2 2	0 0 2 2	0 0 2 2	
Barley hulled. See in Drugs.					
———————— vocat. Beer or Big. By 13 Geo. III. cap. 43, whenever the price of middling British Beer, or Big, shall appear to be at, or above, 24s. per quarter, at the place of importation, according to the method directed for ascertaining the prices of Corn and Grain imported, then is the duty, per quarter ———	0 0 2 2	0 0 2 2	0 0 2 2	0 0 2 2	1 6 8
——— vocat. Beans, not exceeding the price of 3s. 6d. the bushel, or 28s. per quarter, at the place of importation, by the bushel 3s. 4d. which is by the quarter, containing 8 bushels ——— when it shall exceed that by the quarter ———					0 5 0

* But if imported by Aliens Drawback more, 1 s. 3 d. for every 100 l. of the Rate or Value.

‖ If exported within six months.

INWARDS.

Corn and Grain, wheat, Beans:

— By 22 Car. II. cap. 13. when not exceeding 40 s. per quarter, the sum to be paid for Customs instead of Poundage, on the rates above-mentioned, is per quarter, containing 8 bushels, as before-mentioned — Old sub. *l. s. d.* 0 16 0

But by 13 Geo. III. cap. 43. whenever the price of middling British Beans shall appear to be at, or above, 32 s. per quarter, at the place of importation, according to the methods directed for ascertaining the prices of Corn and Grain imported, then the duty on the above rates ceases, and in lieu thereof a duty of three pence a quarter is laid on; so that the net duties payable thereon, under the following circumstances, will be thus:

— not exceeding the price of 26 s. per quarter, the quarter

DUTIES to be paid on IMPORTATION.		Reference to the several Branches, see Page vi.	DRAWBACKS to be repaid on EXPORTATION.*		RATES, or supposed value, by 12 Car. II. cap. 4. 11 Geo. I. cap. 7. from whence the foregoing Duties are computed.
By BRITISH.	By ALIENS.		If exported to any legal place, except as mentioned in the following column.	If the produce of Europe or the East Indies, and exported to the British Colonies in America.	
l. s. d. 20ths	*l. s. d.* 20ths		*l. s. d.* 20ths	*l. s. d.* 20ths	*l. s. d.*
1 1 0	1 1 0	A	0 13 0	0 5 0	

* But if imported by Aliens Drawback more, 1 s. 3 d. for every 100 l. of the Rate or Value.

C [55] C

INWARDS.

———— exceeding 28 s. per quarter, and yet under 32 s. the quarter ———— at, or above, 32 s. per quarter, the quarter ———— *wheat.* Oats, the quarter, containing 8 bushels

And by 22 Car. II. cap. 13. when not exceeding 16 s. per quarter, the sum to be paid for Customs in lieu of pound-age, on the rate above-mentioned, is per quarter, containing 8 bushels, as before-mentioned ———— } Old sub. £. s. d. 0 5 4

But by 13 Geo. III. cap. 43. whenever the price of middling British Oats shall effectuar to be at, or above, 16 s. per quarter, at the place of importation, according to the methods directed for ascertaining the price of Corn and Grain imported, then the duty on the above rate ceases, and in

	DUTIES to be paid on IMPORTATION.		Reference to the several Branches, see Page vi.	DRAWBACKS to be repaid on EXPORTATION.*		RATES, or supposed value, by 12 Car. II. cap. 4. ‡ 11 Geo. I. cap. 7. from whence the foregoing Duties are computed.
	By BRITISH.	By ALIENS.		If exported to any legal place, except as mentioned in the following column.	If the produce of Europe or the East Indies, and exported to the British Colonies in America.	
	£. s. d. 20ths	£. s. d. 20ths		£. s. d. 20ths	£. s. d. 20ths	£. s. d.
	0 17 7 1	0 17 7 1	A	0 9 7 1	0 1 7 1	0 4 0
	0 0 3 3	0 0 3 3	A	0 0 3 3	0 0 3 3	

* But if imported by Aliens Drawback more, 1 s. 3 d. for every 100 l. of the Rate or Value.

† If exported within six months.

[56]

INWARDS.

Corn and Grain, *vocat.* Oats, under 16s. the quarter } *lieu thereof a duty of two pence a quarter is laid on; so that the net duties payable thereon, under the following circumstances, will be thus:*

———— at, or above, 16s. the quarter, *vocat.* Oat-meal, *has practically been charged, under the denomination of Ground Oats, with the same duties as Oats imported; therefore see the like duties as above.*

vizt. Peafe, the quarter, containing 8 bushels

And by 22 Car. II. cap. 13. *when not exceeding 40s. per quarter, the sum to be paid for Customs instead of Poundage, on the rate above-mentioned, is per quarter, containing 8 bushels, as before-mentioned*   *Old sub.*
l. s. d.
0 16 0

	DUTIES to be paid on IMPORTATION.		Reference to the several Branches, see Page vi.	DRAWBACKS to here paid on EXPORTATION.*		RATES or supposed value, by 12 Car. II. cap. 4. § 11 Geo. I. cap. 7. from whence the foregoing Duties are computed.
	By BRITISH.	By ALIENS.		If exported to any legal place, except as mentioned in the following column.	If the produce of Europe or the East Indies, and exported to the British Colonies in America.	
	£. s. d.20ths	£. s. d.20ths		£. s. d.20ths	£. s. d.20ths	£. s. d.
	0 6 2 15 ⅕	0 6 2 15 ⅕	A	0 3 6 15 ⅕	0 0 10 15 ⅖	0 4 0
	0 0 2 2	0 0 2 2	A	0 0 2 2	0 0 2 2	

* But if imported by Aliens Drawback more, 1s. 3d. for every 100l. of the Rate or Value.

‖ If exported within six months.

INWARDS.

DUTIES to be paid on IMPORTATION.		DRAWBACKS to be repaid on EXPORTATION.		RATES, or supposed value, by 12 Car. II. cap. 4. & 11 Geo. I. cap. 7. from whence the foregoing Duties are computed.
By BRITISH.	By ALIENS.	If exported to any legal place, except as mentioned in the following column.	If the produce of Europe or the East Indies, and exported to the British Colonies in America.	
£. s. d./20ths	£. s. d./20ths	£. s. d./20ths	£. s. d./20ths	£. s. d.
0 17 5 3 1/3	0 17 5 3 1/3	0 9 5 3 1/3	0 1 5 3 1/3	1 6 8
0 0 3 3	0 0 3 3 ‖	0 0 3 3 ‖	0 0 3 3	

Reference to the several Branches, fee Page vi. — A A

But by 13 Geo. III. cap. 43, whenever the price of middling British Pease shall appear to be at, or above, 32s. per quarter, at the place of importation, according to the methods directed for ascertaining the prices of Corn and Grain imported, then the duty on the above rate ceases, and in lieu thereof, a duty of three pence a quarter is laid on; so that the net duties payable thereon, under the following circumstances, will be thus:

— not exceeding the price of 40s. the quarter, but under 32s. the quarter ——————
— at, or above, 32s. the quarter ——————
vocat. Rye, not exceeding the price of 4s. 6d. the bushel, or 36s. per quarter, at the place of importation, by the bushel 3s. 4d. which is by the quarter, containing 8 bushels ——

‖ If exported within six months.

INWARDS.

Corn and Grain, *vocat*. Rye:
—— when it shall exceed that rate, by the quarter

And by 22 Car. II. cap. 13. when not exceeding 40s. per quarter, the same to be paid for Customs instead of Poundage, on the rates above-mentioned, is per quarter, containing 8 bushels, and each bushel 8 gallons — Old sub. *l. s. d.* 0 16 0

But by 13 Geo. III. cap. 43. whenever the price of middling British Rye shall appear to be at, or above, 32s. per quarter, at the place of importation, according to the methods directed for ascertaining the prices of Corn and Grain imported, then the duty on the above rates ceases, and in lieu thereof, a duty of three pence a quarter is laid on; so that the net duties payable thereon, under the following circumstances, will be thus:

DUTIES to be paid on IMPORTATION.		Reference to the several Branches, &c. *l.* &c. vi.	DRAWBACKS to be repaid on EXPORTATION.		RATES
By BRITISH.	By ALIENS.		If exported to any legal place, except as mentioned in the following column.	If the produce of Europe or the East Indies, and exported to the British Colonies in America.	
£. s. d. 20ths	£. s. d. 20ths		£. s. d. 20ths	£. s. d. 20ths	£. s. d.
					0 5 0

INWARDS.

	Duties to be paid on IMPORTATION.		References to the several Branches, see Page vi.	Drawbacks to be repaid on EXPORTATION.		Rates or supposed value by 12 Car. II. cap. 4. † 11 Geo. I. cap. 7. from whence the foregoing Duties are computed.
	By BRITISH.	By ALIENS.		If exported to any legal place, except as mentioned in the following column.	If the produce of Europe or the East Indies, and exported to the British Colonies in America.	
	£. s. d. 20ths	£. s. d. 20ths		£. s. d. 20ths	£. s. d. 20ths	£. s. d.
———— not exceeding the price of 40s. the quarter, but under 32s. the quarter	1 1 0	1 1 0	A	0 13 0	0 5 0	
———— at, or above, 32s. the quarter	0 0 3 3	0 0 3 3	A	0 0 3 3	0 0 3 3	2 0 0
———— *wat.* Wheat, not exceeding the price of 5s. 6d. the bushel, or 44s. per quarter at the place of importation, by the bushel, 5s. which is by the quarter, containing 8 bushels ———— when it shall exceed that rate by the quarter ————						0 6 8

And by 22 Car. II. cap. 13. *instead of Poundage on the rates above-mentioned, the sums to be paid for Customs are regulated thus:*

Old sub.

———— not exceeding 53s.	}	0 16 0
4d. per quarter, the quarter ———— exceeding 53s. 4d. and not above 4l. the quarter ————	}	0 8 0

‖ If exported within six months.

C [60] C

INWARDS.

Corn and Grain, vocat. Wheat:

—— *But by 13 Geo. III. cap. 43. whenever the price of middling British Wheat shall appear to be at, or above, 48s. per quarter, at the place of importation, according to the methods directed for ascertaining the prices of Corn and Grain imported, then the duty on the above rates ceases, and in lieu thereof, a duty of six-pence a quarter is laid on; so that the net duties payable thereon, under the following circumstances, will be this:*

	Duties to be paid on IMPORTATION.		Reference to the several Branches, see Page vi.	Drawbacks to be repaid on EXPORTATION.		Rates, or supposed value, by 12 Car. II. cap. 4. § 11 Geo.I. cap. 7. from whence the foregoing Duties are computed.
	By BRITISH.	By ALIENS.		If exported to any legal place, except as mentioned in the following column.	If the produce of Europe or the East Indies, and exported to the British Colonies in America.	
	£. s. d. 20ths	£. s. d. 20ths		£. s. d. 20ths	£. s. d. 20ths	£. s. d.
price of 44s. per quarter, not exceeding the quarter ——	1 3 1 4	1 3 1 4	A	0 15 1 4	0 7 1 4	
exceeding 44s. and yet under 48s. the quarter ——	0 17 10 4	0 17 10 4	A	0 9 10 4	0 1 10 4	
at, or above, 48s. the quarter ——	0 0 6	0 0 6	A	‖ 0 0 6	‖ 0 0 6	

‖ If exported within six months.

INWARDS.

Corn and Grain, *vocat.* Wheat-flour. By 13 *Geo. III. cap.* 43. *whenever the price of middling British Wheat shall appear to be at, or above,* 48 s. *per quarter, at the place of importation, according to the methods directed for ascertaining the prices of Corn and Grain imported, then the duties on Wheat-flour are to cease; and in lieu thereof, a duty of two-pence per Cwt. is laid on; so that the net duties payable thereon, under the following circumstances, will be thus: When Wheat is*

	Duties to be paid on IMPORTATION.		Reference to the several Branches, see Page vi.	Drawbacks to be repaid on EXPORTATION.		Rates, or supposed value, by 12 Car. II. cap. 4. ‡ 11 Geo. I. cap. 7. from whence the foregoing Duties are computed.
	By BRITISH.	By ALIENS.		If exported to any legal place, except as mentioned in the following column.	If the produce of Europe, or the East Indies, and exported to the British Colonies in America.	
	L. s. d. 20ths	*L. s. d.* 20ths		*L. s. d.* 20ths	*L. s. d.* 20ths	*L. s. d.*
—— not exceeding 44 s. the quarter	1 3 1 4	1 3 1 4	A	0 15 1 4	0 7 1 4	
—— exceeding 44 s. and yet under 48 s. the quarter	0 17 10 4	0 17 10 4	A	0 9 10 4	0 1 10 4	
—— at, or above, 48 s. per quarter, then per Cwt.	0 0 2 2	0 0 2 2	A	‖ 0 0 2 2	‖ 0 0 2 2	

‖ If exported within six months.

INWARDS.

	DUTIES to be paid on IMPORTATION.		DRAWBACKS to be repaid on EXPORTATION.		RATES, or suppofed value, by which the foregoing Duties are computed.
Reference to the feveral Branches, fee Page vi.	By BRITISH.	By ALIENS.	If exported to any legal place, except as mentioned in the following column.	If the produce of Europe or the Eaſt Indies, and exported to the Britiſh Colonies in America.	
	£. s. d. 20ths	£. s. d. 20ths	£. s. d. 20ths	£. s. d. 20ths	£. s. d.
A	0 0 1 1	0 0 1 1	∥ 0 0 1 1	∥ 0 0 1 1	

Indian Corn and Maize. By 15 Geo. III. cap. 1. it is declared, That whenever Barley is allowed, by 13 Geo. III. cap. 43. to be imported, on payment of the duty of two pence per quarter, the importation of Indian Corn and Maize be permitted, on payment of a duty of one penny per quarter.

But with reſpect to any Barley, Beer, Big, Beans, Oats, Peaſe, Rye, Wheat, or Wheat-flour, imported into the ports of Beaumaris, Berwick, Biſtol, Dover, Exeter, Falmouth, Harwich, Hull, Lancaſter, Liverpoole, London, Lynn-Regis, Milford, Newcaſtle, Newhaven, Poole, Southampton, Stockton, Whitehaven, and Yarmouth, in South Britain, and into the ports of Aberdeen, Ayr, Leith, Port-Glaſgow, and Kirkwall, in North Britain, or any of them, at any

∥ If exported within ſix months.

INWARDS.						
Reference to the several Branches, see Page vi.	DUTIES to be paid on IMPORTATION.		DRAWBACKS to be repaid on EXPORTATION.		RATES, or supposed value, by 12 Car. II. cap. 4. 11 Geo. I. cap. 7. from whence the foregoing Duties are computed.
	By BRITISH.	By ALIENS.	If exported to any legal place, except as mentioned in the following column.	If the produce of Europe or the East Indies, and exported to the British Colonies in America.	
	L. s. d. 20ths	L. s. d. 20ths	L. s. d. 20ths	L. s. d. 20ths	L. s. d.

time when the duties imposed by the act of 13 Geo. III. cap. 43. are not due and payable, the same may be warehoused under the joint locks of the king and proprietor, and afterwards delivered out, either for exportation or bonne consumption, under the regulations of the said law; and if for the latter, then to pay down in ready money such duties as shall, at the time of taking out such Corn, Grain, or Flour, or any part thereof, be due and payable for the like sort imported into the same port.

And by 18 Geo. III. cap. 25. and 19 Geo. III. cap. 29. this indulgence is extended to the ports of Portsmouth, Sandwich, Chichester, Chester, and Cowes.

Corn-powder. *Vide* Gun-powder.
Corflats. *Vide* Harness.

INWARDS.

	DUTIES to be paid on IMPORTATION.		DUTIES to be paid on IMPORTATION.		Reference to the several Branches, see Page vi.	DRAWBACKS to be repaid on EXPORTATION.*		DRAWBACKS to be repaid on EXPORTATION.*		RATES, or supposed value, by 12 Car. II. cap. 4. † 11 Gen. I. cap. 7. from whence the foregoing Duties are computed.
	By BRITISH.		By ALIENS.			If exported to any legal place, except as mentioned in the following column.		If the produce of Europe or the East Indies, and exported to the British Colonies in America.		
	£. s. d. 20ths		£. s. d. 20ths			£. s. d. 20ths		£. s. d. 20ths		£. s. d.
Cotton, viz. Manufactures of Cotton unrated, and not brought from East India or China, for every 20 s. of their value upon oath And besides for every 20 s. of the value, according to the gross price at the candle	0 5 3		0 5 6 3		C	0 4 9		0 4 3		
—— Manufactures of Cotton from East India or China. Vide East India Goods.	0 3 1 16		0 3 1 16		Q	0 3 1 16		0 3 1 16		0 1 0
Wool. Vide Wool.					.					
Counters of Latten, the pound	0 3 3		0 3 6 1/10		C	0 2 17		0 2 11		
Counters. Vide Cabinets.										
Coverlets of Scotland, the piece, free.										
Cowries. Vide East India goods.										
Cream of Tartar. Vide in Drugs.										
Creepers. Vide Andirons.										
Crofs-bow Laths, the pound	0 0 1 13 3/4		0 0 1 15 7/10		A	0 0 1 9 3/5		0 0 1 7 4/5		0 0 8
And besides, for every Cwt. of Steel	0 0 9 6		0 0 9 6		D	0 0 5 9				
—— Racks, the piece	0 0 2 1 4		0 0 2 15 1/2		A	0 0 1 10 4				0 10 0
—— Thread, the pound	0 0 1 13 3/4		0 0 1 15 7/10		A	0 0 1 9 3/5		0 0 1 5 3/4		0 0 8

* But if imported by Aliens Drawback more, 1 s. 3 d. for every 100 l. of the Rate or Value.

INWARDS

	DUTIES to be paid on IMPORTATION.		Reference to the several Branches, see Page vi.	DRAWBACKS to be repaid on EXPORTATION.*		RATES, or supposed value by 12 Car. II. cap. 4 / 11 Geo. I. cap. 7 from whence foregoing Duties are computed
	By BRITISH.	By ALIENS.		If exported to any legal place, except as mentioned in the following column.	If the produce of Europe or the East Indies, and exported to the British Colonies in America.	
	£. s. d. 20ths	£. s. d. 20ths		£. s. d. 20ths	£. s. d. 20ths	£. s. d.
Cruel ribband. *Vide* Caddas.						
Cruses of Stone, without covers, the hundred, containing five score	0 2 11 4	0 2 15½ 2	A	0 1 10 4	0 1 7 4	0 10 0
—— with covers, the hundred, containing five score	0 5 7 4	0 5 11 8	A	0 4 11 4	0 4 3 4	1 6 8
Chryftal. *Vide in* Drugs.						
K Cucumbers pickled, the gallon	0 0 7 17½	0 0 8 5 ⅜	C	0 0 7 2½	0 0 6 7½	
Culm brought, or imported, from foreign parts, *as by 9 and 10 W. III. cap. 13. §6, 7, and 8, and 8 Ann. cap. 4. and 9 Ann. cap. 6.* for every 20s. of its true value upon oath	0 5 3	0 6 3	C	0 4 9	0 4 3	
And besides, for every chalder, consisting of 36 bushels, Winchester measure —— or Ton, containing 20 Cwt.	0 1 0 12	0 1 0 12	Ha	0 1 0 12	0 1 0 12	† 0 2 6
And besides, for all Culm imported into the port of London, for every { Chalder, containing 36 bushels, Winchester measure	0 3 1 16	0 3 1 16	Vb	0 0 1 16	0 0 1 16	
Curates. *Vide* Harness.	0 3 1 16	0 3 1 16	Vb	0 0 1 16	0 0 1 16	

* But if imported by Aliens Drawback more, 1s. 3d. for every 100l. of the Rate or Value.

INWARDS.

	DUTIES to be paid on IMPORTATION.		Reference to the several Branches, see Page vi.	DRAWBACKS to be repaid on EXPORTATION.*		RATES, or supposed value, by 12 Car. II. cap. 4. ‡ 11 Geo. I. cap. 7. from whence the foregoing Duties are computed.
	By BRITISH.	By ALIENS.		If exported to any legal place, except as mentioned in the following column.	If the produce of Europe or the East Indies, and exported to the British Colonies in America.	
	£. s. d. 20ths	£. s. d. 20ths		£. s. d. 20ths	£. s. d. 20ths	£. s. d.
Currants. *Vide* in Grocery.	0 10 6	0 11 1 17	A	0 9 3	0 8 0	0 10 0
Cushions of Scotland, the dozen, free						
Cushion cloths, coarse, the dozen	1 8 4 4	1 9 6 ½	C	1 6 1 4	1 3 10 4	2 10 0
—— of tapestry, the dozen	0 5 7 4	0 5 11 8	A	0 4 11 4	0 4 3 4	4 10 0
Cuttle bones, the thousand						1 6 8
Cutwork. *Vide* Bands.						
Cyder. *Vide* Syder.						
Cynders, brought or imported from foreign parts, for every 20s. of their true value upon oath	0 5 3	0 5 6 3	C	0 4 9	0 4 3	
And besides, for every chalder, containing 36 bushels, Winchester measure	0 5 3	0 5 3	Ha	0 5 3	0 5 3	

* But, if imported by Aliens Drawback more, 1 s: 3 d: for every 100 l. of the Rate or Value

INWARDS.
D.

	DUTIES to be paid on IMPORTATION.		Reference to the several Branches, see Page vi.	DRAWBACKS to be repaid on EXPORTATION.*		RATES, or supposed value, by 12 Car.II. cap.4. & 11 Geo.I. cap.7. from whence the foregoing Duties are computed.
	By BRITISH.	By ALIENS.		If exported to any legal place, except as mentioned in the following column.	If the produce of Europe or the East Indies, and exported to the British Colonies in America.	
	£. s. d. 20ths	£. s. d. 20ths		£. s. d. 20ths	£. s. d. 20ths	£. s. d.
DAGGERS blades, the dozen	0 5 7 4	0 5 11 8	A	0 4 11 4		1 6 8
And besides for every Cwt. of Iron of bone for children, the dozen	0 5 3	0 5 3	D	0 5 3		0 2 0
——— black, with velvet sheaths, the dozen	0 0 5 0¾	0 0 5 7 1/10	A	0 0 4 8 4/5	0 0 3 16 4/5	3 0 0
And besides for every Cwt. of Iron ——— gilt, with velvet sheaths, the dozen	0 12 7 4	0 13 4 13	A	0 11 1 4		4 0 0
	0 5 3	0 5 3	D	0 5 3		0 0 0
And besides for every Cwt. of Iron for children, the dozen	0 16 9 12	0 17 10 4	D	0 14 9 12		0 4 0
Dags with firelocks, or snaphances, the piece	0 5 3	0 5 3	A	0 5 0 8 17 3/5	0 0 7 13 3/5	1 0 0
And besides for every Cwt. of Iron	0 0 10 1	0 0 10 14 4/5	D	0 0 3 8 8		
Dates. Vide in Grocery.	0 4 2 8	0 4 5 11	A	0 3 8 8		
Davis Streights. See Greenland Seas.	0 5 3	0 5 3		0 5 3		
Deals, vocat. Burgendorp deals, the hundred, containing six score	3 15 7 4	3 18 9	B	3 9 7 4	3 3 7 4	12 0 0
——— Macbro deals, the hundred, containing six score	1 5 2 8	1 6 3	B	1 3 2 8	1 1 2 8	4 0 0

* But if imported by Aliens Drawback more, 1 s. 3 d. for every 100 l. of the Rate or Value.

D [68] D

INWARDS.

	DUTIES to be paid on IMPORTATION.		Reference to the several Branches, see Page vi.	DRAWBACKS to be repaid on EXPORTATION.*		RATES, or supposed value, by 12 Car. II. cap. 4. †11 Geo. I. cap. 7. from whence the foregoing Duties are computed.
	By BRITISH.	By ALIENS.		If exported to any legal place, except as mentioned in the following column.	If the produce of Europe or the East Indies, and exported to the British Colonies in America.	
	$£.$ $s.$ $d.$ 20ths	$£.$ $s.$ $d.$ 20ths		$£.$ $s.$ $d.$ 20ths	$£.$ $s.$ $d.$ 20ths	$£.$ $s.$ $d.$
Deals, viz. Norway deals, the hundred, containing six score	1 11 5	1 12 9 15	B	0 1 9 0	0 1 6 6	5 0 0
———— Spruce deals, the hundred, containing six score	4 14 6	4 18 5 5	B	0 4 7 0	0 3 19 6	15 0 0
———— all other sorts of deals. See in Wood.						
If imported in foreign ships, to pay duty as Aliens.						
Note, Deal-boards of the growth of Germany, imported from thence by any of His Majesty's subjects, in British-built ships, owned by British subjects, and whereof the master, and three fourths of the mariners at least, are British subjects, are to pay the same duties as are payable for Deal boards from Norway.						
Desks, or Stays, for books, the dozen						
———— for women, covered with velvet, the piece	0 10 1 3/5	0 10 14 1 3/5	A	0 0 8 17 4 1/3	0 0 7 13 3 1/5	0 4 0
———— for women, covered with woollen, the piece	0 2 1 4	0 2 2 15 1/2	A	0 0 1 10 2	0 0 1 7 4	0 10 0
———— for women to work on, covered with woollen, the piece	0 1 0 12	0 1 1 7 3/4	A	0 0 0 11 2	0 0 0 9 12	0 5 0

D [69] D

INWARDS.	DUTIES to be paid on IMPORTATION.		Reference to the several Branches, see Page vi.	DRAWBACK's to be repaid on EXPORTATION.*		RATES, or supposed value, by 12 Car.II. cap.4. 11 Geo.I. cap.7. from whence the foregoing Duties are computed.
	By BRITISH.	By ALIENS.		If exported to any legal place, except as mentioned in the following column.	If the produce of Europe or the East Indies, and exported to the British Colonies in America.	
	£. s. d. 20ths	£. s. d. 20ths		£. s. d. 20ths	£. s. d. 20ths	£. s. d.
Dials of bone, the dozen	0. 2. 6 4/5	0. 2. 8 2/5	A	0. 2. 2 4/5	0. 1.11 1/5	0.12. 0
— wood, the dozen	0. 0. 7 11/20	0. 0. 8 13/20	A	0. 0. 6 13/20	0. 0. 6 1/5	0. 3. 0
Diamonds, Pearls, Precious Stones, and Jewels, free.						
Dice, for every 20 s. of the value upon oath	0. 5. 3	0. 6. 3	C	0. 4. 9	0. 4. 3	0. 3. 0
And besides, for every fair	0. 5. 3	0. 5. 3	Ia	0. 0. 3 3/5	0. 0. 3 3/5	
Dimity, the yard	0. 0. 7 11/20	0. 0. 8 13/20	A	0. 0. 6 13/20	0. 0. 5 15/20	
And besides, for every 20 s. of the value, according to the gross price at the candle			Q	0. 3. 1 16/20	0. 2. 2	
But if printed in this kingdom, this drawback is allowed	0. 3. 1 16/20	0. 3. 1 16/20	Q	0. 2. 9	0. 2. 2	
And if of India or China, more, the yard			N	0. 3. 9	0. 0. 9 1/5	
But if flowered, stitched, &c. see the computation under Unrated East India goods.						
Dogs of carts, the gross, containing 12 dozen	0.16. 9	0.17.10 4/5	A	0.14. 9 1/2	0.12. 9 1/2	4. 0. 0
Dornix with caddas, the piece, containing 15 yards	0. 9. 5 8/20	0. 9.10 2/5	C	0. 8. 8	0. 7.11	1.10. 0
— with silk, the piece, containing 15 yards	0.12. 7 4	0.13. 1 10	C	0.11. 7 4	0.10. 4	2. 0. 0

* But if imported by Aliens Drawback more, 1 s. 3 d. for every 100 l. of the Rate or Value.

‖ To Africa.   † To all other legal places.

[70]

INWARDS.

	DUTIES to be paid on IMPORTATION.		Reference to the several Branches, see Page vi.	DRAWBACKS to be repaid on EXPORTATION.*		RATES, or supposed value, by 12 Car. II. cap. 4. 11 Geo... cap. 7. from whence the foregoing Duties are computed.
	By BRITISH.	By ALIENS.		If exported to any legal place, except as mentioned in the following column.	If the produce of Europe, or the East Indies, and exported to the British Colonies in America.	
	£. s. d. 20ths	£. s. d. 20ths		£. s. d. 20ths	£. s. d. 20ths	£. s. d.
Dornix with thread, the piece, containing 15 yards	0 6 3 12	0 6 6 15	C	0 5 6 12	0 5 3 12	1 0 0
—— with wool, the piece, containing 15 yards	0 7 10 10	0 8 2 8	C	0 7 3	0 6 7 10	1 5 0
—— French making, { the ell	0 1 10 1	0 1 10 8 3.4	F	0 1 1 0 11	0 1 1	0 2 6
{ the yard	0 1 5 12 4/5	0 1 5 19 7/10	F	0 0 4 5	0 0 16	0 2 6
Down, the pound	0 0 4 14 1/2	0 0 4 19 4/10	C	0 0 3 8	0 0 2 8	0 1 0
Dudgeon, the hundred pieces, containing five score	0 4 2 8	0 4 5 11	A	0 3 10 4	0 3 7 4	0 10 0
Durance, or Duretty, with silk, the yard	0 2 1 4	0 2 2 15 1/2	A	0 1 2 16	0 1 1 16	0 6 8
—— with thread, the yard	0 1 4 15	0 1 5 17	A	0 0 8 8	0 0 8	
Dutties, the piece	0 4 2 8	0 4 5 11	A	0 3	0 3 2 8	0 10 0

* But if imported by Aliens Drawback more, 1s. 3d. for every 100l. of the Rate or Value.

D R U G S.

NOTES neceffary to be obferved.

DRUGS, rated by 12 Car. II. cap. 4. when imported in Foreign-built fhips, or not directly from the place of their growth, the duty and drawback is treble the fum affixed to them in the following calculations; Pearl Barley, Succus Liquoritiæ, Gum Senega, Gum Arabic, and Verdigreafe, excepted.

But by 7 Ann. cap. 8. all *Drugs*, of the growth and product of America, imported from any of the Britifh Plantations in America, in fhips legally navigated, are to pay duty as if imported directly from the place of their growth.

And by 21 Geo. III. cap 26. *Drugs*, which have heretofore ufually been imported from Turkey, or Egypt, or any of the dominions of the Grand Signior within the Levant Seas, may be imported by perfons free of the Turkey Company, from any port or place whatfoever, in any Britifh fhip, or in any fhip belonging to any ftate in amity with His Majefty, on payment only of fuch duties as would have been due, had the fame been imported directly from the place of their growth in Britifh-built fhips, the Aliens duty when imported in foreign fhips excepted.

And all other *Drugs* of the growth, product, or manufacture, of any place or country within the Streights or Levant Seas, which have heretofore ufually been imported from any port or place in Europe within the Streights of Gibraltar, may be imported by any perfon from any place not within the dominions of the Grand Signior, in any Britifh fhip, or in any fhip belonging to any ftate in amity with His Majefty, on payment of fuch duties as they would have been liable to if imported in Britifh-built fhips directly from the place of their growth. This Act is to continue in force during the prefent hoftilities with France, Spain, or the States General of the United Provinces, or either of them.

DRUGS,

DRUGS, rated by 12 Car. II. cap. 4. having been imported by *Aliens*, directly from the place of their growth, in British-built ships, drawback *more* for every 20 s. of their rate.

	£.	s.	d.
If declared by 3 and 4 Ann. cap. 4. to be for Dyers use, (Gum Senega, Gum Arabic, and Verdigrease excepted) ———————	0	0	0 $\frac{1}{56}$
If not so declared, (Pearl Barley and Succus Liquoritiæ excepted) ———————	0	0	0 $\frac{1}{16}$
And if not imported directly from the place of their growth, or in foreign ships ——————	treble those sums.		
All other *Drugs*, when imported by Aliens, Drawback more, for every 20 s. of their rate or value	0	0	0 $\frac{1}{16}$

DRUGS of the produce of Turkey or Russia, when legally imported by any person in foreign ships, are to be considered as Aliens goods, and subject to duty accordingly.

DRUGS of the growth, production, or manufacture of France, the French colonies, or the East Indies, and not particularly charged as such in the course of the rates, for the duties and drawbacks thereon see the table at the end of Drugs.

D [73] D

INWARDS.

	DUTIES to be paid on IMPORTATION.		Reference to the several Branches, see Page vi.	DRAWBACKS to be repaid on EXPORTATION.*		RATES, or supposed value, by 12 Car. II. cap. 4. ‡ 11 Geo. I. cap. 7. from whence the foregoing Duties are computed.
	From the place of their growth, and in British-built ships. †			If exported to any legal place, except as mentioned in the following column.	If the produce of Europe or the East Indies, and exported to the British Colonies in America.	
	By BRITISH.	By ALIENS.				
	£. s. d. 20ths	£. s. d. 20ths		£. s. d. 20ths	£. s. d. 20ths	£. s. d.
ACACIA, the pound	0 0 10 1	0 0 10 14 3/5	K	0 0 8 17 3/5	0 0 7 13 3/5	0 0 4 0
Acorus, the pound	0 0 2 10	0 0 2 13 10/20	K	0 0 2 4	0 0 1 18	0 0 1 0
Adeps urſi, the pound	0 0 7 6 2/5	0 0 7 12 5/6	L	0 0 6 14 3/5	0 0 6 2 2/5	0 0 2 8
Adianthum Album, the pound	0 0 1 13 3/5	0 0 1 15 7/10		0 0 1 9	0 0 1 5	0 0 0 6
―――― Nigrum, the pound	0 0 1 5 3/8	0 0 1 6 3,0	K	0 0 1 2	0 0 0 19	
Agaricus, or Agarick, for Dyers uſe, *as by 3 and 4 Ann. cap. 4. the pound,* trimmed or pared						0 0 1 0
―――― rough, or untrimmed						0 0 0 0
But by 8 *Geo.* I. cap. 15. § 10. *if regularly imported, entered, and landed,* duty free.						
But *on failure thereof, then to pay,* trimmed, or pared, the pound	0 0 1 4:6	0 0 1 5:7	Ad	0 0 1 2:16	0 0 0 16	0 0 5 0
―――― rough, or untrimmed, the pound	0 0 0 4 4/5	0 0 0 4 9/20	Ad	0 0 0 3 14 2/5	0 0 0 3 4 2/5	
Agnus Caſtus ſeeds, the pound	0 0 1 2 10	0 0 0 2 13 2/3	K	0 0 0 2 4	0 0 0 1 18	0 0 1 0
Alchernes Syrup, the pound	0 0 1 4:16	0 0 1 5:17	K	0 0 1 8:17	0 0 1 7:13	0 6 0
―――― Confectio, the ounce	0 0 0 10 1	0 0 0 10 14 3/5	K	0 0 0 2 4	0 0 0 1 18	0 4 0
Alkanet roots, the pound	0 0 2:10	0 0 2 13:	K	0 0 0 2 4	0 0 0 1 18	0 0 1 0
Alnipict. *Vide* Orcant.						

† If otherwiſe imported. * If imported by Aliens. See the Notes preceding Drugs.

L

[74]

INWARDS.

	DUTIES to be paid, on IMPORTATION.				DRAWBACKS to be repaid on EXPORTATION.*		RATES, or supposed value, by 12 Cr. II. cap. 4. † 11 Geo. I. cap. 7. from whence the foregoing Duties are computed.
	From the place of their growth, and in British-built ships. †		Reference to the several Branches, see Page vi.		If exported to legal place, except as mentioned in the following column.	If the produce of Europe or the East Indies, and exported to the British Colonies in America.	
	By BRITISH.	By ALIENS.					
	£. s. d./20ths	£. s. d./20ths			£. s. d./20ths	£. s. d.	£. s. d.
Drugs, *vocat*.							
Almonds Bitter, the Cwt.	0 8 4.16	0 8 11 2	K		0 7 4.16	0 6 4.16	2 0 0
Aloes Cicotrina, the pound	0 1 0.12	0 1 1	K		0 0 11 2	0 0 9.12	0 5 0
Epatica, the pound	0 0 5 0	0 0 5 7	K		0 0 4.8	0 0 3.16	0 2 0
Alum Romh, or Roch, the Cwt. for Dyers use, *as by 3 and 4 Ann. cap. 4.* Vide Alum in A.	0 1 4.16	0 1 5 17	Ad		0 1 2.16	0 1 0.16	1 0 0
Alumen Plume, the pound, for Dyers use, *as by 3 and 4 Ann. cap. 4.*			Ad				
Ambergrease, black or grey, the ounce troy	0 0 0.16 4/5	0 0 0.17 17/20	K		0 0 0.14 4/5	0 0 0.12 4/5	0 1 0 ‡‡
Arabra Liquida, the pound	0 12 7 4	0 13 4 13	L		0 11 1 4	0 9 7 4	3 0 0
Ameos feed, the pound	0 2 5 4 16/20	0 2 6 9 21/20	K		0 2 2.16 16/20	0 2 0.2 16/20	0 8 0
Aromi feeds, the pound	0 0 1.13 1/2	0 0 1.15 1/5	K		0 0 1.1 1/5	0 0 1.3 1/5	0 0 8
Amacardium, the pound	0 0 8.8 3/5	0 0 8.18 1/5	K		0 0 1.9 1/5	0 0 6.8 1/5	0 0 8
Angelica, the pound	0 0 2.10 2/5	0 0 2.13 2/5	K		0 0 2.4 2/5	0 0 1.18 2/5	0 3 4
Antimonium Crudum, the Cwt. for Dyers use, *as by 3 and 4 Ann. cap. 4.* But by 8 Geo. I. cap. 15. § 10. *if regularly imported, entred and landed,* duty free.			K				0 1 0

† If otherwise imported.   * If imported by Aliens.   See the Notes preceding Drugs.

INWARDS.

	DUTIES to be paid on IMPORTATION.		DRAWBACKS to be repaid on EXPORTATION.*		RATES, or supposed value, by 12 Car. II. cap. 4. †11 Geo. I. cap. 7. from whence the foregoing Duties are computed.
	From the place of their growth, and in British-built ships. †		If exported to any legal place, except as mentioned in the following column.	If the produce of Europe or the East Indies, and exported to the British Colonies in America.	
	By BRITISH.	By ALIENS.			
	£. s. d. 20ths	£. s. d. 20ths	£. s. d. 20ths	£. s. d. 20ths	£. s. d.
DRUGS, vocat.					
But on failure thereof, then to pay					
——— Praeparatum, or Stibium, the pound, for Dyers use, as by 3 and 4 Ann. cap. 4.	0 1 4 16	0 1 5 17	Ad	0 1 2 16	0 1 0 16	‡ 0 0 8
Aqua Fortis, for Dyers use, as by 3 and 4 Ann. cap. 4. the bottle, containing 4 gallons	0 0 0 11 ⅓	0 0 0 11 9/10	Ad	0 0 0 9 13/15	0 0 0 8 8/15	‡ 2 5 0
But by 8 Geo. I. cap. 15. § 10. if regularly imported, entered and landed, duty free.						
But on failure thereof, then to pay						
But if imported in glass bottles, for every dozen quarts	0 7 1 1	0 7 8 2	Bd	0 5 11 11	0 4 10 1	
Argentum sublime, or Limum, or Quicksilver, the pound	0 4 2 8	0 4 2 8	Ze			
Aristolochia longa, and rotunda, the pound	0 0 7 11 ⅕	0 0 8 0	K	0 0 6 13	0 0 5 15 ⅕	0 3 0
Armoniacus. *Vide* Boius communis.	0 0 3 7	0 0 3 11 ⅖	K	0 0 2 19	0 0 2 11 ⅓	0 1 4

† If otherwise imported. *If imported by Aliens. See the Notes preceding Drugs.

INWARDS.

	DUTIES to be paid on IMPORTATION.				DRAWBACKS to be repaid on EXPORTATION.*				RATES, or supposed value, by 12 Car. II. cap. 4. 11 Geo. I. cap. 7. from whence the foregoing Duties are computed.
	From the place of their growth, and in British-built ships. †			Reference to the several Branches, see Page vi.	If exported to any legal place, except as mentioned in the following column.		If the produce of Europe or the East Indies, and exported to the British Colonies in America.		
	By BRITISH.		By ALIENS.						
	£. s. d. 20ths		£. s. d. 20ths		£. s. d. 20ths		£. s. d. 20ths		£. s. d.
DRUGS, *vacat.*									
Arsnick, white or yellow, or Rosalgar, for Dyers use, *as by 3 and 4 Ann. cap. 4.* the pound	0 0 5		0 0 5 $\frac{18}{40}$	Ad					0 0 4
But by 8 Geo. I. cap. 15. §. 10. if regularly imported, entered, and landed, is duty free.									
But on failure thereof, then to pay									
Asarum roots, the pound	0 0 2 10		0 2 13 $\frac{2}{100}$	K	0 0 2 4		0 0 1 18 $\frac{4}{15}$		0 1 0 ‡
Aspalathus, the pound	0 0 3 15		0 0 4 $\frac{1}{40}$	K	0 0 3 6		0 0 2 17 $\frac{5}{15}$		0 1 0 ‡
Asa foetida, the pound	0 0 2 18		0 0 3 2 $\frac{9}{40}$	K	0 0 2 11		0 0 2 4 $\frac{4}{15}$		0 1 2
Auripigmentum. *Vide* Orpiment.									
Auricular Judae, the pound	0 0 3 13		0 0 3 16 $\frac{27}{100}$	L	0 0 3 7		0 0 3 1 $\frac{13}{15}$		0 1 0 ‡
Baccae alkakengi, the pound	0 0 3 13		0 0 3 16 $\frac{73}{100}$	L	0 0 3 7		0 0 3 1 $\frac{1}{15}$		0 1 0 ‡
Balaustium, the pound	0 0 6 6		0 0 6 13 $\frac{17}{100}$	K	0 0 5 11		0 0 4 16 $\frac{3}{15}$		0 2 6 ‡
Balsamum artificial, the pound	0 0 8 8		0 0 8 18 $\frac{1}{100}$	K	0 0 8		0 0 6 8		0 3 4 ‡
— Copaiva, the pound	0 0 9 2		0 0 9 10 $\frac{1}{40}$	L	0 0 8 7		0 0 7 12 $\frac{7}{10}$		0 3 6
— natural, the pound	0 2 1 4		0 0 2 15 $\frac{2}{10}$	K	0 1 10 4		0 0 1 7		0 10 0
Barbadoes tar, the pound	0 0 0 18 $\frac{27}{100}$		0 0 0 19 $\frac{71}{100}$	L	0 0 0 16 $\frac{27}{100}$		0 0 0 15 $\frac{27}{100}$		0 0 3

† *If otherwise imported.*   * *If imported by Aliens.*   See the Notes preceding Drugs.

[77]

INWARDS.	DUTIES to be paid on IMPORTATION.		Reference to the several Branches, see Page vi.	DRAWBACKS to be repaid on EXPORTATION.*		RATES, or supposed value, by 12 Car. II. cap. 4. ‡ 11 Geo. I. cap. 7. from whence the foregoing Duties are computed.
	From the place of their growth, and in British-built ships. †			If exported to any legal place, except as mentioned in the following column.	If the produce of Europe or the East Indies, and exported to the British Colonies in America.	
	By BRITISH.	By ALIENS.				
	£. s. d. 20ths	£. s. d. 20ths		£. s. d. 20ths	£. s. d. 20ths	£. s. d.
DRUGS, viz.						
Barley hulled, or French barley, the Cwt.— Imported from the place of its growth in British ships:						
—— French	0 11 2 8	0 11 2 8	F g	0 7 0 8	0 4 6 8	1 0 0
—— not French	0 8 4 16	0 8 4 16	K	0 5 10 16	0 3 4 16	
Not from the place of its growth, or in foreign ships:						
—— French	1 3 1 4	1 3 1 4	F g	0 15 7 4	0 13 1 4	0 13 4
—— not French	0 14 8 8	0 14 8 8	K	0 12 2 8	0 9 8 8	
Bayberries, the Cwt. for Dyers use, as by 3 and 4 Ann. cap. 4. But by 8 Geo. I. cap. 15. § 10. if regularly imported, entered, and landed, duty free.						
But on failure thereof, then to pay	0 0 11 4	0 0 11 18	Ad	0 0 9 17 ⅓	0 0 8 10 ⅓	0 2 6
Bdellium, the pound	0 0 5 6	0 0 6 13	K	0 0 5 11	0 0 4 16	0 2 0
Ben-album, or Rubrum, the pound	0 0 5 0	0 0 5 7	K	0 0 4 8	0 0 3 16 ⅘	0 0 5
Benjamin of all sorts, the pound	0 0 10 12 ⅘	0 0 11 7	K	0 0 11 2	0 0 9 12	
Bever cods. *Vide* Castoreum.						

† If otherwise imported.   * If imported by Aliens.   See the Notes preceding Drugs.

INWARDS.

DRUGS, vocat.	DUTIES to be paid on IMPORTATION.		Reference to the several Branches, see Page vi.	DRAWBACKS to be repaid on EXPORTATION.*		RATES, or supposed value, by 12 Car. II. cap. 4. 11 Geo. I cap. 7. from whence the foregoing Duties are computed.
	From the place of their growth, and in British-built ships. †			If exported to any legal place, except as mentioned in the following column.	If the produce of Europe or the East Indies, and exported to the British Colonies in America.	
	By BRITISH.	By ALIENS.				
	£. s. d. 20ths	£. s. d. 20ths		£. s. d. 20ths	£. s. d. 20ths	£. s. d.
Bezoar stone, of East India, the ounce troy	0 15 9	0 16 6 ½	K d	0 14 3	0 12 9	3 0 0
— of West India, the ounce troy	0 2 1 4	0 2 15	K	0 1 10 4	0 1 10 4	0 10 0
Bitumen Judaicum, the pound	0 0 1 16 27/30	0 1 18 23/100	L	0 0 1 13 4	0 0 1 10 27	0 0 6
Black lead, the Cwt.	0 6 3 12	0 6 8 6 1/10	K	0 0 5 6 12	0 0 4 9 12	1 10 0
Blatta Bazantia, the pound	0 0 5 0 4/5	0 0 5 7 2/10	K	0 0 4 8 4/5	0 0 3 10	0 2 0
Bolus Communis, or Armoniacus, the Cwt.	0 1 4 16 1/5	0 1 5 17 7/10	K	0 0 1 2 16 3	0 0 1 5	0 6 8
— Verus, or fine Bole, the pound	0 0 1 13 3/5	0 1 15 ½	K	0 0 1 9	0 0 0 6 8	0 8 8
Borax in paste, or unrefined, commonly called Tincall, the pound	0 0 8 8	0 0 8 18	K	0 0 7 8	0 0 0	0 3 4
N. B. By 17 Geo. II. cap. 31, if refined in Great Britain, intitled to the same drawback as unrefined.						
— refined, the pound	0 2 9 12	0 2 11 14		0 2 5 12	0 2 1 12	0 13 4
Bunkins, Holliwortles, or Pistolochia, the pound	0 0 6 6	0 0 6 13 7/8	K	0 0 5 11	0 0 4 16	0 2 6
Cake-lack. Vide Gum-lack.						
Calamus, the pound	0 1 13 3/5	0 1 15 7/10	K	0 0 1 9 3	0 0 1 5 ¾	0 0 8

† If otherwise imported. * If imported by Aliens. See the Notes preceding Drugs.

[79]

INWARDS,

DRUGS, vocat.	DUTIES to be paid on IMPORTATION.		Reference to the several Branches, see Page vi.	DRAWBACKS to be repaid on EXPORTATION.*		RATES, or supposed value, by 12 Car. II. cap. 4. † 11 Geo. I. cap. 7. from whence the foregoing Duties are computed.
	From the place of their growth, and in British-built ships. †			If exported to any legal place, except as mentioned in the following column.	If the produce of Europe or the East Indies, and exported to the British Colonies in America.	
	By BRITISH.	By ALIENS.				
	£. s. d./20ths	£. s. d./20ths		£. s. d./20ths	£. s. d.	£. s. d.
Cal-balfha, for Dyers use, as by 3 and 4 Ann. cap. 4. for every 20s. value upon oath	0 0 6 1 1 3/5	0 0 6 4 4 3/5	L	0 0 5 7 1 3/5	0 0 0 5 1 1 3/5	0 0 3 4
Cambogium, or Gutta Gambr, the pound	0 0 1 8 8	0 0 1 8 18	K	0 0 0 7 8	0 0 0 6 8	0 0 5 0
Camphire refined, the pound	0 0 0 0 12	0 0 1 1 7	K	0 0 0 0 11 2	0 0 0 9 12	0 2 6
N.B. By 17 Geo. II. cap. 31. if refined in Great Britain, intitled to the same drawback as unrefined.						
unrefined, the pound	0 0 0 6 6	0 0 0 6 13 3/5	K	0 0 0 5 11	0 0 0 4 16 3/5	0 0 0
Cancri oculus, the pound	0 0 0 10 1	0 0 0 10 14 3/5	M	0 0 0 8 17 2 3/5	0 0 0 7 13 3/5	0 4 0
Cantharides, the pound	0 0 1 0 12	0 0 1 1 7	K	0 0 0 11 2 3/5	0 0 0 9 12 3/5	0 5 0
Capita papaverum, the thousand	0 0 0 6 5 3/5	0 0 0 7 0	L	0 0 0 4 15 3/5	0 0 0 3 5	0 5 0
Cardamoms, the pound	0 0 0 7 11 2/5	0 0 0 8 0 3/5	K	0 0 0 6 13 4/5	0 0 0 5 15	0 3 0
Carlina, the pound	0 0 0 2 10 3/5	0 0 0 2 13 2/5	K	0 0 0 2 4 4/5	0 0 0 1 18	0 1 0
Carolina, the pound	0 0 0 0 16 1	0 0 0 0 17 2/5	K	0 0 0 0 14 4/5	0 0 0 0 12 3/5	0 0 4
Carpo balfami, the pound	0 0 0 10 1	0 0 0 10 14 3/5	K	0 0 0 8 17 2/5	0 0 0 7 13 3/5	0 4 0
Carrabe, or Succinum, the pound	0 0 0 2 10 3/5	0 0 0 2 13 3/5	K	0 0 0 2 4 4/5	0 0 0 1 18	0 1 0
Carraway feeds, the Cwt.	0 0 5 9	0 0 5 4 5	K	0 0 0 4 5	0 0 0 3 10 1/5	0 4 0
Carthamus feeds, the pound	0 0 0 1 13 7/10	0 0 0 1 15 7/10	L	0 0 0 1 9	0 0 0 1 5	0 0 8

† If otherwise imported.   * If imported by Aliens.   See the Notes preceding Drugs.

INWARDS.

	Duties to be paid on Importation. From the place of their growth, and in British-built ships. † By British. £.	s.	d.	20ths	By Aliens. £.	s.	d.	20ths	Reference to the several Branches, see Page vi.	Drawbacks to be repaid on Exportation. * If exported to any legal place, except as mentioned in the following column. £.	s.	d.	20ths	If the produce of Europe or the East Indies, and exported to the British Colonies in America. £.	s.	d.	20ths	Rates, or supposed value, by 12 Car. II. cap. 4. ‡ 11 Geo. I. cap. 7. from whence the foregoing Duties are computed. £.	s.	d.
Drugs, *vocat.*																					
Cassena, for Dyers use, *as by 3 and 4 Ann. cap. 4. for every 20s. value upon oath*	0	6	1	1 3/5	0	6	4	4 3/5	L	0	5	7	1 1/3	0	5	1	1 1/3			
Cassia fistula, the pound, of all sorts	0	0	3	15 3/5	0	0	4	0 13/40	K	0	0	3	6 1/3	0	0	2	17 1/3	0	1	6
Cassia lignea, the pound	0	0	4	4	0	0	4	9 1/4	K	0	0	3	14	0	0	3	4	0	1	8
Cassumba, for Dyers use, *as by 3 and 4 Ann. cap. 4, for every 20s. of the value upon oath*	0	3	1	16	0	3	4	19	Bd	0	2	7	16	0	2	1	16			
Castoreum, or Bever cods, the pound	0	2	1	4	0	2	2	15 1/2	K	0	1	10	4	0	1	7	4	0	10	0
Cerussa, the Cwt.	0	6	3	12	0	6	8	6 1/2	K	0	5	6	12	0	4	9	12	1	10	0
Cetrach, the pound	0	0	2	10 2/3	0	0	2	13 11/20	K	0	0	2	4 2/3	0	0	1	18 2/3	0	1	0
Chamæpitys, the pound	0	0	1	16 27/50	0	0	1	18 21/200	L	0	0	1	13 27/50	0	0	1	10 27/50	‡ 0	0	6
Chelæ cancrorum, the pound	0	0	0	18 27/100	0	0	0	19 23/400	L	0	0	0	16 77/100	0	0	0	15 27/100	0	0	3
China roots, the pound	0	1	4	16	0	1	5	17	K	0	1	2	16	0	1	0	16	0	6	8
Ciceres, white and red, the pound	0	0	1	5 1/5	0	0	1	6 31/40	K	0	0	1	2 1/3	0	0	0	19 1/3	0	0	6
Cinabrum, or Vermilion, the pound	0	0	6	6	0	0	6	13 7/8	K	0	0	5	11	0	0	4	16	0	2	6
Cinabaris nativa, not of the East Indies, the pound	0	3	0	10 4/5	0	3	2	2 3/10	L	0	2	9	10 4/5	0	2	6	10 4/5	‡ 0	10	0
Ciperus longus and rotundus, the Cwt.	0	7	0		0	7	5	5	K	0	6	2		0	5	4		1	13	4
—— nuts, the pound	0	0	1	13 3/5	0	0	1	15 7/10	K	0	0	1	9 1/3	0	0	1	5 3/4	0	0	8
Citrage, the pound	0	0	2	10 2/3	0	0	2	13 11/20	K	0	0	2	4 2/3	0	0	1	18 2/3	0	1	0

† If otherwise imported. * If imported by Aliens. See the Notes preceding Drugs.

[81]

INWARDS.

DRUGS, vocat.	\multicolumn{2}{c}{DUTIES to be paid on IMPORTATION.}		Reference to the several Branches, see Page vi.	\multicolumn{2}{c}{DRAWBACKS to be repaid on EXPORTATION.*}		RATES, or supposed value, by 12 Car. II. cap. 4. ‡11 Geo. I. cap. 7. from whence the foregoing Duties are computed.
	From the place of their growth, and in British-built ships. †			If exported to any legal place, except as mentioned in the following column.	If the produce of Europe or the East Indies, and exported to the British Colonies in America.	
	By BRITISH.	By ALIENS.				
	£. s. d. 20ths	£. s. d. 20ths		£. s. d. 20ths	£. s. d. 20ths	£. s. d.
Civet, the ounce troy	0 8 4 16	0 8 11 2	K	0 7 4 16	0 6 4 16 4/5	2 0 0
Coculus Indiæ, the pound	0 0 5 0	0 0 5 7 7/10	K	0 0 4 8 4/5	0 0 3 16 4/5	0 0 2
Colophonia, the Cwt.	0 3 0 10	0 3 2 2 3/10	L	0 0 2 9 10 4/5	0 0 2 10 4/5	‡0 0 10
Coloquintida, the pound	0 0 5 0	0 0 5 7 7/10	K	0 0 4 8 4/5	0 0 3 16 4/5	0 0 2
Copperas, for Dyers use, as by 3 and 4 Ann. cap. 4. blue, of Danfk or Hungary, the Cwt.	0 0 10 1	0 0 10 14 1/5	A d	0 0 8 17 3/5	0 0 7 13 3/5	0 0 12 0
green. See its C.						
white, the Cwt.						
Coral, red or white, in fragments, for physical use, the Cwt.	0 2 9 12	0 2 11 14 1/5	A d	0 2 5 12	0 2 1 12	2 0 0
whole, the Cwt.	0 0 8 8	0 0 8 18 1/2	K	0 0 7 8	0 0 6 8	0 3 4
And besides, if polished, the pound	0 0 4 2 8 8/20	0 0 4 5 11 4/5	K	0 0 3 8 6	0 0 3 2 8 4/5	1 0 0
Coriander seeds, the Cwt.	0 0 1 4 16 4/5	0 0 1 4 16 1/5	E	0 0 1 4 8 1/5	0 0 1 4 16 4/5	0 0 0
Cornu cervi calcinatum, the pound	0 0 4 2 8 4/5	0 0 4 5 11 4/5	K	0 0 3 8 2/5	0 0 3 2 8 4/5	1 0 0
unicornu, each	0 0 3 0 10	0 0 3 2 13 4/5	L	0 0 2 9 10	0 0 2 6 10	0 0 10
Cortex caperum, the pound	0 0 0 2 10 1/2	0 0 0 2 13 1/2	L	0 0 2 4	0 0 0 1 8	‡0 0 0 10
cariophyllorum, the pound	0 0 1 16 8/20	0 0 1 18 1/5	K	0 0 1 13 2/5	0 0 1 10 1/5	1 0 6
elatheriæ, the Cwt.	0 0 9 1 12 2/5	0 0 9 6 6 1/5	L	0 0 8 4 12 2/5	0 0 7 12 3/5	‡0 0 11 0

† If otherwise imported. * If imported by Aliens. See the Notes preceding Drugs.

M

INWARDS.

	DUTIES to be paid on IMPORTATION. From the place of their growth, and in British-built ships. †				DRAWBACKS to be repaid on EXPORTATION.*		RATES or supposed value, by 12 Car. II. cap. 4. 11 Geo. I. cap. 7. from whence the foregoing Duties are computed.
	By BRITISH.	By ALIENS.	Reference to the several Branches, see Page vi.	If exported to any legal place, except as mentioned in the following column.	If the produce of Europe or the East Indies, and exported to the British Colonies in America.		
	£. s. d. 20ths	£. s. d. 20ths		£. s. d. 20ths	£. s. d. 20ths	£. s. d.	
DRUGS, vact.							
Cortex guaici, the Cwt.	0 12 7 4	0 13 4 13	K	0 11 1 4	0 0 9 7 4	3 0 0	
—— limonum, vel aurantiorum, the pound	0 0 1 16 $\frac{27}{30}$	0 0 1 18 $\frac{21}{300}$	L	0 0 1 13 $\frac{27}{30}$	0 0 1 10 $\frac{27}{30}$	0 0 6	
—— mandragoræ, the pound	0 0 0 5 $\frac{4}{5}$	0 0 0 5 7 $\frac{10}{300}$	K	0 0 0 4 8 $\frac{4}{5}$	0 0 0 3 16 $\frac{4}{5}$	0 2 0	
—— Peruvianus, or Jesuits bark, the pound	0 0 0 9 2 $\frac{7}{10}$	0 0 0 9 10 $\frac{23}{40}$	L	0 0 0 8 7 $\frac{7}{10}$	0 0 0 7 12 $\frac{7}{10}$	0 2 6	
—— tamerisci, the pound	0 0 0 1 13 $\frac{13}{15}$	0 0 0 1 15 $\frac{7}{100}$	K	0 0 0 1 9 $\frac{3}{5}$	0 0 0 1 5 $\frac{3}{5}$	0 0 3	
—— winteranus, the pound	0 0 0 1 13 $\frac{13}{15}$	0 0 0 1 15 $\frac{7}{100}$	K	0 0 0 1 9 $\frac{3}{5}$	0 0 0 1 5 $\frac{3}{5}$	0 0 3	
Coftus dulcis and amarus, the pound	0 0 0 4 4 $\frac{2}{3}$	0 0 0 4 9 $\frac{2}{100}$	K	0 0 0 3 14 $\frac{4}{15}$	0 0 0 3 4 1	0 1 0	
Cowitch, the pound	0 0 0 3 13 $\frac{13}{15}$	0 0 0 3 16 $\frac{7}{100}$	K	0 0 0 3 7 $\frac{1}{5}$	0 0 0 3 1 $\frac{3}{5}$	0 1 0	
Cranium humanum, each	0 0 0 3 13 $\frac{13}{15}$	0 0 0 3 16 $\frac{7}{100}$	L	0 0 0 3 7 $\frac{1}{15}$	0 0 0 3 1 $\frac{1}{5}$	0 1 0	
Cream of tartar, for Dyers use, as by 3 and 4 Ann. cap. 4. the Cwt. But by 8 Geo. I. cap. 15. § 10. if regularly imported, entered, and landed, duty free. But on failure thereof, then to pay			Bd				
Cryftal in broken pieces for phylick uses, the pound	0 7 10 10	0 8 6 7	K	0 6 7 10	0 5 4 10	2 10 0	
Cubebs, the pound	0 0 3 8	0 0 8 18 $\frac{1}{3}$	K	0 0 7 8	0 0 6 8	0 3 4	
Cummin feeds, the Cwt.	0 0 3 7	0 0 3 11 $\frac{2}{5}$	K	0 0 2 19 $\frac{3}{5}$	0 0 2 11 $\frac{1}{5}$	0 1 4	
	0 7 0	0 7 5 5		0 6 2 2	0 5 4	1 13 4	

† If otherwise imported. * If imported by Aliens. See the Notes preceding Drugs.

INWARDS.

DRUGS, vizt.	DUTIES to be paid on IMPORTATION.				DRAWBACKS to be repaid on EXPORTATION.*				RATES, or supposed value, by 12 Car.II.cap.4. 11 Geo.I.cap.7. from whence the foregoing Duties are computed.
	By BRITISH. From the place of their growth, and in British-built ships.†		By ALIENS.		If exported to any legal place, except as mentioned in the following column.		If the produce of Europe or the East Indies, and exported to the British Colonies in America.	Reference to the several Branches, see Page vi.	
	L. s. d./20ths		*L. s. d.*/20ths		*L. s. d.*/20ths		*L. s. d.*/20ths		*L. s. d.*
Cuscuta, the pound	0 0 2 10		0 0 2 13 2/10		0 0 2 4 8/5		0 0 1 18 3/5	K	0 1 0
Cyclamen, or Paris Fortinus, the pound	0 0 5 0		0 0 5 7 1/10		0 0 4 8 17/20		0 0 3 16 3/5	K	0 2 6
Daucus Creticus, the pound	0 0 10 1 1/2		0 0 10 14 2/10		0 0 8 17 3/4		0 0 7 13 2/5	L	0 4 0
Dens apri, the pound	0 0 7 6 3/4		0 0 7 12 3/10		0 0 6 14 1/5		0 0 6 2 4/5	K	0 2 0
—— equi marini, the pound	0 0 4 2 8/5		0 0 4 5 1/10		0 0 6 14 2/3		0 0 2 8 3/5	K	0 1 0
Diagredium, or Scammony, the pound	0 0 4 2 10		0 0 4 5 11		0 0 3 8		0 0 3 2 17	L	0 1 0
Diptam's leaves, the pound	0 0 6 3 15		0 0 4 0		0 0 5 11 9/5		0 0 4 16 9/10	K	0 2 6
—— roots, the pound	0 0 0 12 2/5		0 0 0 12 4/5		0 0 1 9 3/5		0 0 1 5 5/2	K	0 0 6
Doronicum, the pound	0 0 0 12 2/5		0 0 0 12 4/5		0 0 1 9 3/5		0 0 1 5 5/2	K	0 0 6
Eboris rasura, the pound	0 0 2 13 3/2		0 0 2 15 3/10		0 0 2 4 3/5		0 0 1 13	L	0 1 0
Eleborus albus and niger, the pound	0 0 2 10		0 0 2 13 2/10		0 0 1 10 3/5		0 0 1 18 3/5	K	0 1 0
Epithemum, the pound	0 0 2 0 7		0 0 2 11 1/20		0 0 1 19 3/5		0 0 1 8 7/10	L	0 1 0
Essence of lemons, the pound	0 0 3 7 7/10		0 0 3 11 3/10		0 0 2 19 3/5		0 0 2 11 4/5	K	0 1 6
Æs ustum, the pound	0 0 1 13		0 0 1 15 3/10		0 0 1 9 3/10		0 0 1 5 5/2	L	0 0 6
Euphorbium, the pound	0 0 0 10		0 0 2 6 3/10		0 0 2 2 3/5		0 0 0 19 3/5	L	0 0 10
Fœchia brugnata, th. Cwt.	0 0 3 15 7/2		0 0 4 3 1/5		0 0 3 13 5/2		0 0 3 4 3/5	K	0 1 6
Fennel seeds, the pound	0 0 3 16 5/10		0 0 2 6 3/10		0 0 2 2 3/5		0 0 2 1 3/5	K	0 0 10
Fœnugreek, the Cwt.	0 0 3 16 5/10		0 0 4 3 2/3		0 0 4 3 5/3		0 0 0 19	K	0 15 0
Flores chamæmeli, the pound	0 0 1 16		0 0 1 18		0 0 1 18		0 0 1 10	L	0 0 0
—— meliloti, the pound	0 0 1 16		0 0 1 18		0 0 1 13		0 0 1 10	L	0 0 0

† If otherwise imported.   * If imported by Aliens.   See the Notes preceding Drugs.

INWARDS.

DRUGS, *vizt.*	DUTIES to be paid on IMPORTATION. From the place of their growth, and in British-built ships. †		DRAWBACKS to be repaid on EXPORTATION.*		RATES, or supposed value, by 12 Car. II. cap. 4. 11 Geo. I. cap. 7. from whence the foregoing Duties are computed.
	By BRITISH.	By ALIENS.	Reference to the several Branches, see Page vi.	If exported to any legal place, except as mentioned in the following column.	If the produce of Europe or the East Indies, and exported to the British Colonies in America.
	£. s. d. 20ths	£. s. d. 20ths		£. s. d. 20ths	£. s. d. 20ths	£. s. d.
Flory, the pound	0 0 5 0	0 0 5 7 1/10	K	0 0 4 8 4/5	0 0 3 16 4/5	0 2 0
Folium Indic, the pound	0 0 10 12	0 0 11 7 3/10	K	0 0 11 2	0 0 9 12	0 5 0
Fox lungs, the pound	0 0 7 11	0 0 8 0 2/10	K	0 0 6 13 1/5	0 0 5 15 4/5	0 3 0
Frankincense of France, or	0 0 4 8	0 0 4 5	Fg	0 2 10 16	0 0 2 7 4/5	0 12 0
Parroffin, the Cwt.	0 0 6 4 4/5	0 0 8 2 7/10	K	0 0 2 12 2/5	0 1 11 0 3/5	0 12 0
Galanga, the pound	0 0 3 15	0 0 4 0 4/5	K	0 0 3 6 1/5	0 0 2 17 3/5	0 1 6
Galbanum, the pound	0 0 3 15	0 0 4 0 3/10	K	0 0 3 6 1/5	0 0 2 17 3/5	0 1 6
General, the pound	0 0 3 7 3/10	0 0 3 11 3/10	K	0 0 2 19 1/5	0 0 2 11 1/5	0 1 4
Gentiana, the pound	0 0 1 15	0 0 1 6 4/10	K	0 0 1 2 4/5	0 0 0 19 4/5	0 0 6
Grains of Guinea, or	0 0 6 3 12 1/2	0 0 6 8 1/2	Fg	0 0 5 6 12	0 0 4 9 12	0 10 0
French grains, the Cwt. *Vide in G.*						
Grana pinae, the pound	0 10 6	0 10 10 14 1/2	L	0 7 3	0 6 6	1 10 0
— tinctorum, the pound	0 0 2 10	0 0 2 13 1/20	F g	0 0 2 4 3/5	0 1 18 2/5	0 1 0
Grana Germanica, for Dyers use, as by 3 and 4 Ann. cap. 4. *deemed unrated*, therefor for every 20s. value upon oath	0 0 6 6	0 0 6 13 7/8	K	0 0 5 11	0 0 4 16	0 2 6
Granadilla Peruviana, the pound	0 1 1 1 1/5	0 1 1 4 1/5	L	0 1 1 1 3/5	0 1 1 1 3/5	1 0 0
	0 1 2 12 8/25	0 1 3 4 22/25	L	0 1 1 8 3/25	0 1 0 4 18/25	0 4 0

† If otherwise imported. ⁕ If otherwise imported. ⁂ If imported by Aliens. See the Notes preceding Drugs.

[85]

INWARDS.

DRUGS, vocat.	DUTIES to be paid on IMPORTATION.		References to the several Branches, see Page vi.	DRAWBACKS to be repaid on EXPORTATION.*		RATES, or supposed value by 12 Car. II. cap. 4. † 11 Geo. I. cap. 7. from whence the foregoing Duties are computed.
	From the place of their growth, and in British-built ships. †			If exported to any legal place, except as mentioned in the following column.	If the produce of Europe or the East Indies, and exported to the British Colonies in America.	
	By BRITISH. £. s. d. 20ths	By ALIENS. £. s. d. 20ths		£. s. d. 20ths	£. s. d. 20ths	£. s. d.
Green ginger, the pound	0 0 5 0	0 0 5 7 ½	K	0 0 4 8 ⁴⁄₅	0 0 3 16 ⁴⁄₅	0 2 0
Guinea pepper, the pound	0 0 2 10	0 0 2 13 ½	K	0 0 2 4 ²⁄₅	0 0 1 18 ²⁄₅	0 1 0
Gum animi, the pound	0 0 2 10	0 0 2 13 ½	K	0 0 2 4 ²⁄₅	0 0 1 18 ²⁄₅	0 1 0
Arabick, or Gum Senega, the Cwt. } for Dyers use, as by 3 and 4 Ann. cap. 4. But by 8 Geo. I. cap. 15. § 10. if regularly imported, entered, and landed, duty free. But on failure thereof, then to pay And, by the following laws, the several further duties hereafter mentioned were imposed, viz.						1 10 0
By 5 Geo. III. cap. 37.	0 2 1 4	0 2 15 ½	Ad	0 1 10 4	0 1 7 4	
Gum Senega, or Gum Arabick, the Cwt. averdupois And, by 25 Geo. II. cap. 32.	0 0 6 6	0 0 6 6	Fk			
Gum Senega, from any port or place in Europe, by any of His Majesty's subjects, in British-built ships navigated according to law, the hundred pounds weight	0 10 6	0 10 6	Ff			

† If otherwise imported. * If imported by Aliens. See the Notes preceding Drugs.

INWARDS.

	DUTIES to be paid on IMPORTATION. From the place of their growth, and in British-built ships. †						Reference to the several Branches, see Page vi.	DRAWBACKS to be repaid on EXPORTATION.*						RATES, or supposed value, by 12 Car. II. cap. 4. 11 Geo. I. cap. 7. from whence the foregoing Duties are computed.		
	By BRITISH.			By ALIENS.				If exported to any legal place, except as mentioned in the following column.			If the produce of Europe or the East Indies, and exported to the British Colonies in America.					
	L.	*s.*	*d.*/20ths	*L.*	*s.*	*d.*/20ths		*L.*	*s.*	*d.*/20ths	*L.*	*s.*	*d.*/20ths	*L.*	*s.*	*d.*
DRUGS, vocat.																
Gum armoniack, the pound	0	2	10	0	2	13 1/5	K	0	2	4 1/2	0	1	18 1/3	0	1	0
—— caramen, the pound	0	1	5 1/3	0	1	6 3/5	K	0	1	4 2/5	0	1	19 1/3	0	0	6
—— caranne, the pound	0	10	1 1/3	0	10	14 1/5	K	0	8	17 2/5	0	7	13 1/5	0	4	0
—— coral, the pound	0	3	0	0	3	3 4/5	L	0	2	15	0	2	10 9/10	0	0	10
—— elemni, the pound	0	2	2	0	2	4 1/5	K	0	1	17	0	1	12	0	0	10
—— guaici, the pound	0	10	1 1/3	0	10	14 1/5	K	0	8	17 2/5	0	7	13 1/5	0	4	0
—— hederæ, the pound	0	10	1 1/3	0	10	14 1/5	K	0	8	17 2/5	0	7	13 1/5	0	4	0
—— juniperi. *Vide* Gum Sandrake.																
—— lack, the pound	0	2	10	0	2	13 1/5	K	0	2	4 2/3	0	1	18 1/3	0	1	0
If Stick-lack, for Dyers use, *as by* 3 } *and* 4 *Ann. cap.* 4.																
But by 8 *Geo. I. cap.* 15. § 10. *if regularly imported, enter'd, and landed, duty free.*																
But on failure thereof, then to pay —																
If Cake-lack, for Dyers use, *as by* 3 } *and* 4 *Ann. cap.* 4. the pound	0	0	16 4/5	0	0	17 7/10	Ad	0	0	14 4/5	0	0	12 4/5	0	1	0
—— mount-jack, for Dyers use, *as by* 3 } *and* 4 *Ann. cap.* 4. *deemed unrated*; the pound	0	0	16 4/5	0	0	17 7/10	Ad	0	0	14 4/5	0	0	12 4/5	0	1	0
therefore for every 20s. value upon oath	0	6	1 1/3	0	6	4 3/5	L	0	5	7 1/3	0	5	1 1/3	0	1	0

† If otherwise imported. * If imported by Aliens. See the Notes preceding Drugs.

INWARDS.

	Duties to be paid on Importation. From the place of their growth, and in British-built ships. † By British. £.	s.	d.	20ths	By Aliens. £.	s.	d.	20ths	Reference to the several Branches, see Page vi.	Drawbacks to be repaid on Exportation. * If exported to any legal place, except as mentioned in the following column. £.	s.	d.	20ths	If the produce of Europe or the East Indies, and exported to the British Colonies in America. £.	s.	d.	20ths	Rates, or supposed value, by 12 Car. II. cap. 4. ‡ 11 Geo. I. cap. 7. from whence the foregoing Duties are computed. £.	s.	d.
Drugs, *vocat.*																					
—— opoponax, the pound	0	1	4	16	0	1	5	17	K	0	1	2	16	0	1	0	16	0	6	8
—— sandrake, or juniperi, the Cwt.	0	5	10	11 $\frac{1}{5}$	0	6	2	19 $\frac{2}{5}$	K	0	5	2	3 $\frac{1}{5}$	0	4	5	15 $\frac{1}{5}$	1	8	0
—— sarcocol, the pound	0	0	3	15 $\frac{3}{5}$	0	0	4	0 $\frac{13}{20}$	K	0	0	3	6 $\frac{3}{5}$	0	0	2	17 $\frac{3}{5}$	0	1	6
—— senega. *Vide* Gum Arabick.																				
—— serapinum, or sagapenum, the pound	0	0	3	15 $\frac{3}{5}$	0	0	4	0 $\frac{13}{20}$	K	0	0	3	6 $\frac{3}{5}$	0	0	2	17 $\frac{3}{5}$	0	1	6
—— tacamahaca, the pound	0	0	10	1 $\frac{3}{5}$	0	0	10	14 $\frac{1}{5}$	K	0	0	8	17 $\frac{3}{5}$	0	0	7	13 $\frac{3}{5}$	0	4	0
—— tragacanth, the pound	0	0	2	10 $\frac{2}{5}$	0	0	2	13 $\frac{11}{20}$	K	0	0	2	4 $\frac{2}{5}$	0	0	1	18 $\frac{2}{5}$	0	1	0
Gutta gambæ. *Vide* Cambogium.																				
Hermodactilus, the pound	0	0	5	0 $\frac{4}{5}$	0	0	5	7 $\frac{1}{10}$	K	0	0	4	8 $\frac{4}{5}$	0	0	3	16 $\frac{4}{5}$	0	2	0
Holliwortles. *Vide* Bunkins.																				
Horns of harts or stags, the hundred	0	6	3	12	0	6	8	6 $\frac{1}{2}$	K	0	5	6	12	0	4	9	12	1	10	0
Hypocistis, the pound	0	0	5	0 $\frac{4}{5}$	0	0	5	7 $\frac{1}{10}$	K	0	0	4	8 $\frac{4}{5}$	0	0	3	16 [illegible]	0	2	0
Jesuits bark. *Vide* Cortex Peruvianus.																				
Jessamine ointment, for Dyers use, *as by* 3 *and* 4 *Ann. cap.* 4. *deemed unrated*; therefore for every 20s. value upon oath	0	6	1	1 $\frac{3}{5}$	0	6	4	4 $\frac{3}{5}$	L	0	5	7	1 $\frac{3}{5}$	0	5	1	1 $\frac{3}{5}$			
Incense, or Olibanum, the Cwt.	1	1	0		1	2	3	15	K	0	18	6		0	16	0		5	0	0
Jalop, the pound	0	0	10	1 $\frac{3}{5}$	0	0	10	14 $\frac{1}{5}$	K	0	0	8	17 $\frac{3}{5}$	0	0	7	13 $\frac{2}{5}$	0	4	0
Ireos, the Cwt.	0	10	6		0	11	1	17 $\frac{1}{2}$	K	0	9	3		0	8	0		2	10	0

† If otherwise imported. * If imported by Aliens. See the Notes preceding Drugs.

INWARDS.

	DUTIES to be paid on IMPORTATION.				DRAWBACKS to be repaid on EXPORTATION.		RATES, or supposed value, by 12 Car. II. cap. 4. 11 Geo. I. cap. 7. from whence the foregoing Duties are computed.
	By BRITISH. From the place of their growth, and in British-built ships. †		By ALIENS.		Reference to the several Branches, see Page vi.	If exported to any legal place, except as mentioned in the following column.	If the produce of Europe, or the East Indies, and exported to the British Colonies in America.
	£. s. d./20ths		£. s. d./20ths			£. s. d./20ths	£. s. d./20ths	£. s. d.
DRUGS, vocat.								
Isinglass, for Dyers use, as by 3 and 4 Ann. cap. 4. the Cwt.	0 7 0		0 7 5 $\frac{15}{20}$		Ad	0 6 2	0 5 4	5 0 0
But by 8 Geo. I. cap. 15. § 10. if regularly imported, entered, and landed, is duty free.								
Jujubes, the pound	0 2 10		0 2 13		K	0 2 4 $\frac{2}{5}$	0 5 0 $\frac{2}{5}$	0 1 0
Juniper berries, the Cwt.	0 2 8		0 5 11 $\frac{1}{20}$		K	0 3 8	1 1 8 $\frac{2}{5}$	0 0 0
Lablanum, or Lapadonum, the pound	0 2 10		0 2 13		K	0 2 4	1 1 8	0 1 0
Lack. Vide Gum lack.								
Lapis calaminaris, the Cwt.	0 3 6		0 3 12		K	0 3 1	0 2 8	0 16 8
—— contra yerva, the ounce	0 1 0 12		0 1 7		K	0 0 11 $\frac{2}{5}$	0 9 12	0 5 0
—— hematitis, the pound	0 2 10		0 2 13		K	0 2 4	1 1 8	0 0 1
Vide Blood-stones in S.								
—— hibernicus, the Cwt.	0 6 1		0 6 4 $\frac{1}{5}$		L	0 5 1 $\frac{1}{5}$	0 5 1 $\frac{1}{5}$	0 1 0
—— hyacinthi, the pound	0 2 12		0 3 4		L	0 1 8 $\frac{1}{8}$	1 0 4 $\frac{1}{8}$	0 4 0
—— judicus, the pound	0 2 10		0 2 13		K	0 1 2	0 1 7	0 1 0
—— lazuli, the pound	0 2 14		0 2 15		K	0 1 10	1 0 0	0 10 0
—— magnetis, the pound	0 3 13		0 3 16 $\frac{2}{10}$		L	0 3 7 $\frac{1}{2}$	0 3 1 $\frac{1}{5}$	0 0 1
—— nephriticus, the pound	0 6 5		0 7 1		L	0 4 15	1 3 5	0 1 5

† If otherwise imported.   * If imported by Aliens.   See the Notes preceding Drugs.

[89]

INWARDS.

DRUGS, vocat.	DUTIES to be paid on IMPORTATION. From the place of their growth, and in British-built ships. †				Reference to the several Branches, see Page vi.	DRAWBACKS to be repaid on EXPORTATION.*				RATES, or supposed value, by 12 Car.II.cap.4. ‡ 11 Geo.I.cap.7. from whence the foregoing Duties are computed.		
	By BRITISH.		By ALIENS.			If exported to any legal place, except as mentioned in the following column.		If the produce of Europe or the East Indies, and exported to the British Colonies in America.				
	£ s. d./20ths		£ s. d./20ths			£ s. d./20ths		£ s. d./20ths		£	s.	d.
—— ostiocolla, the pound	0 1 16 2/20		0 1 18 21/20		L	0 1 13 27/20		0 1 10 27/20		1	0	6
—— rubinus, the pound	0 3 13 2/20		0 3 16 21/20		L	0 3 7 25/20		0 3 1 25/20		1	1	0
—— sapphirus, the pound	0 3 13 2/20		0 3 16 21/20		L	0 3 7 25/20		0 3 1 25/20		1	1	0
—— smaragdus, the pound	0 3 13 2/20		0 3 16 21/20		L	0 3 7 25/20		0 3 1 25/20		1	1	0
—— spongiæ, the pound	0 3 13 2/20		0 3 16 21/20		L	0 3 7 25/20		0 3 1 25/20		1	1	0
—— topazæ, the pound	0 3 13 2/20		0 3 16 21/20		L	0 3 7 27/20		0 3 1 27/20		1	1	0
—— tutiæ, the pound	0 2 10 1/20		0 2 13 2/20		K	0 2 4 5/20		1 18 2/20		1	0	8
Leaves of roses, the pound	0 1 3 1/20		0 1 5 7/20		K	0 1 9 2/20		0 1 5 2/20		0	0	3
—— of violets or flowers, the pound	0 0 12 1/20		0 0 13 1/20		K	0 0 11 1/10		0 0 9 3/10		0	0	3
Lentiles, the pound	0 2 4		0 2 5		K	0 2 1 1/10		0 1 7 4/20		0	10	0
Lignum aloes, the pound	0 2 10 1/3		0 2 13		K	0 2 4 1/2		0 1 18 2/5		0	1	0
—— asphaltum, the pound	0 0 1 4		0 0 10 14		K	0 0 17 5/20		0 0 13 4/20		0	10	0
—— nephriticum, the pound	0 2 1 4		0 2 15		K	0 1 10 4		0 1 7 4		0	10	0
—— Rhodium, the Cwt.	0 2 1 1		0 2 15		K	0 1 10 4		0 1 7 4		0	10	0
—— vitæ, the Cwt.												

But by 1 Geo. II. cap. 17. § 5. *if* Lignum vitæ *be regularly imported from the British plantations in America, it is free.*

Linum. Vide Argentum sublime.

† If otherwise imported. * If imported by Aliens. See the Notes preceding Drugs.

INWARDS.

	Duties to be paid on Importation. From the place of their growth, and in British-built ships. † By British. £.	s.	d.	20ths	By Aliens. £.	s.	d.	20ths	Reference to the several Branches, see Page vi.	Drawbacks to be repaid on Exportation. * If exported to any legal place, except as mentioned in the following column. £.	s.	d.	20ths	If the produce of Europe or the East Indies, and exported to the British Colonies in America. £.	s.	d.	20ths	Rates, or supposed value, by 12 Car. II. cap. 4. ‡ 11 Geo. I. cap. 7. from whence the foregoing Duties are computed. £.	s.	d.
Drugs, *viz.*																					
Litharge, for Dyers use, *as by 3 and 4 Ann. cap.* 4. of gold, the Cwt.	0	0	10	1 3/5	0	0	10	14 1/5	A d	0	0	8	17 3/5	0	0	7	13 3/5	0	12	0
—— of silver, the Cwt.	0	0	8	8	0	0	8	18 1/2	A d	0	0	7	8	0	0	6	8	0	10	0
Locust, the pound	0	0	3	7 1/5	0	0	3	11 2/5	K	0	0	2	19 1/5	0	0	2	11 1/5	0	1	4
Lupines, the Cwt.	0	2	1	4	0	2	2	15 1/2	K	0	1	10	4	0	1	7	4	0	10	0
Lyntiscus, or Xylobalsamum, the pound	0	0	4	4	0	0	4	9 1/4	K	0	0	3	14	0	0	3	4	0	1	8
Madder roots, or Rubea tinctorum, for Dyers use, *as by 3 and 4 Ann, cap.* 4. the pound	—	—	—	—	—	—	—	—		—	—	—	—	—	—	—	—	0	1	0
But by 8 Geo. I. cap. 15. § 10. *if regularly imported, entered and landed,* duty free.																				
But on failure thereof, then to pay	0	0	0	16 4/5	0	0	0	17 17/20	A d	0	0	0	14 4/5	0	0	0	12 4/5			
Manna, the pound	0	0	6	6	0	0	6	13 7/8	K	0	0	5	11	0	0	4	16	0	2	6
Marmelade, the pound	0	0	2	10 2/5	0	0	2	13 11/20	K	0	0	2	4 2/5	0	0	1	18 2/5	0	1	0
Mastick, red, the pound	0	0	2	10 2/5	0	0	2	13 11/20	K	0	0	2	4 2/5	0	0	1	18 2/5	0	1	0
—— white, the pound	0	0	8	8	0	0	8	18 1/2	K	0	0	7	8	0	0	6	8	0	3	4
Mechoacana, the pound	0	0	6	6	0	0	6	13 7/8	K	0	0	5	11	0	0	4	16	0	2	6
Mercury precipitat, the pound	0	1	4	16	0	1	5	17	K	0	1	2	16	0	1	0	16	0	6	8
—— sublimat, the pound	0	0	7	11 1/5	0	0	8	0 11/20	K	0	0	6	13 1/5	0	0	5	15 1/5	0	3	0

† If otherwise imported. * If imported by Aliens. See the Notes preceding Drugs.

INWARDS.

	Duties to be paid on Importation. From the place of their growth, and in British-built ships. †								Reference to the several Branches, see Page vi.	Drawbacks to be repaid on Exportation.*								Rates, or supposed value, by 12 Car. II. cap. 4. ‡ 11 Geo. I. cap. 7. from whence the foregoing Duties are computed.		
	By British.				By Aliens.					If exported to any legal place, except as mentioned in the following column.				If the produce of Europe or the East Indies, and exported to the British Colonies in America.						
	£.	s.	d.	20ths	£.	s.	d.	20ths		£.	s.	d.	20ths	£.	s.	d.	20ths	£.	s.	d.
Drugs, *vocat.*																				
Milium solis, the pound	0	0	2	10 2/5	0	0	2	13 11/20	K	0	0	2	4 2/5	0	0	1	18 2/5	0	1	0
Mirabolanes condited, the pound	0	0	4	4	0	0	4	9 1/4	K	0	0	3	14	0	0	3	4	0	1	8
—— dry, the pound	0	0	2	10 2/5	0	0	2	13 11/20	K	0	0	2	4 2/5	0	0	1	18 2/5	0	1	0
Mithridate Venetiæ, the pound	0	2	1	4	0	2	2	15 1/2	K	0	1	10	4	0	1	7	4	0	10	0
Vide letter M *for* Mithridate.																				
Myrtle berries, the pound	0	0	2	10 2/5	0	0	2	13 11/20	K	0	0	2	4 2/5	0	0	1	18 2/5	0	1	0
Mother of pearl shells, not of East-India, the pound	0	0	3	13 2/25	0	0	3	16 23/100	L	0	0	3	7 2/25	0	0	3	1 2/25	‡ 0	1	0
Mummia, the pound	0	0	2	10 2/5	0	0	2	13 11/20	K	0	0	2	4 2/5	0	0	1	18 2/5	0	1	0
Musk, the ounce troy	0	8	4	16	0	8	11	2	K	0	7	4	16	0	6	4	16	2	0	0
—— cods, the dozen	0	8	4	16	0	8	11	2	K	0	7	4	16	0	6	4	16	2	0	0
Myrrha, the pound	0	0	7	11 1/5	0	0	8	0 13/20	K	0	0	6	13 1/5	0	0	5	15 1/5	0	3	0
Nardus Celtica, or Spica Romana, the Cwt.	1	3	6	4 4/5	1	4	11	17 3/5	K	1	0	8	12 4/5	0	17	11	0 4/5	5	12	0
Nigella, the pound	0	0	1	13 3/5	0	0	1	15 7/10	K	0	0	1	9 3/5	0	0	1	5 3/5	0	0	8
Nitrum, the pound	0	0	5	0 4/5	0	0	5	7 1/10	K	0	0	4	8 4/5	0	0	3	16 4/5	0	2	0
Nutmegs condited, the pound	0	0	10	1 1/5	0	0	10	14 1/5	K	0	0	8	17 3/5	0	0	7	13 3/5	0	4	0
Nux de Benne, the pound	0	0	2	10 2/5	0	0	2	13 11/20	K	0	0	2	4 2/5	0	0	1	18 2/5	0	1	0
—— Cupressi, the pound	0	0	1	13 3/5	0	0	1	15 7/10	K	0	0	1	9 3/5	0	0	1	5 3/5	0	0	8
—— Indica, the piece	0	0	1	5 1/5	0	0	1	6 31/40	K	0	0	1	2 1/5	0	0	0	19 1/5	0	0	6
—— pini, or Grana pini, the pound	0	0	2	10 2/5	0	0	2	13 11/20	K	0	0	2	4 2/5	0	0	1	18 2/5	0	1	0

† If otherwise imported. * If imported by Aliens. See the Notes preceding Drugs.

INWARDS.

	Duties to be paid on Importation. From the place of their growth, and in British-built ship. † By British. £.	s.	d.	20ths	By Aliens. £.	s.	d.	20ths	Reference to the several Branches, see Page vi.	Drawbacks to be repaid on Exportation. * If exported to any legal place, except as mentioned in the following column. £.	s.	d.	20ths	If the produce of Europe or the East Indies, and exported to the British Colonies in America. £.	s.	d.	20ths	Rates, or supposed value, by 12 Car. II. cap. 4. ‡ 11 Geo. I. cap. 7. from whence the foregoing Duties are computed. £.	s.	d.
Drugs, *vocat.*																				
Nux pistachiæ. *Vide* Pistachias.																				
—— vomica, the pound	0	0	1	13 3/5	0	0	1	15 7/10	K	0	0	1	9 3/5	0	0	1	5 3/5	0	0	8
Olibanum, or Incense, the Cwt.	1	1	0		1	2	3	15	K	0	18	6		0	16	0		5	0	0
Opium, the pound	0	2	1	4	0	2	2	15 1/2	K	0	1	10	4	0	1	7	4	0	10	0
Orabus, the pound	0	0	1	5 1/5	0	0	1	6 31/40	K	0	0	1	2 1/5	0	0	0	19 1/5	0	0	6
Orange flower ointment, the pound	0	0	6	6	0	0	6	13 7/8	K	0	0	5	11	0	0	4	16	0	2	6
—— water, the gallon	0	1	0	12	0	1	1	7 3/4	K	0	0	11	2	0	0	9	12	0	5	0
Orcant, or Almict, the pound	0	0	2	10 2/5	0	0	2	13 11/20	K	0	0	2	4 2/5	0	0	1	18 2/5	0	1	0
Origanum, the pound	0	0	1	13 3/5	0	0	1	15 7/10	K	0	0	1	9 3/5	0	0	1	5 3/5	0	0	8
Orpiment, or Auripigmentum, the Cwt.	0	8	4	16	0	8	11	2	K	0	7	4	16	0	6	4	16	2	0	0
Osipium huirredum, the pound	0	0	1	5 1/5	0	0	1	6 31/40	K	0	0	1	2 1/5	0	0	0	19 1/5	0	0	6
Ossa de corde cervi, the pound	0	8	4	16	0	8	11	2	K	0	7	4	16	0	6	4	16	2	0	0
Oil of almonds, the pound	0	0	2	10 2/5	0	0	2	13 11/20	K	0	0	2	4 2/5	0	0	1	18 2/5	0	1	0
— of amber, the pound	0	2	5	8	0	2	6	19 1/2	K a	0	2	2	8	0	1	11	8	0	10	0
Oleum annisi, the pound	0	1	6	5 2/5	0	1	7	1 3/20	L	0	1	4	15 2/5	0	1	3	5 2/5	‡ 0	5	0
Oil de Bay, the Cwt.	0	8	4	16	0	8	11	2	K	0	7	4	16	0	6	4	16	2	0	0
— de Ben, the pound	0	1	4	16	0	1	5	17	K	0	1	2	16	0	1	0	16	0	6	8
Oleum cariophyllorum, the pound	0	3	0	10 4/5	0	3	2	2 3/10	L	0	2	9	10 4/5	0	2	6	10 4/5	‡ 0	10	0
—— carui, the pound	0	1	6	5 2/5	0	1	7	1 3/20	L	0	1	4	15 2/5	0	1	3	5 2/5	‡ 0	5	0
—— cinnamomi, the ounce troy	0	1	6	5 2/5	0	1	7	1 3/20	L	0	1	4	15 2/5	0	1	3	5 2/5	‡ 0	5	0

† If otherwise imported. * If imported by Aliens. See the Notes preceding Drugs.

INWARDS.

	DUTIES to be paid on IMPORTATION.				DRAWBACKS to be repaid on EXPORTATION.*		RATES, or supposed value, by 12 Car. II. cap. 4. 11 Geo. I cap. 7. from whence the foregoing Duties are computed.
	By BRITISH. From the place of their growth, and in British-built ships.†	By ALIENS.	Reference to the several Branches, see Page vi.	If exported to any legal place, except as mentioned in the following column.	If the produce of Europe or the East Indies, and exported to the British Colonies in America.	
	£. s. d. /20ths	£. s. d. /20ths		£. s. d. /20ths	£. s. d. /20ths	£. s. d.
DRUGS, *vocat.*						
—— cymini, the pound	0 0 1 2/15	0 0 1 3/15	L	0 0 1 8/15	0 0 1 0 4/15	0 0 4 0
—— juniperi, the pound	0 0 0 7	0 0 0 7 12/15	L	0 0 0 6 14/15	0 0 0 6 2/15	0 0 2 0
—— copaiva. *See* Balsamum copaiva.						
Oil of mace, or nutmegs, the pound	0 0 1 3	0 0 1 4	K	0 0 1 1 8/15	0 0 1 11 10 8/15	0 0 6 0
Oleum nucis muscatæ liquidum, the pound	0 2 2 7 2 15/21	0 2 1 8 1 7/15	L	0 0 1 10 7 2/5	0 0 1 8 7 3/5	0 0 6 8
—— origani, the pound	0 1 6 5 3/15	0 1 6 4 15/21	L	0 0 1 4 15 1/5	0 0 1 3 5 1/5	0 0 5 0
—— palmæ, the Cwt.	0 6 1 1	0 6 4 4	L	0 0 5 7	0 0 5 1	0 1 0 0
Oil of peony, for Dyers use, *as by 3 and 4 Ann. cap. 4. deemed unrated* ; therefore for every 20 s. value upon oath	0 0 1 1	0 0 9 4 9/21	K	0 0 5 7	0 0 5 1	0 1 0 0
Oleum Petroleum, the pound	0 0 15 1 4 2/15	0 0 15 10 9 1/11	L	0 0 13 11 3 14/21	0 0 12 8 3 4/15	0 2 10 0
—— Rhodii, the pound	0 1 8 3 1 11/15	0 1 9 1/21	K	0 0 1 5 15 5 1/21	0 0 1 4 7 4/15	0 0 8 0
Oil of rolemary, the pound	0 0 2 12	0 0 3 7 2/15	L	0 0 1 5 18 5 17/21	0 0 1 0 5 4 2/15	0 0 4 0
Oleum saffafræ, the pound	0 0 2 6 14	0 0 2 6 4 7/15	K	0 0 3 14 3/15	0 0 3 4 2/15	0 0 2 0
Oil of scorpions, the pound	0 0 4 4 5	0 0 4 7 2/15	L	0 0 1 4 15 5/15	0 0 1 3 5/15	0 0 5 0
—— of spike, the pound	0 0 1 1	0 0 1 6	K	0 0 5 7	0 0 5 1	0 0 8 8
Oleum thymæ, the pound	0 0 1 5 2 7/21	0 0 1 6 3 19/15	K	0 0 1 2 5 1 10/15	0 0 1 0 3 4 19/21	0 0 1 6 0
Oil of turpentine, the pound	0 0 3 13 10 5/15	0 0 3 16 10 7/15	L	0 0 3 7 19 1 22/15	0 0 3 19 1 5/15	0 0 1 0

† If otherwife imported. * If imported by Aliens. See the Notes preceding Drugs.

INWARDS.

DRUGS, vocat.	DUTIES to be paid on IMPORTATION.		Reference to the several Branches, see Page vi.	DRAWBACKS to be repaid on EXPORTATION.		RATES, or supposed value, by 12 Car. II. cap. 4. 11 Geol. cap. 7. from whence the foregoing Duties are computed.
	From the place of their growth, and in British-built ships. †			If exported to any legal place, except as mentioned in the following column.	If the produce of Europe or the East Indies, and exported to the British Colonies in America.	
	By BRITISH.	By ALIENS.				
	£. s. d. 20ths	£. s. d. 20ths		£. s. d. 20ths	£. s. d. 20ths	£. s. d.
Oil orange, jessamine, or other perfumed oils, not otherwise rated, the pound	0 1 6 5	0 1 7 1 1/10	L	0 1 4 15 7/5	0 1 3 5 7/5	4 0 5 0
—— chemical oils, not otherwise rated, the pound	0 0 7 6 4/25	0 0 7 12 2 3/10	L	0 0 6 14 4/25	0 0 6 2 4/25	2 0 0 0
Panisporcinus. See Cyclamen.						
Panther, the pound	0 16 9 12	0 17 10 4	K	0 14 9 12	0 12 9 12	4 0 3 4
Parroiin. See Frankincense.						
Pearl beaten, the ounce troy	0 0 8 8 1/4-1/2 1/40	0 0 8 18 1/4-1/2	K	0 0 7 8 1/4-1/2 1/40	0 0 6 8 1/4-1/2 1/40	0 0 3 6
Pellitory, the pound	0 0 1 5 1/2 1/10	0 0 1 1 6 1/2 1/10	K	0 0 1 2 1/2 1/10	0 0 0 19 1/2 1/10	0 0 1 0
Pepper long, the pound	0 0 2 10 1/4-1/2 1/10	0 0 2 13 1/4-1/2 1/10	K	0 0 1 4 1/4-1/2 1/10	0 0 1 1 8 1/4-1/2 1/10	0 0 1 0
Piony seeds, the pound	0 0 1 13 1/2 1/10	0 0 1 15 1/2 1/10	K	0 0 1 9 1/2 1/10	0 0 1 5 1/2 1/10	0 0 1 0
Pistachias, or nux pistachia, the pound	0 0 2 10 1/10	0 0 2 13 1/10	K	0 0 1 4 1/10	0 0 1 18 1/10	0 0 1 0
Pistolochia. Vide Bunkins.						
Pix Burgundiæ, the Cwt.	0 5 3 16 4/5 1/3	0 5 7 4/5 1/7 1/3	F g	0 3 7 10 4/5 1/3 1/3	0 3 3 10 4/5 1/3 1/3	0 15 0 0
Polypodium, the pound	0 0 0 16 3/10 1/10	0 0 0 17 3/10 1/10	K	0 0 0 14 3/10 1/10	0 0 0 12 3/10 1/10	0 0 4 8
Polium montanum, the pound	0 0 1 13 1/3	0 0 1 15 1/3	K	0 0 1 9 1/3	0 0 1 5 1/3	0 0 0 0
Ponatum, for Dyers use, as by 3 and 4 Ann. cap. 4. deemed unrated; therefore for every 20 s. value upon oath	0 6 1 1 1/3	0 6 4 4 3	L	0 5 7 1 1/3	0 5 1 1 1/3	0 0 0 0

† If otherwise imported.   * If imported by Aliens.   See the Notes preceding Drugs.

D   [95]   D

INWARDS.

DRUGS, *vocat.*	DUTIES to be paid on IMPORTATION.		Reference to the several Branches, see Page vi.	DRAWBACKS to be repaid on EXPORTATION.*		RATES, or supposed value, by 12 Car. II. cap. 4. ‡ 11 Geo. I. cap. 7. from whence the foregoing Duties are computed.
	From the place of their growth, and in British-built ships. †			If exported to any legal place, except as mentioned in the following column.	If the produce of Europe or the East Indies, and exported to the British Colonies in America.	
	By BRITISH.	By ALIENS.				
	£. s. d. 20ths	£. s. d. 20ths		£. s. d. 20ths	£. s. d. 20ths	£. s. d.
Pomegranate peels, for Dyers use, *as by 3* and 4 *Ann. cap.* 4. the Cwt. But by 8 *Geo.* I. *cap.* 15. § 10. *if regularly imported, entered and landed, duty free.* But *on failure thereof, then to pay*	0 2 9 12	0 2 11 14 4/10	Ad	0 2 5 12 9 3/5 2/5	0 2 1 12 9 3/5 2/5	2 0 0
Pompholix, the pound	0 0 1 4	0 0 1 5 1/10	L	0 0 1 2 2/5 3/5	0 0 1 1 2/5 3/5	0 0 4 8
Poppy seed, the pound	0 0 1 13	0 0 1 15 1 1/20 7/10	K	0 0 1 9	0 0 1 8	0 0 1 0
Precipitat. *Vide* Mercury precipitat.						
Prunelloes, or Prunes of Brusolia, the pound	0 0 2 10	0 0 2 13 1/10 5/10	K	0 0 2 4 4 1/5 3/5	0 0 2 1 18 4 4/5 1/5	0 0 8 0
Psyllium, the pound	0 0 1 13	0 0 1 15 1 1/20 7/10	K	0 0 1 9	0 0 1 1 18 5	0 0 1 0
Quicksilver. *Vide* Argentum sublime.						
Radix bistortæ, the Cwt.	0 3 0 10 4/5 3/5	0 3 2 2 1/20 3/5	L	0 2 9 10 4/5 3/5	0 0 6 10 4/5 3/5	0 4 0 0
— cassuminar, not of the East-Indies, the pound	0 1 6 5	0 1 7 1 3/20	L	0 1 4 15	0 0 3 5	0 3 6 0
— contra yerva, the pound	0 0 6 8 4/5 3/5	0 0 6 8 18 1/10	K	0 0 5 7 4/10 3/5	0 0 5 8 4 3/5 1/5	0 0 3 0
— enulæ campanæ, the Cwt.	0 0 8 1 2/10 3/5	0 0 8 4 2/5 3/5	L	0 0 7 1	0 0 1 1 1/5 1/5	0 0 0 0
— eringii, the pound	0 0 1 16 1/20 2/10	0 0 1 18 2 6/10 3/20	L	0 0 1 13 3 4/15	0 0 1 10 4 4/15	0 0 1 0
— esulæ, the pound	0 0 2 10	0 0 2 13 1/10 1/20	K	0 0 2 4 4 1/5 3/5	0 0 1 18 4 4/5 1/5	0 0 6 0
— hypocacuanæ, the pound	0 0 0 7	0 0 2 1 8 1/5 1/5	L	0 0 1 10 7 4/5	0 0 0 8 7 4/5	0 0 8 0

† If otherwise imported. * If imported by Aliens. See the Notes preceding Drugs.

[96]

INWARDS.

DRUGS, *vocal.*	DUTIES to be paid on IMPORTATION. By BRITISH. From the place of their growth, and in British-built Ships.†				DUTIES to be paid on IMPORTATION. By ALIENS.				Reference to the several Branches, see Page vi.	DRAWBACKS to be repaid on EXPORTATION.* If exported to any legal place, except as mentioned in the following column.				If the produce of Europe or the East Indies, and exported to the British Colonies in America.				RATES, or supposed value, by 12 Car. II. cap. 4. ‡ 11 Geo. I. cap. 7. from whence the foregoing Duties are computed.		
	£	s.	d.	/20ths	£	s.	d.	/20ths		£	s.	d.	/20ths	£	s.	d.	/20ths	£	s.	d.
Radix mei athamantici, the pound	0	1	16	27/50	0	1	18	21/100	L	0	1	13	27/50	0	1	10	27/50	0	0	6
—— peoniæ, the pound	0	1	13	27/50	0	1	15	7/10	K	0	1	9	27/50	0	1	5	21/50	0	0	8
—— phu, the pound	0	1	16	27/50	0	1	18	21/100	L	0	1	13	27/50	0	1	10	27/50	0	0	6
—— icorcioneræ, the pound	0	0	8	8	0	0	8	21/40	K	0	0	7	8	0	0	6	8	0	0	4
—— serpentariæ, the pound	0	3	9	2	0	3	10	21/40	L	0	3	8	7/10	0	2	7	7/10	0	3	6
—— tormentillæ, the Cwt.	0	3	6	10	0	3	8	12	K	0	2	9	10	0	2	6	10	0	2	6
Red lead, the Cwt.	0	3	0	10	0	3	2	2 3/10	L	0	3	1		0	2	10	4/5	0	16	0
Refinæ jalapii, the pound	0	3	0	10	0	3	2	3/10	L	0	2	9	10	0	2	6	10	0	10	0
—— scamonii, the pound	0	4	2	8	0	4	5	11	L	0	3	10	8	0	2	8	4/5	0	10	0
Rhabarbarum, or Rhubarb, the pound	0	2	9	12	0	2	11	14	K	0	2	5	12	0	2	2	12	0	13	4
Rhaponticum, the pound	0	6	1		0	6	4		L	0	5	7		0	5	1		0	13	4
Rhinchurst, the Cwt.																				
Rosalgar. *Vide* Arsenick.																				
Roslet, the pound	0	1	5	4/5	0	1	6	31/40	K	0	1	2	1/5	0	0	19	11/20	0	0	6
Rubea tinctorum. *Vide* Madder roots.																				
Saccharum Saturni, the pound	0	3	13	27/50	0	3	16	27/100	L	0	3	7	27/50	0	3	1	7/10	0	1	0
Salop, not of the East-Indies, the pound	0	3	13	21/50	0	3	16	21/100	L	0	3	7	21/50	0	3	1	21/50	0	1	0
Sal alkali, the pound	0	10	1	1/5	0	10	14		K	0	8	17	1/5	0	7	13		0	4	0
armoniacum, for Dyers use, *as by* 3 } *and* 4 *Ann. cap.* 4. *the pound* }																		0	1	8

† If otherwise imported.   * If imported by Aliens.   See the Notes preceding Drugs.

D [97] D

INWARDS.

DRUGS	DUTIES to be paid on IMPORTATION.		DRAWBACKS to be repaid on EXPORTATION.*		RATES, or supposed value, by 12 Car. II. cap. 4. ‡ 11 Geo. I. cap. 7. from whence the foregoing Duties are computed.
	From the place of their growth, and in British-built ships. †		If exported to any legal place, except as mentioned in the following column.	If the produce of Europe or the East Indies, and exported to the British Colonies in America.	
	By BRITISH.	By ALIENS.			
	£. s. d. 20ths	£. s. d. 20ths	£. s. d. 20ths	£. s. d. 20ths	£. s. d.
DRUGS, vocat. ——— gem, for Dyers use, as by 3 and 4 Ann. cap. 4. the pound But by 8 Geo. I. cap. 15. § 10. if Sal Armoniacum and Sal Gem are regularly imported, entered, and landed, duty free. But on failure thereof, then to pay,	0 0 1 8	0 0 1 9 3/4	0 0 4 9 2/5	0 1 0 3/5	0 0 8
——— gem, the pound	0 0 0 11	0 0 0 11 3/10	0 0 1 1 1/5		
——— armoniacum, the pound	0 0 3 15	0 0 4 0 2/5	0 0 9 6 2/5	0 2 17 3/5	0 1 0
——— nitre, the pound	0 1 1 16 3/5	0 1 18 23/100	0 3 6 3/5	0 1 10 1/5	0 0 4
——— prunellæ, the pound	0 0 2 12	0 0 3 4 2/5	0 1 13	0 0 4 5 1/5	0 0 4 1/2
——— fuccini, the pound	0 1 6 5	0 0 7 1/5	0 1 1 8	0 0 3 3 2/5	0 1 1
——— tamarisci, the pound	0 0 5 13	0 3 16 7/100	0 4 15	0 0 3 1 2/5	0 1 1
——— tartari, the pound	0 0 3 13	0 0 7 12 2/5	0 3 7 1/5	0 0 3 1 2/5	0 0 2
——— vitrioli, the pound	0 0 7 6 2/5	0 7 12 2/5	0 6 14 2/5	0 0 6 2 2/5	0 0 2
——— volatile, { armoniaci, the pound { cornu cervi, the pound	0 0 7 6	0 0 2 15	0 6 14 4/5	0 0 6 2 2/5	0 0 2
Sandiver, the Cwt.	0 2 1 4		0 1 10 4	0 1 7 4	0 10
Sandaracha, or Gum Sandrcha, or Gum { Juniperi, the Cwt.	0 5 10 11	0 2 6 2 3/5	0 5 2 3	0 4 5 15 1/5	1 8

† If otherwise imported. * If imported by Aliens. See the Notes preceding Drugs.

INWARDS.

INWARDS.	Duties to be paid on Importation. From the place of their growth, and in British-built ships. † By British. £.	s.	d.	20ths	By Aliens. £.	s.	d.	20ths	Reference to the several Branches, see Page vi.	Drawbacks to be repaid on Exportation. If exported to any legal place, except as mentioned in the following column. £.	s.	d.	20ths	If the produce of Europe, or the East Indies, and exported to the British Colonies in America. £.	s.	d.	20ths	Rates, or supposed value, by 12 Car. II. cap. 4. & 11 Geo. I. cap. 7. from whence the foregoing Duties are computed. £.	s.	d.
Drugs, *vocat.*																					
Sanguis draconis, the pound	0	0	8	8	0	0	8	18 ½	K	0	0	7	8	0	0	6	8	0	3	4
—— hirci, the pound	0	0	2	10 ⅖	0	0	2	13 11/20	K	0	0	2	4 ⅖	0	0	1	18 ⅖	0	1	0
Sarsaparilla, the pound	0	0	8	8	0	0	8	18 ½	K	0	0	7	8	0	0	6	8	0	3	4
Sassafras wood, or roots, the Cwt.	0	4	2	8	0	4	5	11	K	0	3	8	8	0	3	2	8	1	0	0
Saunders red, *alias* Stock, for Dyers use, *as by* 3 *and* 4 *Ann. cap.* 4. the Cwt.	—	—	—	—	—	—	—	—		—	—	—	—	—	—	—	—	4	0	0
But by 8 *Geo. I. cap.* 15. § 10. *if regularly imported, entered, and landed,* duty free.																				
But on failure thereof, then to pay	0	5	7	4	0	5	11	8	Ad	0	4	11	4	0	4	3	4			
—— white, the pound	0	0	2	10 ⅖	0	0	2	13 11/20	K	0	0	2	4 ⅖	0	0	1	18 ⅖	0	1	0
—— yellow, the pound	0	0	5	0 ⅘	0	0	5	7 1/10	K	0	0	4	8 ⅘	0	0	3	16 ⅘	0	2	0
Scammony. *Vide* Diagredium.																				
Scincus marinus, the piece	0	0	0	16 ⅘	0	0	0	17 17/20	K	0	0	0	14 ⅘	0	0	0	12 ⅘	0	0	4
Scordium, the pound	0	0	1	5 ⅕	0	0	1	6 31/40	K	0	0	1	2 ⅕	0	0	0	19 ⅕	0	0	6
Scorpions, the piece	0	0	0	12 ⅗	0	0	0	13 31/60	K	0	0	0	11 1/10	0	0	0	9 ⅗	0	0	3
Sebestines, the pound	0	0	2	10 ⅖	0	0	2	13 11/20	K	0	0	2	4 ⅖	0	0	1	18 ⅖	0	1	0
Seeds for gardens, of all sorts, the pound	0	0	1	13 ⅗	0	0	1	15 7/10	K	0	0	1	9 ⅗	0	0	1	5 ⅗	0	0	8
Seler montanus, the pound	0	0	1	13 ⅗	0	0	1	15 7/10	K	0	0	1	9 ⅗	0	0	1	5 ⅕	0	0	8

† If otherwise imported. * If imported by Aliens. See the Notes preceding Drugs.

[99]

INWARDS.

DRUGS, vocat.	DUTIES to be paid on IMPORTATION.				Reference to the several Branches, see Page vi.	DRAWBACKS to be repaid on EXPORTATION.*		RATES or supposed value, by 12 Car. II. cap. 4. † 11 Geo. I. cap. 7. from whence the foregoing Duties are computed.
	From the place of their growth, and in British-built ships. †		By ALIENS.			If exported to any legal place, except as mentioned in the following column.	If the produce of Europe or the East Indies, and exported to the British Colonies in America.	
	By BRITISH.							
	£. s. d. 20ths		£. s. d. 20ths			£. s. d. 20ths	£. s. d. 20ths	£. s. d.
Semen cucumeris, cucurb, citrol, melon, the pound	0 0 1 13		0 0 1 15		K	0 0 1 9	0 0 1 5	0 0 8
Sena, the pound	0 0 6 6 3/5		0 0 6 13 7/20		K	0 0 5 11	0 0 4 16 2/5	0 2 6
Sevum cervinum, the pound	0 0 1 16 27/30		0 0 1 18 21/20		L	0 0 1 13 27/3	0 0 1 10 27/3	0 0 6
Soldonella, vel Sordonella, the pound	0 0 1 13		0 0 1 15 7/20		K	0 0 1 9	0 0 1 5	0 0 8
Spermaceti coarse, oily, the Cwt.	0 0 16 9 12		0 0 17 10 4		K	0 0 14 9 12	0 12 9 12	4 0 0
fine, the pound	0 0 1 0 12		0 0 1 1 7		K	0 0 11 2	0 0 9 12	0 5 0
Spica Celtica, or Romana. *Vide* Nardus Celtica.								
Spikenard, the pound	0 0 1 4 16 4/5		0 0 1 5 17 21/3		K	0 1 2 16 4/3	0 1 0 16 7/5	0 6 8
Spiritus cornu cervi, the pound	0 0 0 7 6 27/32		0 0 0 7 12 21/20		L	0 0 6 14 7/8	0 0 6 2 2/5	0 2 0
vitrioli, the pound	0 0 0 16 8 21/3		0 0 0 1 18		L	0 0 1 13 27/3	0 0 1 10 27/3	0 0 6
Spodium, the pound	0 0 0 3 15		0 0 0 4		K	0 0 3 6	0 0 2 17 2/5	0 1 6
Spunges, the pound	0 0 5 3 8		0 0 4 8 8		K	0 0 4 7 10	0 0 4 6 8	1 5 0
Squilla, the Cwt.	0 0 8 8		0 0 5 6 18		K	0 0 4 7 8	0 0 4 6 8	0 3 6
Squinanthum, the pound	0 0 8 8		0 0 8 18		K	0 0 7 8	0 0 6 8	0 4 0
Staphisager, the Cwt.	0 0 4 16		0 0 8 11 2		K	0 0 7 4 16	0 0 4 16	2 0 0
Stechados, the pound	0 0 2 2		0 0 2 4		K	0 1 17	0 0 1 12	0 0 10
Stibium. *Vide* Antimonium præparat.								
Stick-lack. *Vide* Gum-lack.								

† If otherwise imported. * If imported by Aliens. See the Notes preceding Drugs.

[100]

INWARDS.

	DUTIES to be paid on IMPORTATION.		DRAWBACKS to be repaid on EXPORTATION.*		RATES, or supposed value, by 12 Car. II. cap. 4. 11 Geo. I. cap. 7. from whence the foregoing Duties are computed.
	By BRITISH. From the place of their growth, and in British-built ships.†	By ALIENS.	Reference to the several Branches, see Page vi.	If exported to any legal place, except as mentioned in the following column.	If the produce of Europe or the East Indies, and exported to the British Colonies in America.
	L. s. d. 20ths	*L. s. d.* 20ths		*L. s. d.* 20ths	*L. s. d.* 20ths	*L. s. d.*
DRUGS, vizt.						
Stock. *Vide* Saunders red.						
Storax calamita, the pound	0 1 0 12	0 1 7 3/4+1/20	K	0 0 11 2 2/5	0 0 9 12	0 5 0
—— liquida, the pound	0 2 2 10 1/5	0 0 2 13	K	0 0 2 4	0 0 1 18 2/5	0 1 0
Succinum. *Vide* Carrabe.						
Succus liquoritiæ, the pound But 17, 7 Geo. III. cap. 47. §. 3, 4, and 5, the duties arising upon this rate are repealed, from and after July 20, 1767; and in lieu thereof, a duty is laid upon every Cwt. averdupois of— }	1 11 6	1 11 6				
Sulphur vivum, the pound —— the Cwt.	0 0 1 13 1/5	0 1 15 7/10	K	0 2 1 9 3/5	0 0 1 5 2/5	0 0 10
Talke green, the pound	0 3 0 10 1/5	0 3 5 2 7/10	L	0 2 9 10 4/5	0 0 6 10 4/5	0 10 0
—— white, the pound	0 0 0 5 1/5	0 0 5 6 4/10	K	0 0 4 8 2/5	0 0 3 16 3/5	0 2 6
Tamarinds, the pound	0 0 1 2 2/5	0 0 1 4 3/10 + 5/100	K	0 0 1 1	0 0 0 19 1/5	0 1 0
Tartarum vitriolatum, the pound	0 0 3 13 3/5	0 0 3 16 3/5 + 2/10	K	0 0 11 7 2	0 0 1 12	0 0 10
Terra lemnia, the pound	0 0 1 0 12 1/5	0 0 1 7 3/10	L	0 0 0 11 2 2/25	0 0 9 12	0 1 0
—— figillata, the pound	0 0 7 11 1/5	0 0 8 0	K	0 0 6 13 1/5	0 0 5 15 2/5	0 5 3

† If otherwise imported.   * If imported by Aliens.   See the Notes preceding Drugs.

INWARDS.

	DUTIES to be paid on IMPORTATION. From the place of their growth, and in British-built ships.†				Reference to the several Branches, see Page vi.	DRAWBACKS to be repaid on EXPORTATION.*				RATES, or supposed value, by 12 Car. II. cap. 4. 11: Geo. I. cap. 7. from whence the foregoing Duties are computed.
	By BRITISH.		By ALIENS.			If exported to any legal place, except is mentioned in the following column.		If the produce of Europe or the East Indies, and exported to the British Colonies in America.		
	£. s. d. 20ths		£. s. d. 20ths			£. s. d. 20ths		£. s. d. 20ths		£. s. d.
DRUGS, *vocat.* ――― dulcis, for Dyers use, *as by 3 and 4 Ann. cap. 4. deemed unrated*; therefore for every 20s. value upon oath ―――	0 6 1 1		0 0 6 4 4 $\frac{4}{5}$		L	0 0 5 7 1 $\frac{1}{3}$		0 0 5 1 1 $\frac{1}{3}$		0 1 0
Thiaspii semen, the pound ――― Tincal. *Vide* Borax.	0 0 2 10 $\frac{2}{3}$		0 0 0 2 13 $\frac{1}{10}$		K	0 0 0 2 4 $\frac{2}{3}$		0 0 0 1 8 $\frac{8}{15}$		0 0 8
Tornsal, for Dyers use, *as by 3 and 4 Ann. cat. 4.* the pound ――― But by 8 Geo. I. cap. 15. § 10. *if regularly imported, entered, and landed, duty free.*										
But on failure thereof, then to pay ――― Treacle commor, the pound ――― of Venice, the pound ――― *Vide in* T.	0 0 0 11 0 $\frac{-1}{3}$		0 1 1 0 11 $\frac{9}{10}$		Ad	0 0 0 9 $\frac{1\frac{1}{3}}{3}$		0 0 9 12 $\frac{3}{4}$		0 5 0
Trocisci de vipera, the ounce troy ―――	0 0 1 0 12		0 0 1 1 7 $\frac{3}{4}$		K	0 0 0 4 8		0 0 9 12 $\frac{4}{5}$		0 5 0
Turbith, the pound ―――	0 0 1 0 12		0 0 1 1 7 $\frac{3}{4}$		K	0 0 0 4 8		0 0 3 16		0 2 0
――― thapsia, the pound ―――	0 0 0 5 0		0 0 0 5 7 $\frac{1}{10}$		K	0 0 0 2 4 $\frac{4}{5}$		0 0 1 18 $\frac{2}{3}$		0 1 0
Turmerick, the pound ―――	0 0 2 10 $\frac{2}{3}$		0 0 2 13 $\frac{1}{10}$		K	0 0 1 10		0 0 1 7 4		0 10 0
Turpentine common, the Cwt. ―――	0 2 1 4		0 2 2 15		K	0 0 1 10		0 0 1 7 4		0 10 0

† *If otherwise imported.* * *If imported by Aliens.* See the Notes preceding Drugs.

INWARDS.

	DUTIES to be paid on IMPORTATION.		Reference to the several Branches, see Page 91.	DRAWBACKS to be repaid on EXPORTATION.*		RATES, or supposed value, by 12 Car. II. cap. 4. 11 Geo. I. c. 17. from whence the foregoing Duties are computed.
	From the place of their growth, and in British-built ships. †			If exported to any legal place, except as mentioned in the following column.	If the produce of Europe or the East Indies, and exported to the British Colonies in America.	
	By BRITISH.	By ALIENS.				
	£. s. d. 20ths	£. s. d. 20ths		£. s. d. 20ths	£. s. d. 20ths	£. s. d.
DRUGS, vizt. Turpentine of Venice, Scio, or Cyprus, the pound	0 0 4 4	0 0 4 9 ¼	K	0 3 14	0 0 3 4	0 1 8
of Germany, or from any other place, not otherwise rated, the Cwt.	0 12 2 3	0 12 8 9 ⅓	L	0 11 2 3 ⅓	0 10 2 3 ⅓	2 0 0
Verdigrease, for Dyers use, as by 3 and 4 Ann. cap. 4. the pound						0 4 0
But by 8 Geo. I. cap. 15. § 10. if regularly imported, entered, and landed, duty free.						1 1 0
But on failure thereof, then to pay	0 0 1 8	0 0 1 9	Ad	0 1 4	0 0 1 1	0 1 8
But by 21 Geo. III. cap. 32. the following duties are imposed:						
if common, the pound	0 0 3 3	0 0 3 3 ¾	E c			
if chrystalised, the pound	0 1 0 12	0 1 0 12	E c			
Vermilion. Vide Cinabrium.						
Venish, the Cwt.	8 4 16 1⅓	8 11 2 1⅓	K	7 4 16 1⅓	6 4 16 1⅓	0 0 0
Viscus quercinus, the pound	0 0 1	0 0 14 ⅔	K	0 8 17 ⅔	0 7 13 ⅔	0 4 0
Vitriolum Romanum, the pound	0 0 2 10	0 0 2 13	K	0 0 2 8 ¼	0 0 1 18 ¼	1 1 0
Umber, the Cwt.	0 4 2 8 ⅓	0 4 5 11	K	0 3 2 8	0 0 3 2	1 0 0

† If otherwise imported.   * If imported by Aliens.   See the Notes preceding Drugs.

D   [103]   D

INWARDS.	DUTIES to be paid on IMPORTATION. From the place of their growth, and in British-built ships. †				Reference to the several Branches, fee Page vi.	DRAWBACKS to be repaid on EXPORTATION. *		RATES, or supposed value by 12 Car.II. cap.4. 11 Geo.I. cap.7. from whence the foregoing Duties are computed.
	By BRITISH.		By ALIENS.			If exported to any legal place, except as mentioned in the following column.	If the produce of Europe or the East Indies, and exported to the British Colonies in America.	
	£. s. d. 20ths		£. s. d. 20ths			£. s. d. 20ths	£. s. d. 20ths	£. s. d.
DRUGS, *vocat.*								
Ungulæ alcis, the hundred hoofs	0 3 0 10 4/5		0 3 2 2 7/10		L	0 2 9 10 4/5	0 2 6 10 4/5	0 10 0
White lead, the Cwt.	0 0 4 2 8		0 0 4 5 11		K	0 0 3 0 8	0 0 3 2 8	0 1 0 0
Worm feeds, the pound	0 0 0 8 8		0 0 0 8 18 1/2		K	0 0 0 7 8	0 0 0 6 8	0 0 3 4
Xylobalfamum. *Vide* Lyntifcus.								
Zedoariæ, the pound	0 0 0 8 8		0 0 0 8 18 1/2		K	0 0 0 7 8	0 0 0 6 8	0 0 3 4
All Chymical Salts, Chymical Preparations, Phyfical Oils, and Medicinal Drugs, determined by 3 *and* 4 *Ann. cap.* 4. to be unrated drugs, *and which are not afterwards rated by* 11 *Geo. I. cap.* 7. therefore to pay for every 20 s. of their value upon oath	0 0 6 1 1		0 0 6 4 4 3/5		L	0 0 5 7 1 3/5	0 0 5 1 1 3/5	

† If otherwise imported.   * If imported by Aliens.   See the Notes preceding Drugs.

A TABLE SHEWING THE DUTIES and DRAWBACKS on DRUGS.

By Drugs are meant such goods as are rated under that title in the rates preceding, or any others unrated that are imported for physical use.

DRUGS. Rated by 12 Car. II. cap. 4. for every 20s. of their value.		DUTIES to be paid on IMPORTATION. From the place of their growth, and in British-built ships. †		Reference to the several Branches, See Page vi.	DRAWBACKS to be repaid on EXPORTATION. *	
		By BRITISH. *L. s. d.*/20ths	By ALIENS. *L. s. d.*/20ths		If exported to any legal place, except as mentioned in the following column. *L. s. d.*/20ths	If the produce of Europe or the East Indies, and exported to the British Colonies in America. *L. s. d.*/20ths
of France,	{ declared, by 3 and 4 Ann. cap. 4. to be for Dyers use, and not free, by 8 Geo. I. cap. 15.	0 4 2 8	0 4 3 9	F a	0 2 4 8	0 2 2 8
	not so declared	0 7 0	0 7 3 3	F g	0 4 10	0 4 4 8
of any French plantation,	{ declared, by 3 and 4 Ann. cap. 4. to be for Dyers use, and not free, by 8 Geo. I. cap. 15.	0 2 5 8	0 2 6 9	B d	0 2 3 8	0 2 1 8
	not so declared	0 5 3	0 5 6 3	L	0 4 9	0 4 3
manufactured, and of India or China,	{ declared, by 3 and 4 Ann. cap. 4. to be for Dyers use, and not free, by 8 Geo. I. cap. 15.	0 2 5 8	0 2 6 9	A f	0 2 3 8	0 2 1 8
	not so declared	0 5 11 8	0 6 2 11	K d	0 5 5 8	0 4 11 5
unmanufactured, and of India or China,	{ declared, by 3 and 4 Ann. cap. 4. to be for Dyers use, and not free, by 8 Geo. I. cap. 15.	0 1 0	0 1 10 1	A f	0 1 7	0 1 5
	not so declared	0 5 3 0	0 5 6 3	K d	0 4 9 8	0 4 3 8

† If otherwise imported.   * If imported by Aliens.   See the Notes preceding Drugs.

TABLE of DRUGS continued.

		DUTIES to be paid on IMPORTATION.			DRAWBACKS to be repaid on EXPORTATION.*	
		From the place of their growth, and in British-built ships.†		Reference to the several Branches, see Page vi.	If exported to any legal place, except as mentioned in the following column.	If the produce of Europe or the East Indies, and exported to the British Colonies in America.
		By BRITISH.	By ALIENS.			
		L. s. d./20ths	*L. s. d.*/20ths		*L. s. d.*/20ths	*L. s. d.*/20ths
of all other places,	{ declared, by 3 and 4 Ann. cap. 4. to be for Dyers use, and not free, by 8 Geo. I. cap. 15. }	0 1 4 16	0 1 5 17	Ad	0 1 2 16	0 1 0 16
	not so declared	0 4 2 8	0 4 5 11	K	0 3 8 8	0 3 2 8

Pearl Barley, Succus Liquoritiæ, Gum Senega, Gum Arabick, Oil of Amber, and Verdigrease excepted.

† If otherwise imported.   * If imported by Aliens. See the Notes preceding Drugs.

TABLE of DRUGS continued.

DRUGS.		Reference to the several Branches, see Page vi.	DUTIES to be paid on IMPORTATION.		DRAWBACKS to be repaid on EXPORTATION.[*]	
			By BRITISH. £. s. d. 20ths	By ALIENS. £. s. d. 20ths	If exported to any legal place, except as mentioned in the following column. £. s. d. 20ths	If the produce of Europe or the East Indies, and exported to the British Colonies in America. £. s. d. 20ths
Rated by 11 Geo. I. cap. 7. or unrated, paying duty ad valorem, for every 20s. of their rate or value upon oath.						
of France,	{ declared, by 3 and 4 Ann. cap. 4. to be for Dyers use, and not free, by 8 Geo. I. cap. 15. not so declared	F a	0 12 7 4	0 12 10 7	0 7 1 4	0 6 7 4
			0 15 6 9 ⅓	0 15 9 12 ⅓	0 10 0 9 ⅓	0 9 6 9 ⅓
of any French plantation,	{ declared, by 3 and 4 Ann. cap. 4. to be for Dyers use, and not free, by 8 Geo. I. cap. 15. not so declared	F g	0 7 4 4	0 7 7 7	0 6 10 4	0 6 4 4
of all other places,	{ declared, by 3 and 4 Ann. cap. 4. to be for Dyers use, and not free, by 8 Geo. I. cap. 15. not so declared	B d	0 10 3 9 ⅓	0 10 6 12 ⅓	0 9 9 9 ⅓	0 9 3 9 ⅓
		L	0 3 1 16	0 3 4 19	0 2 7 16	0 2 1 16
Not rated by 12 Car. II. cap. 4.						
manufactured, and of India or China,	{ See the Table of unrated East India goods at the end of the rates inwards.	B d				
unmanufactured, and of India or China,	{ See the Table of unrated East India goods at the end of the rates inwards.	L	0 6 1 1 ⅓	0 6 4 4	0 5 7 1	0 5 1 1 ⅓

[*] If imported by Aliens. See the Notes preceding Drugs.

INWARDS.

E.

Inwards	Duties to be paid on Importation		Reference to the several Branches, see Page vi.	Drawbacks to be repaid on Exportation.*	
	By British *L. s. d. 20ths*	By Aliens *L. s. d. 20ths*		If exported to any legal place, except as mentioned in the following column. *L. s. d. 20ths*	If the produce of Europe or the East Indies, and exported to the British Colonies in America. *L. s. d. 20ths*
EARLINGS, the groce, containing 12 dozen	0 4 2 8	0 4 5 11	A	0 3 8 8	0 3 2 8
Earthen ware, *vocat.* Brick stones, the thousand	0 4 2 8	0 4 5 11	A	0 3 8 8	0 3 2 8
Flanders tiles to scour with, the thousand	0 8 4 16	0 8 11 2	A	0 7 4 16	0 6 4 16
Gally tiles, the foot	0 0 2 10	0 0 2 13 12/20	A	0 0 2 4	0 0 1 18
Paving tiles, the thousand	0 12 7 4	0 13 4 13 3/5	A	0 11 1 4	0 9 7 4
Tiles, called Pantiles, the thousand	2 2 0	2 4 1 4	C	1 18 0	1 14 0
All other sorts of Earthen ware (except India or China) for every 20 s. of the real value upon oath:					
— if French	0 15 10 5	0 16 1 8 1/5	F	0 9 13 3	0 8 9 1 1/5
— if not French	0 7 11 15 1/5	0 8 2 18 3/5	B	0 6 11 3	0 5 10 11 3/5
— if of India or China. See the Table of rated East India goods, at the end of the rates inwards.					
Ebony wood, the Cwt.					

* But if imported by Aliens Drawback more, 1 s. 3 d. for every 100 l. of the Rate or Value.

[108]

INWARDS.	DUTIES to be paid on IMPORTATION.		Reference to the several Branches, see Page vi.	DRAWBACKS to be repaid on EXPORTATION.*		RATES, or supposed value, by 12 Car. II. cap. 4. ‡ 11 Geo. I. cap. 7. from whence the foregoing Duties are computed.
	By BRITISH.	By ALIENS.		If exported to any legal place, except as mentioned in the following column.	If the produce of Europe or the East Indies, and exported to the British Colonies in America.	
	£. s. d. 20ths	£. s. d. 20ths		£. s. d. 20ths	£. s. d. 20ths	£. s. d.
Ebony wood, of, and directly from, any part of America, if regularly entered and landed, free.						
On failure thereof. See in Wood.	0 6 3 12	0 6 6 15	B	0 5 9 12	0 5 3 12	‡ 0 5 6
—— of or from any part of Europe, except Ireland and France	0 4 2 8	0 4 5 11	A	0 3 8 8	0 3 2 8	‡ 0 1 8
—— of Ireland, Africa, or Asia See in Wood.						
—— of France. See in Wood.						
If imported in foreign ships, to pay duty as Aliens.						
Edging for hats of caddas, the dozen	0 1 5 6	0 1 6 3 3/10	C	0 1 3 13 1/2	0 1 2 0 1/2	0 0 0
Eggs, the hundred, containing six score	0 0 4 4	0 0 4 9	A	0 0 3 14	0 0 3 4	0 0 0
Elephants teeth, the Cwt.	1 5 2 8	1 0 6 3 1/4	C	1 3 2 8	1 2 2 8	0 4 0
Emeralds. See Diamonds.						
Emery stones, the Cwt.	0 1 8 3	0 1 9 8 4/5	A	0 1 5 15	0 1 3 7 1/2	‡ 0 8 0
Enamel, the pound French	0 0 3 1 1/2	0 0 3 13 4/5	F	0 0 2 1 4/5	0 0 1 11 4/5	0 0 0
—— not French	0 0 1 9 8	0 0 1 10 1	B	0 0 1 7 12	0 0 1 5 16	‡ 0 4 0
And besides, for every pound weight of Glass	0 0 1 4 16	0 0 1 4 16	Ze	0 0 0 16	0 0 0 16	0 0 0

* But if imported by Aliens Drawback more, 1s. 3d. for every 100l. of the Rate or Value.

[109]

INWARDS.	DUTIES to be paid on IMPORTATION.		Reference to the several Branches, see page vi.	DRAWBACKS to be repaid on EXPORTATION.*		RATES, or supposed value, by 12 Car. II. cap. 4. † 11 Geo. I. cap. 7. from whence the foregoing Duties are computed.
	By BRITISH.	By ALIENS.		If exported to any legal place, except as mentioned in the following column.	If the produce of Europe or the East Indies, and exported to the British Colonies in America.	
	£. s. d. 20ths	£. s. d. 20ths		£. s. d. 20ths	£. s. d. 20ths	£. s. d.
East India goods, rated by 12 Car. II. cap. 4. See them as they severally occur in the course of the rates, except Drugs, for which see the Table at the end of Drugs.						
——— unrated. See the Table of unrated East India goods at the end of the rates inwards.						
F.						
FANS for corn, the piece	0 1 4 16	0 1 5 17	A	0 1 2 16	0 1 0 16	0 6 8
——— of paper, the dozen	0 1 4 16	0 1 5 17	A	0 1 2 16	0 1 0 16	0 6 8
——— for women and children, French } making, the dozen	1 9 4 16	1 9 11 2	F	0 18 4 16	0 17 4 16	2 0 0
Calpins for Fans. *Vide in* C.						
Feather beds, rated by 12 Car. II. cap. 4. rated at 2 l. 13 s. 4 d. the piece, but the rates, and the duties arising therefrom, are, by 16 Geo. III. cap. 4. repealed, and the						

* But if imported by Aliens Drawback more, 1 s. 3 d. for every 100 l. of the Rate or Value.

INWARDS.

	Duties to be paid on Importation. By British. £.	s.	d.	20ths	By Aliens. £.	s.	d.	20ths	Reference to the several Branches, see Page vi.	Drawbacks to be repaid on Exportation.* If exported to any legal place, except as mentioned in the following column. £.	s.	d.	20ths	If the produce of Europe or the East Indies, and exported to the British Colonies in America. £.	s.	d.	20ths	Rates, or supposed value, by 12 Car. II. cap. 4. & 11 Geo. I cap. 7. from whence the foregoing Duties are computed. £.	s.	d.
Feathers *subject to duty as* Feathers for beds.																				
Feathers for beds, the Cwt.	1	5	2	8	1	6	9	6	A	1	2	2	8	0	19	2	8	6	0	0
—— *vocat.* estridge, or ostridge feathers:																				
—— dressed, the pound	0	8	4	16	0	8	11	2	A	0	7	4	16	0	6	4	16	2	0	0
—— undressed, the pound	0	4	2	8	0	4	5	11	A	0	3	8	8	0	3	2	8	1	0	0
Felts for cloaks, French making, 3 ½ yards long, 1 ½ broad, the felt	2	18	9	12	2	19	[illegible]	4	F	1	16	9	12	1	14	9	12	4	0	0
Fiddles for children, the dozen	0	0	10	1 ⅗	0	0	10	14 ⅕	A	0	0	8	17 ⅕	0	0	7	13 ⅗	0	4	0
Figs. *Vide in* Grocery.																				
Figuretto, the yard	0	1	9		0	1	10	6 ¼	A	0	1	6	10	0	1	4		0	8	4
Files, the groce, containing 12 dozen	0	8	4	16	0	8	11	2	A	0	7	4	16	—	—	—	—	2	0	0
And besides for every Cwt. of Iron	0	5	3		0	5	3		D	0	5	3		—	—	—	—			
Fire irons. *Vide in* Iron.																				
Fire shovels, the dozen	0	2	9	12	0	2	11	14	A	0	2	5	12	—	—	—	—	0	13	4
And besides, for every Cwt.	0	5	3		0	5	3		D	0	5	3		—	—	—	—			
Fire shovel plates, the Cwt.	0	8	0	12	0	8	2	14	B	0	7	8	12	—	—	—	—	0	13	4
Fire wood. *See* Wood.																				

* But if imported by Aliens Drawback more, 1s. 3d. for every 100l. of the Rate or Value.

[111]

INWARDS.		DUTIES to be paid on IMPORTATION.		DRAWBACKS to be repaid on EXPORTATION.		RATES, or supposed value, by 12 Car. II. cap. 4. 11 Geo. I. cap. 7. from whence the foregoing Duties are computed.
	Reference to the several Branches, see Page vi.	By BRITISH.	By ALIENS.	If exported to any legal place, except as mentioned in the following column.	If the produce of Europe or the East Indies, and exported to the British Colonies in America.	
		£. s. d. 20ths	£. s. d. 20ths	£. s. d. 20ths	£. s. d. 20ths	£. s. d.
Cod-fish, the barrel						0 13 4
— the last, containing 12 barrels						8 0 0
— the hundred, containing 6 score						2 6 8
— heads, the barrel						0 3 4
Herrings, white, full, or shotten, the barrel						0 8 0
— the last, containing 12 barrels						5 0 0
— red, the cade, containing 500						0 8 0
— the last, containing 20 cades						8 6 8
Lings of all sorts, the hundred, containing 120						3 6 8
Salmon, the barrel						2 0 0
— girls, the barrel						0 15 0
Cole-fish, the hundred, containing 120						1 0 8
Gull-fish, the barrel						0 6 8
Haddocks, the barrel						0 6 8
Lamperns, the piece						0 0 4
Whitings, the barrel						0 3 4

Fish, cont.

INWARDS.

Fish, vocat.

	Reference to the several Branches, see Page vi.	DUTIES to be paid on IMPORTATION.		DRAWBACKS to be repaid on EXPORTATION.		RATES, or supposed value, by 12 Car. II. cap.4. § 11 Geo. I. cap.7. from whence the foregoing Duties are computed.
		By BRITISH.	By ALIENS.	If exported to any legal place, except as mentioned in the following column.	If the produce of Europe or the East Indies, and exported to the British Colonies in America.	
		£. s. d. 20ths	£. s. d. 20ths	£. s. d. 20ths	£. s. d. 20ths	£. s. d.
Seal-fish, the fifth						0 13 4
Newland fish, small, the hundred, containing 120						0 10 0
── middle sort, the like hundred						1 0 0
── great, the like hundred						1 10 0
Eels: Pimper eels, the barrel	La	0 5 9 6	0 5 9 6	0 3 9 6	0 3 3 6	1 0 0
── Shaft, Kine, or Dole eels, the barrel	La	0 8 7 19	0 8 7 19	0 5 7 19	0 4 10 19	1 10 0
── Spruce eels, the barrel	La	0 11 6 12	0 11 6 12	0 7 6 12	0 6 6 12	2 0 8
── Stub eels, the barrel	La	0 13 5 14	0 13 5 14	0 8 9 14	0 7 7 14	2 6 8
── Quick eels, the ship's lading	La	4 9 3	4 9 3	3 14 3	3 4 3	20 0 0
Stock-fish: the hundred, containing 120	La	0 3 10 4	0 3 10 4	0 2 6 4	0 2 2 4	0 13 4
── Croplin the last, containing 10 hundred	La	1 18 6	1 18 6	1 5 2	1 1 10	6 13 4

[113]

INWARDS	DUTIES to be paid on IMPORTATION. By BRITISH	By ALIENS	Reference to the several Branches, see Page vi.	DRAWBACKS to be repaid on EXPORTATION.* If exported to any legal place, except as mentioned in the following column.	If the produce of Europe or the East Indies, and exported to the British Colonies in America.	RATES, or supposed value, by 12 Car. II. cap. 4. † 11 Geo. I. cap. 7. from whence the foregoing Duties are computed.
	£. s. d./20ths	£. s. d./20ths		£. s. d./20ths	£. s. d./20ths	£. s. d.
Fish, vocat. — Lub-fish { the hundred, containing 120	0 7 8	0 7 8	La	0 5 8	0 4 8	1 6 8
the last, containing 10 hundred	3 17 0	3 17 0	La	2 10 4	2 3 8	13 6 8
— Titling, { the hundred, containing 120	0 1 11 2	0 1 11 2	La	0 1 3 2	0 1 1 2	0 6 8
the last, containing 10 hundred	0 19 3	0 19 3	La	0 12 7	0 10 11 16/20	3 6 8
But Note, that Lobsters and Turbets may be imported by any person in any ship, Duty free.						
And also, that all sorts of Fish, British taking, and brought in British ships, ought not to pay any Custom.						
Flannel, the yard	0 0 6 6	0 0 6 11 3/4	C	0 0 15 8 16/20	0 0 5 6	0 8 0
Fustics covered with leather, the dozen	0 1 10 1	0 1 10 16 1/4	B	0 1 8 11	0 1 7 1	0 5 0
And tiffeties, if the leather be the most valuable part, for every 20 s. of the real value thereof upon oath	0 6 3 12	0 6 3 12	Dc	0 0 3 12	0 0 3 12	

* But if imported by Aliens Drawback more, 1 s. 3 d. for every 100 l. of the Rate or Value, except Fish.

F [114] F

INWARDS.	DUTIES to be paid on IMPORTATION.		Reference to the several Branches, see Page vi.	DRAWBACKS to be repaid on EXPORTATION.*		RATES, or supposed value, by 12 Car. II. cap. 4. ‡11Geo.I.cap.7. from whence the foregoing Duties are computed.
	By BRITISH.	By ALIENS.		If exported to any legal place, except as mentioned in the following column.	If the produce of Europe or the East Indies, and exported to the British Colonies in America.	
	£. s. d. 20ths	£. s. d. 20ths		£. s. d. 20ths	£. s. d. 20ths	£. s. d.
Flasks, covered with velvet, the dozen	0 14 8 8	0 15 2 14	B	0 13 8 8	0 12 8 8	2 0 0
And besides, if Glass, for every dozen quarts they contain:						
of horn, the dozen	0 4 2 8	0 4 2 8	Ze	0 0 2 8	0 0 2 8	0 6 0
Flax, dressed or wrought, the Cwt.	0 1 4 16	0 1 5 17	A	0 1 2 16	0 1 0 16	15 0 0
And besides, if not European — Spruce, Muscovy, and all Flax un-dressed or rough, the Cwt.	4 19 9	5 3 8 5	Ac	4 12 3	4 4 9	1 0 0
But if regularly imported, entered, and landed, free.	0 10 6	0 10 6	Mc	0 10 6	0 10 6	
On failure thereof, then to pay						
And besides, if not European	4 0 0	4 0 0	Ac	0 4 0	0 3 6 12	
Note, Flax imported in foreign ships pay duty as Aliens.	0 8 8	0 8 8	Mc	0 3 8	0 8 8	
Flax of the produce of Ireland (or any manufacture made thereof in Ireland) may be imported directly from thence by British or Irish, upon Certificate and Oath, Duty free.						
Fleams to let blood, the piece	0 0 8 8/3	0 0 8 17/40	A	0 0 7 6		0 0 2
And besides, for every Cwt. of Steel	0 5 9 6	0 5 9 6	D	0 5 9 6		

* But if imported by Aliens Drawback more, 1s. 3d. for every 100 l. of the Rate or Value.

[115]

INWARDS.	DUTIES to be paid on IMPORTATION.		Reference to the several Branches, see Page vi.	DRAWBACKS to be repaid on EXPORTATION.*		RATES, or supposed value, by 12 Car. II. cap. 4. [11 Geo. I. cap. 7. from whence the foregoing Duties are computed.
	By BRITISH.	By ALIENS.		If exported to any legal place, except as mentioned in the following column.	If the produce of Europe, or the East Indies, and exported to the British Colonies in America.	
	£. s. d. 20ths	£. s. d. 20ths		£. s. d. 20ths	£. s. d. 20ths	£. s. d.
Flocks, the Cwt.	0 8 4 16	0 8 11 2	A	0 7 4 16	0 6 4 16	2 0 0
Flutes coarse, the grocc containing 12 dozen	0 4 2 8	0 4 5 11	A	0 3 3 8	0 3 2 8	1 0 0
Foils for fencers, the dozen	0 3 1 16	0 3 4 3	A	0 2 2 6		
And besides, for every Cwt.						† 0 15 0
Forceps. Vide Sheers.						
Flowers artificial, for every 20 s. of their true and real value upon oath:	0 5 3	0 5 3 ¼	D	0 5 3		
—— if of silk, and of France	0 15 2 14	0 15 5 17	F h	0 9 8 14	0 9 2 14	
—— and not of France	0 6 9 18	0 7 1 1	C d	0 6 3 18	0 5 9 18	
—— if not of silk, and of France	0 14 8 8	0 14 11 11	F	0 9 2 8	0 8 8 8	
—— and not of France	0 5 3	0 5 6 3	C	0 4 9	0 4 3	
the East Indies						
—— nor the East Indies						
French Goods, viz. rated. See them as they severally occur in the course of the Rates.						
—— Drugs. See the Table at the end of Drugs.						

* But if imported by Aliens Drawback more, 1 s. 3 d. for every 100 l. of the Rate or Value.

[116]

INWARDS.

	DUTIES to be paid on IMPORTATION.		Reference to the several Branches, see Page vi.	DRAWBACKS to be repaid on EXPORTATION.*		RATES, or suppose, value, by 12 Car. II. cap. 4. 11 Geo. I. cap. 7. from whence the foregoing Duties are computed.
	By BRITISH.	By ALIENS.		If exported to any legal place, except as mentioned in the following column.	If the produce of Europe or the East Indies, and exported to the British Colonies in America.	
	£ s. d. 20ths	£ s. d. 20ths		£ s. d. 20ths	£ s. d. 20ths	£ s. d.
All other goods, for every 20s. of their rates or values upon oath:	0 12 7 4	0 12 10 7	F a	0 7 1 4	0 6 7 4	8 0 0 9
If of the product of France, for Dyers use, as by 3 and 4 Ann. cap. 4. and not exempted from duty by 8 Geo. I. cap. 15.	0 14 8 8	0 14 11 11	F	0 9 2 8	0 8 8 8	0 0 0
—— not for Dyers use	0 7 4 4	0 7 7 7		0 6 10 4	0 6 4 4	2 0 0 7
If of the product of any other French dominions, for Dyers use, as by 3 and 4 Ann. cap. 4. and not exempted from duty by 8 Geo. I. cap. 15.	0 9 5 8	0 9 8 11	B d	0 8 11 8	0 8 5 8	0 0 0
—— not for Dyers use	1 13 7 4	1 15 8 8	C	1 9 7 4	1 5 7 4	0 0 0
Frizzado, the piece, containing 24 yards	0 0 5 11 7/10	0 0 5 13 5 7/10	A	0 0 9 6	0 0 8 6	2 0 0 7
Frize, of Ireland, the yard	0 10 6 6	0 11 6 12 1 7/10	C	0 0 9 6	0 0 5 6	1 0 0
Arnins, the timber, containing 40 skins	0 0 6 6	0 0 6 3	C	0 0 4 9	0 0 4 3	2 0 0 6
Fulgers skins, the piece	0 5 3	0 5 11	C	0 4 9	0 4 3	
Bears skins, black or red, the piece	0 10 6	0 11 0	C	0 9 6	0 8 6	
—— white, the piece			C			
Beaver skins; the whole piece But by 8 Geo. I. cap. 15. § 13, the rate was altered, for each skin, to — } £. 0 2 6						

* But if imported by Aliens Drawback more, 1s. 3d. for every 100l. of the Rate or Value.

Furs, vacat.

[117]

INWARDS.

Furs, vocat.

The duties payable whereon will be. But by 4 Geo. III. cap. 9. these duties are repealed from and after April 7. 1764, upon all Beaver skins imported from any of His Majesty's dominions in America, and in lieu thereof, the following duty was imposed:

For every Beaver skin imported from any of His Majesty's dominions in America —

	DUTIES to be paid on IMPORTATION.		Reference to the several Branches, see Page vi.	DRAWBACKS to be repaid on EXPORTATION.*		RATES, or supposed value, by 12 Car. II. cap. 4. 11 Geo. I. cap. 7. from whence the foregoing Duties are computed.
	By BRITISH.	By ALIENS.		If exported to any legal place, except as mentioned in the following column.	If the produce of Europe or the East Indies, and exported to the British Colonies in America.	
	£. s. d./20ths	£. s. d./20ths		£. s. d./20ths	£. s. d./20ths	£. s. d.
	0 7 17 ½	0 0 8 5 3/8	C			0 1 8
						1 6 8
Beaver wombs, the piece	0 0 1 1	0 0 1 1	C	0 0 4 15	0 0 4 5	3 10 0
Budge black {tawed, the dozen skins untawed, the hundred, containing five score skins	0 0 5 5	0 0 5 10 ¼	C	0 0 6 4	0 0 5 8 10	
	0 0 7 0	0 0 7 4	C			
——— white, tawed the hundred, containing 5 score skins	0 18 4 10	0 19 3 10 ½	C	0 16 7 10	0 14 10 10	2 2 0
	0 10 6	0 11 0 6	C	0 9 6	0 8 6	
——— nevern, the hundred less, containing 5 score	0 2 2 5	0 2 3 11 ¼	C	0 1 11 15	0 1 9 5	0 8 4

* But if imported by Aliens, Drawback more, 1s. 5d. for every 20l. of the Rate or Value.

INWARDS.

	DUTIES to be paid on IMPORTATION.		Reference to the several Branches, see Page vi.	DRAWBACKS to be repaid on EXPORTATION.*		RATES or supposed value, by 12 Car. II. cap. 4. & 11 Geo. I. cap. 7. from whence the foregoing Duties are computed.
	By BRITISH.	By ALIENS.		If exported to any legal place, except as mentioned in the following column.	If the produce of Europe or the East Indies, and exported to the British Colonies in America.	
Furs, vocal.	L. s. d./20ths	L. s. d./20ths		L. s. d./20ths	L. s. d./20ths	L. s. d.
Budge poults, the fur, containing 4 pains	0 5 3	0 5 6 3	C	0 4 9	0 4 3	1 0 0
—— rumney, the hundred legs, containing 5 score	0 1 9	0 1 10 1	C	0 1 7	0 1 5	0 0 8
Calaber seasoned, the pain	0 5 3	0 5 6 3	C	0 4 9	0 4 3	1 0 0
—— shubs. Vide in S.						
—— flag, the pain	0 3 3	0 3 5 6½	C	0 2 11 12	0 2 7 17	0 12 6
—— tawed, the timber, containing 40 skins	0 2 1	0 2 2 9	C	0 1 10 16	0 1 8 8	0 8 0
—— untawed, the timber, containing 40 skins	0 1 9	0 1 10 1	C	0 1 7	0 1 5	0 6 8
Cats skins, the hundred, containing 5 score	0 9	0 11 0 6½	C	0 9 6	0 8 6	2 0 0
—— poults { the hundred, containing 5 score / the mantle	0 5 3	0 5 6 3	C	0 4 9	0 4 3	1 0 0
—— wombs, the pain or mantle	0 1 7 13 ¾	0 1 8 13 ⅞	C	0 1 5 16 ¼	0 1 3 18 ¼	0 6 3
Dockerers, the timber, containing 40 skins	0 1 7 13 ¾	0 1 8 13 ⅞	C	0 1 5 16 ¼	0 1 3 18 ¼	0 6 3
Fitches, the timber, containing 40 skins	0 3 6	0 3 8 2	C	0 3 2	0 2 10	0 13 4
skins	0 3 6	0 3 8 2	C	0 3 2	0 2 10	0 13 4

* But if imported by Aliens Drawback more, 1s. 3d. for every 100l. of the Rate or Value.

INWARDS.

Furs, vizct.

		DUTIES to be paid on IMPORTATION.				Reference to the several Branches, see Page vi.	DRAWBACKS to be repaid on EXPORTATION.*				RATES, or supposed value, by 12 Car. II. cap. 4. ‡ 11 Geo. I. cap. 7. from whence the foregoing Duties are computed.
		By BRITISH.		By ALIENS.			If exported to any legal place, except as mentioned in the following column.		If the produce of Europe or the East Indies, and exported to the British Colonies in America.		
		£. s. d. 20ths		£. s. d. 20ths			£. s. d. 20ths		£. s. d. 20ths		£. s. d.
Foxes,	the pain or mantle	0 3 3 7		0 3 5 6	7	C	0 2 11 12		0 2 7 17		0 12 0 6
	the black Fox skin	2 12 6		2 15 1 10		C	0 2 7 6		0 2 6 3	8	10 0 0
	the ordinary skin	0 0 4 4		0 0 4 8		C	0 0 3 16		0 0 3 2	5	0 1 4
	the pain or mantle	0 3 11 5		0 4 1 12		C	0 3 6 15		0 3 2 5		0 15 0
	wombs, poults, or pieces, the pain dressed. *Vide in Skins.*	0 2 7 10		0 2 9 1		C	0 2 4 10		0 2 1 10		0 10 0
Foynes backs, the dozen												
	poults, the hundred, containing 5 score	0 3 6		0 3 8 2		C	0 3 2		0 2 10		0 13 4
	raw, the piece	0 7 0		0 7 4 4		C	0 6 4		0 5 8		1 6 8
	tails, the pain or mantle	0 0 3 3		0 0 3 6		C	0 0 2 17		0 0 2 11		0 1 0 6
	with tails, the piece	0 0 3 7		0 0 3 6		C	0 0 2 11 12		0 0 2 7 17		0 12 6
	without tails, the piece	0 0 10 10		0 0 11 1		C	0 0 9 10		0 0 8 10	4	0 3 4
	wombs seasoned, the pain or mantle	0 1 0 12		0 1 1 1		C	0 0 11 8		0 0 10 4		0 4 0
	wombs, flags, the pain or mantle	0 1 0		0 1 4 4		C	0 6 4		0 5 8		1 6 8
Grays, tawed, the timber, containing 40 skins		0 3 11 5		0 4 1 12		C	0 3 6 15		0 3 2 5		0 15 0
	untawed, the timber containing 40 skins	0 2 5		0 2 3 11		C	0 1 11 15		0 1 9 5		0 8 4

* But if imported by Aliens Drawback more, 1s. 3d. for every 100l. of the Rate or Value.

INWARDS.

Furs, vocat.

	DUTIES to be paid on IMPORTATION.		References to the several Branches, see Page vi.	DRAWBACKS to be repaid on EXPORTATION.*		RATES, or supposed value, by 12 Car. II. cap. 4. ‡ 11 Geo. I. cap. 7. from whence the foregoing Duties are computed.
	By BRITISH.	By ALIENS.		If exported to any legal place, except as mentioned in the following column.	If the produce of Europe or the East Indies, and exported to the British Colonies in America.	
	£. s. d. 20ths	£. s. d. 20ths		£. s. d. 20ths	£. s. d. 20ths	£. s. d.
Jennets black { raw, the skin	0 3 3 7	0 3 5 6 7⁄10	C	0 2 11 12 1⁄2	0 2 7 17	0 12 6
{ seasoned, the skin	0 4 4 10	0 3 7 2 8⁄10	C	0 3 11 10	0 3 6 10	0 16 8
gray { raw, the skin	0 1 0 9	0 0 9 18 10⁄10	C	0 0 8 11	0 0 7 13	0 3 0
{ seasoned, the skin	0 0 0 12	0 0 1 4	C	0 0 0 8	0 0 10 4	0 0 0
Leopards skins, the piece	0 6 6 15	0 6 10 13 3⁄10	C	0 5 11 5	0 5 3 15	1 5 0
wombs, the pain	1 6 3	1 7 6 15 4	C	1 3 9	1 1 3	5 0 0
Letwis tawed, the timber, containing 40 skins	0 2 2 5	0 2 3 11 1⁄4	C	0 1 11 15	0 1 9 5	0 8 4
untawed, the timber, containing 40 skins	0 1 6 18	0 1 7 16 9⁄10	C	0 1 5 2	0 1 3 6	0 6 0
Lewzernes skins, the piece	0 13 1 10	0 13 9 1 1⁄2	C	0 11 10 10	0 10 7 10	2 10 0
Martrons, or Martins, the timber, containing 40 skins	2 12 6	2 15 1 10	C	2 7 6	2 2 6	10 0 0
the pain or mantle	2 7 3	2 9 7 7 4⁄5	C	2 2 9	1 18 3	9 0 0
gills, the timber, containing 40 skins	0 3 1 16	0 3 3 13 1⁄2	C	0 2 10 4	0 2 6 12	0 12 0
poules, the pain or mantle	0 2 7 10	0 2 9 1	C	0 2 4 10	0 2 1 10	0 10 0
tails, the hundred, containing 5 score	0 10 0 6	0 11 0 6	C	0 0 9 6	0 8 6	2 0 0
Miniver, the mantle	0 3 6	0 3 8 2	C	0 3 2	0 2 10	0 13 4

* If imported by Aliens Drawback more, 1 s. 3 d. for every 100 l. of the Rate or Value.

[121]

INWARDS

Furs, vocal.

	DUTIES to be paid on IMPORTATION		Reference to the several Branches, see Page vi.	DRAWBACKS to be repaid on EXPORTATION.*		RATES, or supposed value, by 12 Cur.II. cap.4. 11 Geo.I. cap.7. from whence the foregoing Duties are computed.
	By BRITISH.	By ALIENS.		If exported to any legal place, except as mentioned in the following column.	If the produce of Europe or the East Indies, and exported to the British Colonies in America.	
	£. s. d. /20ths	£. s. d. /20ths		£. s. d. /20ths	£. s. d. /20ths	£. s. d.
Minks tawed, the timber, containing 40 skins	1 1 0	1 2 0 12	C	0 19 0	0 17 0	4 0 0
— untawed, the timber, containing 40 skins	0 15 9	0 16 6 9	C	0 14 3	0 12 9	3 0 0
Mole skins, the dozen	0 1 11	0 1 13 10¾	C	0 1 2 8	0 1 0 5	0 0 6
Otter skins, the piece	0 3 15	0 3 4 6	C	0 2 11 5	0 2 7 5	0 5 0
Ounce skins, the piece	0 3 7	0 3 5 10	C	0 2 11 12	0 2 7 17	0 12 6
Sables of all forts, the timber, containing 40 skins	7 17 6	8 5 4 10	C	7 2 6	6 7 6	30 0 0
— tails, or Tips of Sable. Vide in Skins.						
Weezle skins, the dozen	0 1 1	0 1 2 4	C	0 0 19	0 0 6 17	0 0 4
Wolf skins, tawed, the piece	0 10 10	0 11 8 3 1/20	C	0 7 1 10	0 6 4 10	1 10 0
— untawed, the piece	0 0 9	0 0 6 4 1/20	C	0 0 5 11	0 0 4 13	0 1 3 0
Wolverings, the piece	0 3 7	0 3 5 7½	C	0 2 11 12	0 2 7 17	0 12 6
All other Furs (except those rated amongst Skins) for every 20s. of their value upon oath	0 5 3	0 5 6 3	C	0 4 9	0 4 3	

* But if imported by Aliens Drawback more, 1s. 3d. for every 100l. of the Rate or Value.

[122]

INWARDS.

	DUTIES to be paid on IMPORTATION.		Reference to the several Branches, see Page vi.	DRAWBACKS to be repaid on EXPORTATION.*		RATES, or supposed value, by 12 Car. II. cap. 4. †11 Geo. I. cap. 7. from whence the foregoing Duties are computed.
	By BRITISH.	By ALIENS.		If exported to any legal place, except as mentioned in the following column.	If the produce of Europe or the East Indies, and exported to the British Colonies in America.	
	£. s. d. 20ths	£. s. d. 20ths		£. s. d. 20ths	£. s. d. 20ths	£. s. d.
Furs, vocal. — And if any of the aforesaid Furs, or any other Furs, are tawed or dressed, and are not before charged as such, they are to pay more, for every 20 s. of their real value upon oath	0 6 3 12	0 6 3 12	D c	0 0 3 12	0 0 3 12	0 3 6
Fusties of cloves, the pound	0 0 8 16	0 0 9 17/20	A	0 0 7 15 2/3	0 0 6 14 2/3	8 0 0
Fustians — Amsterdam, Holland, or Dutch Fustians, the piece, containing two half pieces of 15 yards to the half piece	1 13 7 4	1 15 8 8	A	1 9 7 4	1 5 7 4	8 0 0
Barmillians, the piece, containing two half pieces	1 13 7 4	1 15 8 8	A	1 9 7 4	1 5 7 4	8 0 0
Cullen Fustians, the piece, containing two half pieces	1 13 7 4	1 15 8 8	A	1 9 7 4	1 5 7 4	8 0 0
Holmes and Bevernex Fustians, the bale, containing 45 half pieces —— the piece,	16 16 0	17 17 0	A	14 16 0	12 16 0	80 0 0
—— containing two half pieces	0 15 6 9 3/5	0 16 6 2 7/10	A	0 13 8 5	0 11 10	3 14 0
Jean Fustians, the piece, containing two half pieces	0 14 0 16 4/5	0 14 11 7 17/20	A	0 12 4 14 3/5	0 12 8 12 4/5	3 7 0

* But if imported by Aliens Drawback more, 1 s. 3 d. for every 100 l. of the Rate or Value.

INWARDS.

		DUTIES to be paid on IMPORTATION.				Reference to the several Branches, see Page vi.	DRAWBACKS to be repaid on EXPORTATION.*				RATES, or supposed value, by 12 Car. II. cap. 4. ‡ 11 Geo. I. cap. 7. from whence the foregoing Duties are computed.
		By BRITISH.		By ALIENS.			If exported to any legal place, except as mentioned in the following column.		If of the produce of Europe or the East Indies, and exported to the British Colonies in America.		
		£. s. d./20ths		£. s. d./20ths			£. s. d./20ths		£. s. d./20ths		£. s. d.
Fustians	Milan Fustians, the piece, containing two half pieces	1 13 7 4		1 15 8 8		A	1 9 7 4		1 5 7 4		8 0 0
	Naples Fustians: the half piece, containing 7½ yards	0 16 9 12		0 17 10 4		A	0 14 9 12		0 12 9 12		4 0 0
	——— tripe the piece, containing 15 yards	1 13 7 4		1 15 8 8		A	1 9 7 4		1 5 7 4		8 0 0
	——— or velure plain the yard	0 2 1 4		0 2 2 15		A	0 1 10 4		0 1 7 4		0 10 0
	——— wrought, vocat, the half piece, containing 7½ yards	1 5 2 8		1 6 9 6		A	1 2 2 8		0 19 2 8		0 16 0
	Sparta velvet the yard	0 3 4 6		0 3 6 16		A	0 2 11 10 ⅕		0 2 6 14 ⅘		4 10 0
	Oshrow, or Augusta Fustians the piece, containing 2 half pieces with silk, the yard	0 18 10 16		1 0 0 19 ½		A	0 16 7 16		0 14 4 16		0 8 0
	of wcazel, the piece, containing two half pieces										8 0 0
	Fustick. *Vide in* Wood.	1 13 7 4		1 15 8 8		A	1 9 7 4		1 5 7 4		

* But if imported by Aliens Drawback more, 1s. 3d. for every 100 l. of the Rate or Value.

INWARDS.

G.

	Duties to be paid on Importation. By British. £.	s.	d.	20ths	By Aliens. £.	s.	d.	20ths	Reference to the several Branches, see Page vi.	Drawbacks to be repaid on Exportation.* If exported to any legal place, except as mentioned in the following column. £.	s.	d.	20ths	If the produce of Europe or the East Indies, and exported to the British Colonies in America. £.	s.	d.	20ths	Rates, or supposed value, by 12 Car. II. cap. 4. ‡ 11 Geo. I cap. 7. from whence the foregoing Duties are computed. £.	s.	d.
GADZA of all sorts, without gold or silver, the yard	0	0	6	14 2/5	0	0	7	2 4/5	A	0	0	5	18 2/5	0	0	5	2 2/5	0	2	8
—— striped, with gold or silver, the yard	—	—	—	—	—	—	—	—		—	—	—	—	—	—	—	—	0	5	0
Galley dishes, the dozen	0	0	6	6	0	0	6	13 7/8	A	0	0	5	11	0	0	4	16	0	2	6
Gauntlets, the pair	0	0	10	1 3/5	0	0	10	14 1/5	A	0	0	8	17 3/5	—	—	—	—	0	4	0
And besides, for every Cwt. of Iron	0	5	3		0	5	3		D	0	5	3		—	—	—	—			
Garnets of India, small rough, the pound	0	5	3		0	5	6	3	A f	0	4	9		0	4	3		1	0	0
Garnets of India, small or great cut, the pound	1	8	4	4	1	9	1	13	B c	1	6	10	4	1	5	4	4	3	0	0
—— not of India, small rough, the pound	0	4	2	8	0	4	5	11	A	0	3	8	8	0	3	2	8	1	0	0
—— not of India, small or great cut, the pound	0	12	7	4	0	13	4	13	A	0	11	1	4	0	9	7	4	3	0	0
Garters of silk, French making, the dozen pair	—	—	—	—	—	—	—	—		—	—	—	—	—	—	—	—	3	0	0
Galls, for Dyers use, *as by 3 and 4 Ann. cap. 4.* the Cwt.	—	—	—	—	—	—	—	—		—	—	—	—	—	—	—	—	2	0	0
But by 8 Geo. I. cap. 15. § 10. if regularly imported, entered, and landed, duty free.																				
But on failure thereof, then to pay	0	4	2	8	0	4	8	14	B b	0	3	2	8	0	2	2	8			

* But if imported by Aliens Drawback more, 1s. 3d. for every 100l. of the Rate or Value.

INWARDS.

INWARDS.	Duties to be paid on Importation. By British. £.	s.	d.	20ths	By Aliens. £.	s.	d.	20ths	Reference to the several Branches, see Page vi.	Drawbacks to be repaid on Exportation.* If exported to any legal place, except as mentioned in the following column. £.	s.	d.	20ths	If the produce of Europe or the East Indies, and exported to the British Colonies in America. £.	s.	d.	20ths	Rates, or supposed value, by 12 Car. II. cap. 4. ‡ 11 Geo. I. cap. 7. from whence the foregoing Duties are computed. £.	s.	d.
Geneva. *Vide* Spirits.																				
Gimlets for vintners, the dozen	0	1	8	3 1/5	0	1	9	8 2/5	A	0	1	5	15 1/5	—	—	—	—	0	8	0
And besides, for every Cwt. of Iron	0	5	3		0	5	3		D	0	5	3		—	—	—	—			
Ginger. *Vide in* Grocery.																				
—— green. *Vide in* Drugs.																				
Girdles of counterfeit gold and silver, the dozen	0	4	2	8	0	4	5	11	A	0	3	8	8	0	3	2	8	1	0	0
—— cruel, the groce, containing 12 dozen	0	11	2	8	0	11	10	16	A	0	9	10	8	0	8	6	8	2	13	4
—— leather, the groce, containing 12 dozen	0	17	6		0	18	4	10	C	0	15	10		0	14	2		3	6	8
And besides, for every 20 s. of their real value upon oath	0	6	3	12	0	6	3	12	Dc	0	0	3	12	0	0	3	12			
—— silk, the dozen	—	—	—	—	—	—	—	—		—	—	—	—	—	—	—	—	2	0	0
—— velvet, the dozen	—	—	—	—	—	—	—	—		—	—	—	—	—	—	—	—	4	0	0
—— woollen, the dozen	0	6	8	12 4/5	0	7	1	13 3/5	A	0	5	11	0 4/5	0	5	1	8 4/5	1	12	0
Glass and Glasses, *vocat.* Balm glasses, the groce, containing 12 dozen	0	2	9	1 1/2	0	2	10	5 1/8	B	0	2	6	16 1/2	0	2	4	11 1/2	0	7	6
—— Burning glasses, the dozen	0	1	1	4 3/5	0	1	1	14 1/20	B	0	1	0	6 3/5	0	0	11	8 1/5	0	3	0

* But if imported by Aliens Drawback more, 1s. 3d. for every 100 l. of the Rate or Value.

G   [126]   G

INWARDS.

Glass and Glasses, *vizt.*

	DUTIES to be paid on IMPORTATION.		DUTIES to be paid on IMPORTATION.		Reference to the several Branches, see Page vi.	DRAWBACKS to be repaid on EXPORTATION.*		DRAWBACKS to be repaid on EXPORTATION.*		RATES, or supposed value, by 12 Car. II. cap. 4. 11 Geo. I. cap. 7. from whence the foregoing Duties are computed.
	By BRITISH.		By ALIENS.			If exported to any legal place, except as mentioned in the following column.		If the produce of Europe or the East Indies, and exported to the British Colonies in America.		
	£. s. d. 20ths		£. s. d. 20ths			£. s. d. 20ths		£. s. d. 20ths		£. s. d.
Drinking glasses, *vizt.* coarse drinking glasses, the dozen	0 1 4		0 1 14 1/10		B	0 1 0 6		0 0 11 8		0 3 0
Flanders drinking glasses, the hundred glasses	0 0 9		0 0 6 3		B	0 0 8 6 15		0 0 7 11 5		1 5 0
French drinking glasses, the hundred, containing 5 score	0 11 0 6		0 11 2 13		F	0 6 10 16 3/5		0 6 6 6 3/5		0 15 0
Venice drinking glasses, the dozen	0 6 7 7/5		0 6 10 4 3/5		B	0 6 1 19 3/5		0 5 8 11 3/5		0 18 0
Glass pipes great, the Cwt.	2 15 1 10 1		2 17 1 2 10		B B	2 11 4 10 2 6 16		2 7 7 10 2 4 11		7 10 6 0 7 6
small, the pound	0 0 4		0 0 7		B	0 6 10 4		0 0 6 4		0 1 0
Glass plates or lights for looking-glasses, unsilver'd, of chrystal, small, under N° 6, the dozen	0 14 8 1 9 4 11 0 6		0 15 2 14 3/5 1 10 5 4 10		B B B	0 13 8 1 7 8 16 10 5 4 4/5		0 12 8 1 5 10 9 10 4 6 3/5		2 0 0 4 0 0 30 0 0
N° 6, the dozen										
N° 7, 8, 9, 10, the dozen										
N° 11, 12, the dozen										
Glasses for windows, *vizt.* Burgundy: coloured, the chest	3 17 2 2 15 1 10 0 0 5 4/5		3 18 6 12 3/5 2 16 1 1 1 0 5 7 4/5		F F A	2 8 3 12 1 14 6 4 8 0 4 8 4/5		2 5 8 2 1 12 7 10 0 3 16 3/5		5 5 0 3 15 0 0 2 0
white, the chest										
Muscovy glass, or flude, the lb.										

* But if imported by Aliens Drawback more, 1s. 3d. for every 100l. of the Rate or Value.

G   [127]   G

INWARDS	DUTIES to be paid on IMPORTATION		Reference to the several Branches, see Page vi.	DRAWBACKS to be repaid on EXPORTATION		RATES, or supposed value by 12 Car. II. cap. 4. 11 Geo. I. cap. 7. from whence the foregoing Duties are computed.
	By BRITISH.	By ALIENS.		If exported to any legal place, except as mentioned in the following column.	If the produce of Europe or the East Indies, and exported to the British Colonies in America.	
	£ s. d. 20ths	£ s. d. 20ths		£ s. d. 20ths	£ s. d. 20ths	£ s. d.
Glass and Glasses, vizt. { ——Normandy, coloured, the case	2 15 1 10	2 16 1 6 1,4/5	F	1 14 6	1 12 7 10	3 15 0
——— white, the case containing 60 bunches	1 0 12	1 2 5 6 1/2	F	0 13 9 12	0 13 0 12	1 10 0
——Rhenish, the way, or web	0 18 10 16	1 0 0 19	A	0 16 7 16	0 14 4 16	4 10 0
Glass-stone plates for spectacles, rough, the dozen	0 7 4 4	0 7 7 7	B	0 6 10 4	0 6 4 4	1 0 0
Hour-glasses of Flanders making: coarse, the grosse containing 12 dozen	2 0 12	2 10 7 7	B	1 0 6 12	0 19 0 12	3 0 0
——— fine, the dozen	0 7 4 4	0 7 7 7	B	0 6 10 4	0 6 4 4	1 0 0
——— of Venice making, the dozen	1 2 0 12	2 10 1 1/2	B	1 0 6 12	0 19 0 12	3 0 0
Looking-glasses of chrystal, small, the dozen, under N° 6	0 11 0 6	0 11 5 0	B	0 10 3 6	0 9 6 6	1 10 0
——— middle sort, the dozen, N° 6	1 2 0 12	2 10 1 1	B	1 0 6 12	0 19 0 12	3 0 0
——— small, the dozen, N° 7, 8, 9, 10	2 4 1 4	2 5 8 2	B	2 1 1 4	1 18 1 4	6 0 0
——— the dozen, N° 11, 12	16 10 9	17 6 15 4/5	B	15 8 3	14 5 9	45 0 0
Looking-glasses, halfpenny ware, the grosse, containing 12 dozen	0 2 11 5 3/5	0 3 0 10 1/3	B	0 2 8 17	0 2 6	0 8 0
——— penny ware, the grosse, containing 12 dozen	0 5 10 11 1/5	0 6 1 1	B	0 5 5 15 1/3	0 5 0 19 1/3	0 16 0

* But if imported by Aliens Drawback more, 1s. 2d. for every 100l. of the Rate or Value.

INWARDS.

Glass and Glasses, *voat.*

	DUTIES to be paid on IMPORTATION.		DUTIES to be paid on IMPORTATION.		Reference to the several Branches, see Page vi.	DRAWBACKS to be repaid on EXPORTATION.		DRAWBACKS to be repaid on EXPORTATION.		RATES, or supposed value, by 12 Car. II. cap. 4. 11 Geo. I. cap. 7. from whence the foregoing Duties are computed.
	By BRITISH.		By ALIENS.			If exported to any legal place, except as mentioned in the following column.		If the produce of Europe or the East Indies, and exported to the British Colonies in America.		
	£. s. d. 20ths		£. s. d. 20ths			£. s. d. 20ths		£. s. d. 20ths		£. s. d.
Looking-glasses of steel small, the dozen	0 4 10 16		0 5 0 18		B	0 4 6 16				0 13 4
—— large	0 9 9 12		0 10 1 16		B	0 9 1 12				1 6 8
Perspective-glasses: the piece, not exceeding 3 feet in length	0 8 11 2		0 9 2 5		B	0 8 2 2		0 7 5 2		‡ 1 0 0
—— large, the piece, exceeding 3 feet in length	0 17 10 4		0 18 4 10		B	0 16 4 4		0 14 10 4		‡ 2 0 0
—— small, the dozen	0 8 11 2		0 9 2 5		B	0 8 2 2		0 7 5 2		‡ 1 0 0
Vials, the hundred, containing 5 score	0 5 6 3		0 5 8 10		B	0 5 1 13		0 4 9 3		0 15 0
Water glasses, the dozen	0 4 4 18		0 4 6 16		B	0 4 1 6		0 3 9 14		0 12 0
All Glass manufactures, *rated by 11 Geo. I cap. 7. or unrated,* for every 20s. of the rate or value:										
—— if not French	0 16 3 2		0 16 6 9		F	0 10 6 6		0 9 9 6		
—— if French	0 8 11 2		0 9 2 5		B	0 8 2 2		0 7 5 2		
And besides, *for ev ry pound weight of Glass, except green Glass*	0 1 4 16		0 1 4 16		Ze	0 0 16		0 0 16		
For bottles or flasks. *Vide* Bottles.										
Broken glass, the Cwt.	0 1 1 7		0 1 1 15		B	0 1 0 8		0 0 11 2		‡ 0 2 6
Glew, the Cwt.	0 4 2 8		0 4 5 11		A	0 3 3 8		0 3 2 8		1 0 0

* But if imported by Aliens Drawback more, 1 s. 3 d. for every Aliens Drawback more, 2 s. 3 d. for every 20 s. of the Rate or Value.

G   [129]   G

INWARDS.	Duties to be paid on IMPORTATION.		Reference to the several Branches, see Page vi.	Drawbacks to be repaid on EXPORTATION.*		RATES, or supposed value, by 12 Car. II. cap. 4. ‡ 11 Geo. I. cap. 7. from whence the foregoing Duties are computed.
	By BRITISH.	By ALIENS.		If exported to any legal place, except as mentioned in the following column.	If the produce of Europe or the East Indies, and exported to the British Colonies in America.	
	£. s. d. 20ths	£. s. d. 20ths		£. s. d. 20ths	£. s. d. 20ths	£. s. d.
Globes large, the pair	1 5 2 8	1 6 9 6	A	1 2 2 8	0 19 2 8	6 0 0
―― small, the pair	0 12 7 4	0 13 4 13	A	0 11 1 4	0 9 7 4	3 0 0
Gloves of Bridges making, the groce, containing 12 dozen	0 10 6	0 11 1 17 ½	A	0 9 3	0 8 0	2 10 0
―― of Canary, { unwrought, the dozen pair						
Milan, or Venice { wrought with gold or silver, the dozen pair	0 4 2 8	0 4 5 11 ½	A	0 3 8 8	0 3 2 8	1 0 0
―― French making, the groce, containing 12 dozen						
―― French, wrought with gold or silver, the dozen pair	1 16 9	1 17 4 17 ½	F	1 3 0	1 1 9	4 0 0
―― of Spanish, plain, the dozen pair	0 3 1 16	0 3 4 3 ¼+½	A	0 2 9 6	0 2 4 16	2 10 0
―― of Vandon, the dozen pair	0 2 1 4	0 2 2 15 ¾	A	0 1 10 4	0 1 7 4	4 0 0
―― of silk, knit, the dozen pair						0 15 0
Glovers clippings, the Cwt.	0 1 3 15	0 1 4 10	C	0 1 2 5	0 1 0 15	0 10 0
Gold and silver thread:						2 0 0
―― Counterfit, vocat. Bridges gold and silver, the pound, containing 16 ounces averdupois weight	0 3 6	0 3 8 2	C	0 3 2	0 2 10	0 13 4‡

* But if imported by Aliens Drawback more, 1 s. 3 d: for every 100 l. of the Rate or Value.

[130]

INWARDS.

	DUTIES to be paid on IMPORTATION.		Reference to the several Branches, see Page vi.	DRAWBACKS to be repaid on EXPORTATION.*		RATES, or supposed value, by 12 Car. II. cap. 4. 11 Geo. I. cap. 7. from whence the foregoing Duties are computed.
	By BRITISH.	By ALIENS.		If exported to any legal place, except as mentioned in the following column.	If the produce of Europe or the East Indies, and exported to the British Colonies in America.	
	$L. \; s. \; d. \; 20^{ths}$	$L. \; s. \; d. \; 20^{ths}$		$L. \; s. \; d. \; 20^{ths}$	$L. \; s. \; d. \; 20^{ths}$	$L. \; s. \; d.$
Gold and silver thread: Counterfeit, *vizt.* Cap gold and silver, the pound, containing 16 ounces averdupois weight	0 5 3	0 5 6 3	C	0 4 9	0 4 3	1 0 0
Copper gold and silver, upon quills and rolls, or rolls, or in skeins, the pound, containing 16 ounces averdupois weight	0 2 7 10	0 2 9 1½	C	0 2 4 10	0 2 1 10	0 10 0
Cullen gold and silver, the mast, containing 2½ lb. at 12 ounces to the pound	0 7 0	0 7 4 4	C	0 6 4	0 5 8	1 6 3
French copper gold and silver, the mark, containing 8 ounces averdupois	0 3 8 2	0 3 8 17 1¼	F	0 2 3 12	0 2 2	0 5 0
Lyons copper gold and silver, double gilt, the mark, containing 8 ounces averdupois	0 19 7 4	0 19 11 8	F	0 12 3 4	0 11 7 4	1 6 8
Right, *vizt.* French and Paris gold and silver, the mark, containing 11½ ounces Venice weight						2 0 0

* But if imported by Aliens Drawback more, 1 s. 3 d. for every 1 col. of the Rate or Value, except Fish.

[131]

INWARDS.

	DUTIES to be paid on IMPORTATION.		Reference to the several Branches, see Page vi.	DRAWBACKS to be repaid on EXPORTATION.*		RATES, or supposed value, by 12 Car. II. cap. 4. ‡11 Geo. I. cap. 7. from whence the foregoing Duties are computed.
	By BRITISH.	By ALIENS.		If exported to any legal place, except as mentioned in the following column.	If the produce of Europe or the East Indies, and exported to the British Colonies in America.	
	L. s. d. 20ths	*L. s. d.* 20ths		*L. s. d.* 20ths	*L. s. d.* 20ths	*L. s. d.*
Venice, Florence, or Milan gold and silver, the pound, containing 12 ounces Venice weight —	0 1 4 16	0 1 5 17	A	0 1 2 16	0 1 0 16	3 6 8
Gold foil, the small grece, containing 12 dozen —	0 4 2 8	0 4 4 10	B c			0 13 4
paper, the small grece, containing 12 dozen —	0 0 8 8	0 0 9 9	B b	0 0 6 8	0 0 4 8	0 6 8
And besides, for the further duties on Paper, according to the nearest sort above in size and goodness. Vide 10 Ann. cap. 19. and 12 Ann. cap. 9.						
Grain or scarlet powder, for Dyers use, as by 3 and 4 Ann. cap. 4. the pound —	0 0 4 4	0 0 4 14	B b	0 0 3 4	0 0 2 4	0 3 4
of Sevil in berries, and Grains of Portugal or Rotta, for Dyers use, as by 3 and 4 Ann. cap. 4. the pound —	0 0 5 17 1/3 5/3 0 0 1 13 1/3 5/3	0 0 5 19 7/6 7/10 0 0 1 15 7/6 7/10	F	0 0 3 13 3/5 3/3 0 0 3 19 3/5 3/3	0 0 3 9 3/5 5/3 0 0 0 1 3/5 5/3	0 6 8
Grains, French or Guiney, the pound —			A			0 3 8
— if French						
— if Guiney						
Vide Drugs.						
Gravers. *Vide* Punions.						

* But if imported by Aliens Drawback more, 1s. 3d. for every 100l. of the Rate or Value.

S 2

INWARDS.

	DUTIES to be paid on IMPORTATION.		DRAWBACKS to be repaid on EXPORTATION.*		RATES, or supposed value, by 12 Car. II. cap. 4. 11 Geo. I. cap. 7. from whence the foregoing Duties are computed.
	By BRITISH.	By ALIENS.	Reference to the several Branches, see P. & c. vi.	If exported to any legal place, except as mentioned in the following column.	If the produce of Europe or the East Indies, and exported to the British Colonies in America.	
	£. s. d. 20ths	£. s. d. 20ths		£. s. d. 20ths	£. s. d. 20ths	£. s. d.
Graves for dogs, the Cwt.	0 0 10 10	0 0 11 0	C	0 0 9 10	0 0 8 10	0 3 4
Greafe may, by 19 Geo. III. cap. 22. be imported duty free, until 25 March, 1782.						
Grindle stones, the chalder						
Almonds, the Cwt.	0 5 7 4	0 5 11 8	A	0 4 11 4	0 4 3 4	1 6 8
But if of France — bitter. Vide Drugs.	2 4 1 4	2 5 8 2	B e	2 1 1 4	1 18 1 1	6 0 0
Annifeeds, the Cwt.	4 14 6	4 16 0 18	F m	3 1 6	2 13 6	
Cinnamon, the pound	1 2 0 12	1 2 10 1	B e	1 0 6 12	0 19 0 12	3 0 8
Cloves, the pound, by 8 Geo. } £. s. d.	0 4 2 8	0 4 3 9	K c	0 3 9 14	0 3 7 14	0 6 8
I. cap. 15. } 0 4 0	0 2 6 4	0 2 6 17	K c	0 2 3 8	0 2 2 4	
Currants, the Cwt.						
On which the duties are as follows:						
if imported in British-built	1 2 2 12 8/25	1 3 0 2/25	A b	1 0 8 12 8/25	0 16 8 11/25	6 0 0
shipping, legally navigated						
The Drawback when so imported						
by British is — when so imported						
by Aliens is —	1 3 8 0 2/25	1 3 8 0 2/25	L b	1 1 9 10 2/25	0 17 9 11/25	
if imported in ships belonging to the republic of Venice				1 1 9 10 2/25	0 17 9 11/25	

Grocery wares, vocat.

* But if imported by Aliens Drawback more, 1 s. 3 d. for every 100 l. of the Rate or Value, except Currants.

INWARDS.

Grocery wares, vizt. — Grocery wares, vizt.

	DUTIES to be paid on IMPORTATION.		DRAWBACKS to be repaid on EXPORTATION.*		RATES, or (supposed value, by 12 Car. II. cap. 4. † 11 Geo. I. cap. 7. from whence the foregoing Duties are computed.
	By BRITISH.	By ALIENS.	Reference to the several Branches, see Page vi.	If exported to any legal place, except as mentioned in the following column.	If the produce of Europe or the East Indies, and exported to the British Colonies in America.
	L. s. d. 20ths	*L. s. d.* 20ths		*L. s. d.* 20ths	*L. s. d.* 20ths	*L. s. d.*
— if imported in any other foreign ship	1 7 6 7 $\frac{11}{23}$	1 7 6 7 $\frac{11}{23}$	K b	1 5 7 17 $\frac{11}{23}$	1 1 7 12 $\frac{15}{23}$	6 0 0
By 17 Geo. III. cap. 43. an abatement of 8 per Cent. is made out of the duties on Currants in lieu of damage, which allowance has been deducted in the above computations.						
Dates, the Cwt.	1 4	2 5 8 2		2 1 1 4	1 18 1 4	
Figs. See after Plumbs dried.						
Ginger of the East Indies, the pound — of the West Indies, the pound	0 1 1 4 $\frac{3}{5}$ 0 0 5 17	0 1 1 14 $\frac{7}{10}$ 0 0 6 1	B e B e	0 1 0 6 $\frac{3}{5}$ 0 0 5 9	0 0 11 8 0 0 5 9	0 3 0 0 1 4
But if of the British plantations, by a memorandum added at the end of the rules annexed to the Book of Rates of 1660, and also by 9 and 10 W. III. cap. 23. is rated by the Cwt. at 1*l*. 0*s*. 0*d*.	2 4 1 4					
The duties thereon are as follows: Ginger of the British plantations imported directly from thence in British-built ships, the Cwt.	0 10 5 14 $\frac{2}{5}$	0 10 8 17 $\frac{2}{5}$	B e *	0 9 11 14 $\frac{2}{5}$	0 9 11 14 $\frac{2}{5}$	

* But if imported by Aliens Drawback more, 1s. 3d. for every 100l. of the Rate or Value, except Currants.

INWARDS.

Grocery wares, vocat.

	Duties to be paid on Importation. By British. £.	s.	d.	20ths	By Aliens. £.	s.	d.	20ths	Reference to the several Branches, see Page vi.	Drawbacks to be repaid on Exportation.* If exported to any legal place, except as mentioned in the following column. £.	s.	d.	20ths	If the produce of Europe or the East Indies, and exported to the British Colonies in America. £.	s.	d.	20ths	Rates, or supposed value, by 12 Car. II. cap. 4. & 11 Geo. I. cap. 7. from whence the foregoing Duties are computed. £.	s.	d.
Ginger of the British plantations not so imported, the Cwt.	1	0	11	3 1/5	1	1	2	6 1/5	B e	1	0	5	3 1/5	1	0	5	3 1/5			
Liquorice, the Cwt.	1	7	5	14	1	7	10	8 1/2	B e	1	6	8	14	1	5	11	14	1	10	0
—— if French	1	15	4	4	1	15	8	18 1/2	F c	1	7	1	4	1	6	4	4			
—— in powder, the Cwt.	2	9	8	8	2	10	2	14	B e	2	8	8	8	2	7	8	8	‡ 2	0	0
—— if French	3	0	2	8	3	0	8	14	F c	2	9	2	8	2	8	2	8			
Maces, the pound, *by* 8 *Geo. I. cap.* 15. *rated at* l. s. d. 0 6 0	0	3	9	7 1/5	0	3	10	6 1/10	K c	0	3	5	3 1/5	0	3	3	7 1/5			
Nutmegs, the pound, *by* 8 *Geo. I. cap.* 15. *rated at* l. s. d. 0 3 0	0	1	10	13 3/5	0	1	11	3 1/10	K c	0	1	8	11 3/5	0	1	7	13 3/5			
Pepper, the pound	—	—	—	—	—	—	—	—		—	—	—	—	—	—	—	—	0	3	4
—— imported directly from the place of its growth, in British-built shipping, the pound	—	—	—	—	—	—	—	—		—	—	—	—	—	—	—	—	0	1	8
The duties payable on Pepper, when not imported directly from the place of its growth in British-built shipping, by 8 *Ann. cap.* 7. *are as follows:*																				
—— at importation to be warehoused, the pound	0	0	1		0	0	1		M	—	—	—	—	—	—	—	—			

* But if imported by Aliens Drawback more, 1s. 3d. for every 100l. of the Rate or Value.

[135]

INWARDS.		DUTIES to be paid on IMPORTATION.		Reference to the several Branches, see Page vi.	DRAWBACKS to be repaid on EXPORTATION.*		RATES, or supposed value, by 12 Car. II. cap. 4. 11 Geo. I. cap. 7. from whence the foregoing Duties are computed.
		By BRITISH.	By ALIENS.		If exported to any legal place, except as mentioned in the following column.	If the produce of Europe or the East Indies, and exported to the British Colonies in America.	
		£. s. d. 20ths	£. s. d. 20ths		£. s. d. 20ths	£. s. d. 20ths	£. s. d.
Grocery wares, vocat,	⎧ on delivery out of the warehouse for home consumption, the pound	0 2 7 11	0 2 8 1½	L c			
	But by 8 Geo. I. cap. 15. the duties on Pepper, imported directly from the place of its growth, in British-built shipping, are as follows:						
	at importation to be warehoused, the pound	0 0 0.10	0 0 0.10	M			
	on delivery out of the warehouse for home consumption, being by that act rated at, the pound 3d. ⅓	0 4 11 1½	0 4 12 3/6	L c			
	All Spicery, except Pepper, imported directly from the place of its growth, in British-built shipping, to be rated one third part of what is charged in this book, and no more.						
	Note, That the aforegoing clause doth not affect the rates on Cloves, Mace, and Nutmegs; nor does it affect the rate on Ginger of the British plantations						

* But if imported by Aliens Drawback more, 1 s. 3 d. for every 100 l. of the Rate or Value.

INWARDS.

Grocery wares, viast.

	DUTIES to be paid on IMPORTATION.			Reference to the several Branches, see Page vi.	DRAWBACKS to be repaid on EXPORTATION.*		RATES, or supposed value, by 12 C. r. ll. cap. 4. 11 Geo. I. from whence the foregoing Duties are computed.
	By BRITISH.		By ALIENS.		If exported to any legal place, except as mentioned in the following column.	If the produce of Europe or the East Indies, and exported to the British Colonies in America.	
	£. s. d. 20ths		£. s. d. 20ths		£. s. d. 20ths	£. s. d. 20ths	£. s. d.
lations, the said articles being now otherwise regulated.							
Pimento, of and from the British plantations, the pound	0 0 1 17 4/5		0 0 1 19 1/8	C c	0 0 1 14 4/5	0 0 1 14 4/5	‡ 0 0 6
Plumbs dried, the pound	0 0 1 17 4/5		0 0 1 19 1/8	C c	0 0 1 14 4/5	0 0 1 11 1/2	‡ 0 0 6
Best if of France	0 0 4 14 4/5		0 0 4 16 4/40	F m	0 0 3 1	0 0 2 18 1/2	
Figs, the Cwt.	0 12 3		0 12 5 1/4 1/4	B e	0 11 5 1/4	0 10 7 2/3	1 13 4
Prunes, the Cwt.	0 5 6 3		0 5 8 1/4	B e	0 5 1 3	0 4 9 3	0 15 0
Best if of France	0 11 9 15		0 11 0 3 1/4	F m	0 10 8 5	0 9 3 5	
Raisins great, the Cwt. by 14 £. s. d. Geo. III. cap. 74. rated at 0 10 0	0 7 6 14 2/5		0 7 8 3 1/2	L c	0 7 4	0 7 1	
of Smyrna { black, the Cwt. red, the Cwt.	0 10 10 5 17/25 0 10 10 5 17/25		0 11 1 4 7/10 0 11 1 4 9/10	L c L c	0 10 4 12 22/25 0 10 4 12 22/25	0 10 4 12 22/25 0 10 4 12 22/25	1 0 0 1 0 0
of the sun, the Cwt.	0 17 8 1 1/5		0 18 2 5 3/10	L c	0 16 8 3 1/2	0 15 8 5 1/2	2 0 0
Fara and Lexia raisins, the Cwt.	0 7 6 14 4/5		0 7 8 3 1/2	L c	0 7 4	0 7 1	
Raisins of Alicant, Denia, and other raisins, not otherwise rated, the Cwt.	0 6 8 12 4/5		0 6 9 18 5/8	L c	0 6 4	0 6 3 16	‡ 0 10 0
of Lipra, or Belvadera, the Cwt.	0 7 10 2 11/25		0 7 11 13 5/8	L c	0 7 7 3 1/15	0 7 4 3 16/15	‡ 0 11 0

Note. By 17 Geo. III. cap. 43. the following abatements are made out Cwt.

* But if imported by Aliens Drawback more, 1 s. 3 d. for every 100 l. of the Rate or Value, but from Raisins the allowance for Damage must be deducted.

INWARDS.

Grocery wares, *vizt.*

	DUTIES to be paid on IMPORTATION.		Reference to the several Branches, see Page vi.	DRAWBACKS to be repaid on EXPORTATION.*		RATES, or supposed value, by 12 Car.II.cap.4. & 11Geo.I.cap.7. from whence the foregoing Duties are computed.
	By BRITISH.	By ALIENS.		If exported to any legal place, except as mentioned in the following column.	If the produce of Europe or the East Indies, and exported to the British Colonies in America.	
	£. s. d.20ths	£. s. d.20ths		£. s. d.20ths	£. s. d.20ths	£. s. d.
of the duties on Raisins, *in lieu of damage, which allowances have been deducted in the above computations:*						
On Raisins solis, *One per Cent.*	2 12 6	2 15 1 10	Af	2 7 6	2 2 6	10 0 0
Smyrna Raisins, *Six per Cent.*	4 14 6	4 17 1 10	Be	4 9 6	4 4 6	
Lipari, Faro, Belvidere, and Great or Lexia Raisins, *Ten p.r Cent.*	3 18 9	4 2 8 5	Af	3 11 3	3 3 9	15 0 0
Denia Raisins, *Twenty per Cent.*	7 1 9	7 5 8 5	Be	6 14 3	6 6 9	
Sugar candy, brown, the Cwt.						
If from the East Indies	1 5 10 16	1 6 11 8	Nc	1 3 10 16	1 3 10 16	4 0 0
—— white, the Cwt.						
If from the East Indies				1 1 10 16		
Sugar Muscovadoes, the Cwt.						
But if exported to Ireland, the drawback is						
—— refined, double or single, in loaves, the Cwt.	4 14 1 16	4 18 7 7	Nc	4 5 7 16	4 5 7 16	17 0 0
But if exported to Ireland, the drawback is				3 17 1 16		

* But if imported by Aliens Drawback more, 1s. 3d. for every 100 l. of the Rate or Value.

INWARDS

Grocery wares, vocat.

	Duties to be paid on Importation		Reference to the several Branches, see Page vi.	Drawbacks to be repaid on Exportation.*		Rates, or supposed value, by 12 Car. II. cap. 4. 11 Geo. I. cap. 7. from whence the foregoing Duties are computed.
	By British	By Aliens		If exported to any legal place, except as mentioned in the following column.	If the produce of Europe or the East Indies, and exported to the British Colonies in America.	
	£. s. d. 20ths	£. s. d. 20ths		£. s. d. 20ths	£. s. d. 20ths	£. s. d.
St. Thome and Paneles, the Cwt.	0 15 4 16	0 15 11 2	Nc	0 14 4 16	0 14 4 16	2 0 0
But if exported to Ireland, the drawback is — white, the Cwt.	2 3 4 16	2 5 3 18		0 13 4 16	1 19 8 16	7 6 8
But if exported to Ireland, the drawback is — white Sugars from the British plantations, the Cwt.	1 7 7 16	1 8 11 11	Nd	1 19 8 16	1 5 1 16	
But if exported within one year, the drawback is — brown Sugars, and Muscovadoes, from the British plantations, the Cwt.				1 16 0 16	1 7 7 16	5 0 0
		0 12 1 8	Nd	1 5 1 16		
But if exported within one year, the drawback is — Paneles, from the British plantations, the Cwt.	0 11 8 14			1 7 7 16	0 10 11 14	1 10 0
				0 10 11 14	0 11 8 14	
But if exported within one year, the drawback is	0 15 4 16	0 15 11 2	Nc	0 11 8 14	0 14 4 16	2 0 0
				0 14 4 16	0 15 4 16	
				0 15 4 16		

* But if imported by Aliens Drawback more, 1s. 3d. for every 100l. of the Rate or Value.

INWARDS

Grocery wares, viscat.

But by 18 Geo. III. cap. 58. Sugars or Panneles imported from any British colony or plantation in America without a certificate, as required by 4 Geo. III. shall be deemed and taken to be Sugars, &c. of any French colony or plantation.

The duties therefore for such goods will stand as follows:

— brown and Muscovadoes, the Cwt.
But if exported to Ireland, the drawback is
— refined, double or single, in loaves, the Cwt.
But if exported to Ireland, the drawback is
— white, the Cwt.
But if exported to Ireland, the drawback is

	DUTIES to be paid on IMPORTATION.		Reference to the several Branches, see Page vi.	DRAWBACKS to be repaid on EXPORTATION.*		RATES, or supposed value, by 12 Car. II. cap. 4. 11 Geo. I cap. 7. from whence the foregoing Duties are computed.
	By BRITISH.	By ALIENS.		If exported to any legal place, except as mentioned in the following column.	If the produce of Europe or the East Indies, and exported to the British Colonies in America.	
	£. s. d. 20ths	£. s. d. 20ths		£. s. d. 20ths	£. s. d. 20ths	£. s. d.
brown and Muscovadoes	2 6 10.16	2 7 11 8	N f	2 4 10.16	2 4 10.16	4 0 0
exp. to Ireland				2 2 10.16		
refined	9 3 4.16	9 7 10 7	N f	8 14 10.16	8 14 10.16	17 0 0
exp. to Ireland				8 6 4.16		
white	4 1 10.16	4 3 9 18	N f	3 18 2.16	3 18 2.16	7 6 8
exp. to Ireland				3 14 6.16		

* But if imported by Aliens Drawback more, 1s. 3d. for every 100l. of the Rate or Value.

[140]

INWARDS.		DUTIES to be paid on IMPORTATION.		Reference to the several Branches, see Page vi.	DRAWBACKS to be repaid on EXPORTATION.*		RATES, or supposed value, by 12 Car. II. cap. 4. 11 Geo. I. cap. 7. from whence the foregoing Duties are computed.
		By BRITISH.	By ALIENS.		If exported to any legal place, except as mentioned in the following column.	if the produce of Europe or the East Indies, and exported to the British Colonies in America.	
		£. s. d. /20ths	£. s. d. /20ths		£. s. d. /20ths	£. s. d. /20ths	£. s. d.
Grocery wares, vocat.	Paneles, the Cwt. ——— But if exported to Ireland, the drawback is	1 5 10 16	1 6 5 2	N f	1 4 10 16	1 4 10 16	2 0 0
	By 6 Geo. III. cap. 52. § 23. Sugars imported from any of the British colonies on the continent of America may be warehoused for exportation on payment of, the Cwt. ——— But if taken out of such warehouse to be used in this kingdom, then the remainder of the duties are to be paid up as if the goods were the produce of the French plantations.	0 0 3	0 0 3	B a	1 3 10 16		
	Note. Figs, Prunes, Raisins, and Sugar, when imported in foreign ships, pay duty as Aliens.						
	Grograms, vocat. Lile grograms. Vide Buffins.						
	——— Turkey, the yard	0 0 9	0 0 10 ½	A	0 0 8 ½	0 0 7	0 3 0
	Gun-powder, vocat. Corn-powder, the Cwt.	1 13 7	1 15 8	A	0 17 6	1 5 7	0 8 0
	——— Serpentine, the Cwt. ———	1 1 0	1 2 3 15/11	A	0 18 6	0 10 0	0 5 0

* But if imported by Aliens Drawback more, 1s. 3d. for every 100 L. of the Rate or Value.

G [141] H

INWARDS.

	DUTIES to be paid on IMPORTATION.		DRAWBACKS to be repaid on EXPORTATION.*			
	By BRITISH.	By ALIENS.	Reference to the several Branches, see Page vi.	If exported to any legal place, except as mentioned in the following column.	If the produce of Europe or the East Indies, and exported to the British Colonies in America.	RATES, or supposed value, by 12 Car. II. cap. 4. & 11 Geo. I. cap. 7. from whence the foregoing Duties are computed.
	£ s. d. 20ths	£ s. d. 20ths		£ s. d. 20ths	£ s. d. 20ths	£ s. d.
Guns, *vocat.* Callivers, the piece	0 1 0 12	0 1 7	A	0 0 11 2		0 5 0
—— Muskets, the piece	0 2 1 4	0 2 15	A	0 1 10 4		0 10 0
And besides for every Cwt. of Iron in the aforesaid Guns	0 5 3	0 5 3	D	0 5 3		

H.

HAIR, *vocat.* Camels hair, the pound	0 0 7 11	0 0 8 0 1/2	A	0 0 7	0 0 6 5 15/20	0 3 0
—— Cow or Ox hair, the Cwt.	0 7 10 10	0 8 3	C	0 7 1 10	0 0 6 4 10/20	1 10 0
—— Elks hair for saddles, the Cwt.	0 2 7 10	0 2 9 3/4	A	0 2 3 15	0 0 2 0	0 12 6
Cwt. —— Goats hair, the pound	0 0 7 2	0 0 7 8 1/2	C	0 0 6 15	0 0 0 6 15/20	0 1 2
if Carmenia wool, the pound	0 0 5 0	0 0 5 8 1/2	C	0 0 4 13	0 0 0 4 13/20	
of any other sort, the pound	0 0 7 17	0 0 8 5 1/2	C	0 0 7 2	0 0 0 7 2/20	0 2 6
—— Horse hair, the pound			C			
—— Human hair for perukes, the pound	0 1 9	0 1 10 1/2	C	0 1 7	0 0 1 5	0 6 8

* But if imported by Aliens Drawback more, 1s. 3d. for every 1col. of the Rate or Value.

INWARDS.

	DUTIES to be paid on IMPORTATION.				Reference to the several Branches, See Page vi.	DRAWBACKS to be repaid on EXPORTATION.*	
	By BRITISH.		By ALIENS.			If exported to any legal place, except as mentioned in the following column.	If the produce of Europe or the East Indies, and exported to the British Colonies in America.
	£. s. d. 20ths		£. s. d. 20ths			£. s. d. 20ths	£. s. d. 20ths
Hair bottoms for fieves, the groce, containing 12 dozen	0 2 1	4	0 2 2 15	½	A	0 1 10	4	0 1 7	4
Hair powder. *Vide* Powder.							
Halberds gilt, the piece	0 2 9	12	0 2 11	14	A	0 2 5	12	—
———— ungilt, the piece	0 0 8	8	0 0 8	18	A	0 0 7	8	—
N.B. besides, for every Cwt. of Iron, contained in the Halberds					D		
Hairs. *Vide* Bacon.	0 5 3		0 5 3			0 5 3	—
Hammers with wooden handles, or without, the dozen	0 10 1	3/5	0 10 14	4/5	A	0 8 17	3/5	—
viat. Horsemen's hammers, the dozen	0 2 9	12	0 2 11	14	A	0 2 5	12	—
And besides, for every Cwt. of Iron					D		
Handbaskets. *Vide* Baskets.	0 5 3		0 5 3			0 5 3	—
Handkerchers, *vel* Handkerchiefs, the dozen	0 12 7	4	0 13 4	13	A	0 11 1	4	0 9 7	4
Handicoots } *Vide* Wood.							
Handspikes }							
Hand vices. *Vide* Vice tongues.							
Harness, *scoet.* Corslets, compleat, the piece	0 5 3		0 5 6	7/8	C	0 4 9		0 4 3	
———— Curates, the piece	0 3 3	7	0 3 5	½	C	0 2 11	12	0 2 7	17	½

*But if imported by Aliens Drawback more, 1 s. 3 d. for every 20 s. of the Rate or Value.

INWARDS.

	DUTIES to be paid on IMPORTATION.		Reference to the several Branches, see Page vi.	DRAWBACKS to be repaid on EXPORTATION.*		RATES, or supposed value by 12 Car. II. cap. 4. ‡ 11 Geo. I. cap. 7. from whence the foregoing Duties are computed.
	By BRITISH.	By ALIENS.		If exported to any legal place, except as mentioned in the following column.	If the produce of Europe or the East Indies, and exported to the British Colonies in America.	
	£. s. d. 20ths	£. s. d. 20ths		£. s. d. 20ths	£. s. d. 20ths	£. s. d.
—— Morians, {graven, the piece	0 2 7 10	0 2 9 1	C	0 2 4 10	0 2 1 10	0 10 0
or Head-pieces {plain, the piece	0 1 3 15	0 1 4 10	C	0 1 2 5	0 1 0 15	0 5 0
—— Harnefs plates. *Vide* Plates.						
Harnefs rofes, the thoufand	0 0 3 3	0 0 3 6 3/20	C	0 0 2 17	0 0 2 11	0 1 0
Harpftrings, or Catlings, the groce, containing 12 dozen ——	0 2 7 10	0 2 8 5 3/4	C	0 0 2 6	0 0 2 4 10	0 5 0
—— if French *Vide* Luteftrings.	0 3 11 5	0 4 0 0 3/4	Fr	0 0 2 6 15	0 0 2 5 5	
Hatbands, the groce, containing 12 dozen						
Hatchets. *Vide* Axes.	1 1 0	1 2 3 15	A	0 18 6	0 16 0	5 0 0
Hats of chip, cane, or horfe hair } See *page 14.*						
—— of ftraw ——						
—— of beaver wool or hair, the hat	2 2 0	2 4 7 10	A	1 17 0	1 12 0	10 0 0
—— of Bridges, the dozen	2 2 0	2 4 7 10	A	1 17 0	1 12 0	10 0 0
Dutch felts, or hats made of wool, } the piece	0 4 2 8	0 4 5 11	A	0 3 8 8	0 3 2 8	1 0 0
—— of filk, French making, the dozen						
—— Spanifh or Portugal felts, the dozen	1 1 0	1-2 3 15	A	0 18 6	0 16 0	3 0 0
—— of Venice, the dozen	0 12 7 4	0 13 4 13	A	0 11 1 4	0 9 7 4	5 0 0
						3 0 0

* But if imported by Aliens Draws back more, 1s. 3d. for every 100l. of the Rate or Value.

INWARDS.

	DUTIES to be paid on IMPORTATION.		Reference to the several Branches, see Page vi.	DRAWBACKS to be repaid on EXPORTATION.*		RATES, or supposed value, by 12 Car.II.cap.4. 11 Geo.I.cap.7. from whence the foregoing Duties are computed.
	By BRITISH.	By ALIENS.		If exported to any legal place, except as mentioned in the following column.	If the produce of Europe or the East Indies, and exported to the British Colonies in America.	
	£. s. d. 20ths	£. s. d. 20ths		£. s. d. 20ths	£. s. d. 20ths	£. s. d.
Hats of wool or worsted, trimmed, the dozen	0 12 7 4	0 13 4 13	A	0 11 1 4	0 9 7 4	3 0 0
Hawks, *vocat.* Faulcons, the hawk	0 16 9 12	0 17 10 4	A	0 14 9 12	0 12 9 12	4 0 8
———— Goshawks, the hawk	0 14 0	0 14 10 10	A	0 12 4	0 10 8	3 6 8
———— Jerfaulcons, the hawk	0 18 10 16	0 19 10 10 ½	A	0 16 7 16	0 14 4 16	4 10 8
———— Jerkins, the hawk	0 14 0	0 14 10 10	A	0 12 4	0 10 8	3 6 8
———— Lanners, the hawk	0 16 9 12	0 17 10 4	A	0 14 9 12	0 12 9 12	4 0 0
———— Lannerets, the hawk	0 8 4 16	0 8 11 2	A	0 7 4 16	0 6 4 16	2 0 0
———— Tassels of all sorts, the hawk	0 8 4 16	0 8 11 2	A	0 7 4 16	0 6 4 16	2 0 0
Hawks hoods, the groce, containing 12 dozen	0 5 7 4	0 5 11 8	A	0 4 11 4	0 4 3 4	1 6 8
Hay, the load, containing 36 trusses, each truss being 56 lb.	0 10 6	0 11 0 6	C	0 9 6	0 8 6	
Headings for pipes, hogsheads, or barrels, the hundred, containing six score ——— of, and directly from, any part of America, if regularly entered and landed, free. *On failure thereof. See in* Wood. ——— of or from any part of Europe, except Ireland and France			B			‡ 2 0 0
	0 2 1 4	0 2 2 5		0 1 11 4	0 1 9 4	0 6 8

* But if imported by Aliens Drawback more, 1s. 3d. for every 100 l. of the Rate or Value.

INWARDS.

	DUTIES to be paid on IMPORTATION.		Reference to the several Branches, See Page vi.	DRAWBACKS to be repaid on EXPORTATION.*		RATES, or supposed value, by 12 Car. II. cap. 4. & 11 Geo. I. cap. 7. from whence the foregoing Duties are computed.
	By BRITISH.	By ALIENS.		If exported to any legal place, except as mentioned in the following column.	If the produce of Europe or the East Indies, and exported to the British Colonies in America.	
	£. s. d. 20ths	£. s. d. 20ths		£. s. d. 20ths	£. s. d. 20ths	£. s. d.
—— of Ireland, Africa, or Asia ——	0 1 4 16	0 1 5 17	A	0 1 2 16	0 1 0 16	1 0 0
—— of France. *See in Wood.*						
If imported in foreign ships, to pay duty as Aliens.						
Head pieces. *Vide Harness.*						
Heath for brushes, the Cwt.	0 4 2 8	0 4 5 11	A	0 3 8 8	0 3 2 8	
Hemp, *vect.* of the British plantations in America, is by 8 Geo. I. cap. 12. duty free.						
—— of the growth of Ireland, (and all the production thereof, as thread, yarn, and linen of the manufacture of Ireland) may be imported by British or Irish directly from thence into Great Britain, under the certificates and proofs upon oath preferred by law, duty free.						
—— Cullen and Steel hemp, and short dressed, the Cwt.	2 2 0	2 4 7 10	A	1 17 0	1 12 0	10 0 0
all other sorts of dressed hemp, the Cwt.	1 13 7 4	1 15 8 8	A.	1 9 7 4	1 5 7 4	8 0 0
Spruce, Muscovia, and all other rough hemp, the Cwt.	0 3 6	0 3 8 2	C	0 3 2		0 13 4

* But if imported by Aliens Drawback more, 1s. 3d. for every 100l. of the Rate or Value.

H [146] H

INWARDS.

Hides, viz.

	DUTIES to be paid on IMPORTATION.		Reference to the several Branches, see Page vi.	DRAWBACKS to be repaid on EXPORTATION.*		RATES, or supposed value, by 12 Car.II.cap.4. 11 Geo.I.cap.7. from whence the foregoing Duties are computed.
	By BRITISH.	By ALIENS.		If exported to any legal place, except as mentioned in the following column.	If the produce of Europe or the East Indies, and exported to the British Colonies in America.	
	£ s. d. 20ths	£ s. d. 20ths		£ s. d. 20ths	£ s. d. 20ths	£ s. d.
But if imported in foreign ships, to pay duty as Aliens.						
Buff hides, the hide	0 4 2 8	0 4 3 19	C	0 3 11 8	0 3 8 8	0 10 0
And besides, for every pound weight Cow, or Horse hides in the hair, the piece	0 0 7 7	0 0 7 7	D	0 0 5 —	0 0 5 —	0 2 6
tanned, the piece	0 0 7 17½	0 0 8 8½	C	0 0 7 2	0 0 6 7	0 10 0
And besides, for every pound weight hides of Barbary and Muscovia, the hide	0 2 7 10¼	0 2 9 1¼	C	0 2 4 10	0 2 1 10	
	0 0 3 13¼	0 0 3 13¼	D			
And besides, if { dressed in oil, the poma tanned, the pound tawed, the hide	0 0 7 17½	0 0 8 5	C	0 0 7 2	0 0 6 7½	0 2 6
	0 0 7 7	0 0 7 7	D D	0 0 5 2	0 0 5 2	
	0 0 3 13¼	0 0 3 13¼	D	0 0 2 6	0 0 2 6	
Elk hides. Vide in Skins.						
Indian hides, the hide	0 1 2 —	0 1 15	C	0 0 11 17	0 0 10 12	
And besides, if { dressed in oil, the pound tanned, the pound tawed, the hide	0 0 7 7	0 0 7 13	D	0 0 5 2	0 0 5 2	
	0 0 3 13¼	0 0 3 13 2	D	0 0 2 6	0 0 2 6	
	0 3 8	0 3 8	D	0 0 2 6	0 0 2 6	
of horses, mares, and geldings, tawed, for every 20s. of their value upon cath	0 5 3	0 5 6 3	C	0 4 9	0 4 3	0 4 2

* But if imported by Aliens Drawback more, 1s. 3d. for every 100l. of the Rate or Value.

INWARDS

Hides, viz:

	DUTIES to be paid on IMPORTATION.		Reference to the several Branches, see Page vi.	DRAWBACKS to be repaid on EXPORTATION.*		RATES, or supposed value by 12 Car.II. cap.4. & 11 Geo.I. cap.7. from whence the foregoing Duties are computed.
	By BRITISH.	By ALIENS.		If exported to any legal place, except as mentioned in the following column.	If the produce of Europe or the East Indies, and exported to the British Colonies in America.	
	£ s d/20ths	£ s d/20ths		£ s d/20ths	£ s d/20ths	£ s d
And besides, for every hide ——— Lofh hides, the piece	0 2 1 4 0 0 4	0 2 1 9 0 0 7 7	D c C c	0 1 5 4 0 1 11 14	0 1 5 4 0 1 10 4	0 5 0
And besides, for every pound weight ——— Red or Muscovia hides, tanned, coloured, or uncoloured, the hide	0 0 7	0 0 7 ½ 0 1 10 1	D c C	0 0 5 3 0 1 7	0 0 5 10 0 1 5	
And besides, for every pound weight ——— All other hides and pieces of hides, not before particularly charged, for every 20s. of their value upon oath	0 1 9 0 3 3	0 3 3 0 6 3	D c C	0 0 2 5 0 4 9	0 0 2 5 0 4 3	0 6 8
And besides, if tanned, the pound — dressed in oil, the pound tawed, the hide	0 5 3	0 5 3	D c	0 5 3	0 5 3	
All other hides in the hair or undressed, half custom.	0 0 7 7 0 3 13 2 0 0 2	0 0 7 7 0 3 13 2 0 0 3	D c D c D c	0 0 2 10 0 0 2 6 0 0 2	0 0 2 10 0 0 2 6 0 0 2	

N.B. By 21 Geo. III. cap. 29, raw or undressed hides of Steers, Cows, or any other cattle (*except of* Horses, Mares, *or* Geldings) *may be imported from Ireland and the British plantations in America, if regularly entered and landed, duty free, until half custom.*

* But if imported by Aliens Drawback more, 1s. 3d. for every 100l. of the Rate or Value.

INWARDS.

	DUTIES to be paid on IMPORTATION.		Reference to the several Branches, see Page vi.	DRAWBACKS to be repaid on EXPORTATION.*		RATES, or supposed value, by 12 C. II. cap. 4. 11 Geo. I. c. 7. from whence the foregoing Duties are computed.
	By BRITISH.	By ALIENS.		If exported to any legal place, except as mentioned in the following column.	If the produce of Europe or the East Indies, and exported to the British Colonies in America.	
	£. s. d. 20ths	£. s. d. 20ths		£. s. d. 20ths	£. s. d. 20ths	£. s. d.
June 1, 1786, and from thence to the end of the then next *sessions of parliament.*						
Hilts for swords or daggers, the dozen ‖	0 10 6	0 11 0 6	C	0 9 6	0 8 6	2 0 0
Hoans, the hundred, containing five score	0 10 6	0 11 0 6	C	0 9 6	0 8 6	2 0 0
Honey, the barrel	0 8 4 16	0 8 11 2	A	0 7 4 16	0 6 4 16	4 0 0
— the ton	2 10 4 16	2 13 6 12	A	2 4 4 16	1 18 4 16	12 0 0
Hook ends. *Vide* Cap hooks.						
Hooks, *vacat.* Tenter hooks. *Vide* Nails.						
Hoops of iron for pipes or hogsheads, the Cwt.	0 10 10 4	0 11 2 8	B	0 10 2 4	—	1 6 8
Racket hoops. *Vide in* R.						
Hoops for coopers, the thousand	0 5 7 4	0 5 11 8	A	0 4 11 4	0 4 3 4	1 6 8
Hops, the Cwt.	5 13 4 16	5 17 4 1	M a	3 17 10 16	3 10 4 16	15 0 0
Horns of cows or oxen, the hundred, containing five score	0 1 9	0 1 10 1	C	0 1 7	0 1 5	0 6 8
— of harts. *Vide in* Drugs.						
Horn tips, the hundred, containing 5 score	0 0 6	0 0 6 12 10	C	0 0 5 14	0 0 5 2	0 2 0
Horses and Mares, the horse or mare	2 2 0	2 4 7 10	A	1 17 0	1 12 0	10 0 0
But by 16 *Geo.* III. *cap.* 8. *from Ireland,* duty free.						

* But if imported by Aliens Drawback more, 1s. 3d. for every 100l. of the Rate or Value.   ‖ If Iron or Steel no Drawback to the British Colonies in America.

[149]

INWARDS.

	DUTIES to be paid on IMPORTATION.		Reference to the several Branches, see Page vi.	DRAWBACKS to be repaid on EXPORTATION.*		RATES, or supposed value, by 12 Car. II. cap. 4. ‡ 11 Geo. I. cap. 7. from whence the foregoing Duties are computed.
	By BRITISH.	By ALIENS.		If exported to any legal place, except as mentioned in the following column.	If the produce of Europe or the East Indies, and exported to the British Colonies in America.	
	£. s. d. 20ths	£. s. d. 20ths		£. s. d. 20ths	£. s. d. 20ths	£. s. d.
Hose of cruel, *vicat.* Mantua hose, the pair Hungary water. *Vide* Spirits.	0 2 1 4	0 2 15 ½	A	0 1 10 4	0 1 7 4	0 10 0
J.						
JAPANNED and lacquered wares of the manufacture of India or China. *See the Table of* unrated East India goods.						
Jet, the pound	0 0 8 8	0 0 8 18 ½	A	0 0 7 8	0 0 6 8	0 3 4
Jewels. *Vide* Diamonds.						
Jews trumps, the groce, containing 12 dozen ‖	0 2 1 4	0 2 15 ½	A	0 1 10 4	0 1 7 4	0 10 0
And besides, if { Iron, for every Cwt. made of { Brass, for every Groce	0 5 3 6	0 5 3 6	D	0 5 0 0	0 0 4 6	1 10 0
Imperlings, blue or red, the dozen	0 0 6 6	0 0 6 6	E	0 0 6 6	0 0 6 6	
Incle rolls, the dozen pieces, containing 36 yards, the piece	0 6 3 12	0 6 3 12	A	0 5 6 12	0 4 9 12	6 0 0
unwrought, the pound	0 1 1 0	0 1 2 6 18	Aa	0 0 18 0	0 0 15 0	0 2 6

* But if imported by Aliens Drawback more, 1s. 3d. for every 20s. of the Rate or Value.

‖ If Iron no Drawback to the British Colonies in America.

INWARDS.

	DUTIES to be paid on IMPORTATION.		Reference to the several Branches, see Page vi.	DRAWBACKS to be repaid on EXPORTATION.*		RATES, or supposed value, by 12 Car. II. cap. 4. § 11 Geo. I cap. 7. from whence the foregoing Duties are computed.
	By BRITISH.	By ALIENS.		If exported to any legal place, except as mentioned in the following column.	If the produce of Europe or the East Indies, and exported to the British Colonies in America.	
	£. s. d. 20ths	£. s. d. 20ths		£. s. d. 20ths	£. s. d. 20ths	£. s. d.
But by 24 Geo. II. cap. 46. the duties upon unwrought Incle and short Spinnel were repealed, and in lieu thereof, the following duty was imposed:	0 0 3 3	0 0 3 3				0 8 0
Upon all whitened or bleached Linen-yarn, known by the name of unwrought Incle, or short Spinnel, if the manufacture of any part or place not belonging to the crown of Great Britain, the pound weight			W a			
Incle wrought, the dozen pound	1 8 0	1 10 1 4	A a	1 4 0	1 0 0	0 3 4
More, if French	4 4 0	4 4 0	F b	2 4 0	2 4 0	1 8
Indigo of the British plantations, the pound — if not European — of Turkey, of the West Indies, or Rich Indigo, the pound	1 13 7 4	1 15 8 3	A	1 9 7 4	1 5 7 4	0 0 0
—— Duff, the pound						
But Indigo of all sorts is duty free.						
Ink for printers, the Cwt.	0 8 4 16	0 8 11 2	A	0 7 4 16	0 6 4 16	2 0 0
Ink-horns, the grocc, containing 12 dozen	0 12 7 4	0 13 4 13	A	0 11 1 4	0 9 7 4	3 0 0
—— of brass, the dozen	0 3 1 16	0 3 3 13	C	0 2 10 4	0 2 6 12	0 12 0

* But if imported by Alien: Drawback more, 1s. 3d. for every 20s. of the Rate or Value.

[157]

INWARDS.

		DUTIES to be paid on IMPORTATION.		DRAWBACKS to be repaid on EXPORTATION.*		RATES, or supposed value, by 12 Car. II. cap. 4. 11 Geo. I. cap. 7. from whence the foregoing Duties are computed.
		By BRITISH.	By ALIENS.	Reference to the several Branches, see Page vi.	If exported to any legal place, except as mentioned in the following column.	If the produce of Europe or the East Indies, and exported to the British Colonies in America.
		£. s. d. 20ths	£. s. d. 20ths		£. s. d. 20ths	£. s. d. 20ths	£. s. d.
Instruments for barbers and furgeons, *viz.*	Bullet fcrews, the dozen	0 0 10 1 3/5	0 0 10 14 3/5	A	0 0 8 17 3/5		0 4 0
	Incifion fheers, the dozen	0 0 1 12	0 0 1 7	A	0 0 0 11 2		0 5 0
	Paices, or Tooth-drawers, the dozen	0 0 1 12	0 0 1 7	A	0 0 0 11 2		0 5 0
	Plulicanes, the dozen	0 0 1 12	0 0 1 7	A	0 0 0 11 2		0 5 0
	Sets, the bundle, containing 16	0 0 5 0 4/5	0 0 5 5 1/5	A	0 0 4 8		0 5 2
	Trepans, the dozen	0 0 2 1 4	0 0 2 2 15	A	0 0 1 10 4		0 10 0
	And befides, for fuch infruments as are made of { Iron, the Cwt. Steel, the Cwt.			D			
	Amys, Spanifh, Spruce, and Swedifh, the ton	0 5 3	0 5 3	D	0 5 3		0 7 0
Iron, *viz.*	Imported in { Britifh-built fhips, legally navigated, the ton Foreign-built fhips, the ton	0 5 9 6 2 13 6 12	0 5 9 6 2 15 9 13	B B	0 5 9 6 2 10 0 12 2 10 6 12		
	of Ireland, and all other places, unwrought, not otherwife rated, the ton, containing 20 Cwt.	3 4 0 12	3 5 10 13				
	of Ireland	1 9 4 16	1 11 2 17	A	1 5 10 16		0 7 0

* But if imported by Aliens Drawback more, 1s. 3d. for every ton. of the Rate or Value.

[152]

INWARDS.	DUTIES to be paid on IMPORTATION.		Reference to the several Branches, see Page vi.	DRAWBACKS to be repaid on EXPORTATION.*		RATES, or supposed value, by 12 Car. II. cap. 4. ‡ 11 Geo. I. cap. 7. from whence the foregoing Duties are computed.
	By BRITISH.	By ALIENS.		If exported to any legal place, except as mentioned in the following column.	If the produce of Europe or the East Indies, and exported to the British Colonies in America.	
	L. s. d./20ths	*L. s. d.*/20ths		*L. s. d.*/20ths	*L. s. d.*/20ths	*L. s. d.*
Iron, viz. From any other foreign parts, imported in { British-built ships, legally navigated } { Foreign-built ships }	2 13 6 12 3 4 0 12	2 15 4 13 3 5 10 13	B B	2 10 0 12 2 10 6 12		0 13 4 0 6 8 0 2 0
But Bar Iron made in, and imported from, the British colonies in America, according to the regulations directed by 23 Geo. II. cap. 29. is duty free.						
Backs for chimneys, large, the piece — small, the piece —	0 5 3 0 2 7 10 0 13 7 16	0 5 5 2 0 2 8 11 0 14 2 2	B B B	0 4 11 0 2 5 10 0 12 7 16		
Bands for kettles, the Cwt. Caskets. *Vide* in C. Chests. *Vide* in C. Doubles. *Vide* Plates.						0 10 0
Fire irons, the groce, containing 12 dozen And besides, for every Cwt.		½				1 6 8
Hoops, the Cwt. Iron flit or hammered into rods, called Rod Iron, and Iron drawn or hammered less than ¼ of an inch square, the Cwt.	0 2 1 4 0 5 3 0 10 10 4	0 2 2 15 0 5 3 2 0 11 2 8	B D B	0 1 10 4 0 5 3 0 10 2 4		1 0 0 ‡

* But if imported by Aliens Drawback more, 1 s. 3 d. for every 100 l. of the Rate or Value.

[153]

INWARDS.

Iron, viz.

Description	Duties to be paid on Importation — By British (£. s. d.|20ths)	By Aliens (£. s. d.|20ths)	Reference to the several Branches, see Page vi.	Drawbacks to be repaid on Exportation.* — If exported to any legal place, except as mentioned in the following column. (£. s. d.|20ths)	If the produce of Europe or the East Indies, and exported to the British Colonies in America. (£. s. d.|20ths)	Rates, or supposed value, by 12 Car. II. cap. 4. 11 Geo I. cap. 7. from whence the forgoing Duties are computed. (£. s. d.)
⎰ slit or hammered into rods ⎱ of Ireland ⎱ drawn or hammered less than ¼ of an inch square	0 4 2|8	0 4 5|11	A	0 3 8|8	—	‡ 2 0 0
of all other places	0 9 5|8	0 9 8|11	B	0 8 11|8	—	
Iron wares manufactured, not otherwise rated, or not prohibited by law to be imported, the Cwt.	0 9 5|8	0 9 8|11	B	0 8 11|8	—	
Besides ⎰ for Kettles, the piece	0 8 4|16	0 8 11 2	A	0 7 4|16	—	‡ 0 10 0
for other Manufactures, the Cwt.	0 1 3|15	0 1 3|15 ½	D	0 1 3|15	—	‡ 2 10 0
Iron ore, the ton, containing 20 Cwt.	0 5 3	0 5 3 ½	D	0 5 3	—	
Old bushel, broken, and old cast iron, the ton	0 2 7|10	0 2 9	C	0 2 4|10	—	‡ 1 0 0
Iron, called Pig Iron, from the British plantations, the ton, containing 20 Cwt.	0 13 1|10	0 13 9 7	C	0 11 10|10	—	
But Pig Iron made in, and imported from, the British colonies in America, Cwt.	0 5 3	0 5 6 3	C	0 4 9	—	

* But if imported by Aliens Drawback more, 1s. 3d. for every 100l. of the Rate or Value.

INWARDS.

		DUTIES to be paid on IMPORTATION.		DRAWBACKS to be repaid on EXPORTATION.*		RATES, or supposed value, by 12 Car. II. cap. 4. 11 Geo. I. cap. 7. from whence the foregoing Duties are computed.
	Reference to the several Branches, see Page vi.	By BRITISH.	By ALIENS.	If exported to any legal place, except as mentioned in the following column.	If the produce of Europe or the East Indies, and exported to the British Colonies in America.	
		L. s. d. 20ths	*L. s. d.* 20ths	*L. s. d.* 20ths	*L. s. d.* 20ths	*L. s. d.*
Iron, viz. { according to the regulations directed by 23 Geo. II. cap. 29. is duty free.						
Iron pots. *Vide* Pots.						
Iron stoves, the piece		1 1 0	1 2 3·15	0 18 6	— — —	5 0 0
All these, for every Cwt.		0 5 3	0 5 3	0 5 3	— — —	
Note. By the acts of 2 and 3 Ann. cap. 9. and 9 Ann. cap. 6. no drawback is to be allowed upon the exportation of Iron, or of any wares made of wrought Iron in foreign parts, exported to the British colonies or plantations in America.						
Juice of lemons, the pipe	A	1 13 7 4	1 14 7 16	1 11 7 4	1 9 7 4	4 0 0
— limes, the gallon	D	0 0 2 10⅔	0 0 2 11 3·9/10½	0 0 2 3	0 0 2 2⅔	0 6 0
Ivory, the pound	C	0 0 1 4	0 0 2 2·15	0 0 1 10	0 0 1 7	0 10 0
Isle of Man:	C					
Note. As by 5 Geo. III. cap. 43. the importation of Bestials, or any goods, wares, or merchandise, of the growth, produce, and manufacture of the Isle of	A					

* But if imported by Aliens Drawback more, 1s. 3d. for every 100l. of the Rate or Value.

[155]

INWARDS.

Man (except such as are prohibited to be imported by any act of that session of parliament, and also except Woollen manufactures, Beer and Ale) is, from and after the 1st day of July, 1765, admitted directly from the said island, under the certificates and oaths thereby prescribed and required, without paying any customs, subsidies, or duties for or in respect thereof, except such Excise or other duty as shall be due and payable for the like goods, wares, and merchandises of the growth, produce, and manufacture of Great Britain, all Hides tanned, tawed, or dressed in oil, imported from the Isle of Man, will be subject to the same duty as those articles respectively are charged in Great Britain, by the acts of 9 Ann. cap. 11. and 10 Ann. cap. 26. but on failure of the performance of the requisit's prescribed by said law, then the said

Reference to the several Branches, see Page vi.	DUTIES to be paid on IMPORTATION.		DRAWBACKS to be repaid on EXPORTATION.		RATES, or supposed value, by { 12 Car. II. cap. 4. { 11 Geo. I. cap. 7. from whence the foregoing Duties are computed.
	By BRITISH.	By ALIENS.	If exported to any legal place, except as mentioned in the following column.	If the produce of Europe, or the East Indies, and exported to the British Colonies in America.	
	£. s. d. 20ths	£. s. d. 20ths	£. s. d. 20ths	£. s. d. 20ths	£. s. d.

INWARDS.

	DUTIES to be paid on IMPORTATION.		DRAWBACKS to be repaid on EXPORTATION.*		RATES, or supposed value, by 12 Car. II. cap. 4. 11 Geo. I. cap. 7. from whence the foregoing Duties are computed.
Reference to the several Branches, see Page vi.	By BRITISH.	By ALIENS.	If exported to any legal place, except as mentioned in the following column.	If the produce of Europe or the East Indies, and exported to the British Colonies in America.	
	£. s. d. 20ths	£. s. d. 20ths	£. s. d. 20ths	£. s. d. 20ths	£. s. d.

Beastials, goods, wares, *and merchan-dises, are to be subject to the same duties penalties and forfeitures, as if said laws had never been made; and no manufactures of goods in said island, from materials of the growth or product of any foreign nation or country, can be imported from thence, except Linen manufactures made there of Hemp or Flax, not being the produce of said island.*

K.

KELP, the ton, containing 20 Cwt. ——— C | 0 15 9 | 0 16 6 9 | 0 14 3 | 0 12 9 | 1 3 0 0
Kettles. *Vide* Battery.
——— of iron. *Vide* Iron.
Key knops, the groce, containing 12 dozen | A | 0 4 2 8 | 0 4 5 11 | 0 3 8 8 | | 1 0 0

* But if imported by Aliens. Drawback more, 1s. 3d. for every 100l. of the Rate or Value.

K [157] K

INWARDS.

	DUTIES to be paid on IMPORTATION.		Reference to the several Branches, see Page vi.	DRAWBACKS to be repaid on EXPORTATION.*		RATES, or supposed value, by 12 Car. II. cap. 4. 11 Geo. I. cap. 7. from whence the foregoing Duties are computed.
	By BRITISH.	By ALIENS.		If exported to any legal place, except as mentioned in the following column.	If the produce of Europe or the East Indies, and exported to the British Colonies in America.	
	£. s. d. 20ths	£. s. d. 20ths		£. s. d. 20ths	£. s. d. 20ths	£. s. d.
And besides { if made of Iron, the Cwt. — if made of Steel, the Cwt. —	0 5 3 9	0 5 3 9	D	0 5 3 6		0 3 0
Kits of wood. *Vide* Pails.	0 5 9 6	0 5 9 6	D	0 5 9 6		0 3 0
Knees of oak. *Vide* Wood.						
Knives, viz. Almain, Bohemia, and all other coarse knives, the dicker, containing 10 knives —	0 7 11 ½	0 8 6 13/20	A	0 0 0 ⅓		3 0 0
—————— Butchers knives, the dicker, containing 10 knives —	0 7 11 ⅕	0 8 6 13/20	A	0 0 0		3 0 0
—————— Carving knives, the dozen —	0 12 7 4	0 13 4 13	A	0 11 1		8 0 0
—————— Collen knives, the groce, containing 12 dozen —	0 13 7 4	1 15 3 8	A	1 9 7		1 10 0
—————— Glovers knives, the bundle, containing 6 knives —	0 6 3 12	0 6 8 6	A	0 5 6 12		1 10 0
—————— Pen knives, the groce, containing 12 dozen —	0 6 3 12	0 6 8 6	A	0 5 6 12		
—————— Sker knives, the dicker, containing 10 knives —	0 7 11 ⅕	0 8 6 13/20	A	0 6 13 ⅓		0 3 0

* But if imported by Aliens Drawback more, 1s. 3d. for every 100l. of the Rate or Value.

K [158] K

INWARDS.

		DUTIES to be paid on IMPORTATION.					Reference to the several Branches, see Page vi.	DRAWBACKS to be repaid on EXPORTATION.*						RATES, or supposed value, by 12 Car. II. cap. 4. ‡11 Geo.I. cap.7. from whence the foregoing Duties are computed.	
		By BRITISH.			By ALIENS.			If exported to any legal place, except as mentioned in the following column.			If the produce of Europe or the East Indies, and exported to the British Colonies in America.				
		L.	*s.*	*d.*	20ths	*L.*	*s.*	*d.*	20ths		*L.*	*s.*	*d.*	20ths	*L.*	*s.*	*d.*	20ths	*L.*	*s.*	*d.*
Stock knives { gilt, the dozen flocks ungilt, the dozen flocks		1	5	2	8	1	6	9	6	A	1	2	2	8					0	6	0
		0	16	9	12	0	17	10	4	A	0	14	9	12					0	4	0
And besides, for such of the aforesaid knives as are made of { Iron, for every Cwt. Steel, for every Cwt.		0	5	3		0	5	3		D	0	5	3								
		0	5	9	6	0	5	9	6	D	0	5	9	6							
French knives, the grocc, containing 12 dozen		2	18	9	12	2	19	10	4	F	1	16	9	12							

L.

LACE, *vizt.* Bone lace, of thread, the dozen yards		0	16	9	12	0	17	10	4	A	0	14	9	12	0	12	9	12	0	4	0
——— Britain lace, the grocc, containing 12 dozen yards		4	8	2	8	4	9	9	6	F	2	15	2	8	2	12	2	8	0	6	0
——— Bugle lace. *Vide* Bugle.																					

* But if imported by Aliens Drawback more, 1 s. 3 d. for every 100 l. of the Rate or Value,

INWARDS.

	Reference to the several Branches, see Page vi.	DUTIES to be paid on IMPORTATION.		DRAWBACKS to be repaid on EXPORTATION.*		RATES, or supposed value, by 12 Car. II. cap. 4. 11 Geo. I. cap. 7. from whence the foregoing Duties are computed.
		By BRITISH.	By ALIENS.	If exported to any legal place, except as mentioned in the following column.	If the produce of Europe or the East Indies, and exported to the British Colonies in America.	
		£. s. d.20ths	£. s. d.20ths	£. s. d.20ths	£. s. d.20ths	£. s. d.
―― Cruel lace, the small groce, containing 12 dozen	A	1 13 7 4	1 15 8 8	1 9 7 4	1 5 7 4	8 0 0
―― Gold { the pound, containing 12 ounces troy and Silver lace { the ounce troy						12 0 0
						1 0 0
―― Pomet lace, the groce, containing 12 dozen yards	A	0 8 4 16	0 8 11 2	0 7 4 16	0 6 4 16	2 0 0
―― Purle, or Antlet lace of thread, the groce, containing 12 dozen	A	0 4 2 8	0 4 5 11	0 3 8 8	0 3 2 8	1 0 0
―― Bone lace, the pound, containing 16 ounces						
―― Silk { Lace of all other sorts, the pound, containing 16 ounces	B		0 14 2 2			40 0 0
Ladles, vocat. Melting ladles, the Cwt.	A	0 13 7 16		0 12 7 16		10 0 0
Lamp black. *Vide* Blacking.						
Lamps. *Vide* Brass.						
Lapis magnetis fulv., the pound	C	0 0 7 11 ⅓	0 0 8 0 ¼⁰⁄₂₀	0 0 6 13 ⅓	0 0 5 15	2 0 0
Lard, the pound		0 0 0 15	0 0 0 16 4⁰⁄₂₀	0 0 0 14 ¼	0 0 5 12	0 3 0
But by 19 Geo. III. cap. 22. Hogs lard, if regularly imported, entered, and				0 0 0 0	0 0 0 0	+ 0 0

* But if imported by Aliens Drawback more, 1 s. 3 d. for every 100l. of the Rate or Value.

INWARDS.

	DUTIES to be paid on IMPORTATION.		Reference to the several Branches, see Page vi.	DRAWBACKS to be repaid on EXPORTATION.*		RATES, or supposed value, by 12 Car. II. cap. 4. 11 Geo. I. cap. 7. from whence the foregoing Duties are computed.
	By BRITISH.	By ALIENS.		If exported to any legal place, except as mentioned in the following column.	If the produce of Europe or the East Indies, and exported to the British Colonies in America.	
	£. s. d. 20ths	£. s. d. 20ths		£. s. d. 20ths	£. s. d. 20ths	£. s. d.
landed, is duty free, until March 25, 1762.						
Lathwood. *Vide* Wood.						
Latten, *vocat.* Black latten, the Cwt.	0 12 7 4	0 13 1 10	C	0 11 7 4	0 10 7 4	2 0 0
Shaven latten, the Cwt.	1 1 0	1 1 10 10	C	0 19 4	0 17 8	3 6 8
Laver cocks. *Vide* Brass.						
Lead ore, the ton	0 16 9 12	0 17 10 4	A	0 14 9 12	0 12 9 12	4 0 0
Lead, black, red, and white. *Vide in* Drugs.						
Leather, *vocat.* Basil leather, the dozen	5 5 0	5 10 3	C	4 15 0	4 5 0	20 0 0
And besides, if not particularly charged, *for every 20s. of their real value upon oath*	0 6 3 12	0 6 3 12	D c	0 0 0	0 0 0	0 0 0
Turkey and East India Cordivant, the dozen	1 4 16	1 9 11 2	O	1 0 4 16	0 19 4 16	2 0 0
of East India, the dozen	0 18 10 16	0 19 5 2	O	0 9 10 16	0 8 10 16	
of Turkey, the dozen						
See in Skins.						
Hangings gilt, the piece	1 1 0	1 2 0 12	C	0 19 0	0 17 0	4 0 0
And besides, for every 20s. of their real value upon oath	0 6 3 12	0 6 3 12	D c	0 0 3 12	0 0 3 12	
Leather for masks, the pound	0 1 9	0 1 10 1	C	0 1 7	0 1 5	0 6 8

* If imported by Aliens Drawback more, 1s. 3d. for every 100l. of the Rate or Value.

INWARDS.

	DUTIES to be paid on IMPORTATION.		Reference to the several Branches, see Page vi.	DRAWBACKS to be repaid on EXPORTATION.*		RATES, or supposed value, by 12 Car. II. cap. 4. ‡ 11 Geo. I. caf. 7. from whence the foregoing Duties are computed.
	By BRITISH.	By ALIENS.		If exported to any legal place, except as mentioned in the following column.	If the produce of Europe or the East Indies, and exported to the British Colonies in America.	
	£. s. d. 20ths	£. s. d. 20ths		£. s. d. 20ths	£. s. d. 20ths	£. s. d.
And besides, if not particularly charged, for every 20s. of their real value upon oath	0 6 3 12	0 6 3 12	D c	0 0 3 12	0 0 3 12	5 0 0
Spanish leather, or Cordivant, the dozen skins *Vide in Skins*.	1 14 7 16	1 15 11 11	O	1 4 1 16	1 1 7 16	2 0 0
Spruce, or Danske leather, the dozen skins *Vide in Skins*.	0 10 6	0 11 6	C	0 9 6	0 8 6	
And besides, if not particularly charged, for every 20s. of their real value upon oath	0 6 3 12	0 6 3 12	D c	0 0 3 12	0 0 3 12	
All other Leather, and manufactures of Leather, unrated, and whereof the most valuable part is Leather { For every 20s. of the value upon oath / For every 20s. of the real value upon oath }	0 5 3 / 0 6 3 12	0 5 6 / 0 6 3 12	C. / D c	0 4 9 / 0 0 3 12	0 4 3 / 0 0 3 12	
Leaves of gold, the hundred leaves, containing five score	0 1 0 12	0 1 7 3,4	A	0 11 2	0 0 9 12	0 5 0
Lemons pickled, the pipe	0 16 9 12	0 17 10 4	A	0 14 9 12	0 12 9 12	4 0 0

* But if imported by Aliens Drawback more, 1s. 3d. for every 100l. of the Rate or Value.

INWARDS.

INWARDS.	Duties to be paid on Importation. By British. £. s. d. 20ths	Duties to be paid on Importation. By Aliens. £. s. d. 20ths	Reference to the several Branches, see Page vi.	Drawbacks to be repaid on Exportation.* If exported to any legal place, except as mentioned in the following column. £. s. d. 20ths	Drawbacks to be repaid on Exportation.* If the produce of Europe or the East Indies, and exported to the British Colonies in America. £. s. d. 20ths	Rates, or supposed value, by 12 Car. II. cap. 4. † 11 Geo. I. cap. 7. from whence the foregoing Duties are computed. £. s. d.
Lemon water, the ton	2 4 9 12	2 7 7 4	A	1 19 5 12	1 14 1 12	10 13 4
——— the gallon	0 0 2 6 1/5	0 0 2 9 7/10	A	0 0 2 0 7/10	0 0 1 15 1/5	0 0 11
Lemon juice. *Vide* Juice of lemons.						
Lewers for hawks, the piece	0 0 3 7 1/5	0 0 3 11 2/5	A	0 0 2 19 1/5	0 0 2 11 1/3	0 1 4
Lime juice. *Vide* Juice of limes.						
Lime. *See* Lyme.						
Lines of Hamburgh for ships, the piece	0 0 1 5 1/5	0 0 1 6 11/20	A	0 0 1 2 1/5	0 0 0 19 1/3	0 0 6
Linen cloth, or Alexandria or Turkey linen, the ell	0 0 5 18 1/8	0 0 6 2 17/20	Cd	0 0 5 9 1/8	0 0 5 0 1/8	‡ 0 1 6
Linen cloth, or Borelaps (not exceeding 28 1/2 inches in breadth, nor 12*d.* an English ell in value, *as by 7 and 8 W. III. cap.* 10. 1 *Ann. cap.* 8.) the ell	0 0 3 1 1/4	0 0 3 3 7/8	Cc	0 0 2 16 1/4	0 0 2 11 3/4	‡ 0 0 10
Linen cloth, or British, the hundred ells, containing five score	—	—		—	—	6 13 4
Linen cloth, or Callicoes fine, or coarse, the piece	0 4 11 17	0 5 1 8 1/2	Cd	0 4 8 17	0 4 8 17	0 10 0
And besides, for these species called Muslins — *For every 20s. of their gross price at the candle*	0 3 1 16	0 3 1 16	P	0 2 9	0 2 2 8	
or White callicoes — *For every 20s. of their gross price at the candle*	0 3 1 16	0 3 1 16	Q	0 2 9	0 2 2 8	
But if exported to Africa, the drawback is	—	—		0 3 1 16	—	

* But if imported by Aliens Drawback more, 1s. 3d. for every 100l. of the Rate or Value.

[163]

Linen cloth, or

INWARDS.

	Reference to the several Branches, see Page vi.	DUTIES to be paid on IMPORTATION.		DRAWBACKS to be repaid on EXPORTATION.		RATES, or supposed value, by 12 Car. II. cap. 4. 11 Geo. I. cap. 7. from whence the foregoing Duties are computed.
		By BRITISH.	By ALIENS.	If exported to any legal place, except as mentioned in the following column.	If the produce of Europe or the East Indies, and exported to the British Colonies in America.	
		£. s. d. 20ths	£. s. d. 20ths	£. s. d. 20ths	£. s. d. 20ths	£. s. d.
But if printed, stained, painted, or dyed in this kingdom, this draw-back is allowed —— But if printed, dyed, painted, or stained in Persia, China, or East India, the like piece —— And besides, for every 20 s. of the true and real value of such printed, dyed, painted, or stained Callicoes, according to the gross price at which the same shall be sold at the public and legal sales thereof: If at the sales of the United Company of merchants of England trading to the East Indies. See the Table of Unrated East-India goods.	M	0 0 3	0 0 3	0 3 16	0 2 8	0 0 0 0 0 0 1 0
If at any other public legal sales in this kingdom —— Cambrick, the half piece, containing 6½ ells —— the piece, containing 13 ells	Pc	0 1 0	0 1 0			2 0

[164]

INWARDS.

Linen cloth, or

	DUTIES to be paid on IMPORTATION.				Reference to the several Branches, see Page vi.	DRAWBACKS to be repaid on EXPORTATION.*				RATES, or supposed value, by 12 Car. II. cap. 4. 11 Geo. I. cap. 7. from whence Duties are computed.
	By BRITISH.		By ALIENS.			If exported to any legal place, except as mentioned in the following column.		If the produce of Europe or the East Indies, and exported to the British Colonies in America.		
	£. s. d. 20ths		£. s. d. 20ths			£. s. d. 20ths		£. s. d. 20ths		£. s. d.
Cambricks may be imported for exportation only, and under the regulations directed by 32 Geo. II. cap. 32. and 7 Geo. III. cap. 43. on payment of the following duty:										
—— the half piece, containing 6½ ells	0 0 6		0 0 6		M					
—— the piece, containing 13 ells	0 1 0		0 1 0		M					
Canvas, vocat. Dutch barrass, and Hessens canvas, the hundred ells, containing six score	1 5 9	4	1 6 8	5	Cf	1 4 0	4	1 2 3	4	3 10 0
—— French canvas, and Line broad, for tabling, being 1 ⅛ ell, and upwards, the hundred ells, containing six score	13 5 1	10	13 9 0	15	Fn	9 2 7	10	8 15 1	10	15 0 0
—— French or Normandy canvas, and Line narrow, brown, or white, the hundred ells, containing six score	4 13 5	8	4 15 0	6	Fh	3 0 5	8	2 17 5	8	6 0 0
—— if above yard wide	1 11 6		1 11 6		Gd	1 - 11		1 11 6		

* But if imported by Aliens Drawback more, 1s. 3d. for every 100l. of the Rate or Value.

[165]

INWARDS.

	DUTIES to be paid on IMPORTATION.		Reference to the several Branches, See Page vi.	DRAWBACKS to be repaid on EXPORTATION.*		RATES, or supposed value, by 12 Car. II. cap. 4. 11 Geo. I. cap. 7. from whence the foregoing Duties are computed.
	By BRITISH.	By ALIENS.		If exported to any legal place, except as mentioned in the following column.	If the produce of Europe or the East Indies, and exported to the British Colonies in America.	
	£. s. d. 20ths	£. s. d. 20ths		£. s. d. 20ths	£. s. d. 20ths	£. s. d.
Linen cloth, or — Heffens canvas. *Vide* Dutch briefs.						
Packing canvas, Guttings, and Spruce canvas, the hundred ells, containing six score —	0 17 3 7	0 17 11 5	Cf	0 16 0 7	0 14 9 7	2 10 0
Poldavies, the bolt, containing 28 ells — *Note.* Poldavies, or Powle Davies, is, by 1 *Jac.* I. cap. 24. deemed to be Sail-cloth.	0 8 3 15	0 8 6 18	R	0 4 1 5½	0 4 3 2	1 0 0
Spruce, Elbing, or Queensborough canvas, the bolt, containing 28 ells	0 5 0 2	0 5 2 9	Cf	0 4 7 12		0 15 0
Striped canvas with copper, the piece, containing 15 yards	1 3 5 8	1 4 6	Cb	1 1 5 8	0 19 5 8	4 0 0
Striped or Tufted canvas, with thread, the piece, containing 15 yards	0 11 8 14	0 12 3	Cb	0 10 8 14	0 9 8 14	2 0 0
Striped, Tufted, or Quilted canvas, with silk, the piece, containing 15 yards						4 0 0

* But if imported by Aliens Drawback more, 1 s. 3 d. for every 20 s. of the Rate or Value.

[166]

INWARDS.		Reference to the several Branches, see Page vi.	Duties to be paid on IMPORTATION.		Drawbacks to be repaid on EXPORTATION.*		RATES, or supposed value, by 12 Car. II. cap. 4. ‡ 11 Gen. I. cap. 7. from whence the foregoing Duties are computed.
			By BRITISH.	By ALIENS.	If exported to any legal place, except as mentioned in the following column.	If the produce of Europe or the East Indies, and exported to the British Colonies in America.	
			£. s. d. 20ths	£. s. d. 20ths	£. s. d. 20ths	£. s. d. 20ths	£. s. d.
Linen cloth, or	Canvas, vizat. Vandolose or Vitery canvas, the hundred ells, containing six score	R c	4 8 4 10	4 9 8 5	0 16 1 1	0 14 7 1	5 0 0
	Working canvas { for cushions, narrow, the hundred ells, containing six score	C b	0 17 7 1	0 18 4 10	1 6 9 15	1 4 3 15	3 0 0
	{ broad, the hundred ells, containing six score	C b	1 9 3 15	1 10 7 10	1 12 2 2	1 9 2 2	5 0 0
	{ of the broadest fort, the hundred ells, containing six score	C b	1 15 2 2	1 16 9	0 0 5 7¼	0 0 4 17	6 0 0
	Cowsfield cloth or plats, the ell	C b	0 0 5 17¼	0 0 6 2	0 0 4 6⅛	0 0 4 0 18	0 1 8
	Damask Tabling of Holland making, the yard	C a	0 5 0 18	0 0 4 1			
	{ above 1½ ell English in breadth, and under 2 ells, the yard	D	0 0 9 9	0 0 9 9	0 0 9 9	0 0 9 9	1 0 0
	And besides, if { of the breadth of 2 ells, or upwards, and under 3 ells, the yard	D	0 1 6 18	0 1 6 18	0 1 6 18	0 1 6 18	

* But if imported by Aliens Drawback more, 1s. 3d. for every 100l. of the Rate or Value.

INWARDS.

		DUTIES to be paid on IMPORTATION.				Reference to the several Branches, see Page vi.	DRAWBACKS to be repaid on EXPORTATION.*				RATES, or supposed value, by 12 Car. II. cap. 4. ‡ 11 Geo. I. cap. 7. from whence the foregoing Duties are computed.
		By BRITISH.		By ALIENS.			If exported to any legal place, except as mentioned in the following column.		If the produce of Europe or the East Indies, and exported to the British Colonies in America.		
		£. s. d. 20ths		£. s. d. 20ths			£. s. d. 20ths		£. s. d. 20ths		£. s. d.
Linen cloth, of,	And besides, if of the breadth of 3 ells, or upwards, the yard ——— Tabling of Silesia making, the yard	0 4 8 14		0 4 8 14		D	0 4 8 14		0 4 8 14		0 4 0
	Tabling of all other places, except Ireland and Russia. *Vide after* Diaper.	0 1 2 1 2/3		0 1 2 14		Cb	0 1 0 17 4/5		0 0 11 13 4/3		
	Towelling and Napkining ——— { of Silesia making, the yard	0 0 4 13 4/5		0 0 4 18		Cb	0 0 4 5		0 0 3 17 7/5		
	{ of Holland making, the yard	0 1 9 6 1/10		0 1 10 8 7/20		Ca	0 1 7 4 4/10		0 1 5 2 3/10		0 7 0
	{ of the manufacture of Russia, not exceeding half an ell in breadth of all other places, except Ireland and Russia. *Vide after* Diaper.	0 0 1 3 2/20		0 0 1 4 1/2		Cb	0 0 1 1 9/20		0 0 0 19 9/20		† 0 0 4
	Diaper of Russia. *See* Linen of Russia *hereafter following.*										

* But if imported by Aliens Drawback more, 1s. 3d. for every 100l. of the Rate or Value.

INWARDS.

Linen cloth, or

	DUTIES to be paid on IMPORTATION.		DUTIES to be paid on IMPORTATION.		Reference to the several Branches, see Page vi.	DRAWBACKS to be repaid on EXPORTATION.		DRAWBACKS to be repaid on EXPORTATION.		RATES, or supposed value, by 12 Car.II. cap.4. 11 Geo.I. cap.7. from whence the foregoing Duties are computed.
	By BRITISH.		By ALIENS.			If exported to any legal place, except as mentioned in the following column.		If the produce of Europe or the East Indies, and exported to the British Colonies in America.		
	£. s. d./20ths		£. s. d./20ths			£. s. d./20ths		£. s. d./20ths		£. s. d.
Diaper Napkining of Holland making, the dozen	0	9 1 12 4/5	0	9 7 5 4/5	Ca	0	8 2 16 2/5	0	7 4 0 2/5	1 16 0
Tabling of Holland making, the yard	0	2 3 8 1/10	0	2 4 16 9/20	Ca	0	2 0 14 1/10	0	1 10 0 1/10	0 9 0
And besides, if { above 1¼ ell English in breadth, and under 2 ells, the yard	0	0 4 5 1/20	0	0 4 5 1/10	D	0	0 4 5 1/20	0	0 4 0 3/20	
of the breadth of 2 ells, or upwards, and under 3 ells, the yard	0	0 8 10 1/10	0	0 8 10 1/10	D	0	0 8 10 1/10	0	0 8 10,5	
of the breadth of 3 ells or upwards, the yard	0	2 1 10 1/10	0	2 1 10 1/10	D	0	2 1 10 1/10	0	2 1 10,5	
Tabling of Silesia making, the yard	0	0 11 14 1/2	0	0 9 12 1/20	Cb	0	0 10 14 1/2	0	0 9 14 1/2	0 3 4
Towelling and Napkining { of Holland making, the yard of Silesia making, the yard of the manufacture of Russia, not exceeding half an ell English in breadth, the yard	0 0 0	0 2 7 4/5 0 4 13 4/5 0 1 3 9/20	0 0 0	0 9 12 1/20 0 4 18 0 1 4 1/2	Ca Cb Cb	0 0 , 0	0 8 4 7 4/5 0 4 5 0 1 1 2/20	0 0 0	0 7 6 4/5 0 3 17 5 0 0 19 2/20	0 3 4 0 1 4 0 0 4

● But if imported by Aliens Drawback more, 1s. 3d. for every 100l. of the Rate or Value.

INWARDS

Linen cloth, or

	Duties to be paid on IMPORTATION.		Reference to the several Branches, see Page vi.	Drawbacks to be repaid on EXPORTATION.		RATES, or supposed value, by 12 Car. II. cap. 4. ‡ 11 Geo. I. cap. 7. from whence the foregoing Duties are computed.
	By BRITISH.	By ALIENS.		If exported to any legal place, except as mentioned in the following column.	If the produce of Europe, or the East Indies, and exported to the British Colonies in America.	
	£ s. d.¦20ths	£ s. d.¦20ths		£ s. d.¦20ths	£ s. d.¦20ths	£ s. d.
By the Additional Book of Rates of 11 Geo. I. cap. 7. it is declared, That Diaper, or Damask tabling or napkining, and towelling of any place (except Ireland and Russia) not otherwise rated, to be rated at the several rates of Damask or Diaper, of Silesia making, in the Book of Rates.						
From Ireland, being free by proper certificate and oath; and from Russia. See the Rates under Linen of Russia hereafter following.						
Dowlas. Vide Lockrams.						
Drilling and Packduck, the hundred ells, containing six score	2 3 2¼	2 3 9	Ge	2 2 2¼	2 1 2¼	2 0 0
Elbing or Dansk cloth, double ploy, the ell	0 0 5 17¼	0 0 6 2½	Cb	0 0 5 7¼	0 0 4 17¼	0 1 8

* But if imported by Aliens Drawback more, 1 s. 3 d. for every 100 l. of the Rate or Value.

[170]

INWARDS.

Linen cloth, or

		DUTIES to be paid on IMPORTATION.		Reference to the several Branches, fee Page vi.	DRAWBACKS to be repaid on EXPORTATION.*		RATES, or supposed value, by 12 Car. II. cap. 4. 11 Geo. I. cap. 7. from whence the foregoing Duties are computed.
		By BRITISH.	By ALIENS.		If exported to any legal place, except as mentioned in the following column.	If the produce of Europe or the East Indies, and exported to the British Colonies in America.	
		£. s. d. 20ths	£. s. d. 20ths		£. s. d. 20ths	£. s. d. 20ths	£. s. d.
Flanders Holland cloth	Flemish cloth ⎫ Gentish cloth ⎪ Ifingham cloth ⎬ the ell Overissel cloth ⎪ Roufe cloth ⎭	0 1 3 4 ½	0 1 4 0 ¾	Ca	0 1 1 14 ½	0 1 0 4 ½	0 5 0
	Brabant cloth ⎫ Emblen cloth ⎬ Freeze cloth ⎪ Bag Holland ⎭ Brown Holland	0 0 2 7 ½	0 0 2 7 ¼	D	0 0 2 7 ½	0 0 2 7 ½	
	above 1 ⅛ ell English in breadth, and under 2 ells, the ell	0 0 4 14 ½	0 0 4 14 ½	D	0 0 4 14 ½	0 0 4 14 ½	
And besides, if	of the breadth of 2 ells or upwards, and under 3 ells, the ell	0 1 2 3 ½	0 1 2 3 ½	D	0 1 2 3 ½	0 1 2 3 ½	
	of the breadth of 3 ells or upwards, the ell						
	Hamburgh and Silesia cloth, broad, white or brown the hundred ells, containing 120,	2 18 7 10	3 1 3	Cb	2 13 7 10	2 8 7 10	10 0 0

* But if imported by Aliens Drawback more, 1s. 3d. for every 100l. of the Rate or Value.

[171]

Linen cloth, or

INWARDS.	DUTIES to be paid on IMPORTATION.		Reference to the several Branches, see Page vi.	DRAWBACKS to be repaid on EXPORTATION.*		RATES, or supposed value, by 12 Car. II. cap. 4. & 11 Geo. I. cap. 7. from whence the foregoing Duties are computed.
	By BRITISH.	By ALIENS.		If exported to any legal place, except as mentioned in the following column.	If the produce of Europe or the East Indies, and exported to the British Colonies in America.	
	£. s. d. 20ths	£. s. d. 20ths		£. s. d. 20ths	£. s. d. 20ths	£. s. d.
more, if above yard wide	1 11 6	1 11 6	G d	1 11 6	1 11 6	
Hamburgh cloth, narrow, the hundred ells, containing six score	2 6 10 16	2 9 0	C b	2 2 10 16	1 18 10 16	8 0 0
more, if above yard wide	1 11 6	1 11 6	G d	1 11 6	1 11 6	
Hinderlands, Middlegood, Headlake, and Muscovia linen, narrow, (viz. under 22½ inches) the hundred ells, containing six score, if brown	0 15 7 12	0 16 4	C b	0 14 3 12	0 12 11 12	2 13 4
if Whited, from Prussia, Polonia, or any part of the East country (except Russia) under the breadth of ⅞ of a yard, are to pay as narrow East Country Linen, 4 and 5 W. & M. cap. 5. which is rated at 4 l. the hundred ells, as hereafter following.						
Irish cloth, the hundred ells, containing six score	0 11 8 14	0 12 3	C b	0 10 8 14	0 9 8 14	
And more, if above one yard English in width	1 11 6	1 11 6	G d	1 11 6	1 11 6	2 0 0
But by 7 and 8 W. III. cap. 39. and 16 Geo. II. cap. 26. all Linens of						

* But if imported by Aliens Drawback more, 1s. 3d. for every 100 l. of the Rate or Value,

[172]

INWARDS.

	DUTIES to be paid on IMPORTATION.		Reference to the several Branches, see Page vi.	DRAWBACKS to be repaid on EXPORTATION.*		RATES, or supposed value, by 12 Car. II. cap. 4. 11 Geo. I. cap. 7. from whence the foreign Duties are computed.
	By BRITISH.	By ALIENS.		If exported to any legal place, except as mentioned in the following column.	If the produce of Europe or the East Indies, and exported to the British Colonies in America.	
	£. s. d. 20ths	£. s. d. 20ths		£. s. d. 20ths	£. s. d. 20ths	£. s. d.
Linen cloth, or the manufacture of Ireland may be imported by British or Irish directly into Great-Britain, free of all duties, under the certificates and oaths therein directed, except those in consideration of their being chequered, striped, printed, painted, stained, or dyed, and except such Canvas or Sail-cloth of the manufacture of Ireland, on which the bounties have been allowed on exportation from thence; and also except Cambricks and Lawns.						3 0 0
Lawns, the half piece, containing 6½ ells						6 0 0
——— the piece, containing 13 ells						1 6 8
——— vocat. Callico lawns, the piece.						
See Silesia Lawns.						
——— vocat. French lawns, the piece						1 10 0
See Cambricks.						

* But if imported by Aliens Drawback more, 1 s. 3 d. for every 100 l. of the Rate or Value.

INWARDS.

		DUTIES to be paid on IMPORTATION.		DRAWBACKS to be repaid on EXPORTATION.*		RATES, or supposed value, by 12 Car.II. cap.4. ‡11Geo.I.cap.7. from whence the foregoing Duties are computed.
	Reference to the several Branches, see Page vi.	By BRITISH.	By ALIENS.	If exported to any legal place, except as mentioned in the following column.	If the produce of Europe or the East Indies, and exported to the British Colonies in America.	
		£. s. d. 20ths	£. s. d. 20ths	£. s. d. 20ths	£. s. d. 20ths	£. s. d.
Linen cloth, or { *vocat.* Silesia lawns, the piece, between 4 and 8 yards ——— By 7 Geo.III. cap. 58. it is enacted and declared, That from and after the first day of August, 1767, all foreign Lawns imported into Great-Britain, are to be rated and entered as Silesia Lawns, and pay duty accordingly. *And,* By the said act is imposed a duty upon every yard of foreign Lawn bleached in Holland, commonly called Holland Whited Lawn, imported, of ——— Lockrams, *vocat.* Dowlas, broad, the piece, containing 106 ells ——— Treger, greit, and narrow, or common dowlas, the piece, containing 106 ells ——— French Not French }	Cb	0 2 11 3	0 3 0 15	0 2 8 3½	0 2 5 3	0 10 0
		0 0 1 1	0 0 1 1	0 0 1 1	0 0 1 1	
	Qc					
		0 0 1 1	0 0 1 1	0 0 1 1	0 0 1 1	
	Fh Cb	3 17 10 10 1 9 3 15	3 19 2 5 1 10 7 10	2 10 4 10 1 6 9 15	2 7 10 10 1 4 3 15	5 0 0

* But if imported by Aliens Drawback more, 1s. 3d. for every 100l. of the Rate or Value.

INWARDS.

Linen cloth, or

Description	Duties to be paid on Importation — By British £ s. d. 20ths	By Aliens £ s. d. 20ths	Reference to the several Branches, see Page vi.	Drawbacks to be repaid on Exportation.* — If exported to any legal place, except as mentioned in the following column £ s. d. 20ths	If the produce of Europe or the East Indies, and exported to the British Colonies in America £ s. d. 20ths	RATES, or supposed value, by 12 Car. II. cap. 4. 11 Geo. I. cap. 7. from whence the foregoing Duties are computed £ s. d.
Minsters, the roll, containing 1500 ells, at five score to the hundred — Napkins, French making. Vide in Neckcloths	16 12 2 10	17 7 1	Cb	15 3 10 10	13 15 6 10	56 13 4
of Silesia, or any other country (except India) the dozen	0 2 7 13 2/5	0 2 9 1 1/4		0 2 4 19 13	0 2 2 5 1/20	+0 9 0
of Silesia, or any other country, other than the Spanish Netherlands, or the United Provinces, the dozen	0 2 9 1 1/4	0 2 10 9 17/20	Cb	0 2 6 7 1/2	0 2 3 13 1/2	
of the manufacture of the Spanish Netherlands, or United Provinces, the dozen		0 0 3 16 13/20	Cc	0 0 3 7	0 0 3 1 1/2	
Oil cloth, the ell		0 0 3 13 1/2	Cc	0 0 3 4 7/20	0 0 2 18 7/20	+0 1 0
of the manufacture of the Spanish Netherlands, or of the United Provinces, the ell	0 0 3 10 7/16	0 0 3 6	Cb	0 0 3 9	0 0 2 18	
of any other country (except India and France) the ell						
Ozenbrigs, the roll, containing 1500 ells, at five score to the hundred — Packduck. Vide Drilling.	17 11 9	18 7	Cb	16 1 9	14 11 9	60 0 0

* But if imported by Aliens Drawback more, 1s. 3d. for every 100l. of the Rate or Value.

[175]

INWARDS. — Linen cloth, or

Polonia, Ulsters, Hanovers, Lubeck, narrow Silesia, narrow Westphalia, narrow Hartford, plain Napkining, and all other narrow cloth of High Dutchland and the East Country, white or brown, and not otherwise rated, the hundred ells, containing six score ————
Note. All Linen of Germany or High Dutchland, and Silesia, not above three quarters and a half broad, shall be accounted narrow Linen; and all above that breadth shall be accounted broad, and pay accordingly.
Note. All Linen of *Prussia, Polonia,* or any part of the East country (except *Russia*) above the bread[th] of 7/8 of a yard, is to pay as broad German Linen. 4 and 5 W. & M. cap. 5.

	Duties to be paid on Importation.		Reference to the several Branches, see Page vi.	Drawbacks to be repaid on Exportation.*		Rates, or supposed value, by 12 Car. II. cap. 4. ‡ 11 Geo I. cap. 7. from whence the foregoing Duties are computed.
	By British.	By Aliens.		If exported to any legal place, except as mentioned in the following column.	If the produce of Europe or the East Indies, and exported to the British Colonies in America.	
	£. s. d. 20ths	£. s. d. 20ths		£. s. d. 20ths	£. s. d. 20ths	£. s. d.
	1 3 5 9	1 4 6	Cb	1 1 5 8	0 19 5 8	4 0 0

* But if imported by Aliens Drawback more, 1s. 3d. for every 100l. of the Rate or Value.

INWARDS.		DUTIES to be paid on IMPORTATION.		Reference to the several Branches, see Page vi.	DRAWBACKS to be repaid on EXPORTATION.*		RATES, or supposed value, by 12 Car. II. cap. 4. 11 Geo. I. cap. 7. from whence the foregoing Duties are computed.
		By BRITISH.	By ALIENS.		If exported to any legal place, except as mentioned in the following column.	If the produce of Europe or the East Indies, and exported to the British Colonies in America.	
		£. s. d. 20ths	£. s. d. 20ths		£. s. d. 20ths	£. s. d. 20ths	£. s. d.
Linen cloth, or {	By the act of 6 Geo. III. cap. 13. the following Russia Linen was rated at four pounds the 120 English ells, which before paid duty ad valorem. Linen cloth and Diaper of Russia, not otherwise rated, exceeding 22½ inches, and not exceeding 31¼ inches in breadth, for every 120 English ells	1 3 5 8	1 4 6	Cb	1 1 5 8	0 19 5 8	
	By the act of 5 Geo. III. cap. 43. the following sorts were also rated, which before paid duty ad valorem. Linen cloth and Diaper of Russia, not otherwise rated, exceeding 31¼ inches in breadth, and not exceeding 45 inches in breadth, for every 120 English ells 6l. 0s. 0d. ────── exceeding 45 inches in breadth, for every 120 English ells 10l. 0s. 0d. And in that proportion for any greater						

* If imported by Aliens Drawback more, 1s. 3d. for every 100l. of the Rate or Value.

L [177] L

INWARDS.

Linen cloth, or lesser quantity of any of the said goods on which said last two rates, the duties will stand as follow:	DUTIES to be paid on IMPORTATION.		Reference to the several Branches, See Page vi.	DRAWBACKS to be repaid on EXPORTATION.*		RATES, or supposed value, by 12 Car.II.cap.4. ‡11Geo.I cap.7. from whence the foregoing Duties are computed.
	By BRITISH.	By ALIENS.		If exported to any legal place, except as mentioned in the following column.	If the produce of Europe or the East Indies, and exported to the British Colonies in America.	
	£. s. d. 20ths	£. s. d. 20ths		£. s. d. 20ths	£. s. d. 20ths	£. s. d.
exceeding 31½ inches, and not exceeding 45 inches in breadth, but under 36, or 1 yard English, the 120 English ells	1 15 2 2	1 16 9	C b	1 12 2 2	1 9 2 2	0 0
exceeding 31¼ inches, and not exceeding 45 inches in breadth, but above 36, or 1 yard English, the 120 English ells	3 6 8 2	3 8 3	G e	3 3 8 2	3 0 8 2	
exceeding 45 inches in breadth, the 120 English ells	4 10 1 10	4 12 9	G e	4 5 1 10	4 0 1 10	
Sack-cloth, Sail-cloth, commonly called Sail-duck, or Holland-duck, from all places (except from India) the hundred, containing 120 ells						1 5 0 0
of Holland { if of or under 1 yard English in width	2 1 11 10	2 2 5 5	R g			

* But if imported by Aliens Drawback more, 1s. 3d. for every 100l. of the Rate or Value.

A 2

[178]

INWARDS.

Linen cloth, or

	DUTIES to be paid on IMPORTATION.		Reference to the several Branches, see Page vi.	DRAWBACKS to be repaid on EXPORTATION.*		RATES, or supposed value, by 12 Car. II. cap. 4. 11 Geo. I. cap. 7. from whence the foregoing Duties are computed.
	By BRITISH.	By ALIENS.		If exported to any legal place, except as mentioned in the following column.	If the produce of Europe or the East Indies, and exported to the British Colonies in America.	
	£. s. d. 20ths	£. s. d. 20ths		£. s. d. 20ths	£. s. d. 20ths	£. s. d.
Sail-cloth of Holland { if above 1 yard English in width, and yet under the 1 s ell English in breadth	3 12 7 10	3 13 11 5	R h			
———— of France. See Vandolose or Vitry canvas.						
———— of all other places (except India, the hundred, containing 120 ells	1 19 9 15	2 1 1 10	R			
Foreign-made Sails, for every 20s. of their true and real value upon oath	1 11 11 6	1 11 1 6	G d			
———— if French	0 6 9 18	0 7 1 1	F w			
And besides, if imported by way of merchandise, for every ill ———— if used in, or being on board any ship or vessel belonging to any of his Majesty's subjects, except such as come from the East-Indies, for every ill	0 16 3 6 0 0	0 16 6 9 0 0	W b V			
	0 1 1	0 1 1	V			

*But if imported by Aliens Drawback more, 1s. 3d. for every 100l. of the Rate or Value.

INWARDS.

Linen cloth, or	Duties to be paid on Importation — By British	Duties to be paid on Importation — By Aliens	Reference to the several Branches, see Page vi.	Drawbacks to be repaid on Exportation — If exported to any legal place, except as mentioned in the following column	Drawbacks to be repaid on Exportation — If the produce of Europe or the East Indies, and exported to the British Colonies in America	RATES, or supposed value, by 12 Car. II. cap. 4. / 11 Geo. I. cap. 7. from whence the foregoing Duties are computed
	£ s. d. 20ths	£ s. d. 20ths		£ s. d. 20ths	£ s. d. 20ths	£ s. d.
Sail-cloth, or Canvas, of the manufacture of Ireland, on which the several bounties of 4d. and 2d. a yard respectively have been there granted, of the value of 14d. a yard and upwards, for each yard	0 0 4	0 0 4	V			0 1 6
— of the value of 10d. a yard, and under 14d. a yard, for each yard						0 0 0
Sheets old, the piece	0 0 2	0 0 2	V			4 0 0
Soultwich, the hundred ells, containing six score	1 3 5 / 5 10¼	1 4 6 / 5 14 32/20	C c	0 1 1 8/20 / 5 1 8	0 19 0 / 4 12 7/20	0 1 4
Spanish or Portugal linen, the ell	0 0 5 8 / 5 8 4/20	0 0 4 18 / 4 18 ½	C b	0 0 4 5/20	0 0 5 / 3 17 3/20	0 3 0
Strafburgh or Hamburgh linen, the ell	0 0 4 13 4/20 / 4 13	0 0 4 18 / 4 18	C b	0 0 9 13/20	0 0 8 15/20	0 1 0
Tiillets, the ell	0 0 10 11 / 0 11	0 0 11 0 / 0 11	C b			
Spanish Netherlands, or of the manufacture of the United Provinces, the ell	0 0 6 2 ½	0 0 6 7	C c	0 0 5 12 / 5 12 ½	0 0 5 / 2 7/10	0 1 4
Turkey linen. Vide Alexandria linen — of any other country, the ell	0 0 5 7 ¼	0 0 6 2	C b	0 0 5 7 / 5 7 ⅓	0 0 0 / 4 17	0 0 8

* But if imported by Aliens Drawback more, 1s. 3d. for every 100l. of the Rate or Value.

INWARDS.	DUTIES to be paid on IMPORTATION.		Reference to the several Branches, see Page vi.	DRAWBACKS to be repaid on EXPORTATION.*		RATES, or imposed value, by 12 Car. II. cap. 4. § 11 Geo... cap. 7. from whence the foregoing Duties are computed.
	By BRITISH.	By ALIENS.		If exported to any legal place, except as mentioned in the following column.	If the produce of Europe or the East Indies, and exported to the British Colonies in America.	
	£. s. d. 20ths	£. s. d. 20ths		£. s. d. 20ths	£. s. d. 20ths	£. s. d.
Twill and Ticking of Scotland, the hundred ells, containing six score, free.						
All other Linens, for of France of another part of Europe, if not European	0 15 6 18	0 15 10 1	F h	0 10 0 18	0 9 6 18	
every 20 s. of their value upon oath,	0 5 10 7	0 6 1 10	C b	0 5 4 7	0 4 10 7	
And besides, for all such as is above 1 yard English in width, the ell—	0 6 6 15	0 6 9 18	C d	0 6 0 15	0 5 6 15	
And besides the aforesaid duties, all Linens chequered and striped, and all Linens printed, painted, stained, or dec ast er the manufacture, or in the thread or yarn before the manufacture, in foreign parts, and which may be lawfully used or worn in Great-Britain, are to pay for every 20 s. of their real value upon oath	0 0 3 3	0 0 3 3	G d	0 0 3 3	0 0 3 3	
Except all Lawns, and striped or chequered Linens, being all white, and Neckcloths striped at the end only; and also Barras or Packing Canvas, and Buckrams.	0 6 3 12	0 6 3 12	E a	0 6 3 12	0 6 3 12	

* But if imported by Aliens Drawback more, 1 s. 3 d. for every 20 s. of the Rate or Value.

INWARDS.

	DUTIES to be paid on IMPORTATION.		Reference to the several Branches, see Page vi.	DRAWBACKS to be repaid on EXPORTATION.*		RATES, or supposed value by 12 Car.II. cap.4. ‡11 Geo.I.cap.7. from whence the foregoing Duties are computed.
	By BRITISH.	By ALIENS.		If exported to any legal place, except as mentioned in the following column.	If the produce of Europe or the East Indies, and exported to the British Colonies in America.	
	£. s. d. 20ths	£. s. d. 20ths		£. s. d. 20ths	£. s. d. 20ths	£. s. d.
Linns, blue or red, the dozen	0 6 3 12	0 6 8 6 ½	A	0 5 6 12	0 4 9 12	1 10 0
Linseed, the bushel, *free*						0 5 0
Liquorice. *Vide in Grocery.*						
juice. *Vide in Drugs.*						
Litharge of gold and silver. *Vide in Dyers use,* as by 3 and 4 Ann. cap. 4. for every 20s. of their value upon oath	0 3 1 16	0 3 4 19	B d	0 2 7 16	0 2 1 16	1 0 0
Litmus, the Cwt. for Dyers use, *as by 3 and 4 Ann. cap. 4.*	0 3 1 16	0 3 4 19	B d	0 2 7 16	0 2 1 16	
But by 8 Geo. I. cap. 15. if regularly imported, entered, and landed, duty free. But on failure thereof, then to pay	0 3 6	0 3 8 2	C	0 3 2	0 2 10	0 13 4
Lockets or Chapes for daggers, the groce, containing 12 dozen	0 6 3 12	0 6 8 6 ½	A	0 5 6 12		1 10 0
Locks, *vocat.* Budget or Hanging locks, small, the groce, containing 12 dozen	0 12 7 4	0 13 4 13	A	0 11 1 4		3 0 0
Hanging locks, large, the groce, containing 12 dozen	0 5 3	0 5 3	D	0 5 3		
And besides, for every Cwt. of Iron						

* But if imported by Aliens Drawback more, 1s. 3d. for every 1 col. of the Rate or Value.

[182]

INWARDS.

	DUTIES to be paid on IMPORTATION.		Reference to the several Branches, see Page vi.	DRAWBACKS to be repaid on EXPORTATION.*		RATES, or supposed value, by 12 Car. II. cap. 4. ‡11 Geo. I. cap. 7. from whence the foregoing Duties are computed.
	By BRITISH.	By ALIENS.		If exported to any legal place, except as mentioned in the following column.	If the produce of Europe or the East Indies, and exported to the British Colonies in America.	
	£. s. d. 20ths	£. s. d. 20ths		£. s. d. 20ths	£. s. d. 20ths	£. s. d.
Logwood, by 13 and 14 Car. II. cap. 11. for Dyers use, *was rated* 5 0 0 to pay the ten.	10 10 0	11 16 3	Bb	9 10 0	5 10 0	8 0 0
And on exportation, to draw back —— 4 0 0						
But by 8 Geo. I. cap. 15. if regularly imported, entered and landed, duty free.						
And on failure thereof, then to pay						
But by 11 Geo. III. cap. 41. any sort of unmanufactured Wood may be imported directly from any part of America, being the growth and product thereof, in British vessels (navigated according to law)						
by any persons, duty free, Masts, Yards, and Bowsprits, excepted.						24 0 0
Lutes, Cullen making, with cases, the dozen	1 13 7 4	1 15 8 8	A	1 9 7 4	1 5 7 4	
—— Venice making, with cases, the dozen	5 0 9 12	5 7 4	A	4 8 9 12	3 16 9 12	
Lutestrings, *vocat.* Catlings, the groce, containing 12 dozen knots			F			0 2 8
—— French	0 0 2 10 0	0 0 2 10 0	C	0 0 2 2 0	0 0 2 2 0	
—— not French	0 0 2 1 12	0 0 2 2 0		0 0 2 2 0	0 0 2 2 0	

* But if imported by Aliens Drawback more, 1s. 3d. for every 100l. of the Rate or Value.

[183]

INWARDS.

	DUTIES to be paid on IMPORTATION.		DRAWBACKS to be repaid on EXPORTATION.*			RATES, or supposed value, by 12 Car. II. cap. 4. 11 Geo. I. cap. 7. from whence the foregoing Duties are computed.
	By BRITISH.	By ALIENS.	Reference to the several Branches, see Page vi.	If exported to any legal place, except as mentioned in the following column.	If the produce of Europe or the East Indies, and exported to the British Colonies in America.	
	£. s. d. 20ths	£. s. d. 20ths		£. s. d. 20ths	£. s. d. 20ths	£. s. d.
——— Minikins, the groce, containing 12 dozen knots	0 7 2 2	0 7 6 6	C	0 6 6 2	0 5 10 2	1 6 8
Vide Harpstrings.						
Lyme for Dyers, the barrel	0 1 0 12	0 1 1 7 ¾	A	0 0 11 2	0 0 9 12	0 5 0

M.

MACES. *Vide in* Grocery.
Madder, for Dyers use, as by 3 and 4 *Ann.* cap. 4. *vocat.* Crop madder, and all other Bale madder, the Cwt.
But by 8 *Geo.* I. *cap.* 15. *if regularly imported, entered, and landed,* duty free.
But on failure thereof, then to pay

	0 4 8 14	0 5 1 8 ½	Bd	0 3 11 14	0 3 2 14	1 10 0

——— Fat madder, the Cwt.
But by 8 *Geo.* I. *cap.* 15. *if regularly imported, entered, and landed,* duty free.
But on failure thereof, then to pay

	0 2 7 10	0 2 10 2 ½	Bd	0 2 2 10	0 1 9 10	0 16 8

* But if imported by Aliens Drawback more, 1s. 3d. for every 100 l. of the Rate or Value.

M [184] M

INWARDS.	DUTIES to be paid on IMPORTATION.		DRAWBACKS to be repaid on EXPORTATION.*		RATES, or supposed value, by 12 Car. II. cap. 4. † 11 Geo. I. cap. 7. from whence the foregoing Duties are computed.
	By BRITISH.	By ALIENS.	Reference to the several Branches, fee Page vi.	If exported to any legal place, except as mentioned in the following column.	If the produce of Europe or the East Indies, and exported to the British Colonies in America.
	£. s. d. /20ths	£. s. d. /20ths		£. s. d. /20ths	£. s. d. /20ths
Madder, weat. Mull madder, the Cwt. ——— But by 8 Geo. I. cap. 15. if regularly imported, entered, and landed, duty free. But on failure thereof, then to pay	0 3 1 16	0 3 4 19	Bd	0 2 7 16	0 2 1 16	1 0 0
Madder roots. Vide in Drugs.						
Magnus, the Cwt. ———	0 4 2 8	0 4 5 11	A	0 3 8 8	0 3 2 8	1 0 0
Males. Vide Andlets.						
Malt and Barley. Vide Corn.						
Mantles. Vide Blankets.						
Maps printed, the ream ——— in frames, the map and frame	0 16 9 12 0 1 3 15	0 17 10 4 0 1 4 10	A C	0 14 9 12 0 1 2 5	0 12 9 12 0 1 0 15	4 0 0 ‡ 0 5 0
Marble. Vide Stones.						
Mares. Vide Horses.						
Masks of sattin, the dozen ———						2 0 0
of velvet, the dozen						3 0 0
Masts for ships, small, the mast ——— of or from any part of Europe, except Ireland or France	0 1 0 12	0 1 1 2	B	0 0 11 12	0 0 10 12	0 3 4
of Ireland, Africa, Asia, or America (except the French plantations)	0 0 8 8	0 0 8 18	A	0 0 7 8	0 0 6 8	

* But if imported by Aliens Drawback more, 1 s. 3 d. for every 100 l. of the Rate or Value.

INWARDS.

INWARDS	Duties to be paid on IMPORTATION. By BRITISH. £. s. d. /20ths	Duties to be paid on IMPORTATION. By ALIENS. £. s. d. /20ths	Reference to the several Branches, fee Page vi.	DRAWBACKS to be repaid on EXPORTATION.* If exported to any legal place, except as mentioned in the following column. £. s. d. /20ths	DRAWBACKS to be repaid on EXPORTATION.* If the produce of Europe or the East Indies, and exported to the British Colonies in America. £. s. d. /20ths	RATES, or supposed value, by 12 Car. II. cap. 4. † 11 Geo. I. cap. 7. from whence the foregoing Duties are computed. £. s. d.
———— of France, or French plantations. *See in Wood.*						
middle, the mast ———— of or from any part of Europe, except Ireland or France	0 3 1 16	0 3 3 7	B	0 2 10 16	0 2 7 16	0 10 0
———— of Ireland, Africa, Asia, or America (except the French plantations)	0 2 1 4	0 2 2 15 ½	A	0 1 10 4	0 1 7 4	
———— of France, or French plantations. *See in Wood.*						
great, the mast ———— of or from and part of Europe, except Ireland or France	0 6 3 12	0 6 6 15	B	0 5 9 12	0 5 3 12	1 0 0
———— of Ireland, Africa, Asia, or America (except the French plantations)	0 4 2 8	0 4 5 11	A	0 3 8 8	0 3 2 8	
———— of France, or French plantations. *See in Wood.*						
Note. All Masts imported in foreign ships pay duty as Aliens.						
Match for guns, the pound		0 0 8 3 7/10	A	0 0 7 2/5	0 0 6 2/5	0 0 2
Mats of Russia, the mat	0 0 1 5	0 0 6 3 4/10	A	0 0 1 2	0 0 0 19 3/5	0 0 6
If imported in foreign ships, pay duty as Aliens.						

* But if imported by Aliens Drawback more, 1s. 3d. for every 100l. of the Rate or Value.

M [186] M

INWARDS.	DUTIES to be paid on IMPORTATION.		Reference to the several Branches, see Page vi.	DRAWBACKS to be repaid on EXPORTATION.*		RATES, or supposed value, by 12 Car. II. cap. 4. 11 Geo. I. cap. 7. from whence the foregoing Duties are computed.
	By BRITISH. £. s. d. /20ths	By ALIENS. £. s. d. /20ths		If exported to any legal place, except as mentioned in the following column. £. s. d. /20ths	If the produce of Europe or the East Indies, and exported to the British Colonies in America. £. s. d. /20ths	£. s. d.
Matting of Barbary or Portugal, the yard	0 0 4 14	0 0 4 19 9/40	C	0 0 4 5 1/2	0 0 3 16 1/2	0 0 1 6
—— of Holland, the yard	0 0 1 11	0 0 1 13 1/40	C	0 0 1 8 1/2	0 0 1 5	0 0 0 6
Meal of wheat or rye, the last, containing 12 barrels						3 0 0
See Corn and Grain, page 61.						
Medlars, the basket, containing two bushels	0 2 1 4	0 2 15 1/2	A	0 1 10 4	0 1 7 4	0 10 0
Melasses of Rameals, the ton	2 16 0	2 19 6	A	2 9 1	0 2 2	13 6 8
And if imported from any other place than the British plantations in America, more the ton	8 8 0	8 8 0	D	8 8 0	8 8 0	
Mesielanes, the piece, containing 30 yards	1 17 9 12	2 0 8 2/5	A	1 13 3 12	1 8 9 12	9 0 0
—— the single piece, containing 14 yards of Silesia making	0 7 6 14	0 8 0	A	0 6 7 18	0 0 5 2	1 16 0
Metal, viz. Leaf metal (except of Leaf gold) the packet, containing 250 leaves prepared for battery, the Cwt.	0 0 1 11	0 0 1 13 3/40	C	0 0 1 8	0 0 1 5 8	0 0 6
Metheglin, the hogshead	1 10 5 8	1 12 0 6	C	1 7 5 8	0 4 5 8	0 6 0
Minikins. Vide Lutestrings.	0 8 4 16	0 8 11 2	A	0 7 4 16	0 6 4 16	0 2 0
Mithridate, the pound	0 4 2 8	0 4 5 11		0 3 8 8	0 3 2 8	1 0 0
Mithridate Venetia. Vide in Drugs.		0 2 0	C			
Mittins of Wadmol, the dozen pair	0 1 10 13 3/5	0 1 2 1 9/20	A	0 1 7 19 7/5	0 1 5 5 3/5	0 9 0

* But if imported by Aliens Drawback more, 1s. 3d. for every 100l. of the Rate or Value.

M   [187]   M

INWARDS.

	Reference to the several Branches, see Page vi.	Duties to be paid on Importation		Drawbacks to be repaid on Exportation.*		Rates, or supposed value, by 12 Car. II. cap. 4. 11 Geo. I. cap. 7. from whence the foregoing Duties are computed.
		By British	By Aliens	If exported to any legal place, except as mentioned in the following column.	If the produce of Europe or the East Indies, and exported to the British Colonies in America.	
		£. s. d. 20ths	£. s. d. 20ths	£. s. d. 20ths	£. s. d. 20ths	£. s. d.
Moccadoes. *Vide* Buffins.						
Moccalo ends, the dozen pounds	A	0 16 9½	0 17 10 4	0 14 9½	0 12 9½	4 0 0
Mohairs. *Vide* Camlets.						
Mohogany timber, or plank. *Vide* Wood.						
Morels, the pound	C	0 1 0½	0 1 1 4 ⅕	0 0 11 8	0 0 10 4	0 4 0
Morians. *Vide* Harness.						
Mortars and Pestles of brass, the pound	C	0 0 4 4	0 0 4 8 ⅕⅕	0 0 3 16	0 0 3 8	0 1 4
Mum, the barrel, containing 42 gallons	L	0 12 3	0 12 10 17	0 0 11 0	0 0 9 9	2 10 0
Subject also to the Excise duties.						
But of and from *Guernsey*, *Jersey*, *Alderney* and *Sark*, may be imported from thence without payment of any other duty, than such Excise as is chargeable for the time being on the like liquor made in this kingdom.						
Muskets. *Vide* Guns.						
Muslins as Callicoes, which see in Linen.						
——— flowered, &c. *Vide the Table of Unrated East India goods.*						
Mustard feed, the Cwt.	A	0 2 1 4	0 2 15 ½	0 1 10 4	0 1 7 4	0 10 0

* But if imported by Aliens Drawback more, 1s. 3d. for every 100 l. of the Rate or Value.

INWARDS.

N.

	DUTIES to be paid on IMPORTATION.						Reference to the several Branches, see Page vi.	DRAWBACKS to be repaid on EXPORTATION.*						RATES, or supposed value, by 12 Car. II. cap. 4. 11 Geo. I. cap. 7. from whence the foregoing Duties are computed.
	By BRITISH.			By ALIENS.				If exported to any legal place, except as mentioned in the following column.			If the produce of Europe or the East Indies, and exported to the British Colonies in America.			
	£.	s.	d.|20ths	£.	s.	d.|20ths		£.	s.	d.|20ths	£.	s.	d.|20ths	£. s. d.
NAILS, vocat. Chair nails, the thousand And besides, if ⎱ Iron, the Cwt. ⎰ made of ⎱ Brass, the thousand ⎰	0	2	9|12	0	2	11|14	A	0	0	2|5|12	0	0	2 1|12	0 13 4
Copper nails, the sum, containing ten thousand	0	5	3|8	0	5	3|8	D	0	5	3|8				
And besides, for every Cwt.	0	0	8|8	0	0	8|8	E	0	0	8|8	0	0	8|8	
Harness nails, the sum, containing ten thousand	0	2	9|12	0	2	11|14	A	0	2	5|12	0	0	2 1|12	0 13 4
Head nails, the barrel	0	18	4|10	0	18	4|10	E	0	18	4|10	0	18	4|10	1 0 0
Rose and Sadlers nails, the sum, containing ten thousand	0	4	2|8	0	4	5|11	A	0	3	8|8	0	3	2|8	8 0 0
Small nails, the half barrel	1	13	7|4	1	15	8|8	A	1	9	7|4	1	5	7|4	0 13 4
Sprig nails, the sum, containing ten thousand	0	2	9|12	0	2	11|14	A	0	2	5|12	0	2	1|12	8 0 0
Tenter hooks, the thousand	0	1	4|16	0	1	5|17 3/4	A	0	1	2|16	0	1	0|16	0 6 8
And besides, for every Cwt. of Iron	0	0	12	0	0	12	A	0	0	11 2				0 5 0
And besides, for such of the Harness, Head, Rose, Sadlers, Small, and Sprig nails, as are made of Iron, for every Cwt.	0	5	3	0	5	3	D	0	5	3				
Brass, for every 20 s. of their respective rates	0	5	3	0	5	3	D	0	5	3				
	0	1	0|12	0	1	0|12	E	0	1	0|12	0	1	0|12	

* But if imported by Aliens Drawback more, 1 s. 3 d. for every 100 l. of the Rate or Value.

‖ If Iron no Drawback to the British Colonies in America.

INWARDS.

	DUTIES to be paid on IMPORTATION.		Reference to the several Branches, See Page vi.	DRAWBACKS to be repaid on EXPORTATION.*		RATES, or supposed value, by 12 Car. II. cap. 4. ‡ 11 Geo. I. caf. 7. from whence the foregoing Duties are computed.
	By BRITISH.	By ALIENS.		If exported to any legal place, except as mentioned in the following column.	If the produce of Europe or the East Indies, and exported to the British Colonies in America.	
	£. s. d. 20ths	£. s. d. 20ths		£. s. d. 20ths	£. s. d. 20ths	£. s. d.
Napkins, French making, the dozen	0 9 4 2	0 9 6 0	F h	0 6 0 10	0 5 8 18 4/5	0 0 12 0
Neats tongues of Ruffia, the piece	0 0 0 8 3/5	0 0 0 8 3/5	A	0 0 0 7 2/5	0 0 0 6 4/5	0 0 0 2
— the barrel	0 2 1 4	0 2 15 0	A	0 1 10 4	0 0 1 7 4	0 0 10 0
— the dozen	0 0 4 6	0 0 6 13 1/2	A	0 0 5 11	0 0 4 16	0 0 2 6
Note, Irish Salted Beef is duty free.						
Neckerchers of Flanders making, the dozen	1 5 2 8	1 6 9 6	A	1 2 2 8	0 19 2 8	6 0 0
Necklaces. Vide Bracelets.						
Needles, the dozen thousand	0 12 7 4	0 13 4 13	A	0 11 1 4	—	3 0 0
vocat. Pack needles, the thousand	0 2 9 12	0 2 11 14	A	0 2 5 12	—	0 13 4
— Sail needles, the thousand	0 1 4 16	0 1 5 17	A	0 1 2 16	—	0 6 8
And besides, for every Cwt. of Iron, contained in any of the aforesaid needles.						
Nicorago wood. Vide Wood for dying.	0 5 3	0 5 3	D	0 5 3		
Nutmegs. Vide in Grocery.						
— condited. Vide in Drugs.						
— pickled, the piece	0 0 0 16 4/5	0 0 0 17 17/20	A	0 0 0 14	0 0 0 12 4/5	0 0 4 0
Nuts, vocat. Chestnuts, the bushel	0 1 3 15	0 1 4 10	C	0 1 2 5	0 1 1 15	0 5 0
— Small nuts, the barrel	0 2 1 4	0 2 15	A	0 1 10 4	0 1 7 4	0 10 0
— Walnuts, the barrel	0 4 4 16	0 1 5 17	A	0 1 2 16	0 0 4 16	0 6 8

* But if imported by Aliens Drawback more, 1s. 3d. for every 100l. of the Rate or Value.

I N W A R D S.

O.

	DUTIES to be paid on IMPORTATION.		Reference to the several Branches, see Page vi.	DRAWBACKS to be repaid on EXPORTATION.*		RATES, or supposed value, by 12 Car. II. cap. 4. 11 Geo I. cap. 7. from whence the foregoing Duties are computed.
	By BRITISH.	By ALIENS.		If exported to any legal place, except as mentioned in the following column.	If the produce of Europe or the East Indies, and exported to the British Colonies in America.	
	£. s. d. 20ths	£. s. d. 20ths		£. s. d. 20ths	£. s. d. 20ths	£. s. d.
OAKER, the barrel	0 5 7 4	0 5 11 8	A	0 4 11 4	0 4 3 4	1 6 8
Oakham, the Cwt.	0 2 1 4	0 2 2 15	A	0 1 10 4	0 1 7 4	0 10 0
Oars, the piece						0 1 0
—— of and directly from any part of America, if regularly entered and landed, free. On failure thereof. See in Wood.						
—— of or from any part of Europe, except Ireland and France	0 0 3 15	0 0 3 18 1¼	B	0 0 3 9 1½	0 0 3 3 1½	
—— of Ireland, Africa, or Asia	0 0 2 10 ⅖	0 0 2 13 ⅘	A	0 0 2 4 1½	0 0 1 18 ⅕	6 0 0
—— of France. See in Wood.						
If imported in foreign ships, to pay duty as Aliens.						
—— the hundred, containing six score						
—— of and directly from any part of America, if regularly entered and landed, free. On failure thereof. See in Wood.						
—— of or from any part of Europe, except Ireland and France	1 17 9 12	1 19 4 10	B	1 14 9 12	1 11 9 12	
—— of Ireland, Africa, or Asia	1 5 2 8	1 6 9 6	A	1 2 2 8	0 19 2 8	
—— of France. See in Wood.						
If imported in foreign ships, to pay duty as Aliens.						

* But if imported by Aliens Drawback more, 1s. 3d. for every 100l. of the Rate or Value.

O [191] O

INWARDS.

Oats. *Vide in Corn.*

Oils, vocat.

	DUTIES to be paid on IMPORTATION.		DRAWBACKS to be repaid on EXPORTATION.*		RATES, or supposed value, by 12 Car. II. cap. 4. 11 Geo. I. cap. 7. from whence the foregoing Duties are computed.
	By BRITISH.	By ALIENS.	Reference to the several Branches, See Page vi.	If exported to any legal place, except as mentioned in the following column.	If the produce of Europe or the East Indies, and exported to the British Colonies in America.	
	£. s. d. 20ths	£. s. d. 20ths		£. s. d. 20ths	£. s. d. 20ths	£. s. d.
Sallet oil, the gallon, French	0 3 8 2	0 3 8 17	F	0 2 3 12	0 2 2 2	0 5 0
not French	0 1 0 12	0 1 1 7¾	A	0 0 11 2	0 0 9 12	0 5 0
And besides if in Glass Bottles or Flasks, for every dozen quarts of Glass	0 4 2 8	0 4 2 7¼ 8	Ze			
Sevil oil, Majorca oil, Minorca oil, Apuglia, Provence oil, and Portugal oil, the ton	6 14 4 16	7 2 9 12	A	5 18 4 16	5 2 4 16	32 0 0
Ordinary oil of olives from any place, not otherwise rated, the ton, containing 252 gallons	6 14 4 16	7 2 9 12	A	5 18 4 16	5 2 4 16	† 32 0 0
But Provence, and all other oils of France, more the ton	16 16 0	16 16 0	F b	8 16 0	8 16 0	
If imported in foreign ships, to pay duty as Aliens.						
Rape and Linseed oil, the ton	23 2 0	24 0 4 10	B	21 7 0	19 12 0	70 0 0
Oil of Hempseed, the ton, containing 252 gallons	12 12 0	12 17 3	B	12 2 0	11 12 0	† 20 0 0
Other seed oil, *for every 20s. value upon oath*	0 4 2 8	0 4 5 11	A	0 3 8 8	0 3 2 8	
And besides, for every ton	8 8 0	8 8 0	D	8 8 0	8 8 0	

* If imported by Aliens Drawback more, 1s. 3d. for every 100l. of the Rate or Value.

[192]

INWARDS.

	By BRITISH. £. s. d./20ths	By ALIENS. £. s. d./20ths	Reference to the several Branches, see Page vi.	If exported to any legal place, except as mentioned in the following column. £. s. d./20ths	If the produce of Europe, or the East Indies, and exported to the British Colonies in America. £. s. d./20ths	RATES, or supposed value, by 12 Car. II. cap. 4. 11 Geo. I. cap. 7. from whence the foregoing Duties are computed. £. s. d.
Oil, vocat. Train Oil or Blubber. Oil, vocat. {Train oil, of Greenland, the ton — of Newfoundland, and like fort —	17 6 6	17 6 6	A	12 16 6	8 6 6	8 0 0
All Train oil, or Fish oil, of foreign fishing, the ton — of Greenland and parts adjacent, made of fish, or of any other creature living in the seas, caught in any ships or vessels truly and properly belonging to Great-Britain, and imported in such ships, free. — taken by any shipping belonging to any of his Majesty's colonies and plantations, and imported in such shipping, the ton —	0 14 8 8	0 14 8 8	B b	0 11 8 8	0 8 8 8	6 0 0
taken by any shipping belonging to any of his Majesty's colonies and plantations, but imported in shipping belonging to Great-Britain, the ton —	0 11 6 12	0 11 6 12	B b	0 10 0 12	0 8 6 12	50 0 0

Oil, except Train Oil or Blubber.

INWARDS.

	Duties to be paid on Importation.		Reference to the several Branches, see Page vi.	Drawbacks to be repaid on Exportation.		Rates, or supposed value, by 12 Car. II. cap. 4. 11 Geo. I. cap. 7. from whence the foregoing Duties are computed.
	By British.	By Aliens.		If exported to any legal place, except as mentioned in the following column.	If the produce of Europe or the East Indies, and exported to the British Colonies in America.	
	£. s. d. 20ths	£. s. d. 20ths		£. s. d. 20ths	£. s. d. 20ths	£. s. d.
Of Newfoundland, or of any other his Majesty's colonies and plantations, made of fish, or of any other creature living in the seas, caught in any ships or vessels truly and properly belonging to Great-Britain, and imported in such ships, free.						
— taken by any shipping belonging to any of his Majesty's colonies and plantations, and imported in such shipping, the ton ———	0 12 7 4	0 12 7 4	Bb	0 9 7 4	0 9 7 4	
— taken by any shipping belonging to any of his Majesty's colonies and plantations, but imported in shipping belonging to Great-Britain, the ton ———	0 9 5 8	0 9 5 8	Bb	0 7 11 8	0 7 11 8	
By 15 Geo. III. cap. 31. Train Oil or Blubber taken in any part of the ocean by, and imported in, any ship belonging to his Majesty's subjects of Great Britain, Ireland, Guernsey, Jersey, or Man, may be imported duty free.						

INWARDS.

	DUTIES to be paid on IMPORTATION.		Reference to the several Branches, see Page vi.	DRAWBACKS to be repaid on EXPORTATION.*		RATES, or supposed value, by 12 Car. II. cap. 4. ‡11 Geo. I. cap. 7. from whence the foregoing Duties are computed.
	By BRITISH.	By ALIENS.		If exported to any legal place, except as mentioned in the following column.	If the produce of Europe or the East Indies, and exported to the British Colonies in America.	
	£. s. d. 20ths	£. s. d. 20ths		£. s. d. 20ths	£. s. d. 20ths	£. s. d.
Olives, the hogshead	1 13 7 4	1 15 8 8	A	1 9 7 4	1 5 7 4	8 0 0
Onions, the barrel	0 0 8 8	0 0 8 18	A	0 0 7 8	0 0 6 8	0 3 4
— the hundred bunches	0 3 6	0 3 8 12	A	0 3 1	0 2 8	0 16 8
— feed, the Cwt.	0 16 9 12	0 17 10 4	A	0 14 9 12	0 12 9 12	4 0 0
Oranges and Lemons, the thousand	0 4 2 8	0 4 5 11	A	0 3 8 8	0 3 2 8	1 0 0
Orchal, the Cwt. *for dyers ufe, as by 3 & 4 Ann. cap. 4.*						2 0 0
But by 8 Geo. I. cap. 15. §. 10. if regularly imported, entered, and landed, duty free.						
But on failure thereof, then to pay Orchelia. *Vide Archelia.*	0 6 3 12	0 6 9 18	Rd	0 5 3 12	0 4 3 12	
Orfedew, the dozen pound	0 5 7 4	0 5 11 8	A	0 4 11 4	0 4 3 4	
Oyfters from France, *by 10 Geo. II. cap. 30.* the bufhel, ftrike meafure, according to the Winchefter corn bufhel, to be rated at } £. s. d. 0 0 7			F			
— of all other places, *for every 20s. of their real value, upon aath*	0 5 3	0 5 6 3	C	0 4 9	0 4 3	1 6 8
Orange peel. *See* Cortex Limonum *vel* Aurantiorum.						

* But if imported by Aliens Drawback more, 1s. 16s. 3d. for every 100l. of the Rate or Value.

INWARDS.
P.

	Duties to be paid on IMPORTATION. By BRITISH.	Duties to be paid on IMPORTATION. By ALIENS.	Reference to the several Branches, see Page vi.	DRAWBACKS to be repaid on EXPORTATION.* If exported to any legal place, except as mentioned in the following column.	DRAWBACKS to be repaid on EXPORTATION.* If the produce of Europe or the East Indies, and exported to the British Colonies in America.	RATES, or supposed value by 12 Car. II. cap. 4. & 11 Geo. I. cap. 7. from whence the foregoing Duties are computed.
	£. s. d. 20ths	£. s. d. 20ths		£. s. d. 20ths	£. s. d. 20ths	£. s. d.
Packthread in skeins, the hundred pounds vocat. Bottomthread, the hundred pounds	0 12 7 4	0 13 4 13	A	0 11 1 4	0 9 7 4	3 0 0
	0 10 6	0 11 1 17	A	0 9 3	0 8 0	2 10 0
Pailing boards. Vide Wood.						
Pails of wood, or Kits of wood, the dozen	0 1 9	0 1 10 ½	C	0 1 7	0 1 5	0 6 8 ‡
Painters colours of all sorts, not otherwise rated, the pound	0 0 1 11	0 0 1 13 1/40	C	0 0 1 8 ½	0 0 1 5 ½	0 0 6 ‡
Pans, vocat. Dripping pans, the Cwt.	0 17 10 4	0 18 7 13	B	0 16 4 4	0 12 9	3 0 0
Frying pans, the Cwt.	0 16 9 12	0 17 7 1	B	0 15 3 12	0 9 7 4	3 0 0
Warming pans, the dozen	0 15 9	0 16 6 9	C	0 14 3	0 18 4 10	3 0 0
(if Brass) But if of Copper, the dozen	0 18 7 4	0 13 4 13	A	0 11 1 4		
And besides for every Cwt.	0 18 4 10	0 18 4 10	E	0 18 4 10		
Atlas ordinary, the ream	0 17 0	0 17 2 6	W			
Paper, vocat. Blue paper, the ream	0 7 4	0 7 5 15	W			0 14 0 ‡
— if Blue royal, not French — the single ream, for sugar-bakers	0 6 9	0 6 2 0	Wc			0 10 0 ‡
— Blue paper for sugar-bakers, not French	0 6 6		W			
— if Blue royal, French — the single ream	0 11 6	0 11 1 17	Wc			
— Blue paper for sugar-bakers, French — the single ream, French	0 9 8 11	0 9 10 2	Wc			

* But if imported by Aliens Drawback more, 1 s. 3 d. for every 20 s. of the Rate or Value.

[196]

INWARDS.

Paper, vocat.

	DUTIES to be paid on IMPORTATION.		Reference to the several Branches, see l. geo vi.	DRAWBACKS to be repaid on EXPORTATION.		RATES, or supposed value, by 12 Car. II. cap. 4. 11 Geo. I. cap. 7. from whence the foregoing Duties are computed.
	By BRITISH.	By ALIENS.		If exported to any legal place, except as mentioned in the following column.	If the produce of Europe or the East Indies, and exported to the British Colonies in America.	
	£ s. d. 20ths	£ s. d. 20ths		£ s. d. 20ths	£ s. d. 20ths	£ s. d.
Brown paper, the bundle	0 2 0 3	0 2 0 12 2/20	W c			0 3 0
— if French	0 4 19	0 5 8 8/20	W			0 7 6
Cap paper, called Brown cap, the ream	0 3 11 5	0 4 0 8 5/20	W			0 7 6 ‡
Cartridge paper, the ream	0 4 8 14	0 4 9 17 5/20	W			0 5 0 ‡
Chancery double, the ream	0 4 8 14	0 4 9 9 4/20	W			0 12 0
Demy paper, the ream						
— if Demy fine, not French	0 11 6	0 11 2 3 4/20	W			0 7 6 ‡
— Demy second, not French	0 8 7 19	0 8 9 16 5/20	W			
— Demy fine, French	0 15 9	0 15 10 17 5/20	W c			
— Demy second, French	0 13 4 13 1/2	0 13 6 10 6/20	W c			0 14 0 ‡
Elephant ordinary, the ream	0 7 5 15 3/4	0 7 7 6 19 3/20	W			
Gold paper. Vide in G.						
Medium paper, the ream						
— if Medium fine	0 13 10 6	0 14 0 10 1/4	W			0 14 0 ‡‡
— Second writing medium	0 10 8 10 3/4	0 10 10 14 1/4	W			0 10 0 ‡‡
Genoa medium fine	0 8 4 3 3/4	0 8 6 7 1/4	W			
Second Genoa medium	0 7 1 1 1/4	0 7 2 12 1/4	W			0 4 6
Ordinary printing and Copy paper, the ream						
— if Bastard, or Double copy	0 4 6 16 3/4	0 4 7 10 3/4	W			

[197]

INWARDS.

Paper, viz.

		DUTIES to be paid on IMPORTATION.		Reference to the several Branches, see Page vi.	DRAWBACKS to be repaid on EXPORTATION.		RATES, or supposed value, by 12 Car. II. cap. 4. 11 Geo. I. cap. 7. from whence the foregoing Duties are computed.
		By BRITISH.	By ALIENS.		If exported to any legal place, except as mentioned in the following column.	If the produce of Europe or the East Indies, and exported to the British Colonies in America.	
		£. s. d. 20ths	£. s. d. 20ths		£. s. d. 20ths	£. s. d. 20ths	£. s. d.
— if Crown, viz.	Genoa fine	0 3 9 7	0 3 10 1 ⅜	W			
	Genoa second	0 2 11 18	0 3 0 12	W			
	German	0 2 11 18	0 3 0 12	W			
	Printing crown, fine	0 2 7 3 7/10	0 2 7 17	W			
	Printing crown, second ordinary						
— if Demy, viz.	Genoa fine	0 4 6 16	0 4 7 10	W			
	Genoa second	0 3 9 7	0 3 10 1	W			
	German	0 3 9 7	0 3 10 1	W			
	Printing	0 4 0 10	0 4 1 4	W			
	Fine	0 5 4 5	0 5 4 19	W			
	Second	0 4 6 16	0 4 7 10	W			
— if Foolscap, viz.	Genoa fine	0 3 9 7	0 3 10 1	W			
	Genoa second	0 2 11 18	0 3 0 12	W			
	German	0 2 11 18	0 3 0 12	W			
	Printing fine	0 3 0 3	0 3 0 3	W			
	Printing second or dinary	0 2 7 7/10	0 2 7 17	W			
— if Lombard, viz. German Lombard		0 2 11 18	0 3 0 12	W			

INWARDS (Paper, viz.)	DUTIES to be paid on IMPORTATION.				Reference to the several Branches, see Page vi.	DRAWBACKS to be repaid on EXPORTATION.		RATES, or supposed value, by 12 Car. II. cap. 4. 11 Geo. I. cap. 7. from whence the foregoing Duties are computed.
	By BRITISH.		By ALIENS.			If exported to any legal place, except as mentioned in the following column.	If the produce of Europe or the East Indies, and exported to the British Colonies in America.	
	£. s. d. 20ths		£. s. d. 20ths			£. s. d. 20ths	£. s. d. 20ths	£. s. d.
Ordinary printing and Copy paper, the ream, if Pot, viz. — Genoa fine	0 2 7 3 7/10		0 2 7 17 7/10		W			0 13 4
Genoa second	0 2 7 3 7/10		0 2 7 17 7/10		W			
Ordinary	0 2 7 3 7/10		0 2 7 17 7/10		W			
Superfine	0 4 6 16 1/2		0 4 7 10 1/2		W			
Second fine	0 3 9 7 5/8		0 3 10 1 5/8		W			
Small post	0 3 9 7 5/8		0 3 10 1 5/8		W			
Painted paper, the ream	0 17 8 2 1/8		0 17 10 4 1/8		W			
if French	1 3 1 4		1 3 3 6		Wc			
Pressing paper, the 100 leaves And more, by 13 Geo. III. cap. 67. when imported as merchandize, and not painted in and brought from the East Indies, the yard square	0 1 1 1 1/2		0 1 1 1 1/2		E a			0 13 4
And besides, for every Cwt. as Pasteboards or Millboards	0 4 2 8		0 4 4 10		B e			
Post, viz. Fine large post, weighing 15 pounds per ream and upwards, the ream	0 7 10 10		0 7 10 10		E a			0 10 0
Fine large post, weighing 15 pounds per ream, the ream	0 7 1 1 1/2		0 7 2 12 1/2		W			
under 15 pounds per ream, the ream	0 6 3 12 5/2		0 6 4 15 5/2		W			0 7 6

INWARDS

Paper, uncut.

	DUTIES to be paid on IMPORTATION								Reference to the several Branches, see Page vi.	DRAWBACKS to be repaid on EXPORTATION								RATES, or supposed value, by 12 Car. II. cap. 4. 11 Geo. I. cap. 7. from whence the foregoing Duties are computed.		
	By BRITISH				By ALIENS					If exported to any legal place, except as mentioned in the following column.				If the produce of Europe or the East Indies, and exported to the British Colonies in America.						
	L.	s.	d.	20ths	L.	s.	d.	20ths		L.	s.	d.	20ths	L.	s.	d.	20ths	L.	s.	d.
Royal paper, the ream	1	12	6	12	1	12	9	15	W	—	—	—	—	—	—	—	—			
— if Atlas fine	0	19	11	8	1	0	2	11	W	—	—	—	—	—	—	—	—			
— Elephant fine	1	12	6	12	1	12	9	15	W	—	—	—	—	—	—	—	—			
— Imperial { fine	1	4	8	2	1	4	11	5	W	—	—	—	—	—	—	—	—			
second writing imperial	0	19	11	8	1	0	2	11	W	—	—	—	—	—	—	—	—			
— Royal fine	1	16	3		1	6	6	3	W	—	—	—	—	—	—	—	—			
— Super royal fine	0	16	0		0	16	3	6	W	—	—	—	—	—	—	—	—			
— Second writing royal	0	19	11	8	1	0	2	11	W	—	—	—	—	—	—	—	—			
— Second writing super royal	0	8	4	16	0	8	4	16	W	—	—	—	—	—	—	—	—			
If any of the above Royal Paper is French, it is to pay more for every ream —																		1	0	0
In which case the whole duties are to be appropriated to —									W											
— Genoa royal { fine	0	6	6		0	9	8	11	W	—	—	—	—	—	—	—	—	0	14	0
second	0	3	4		0	8	4	16	W	—	—	—	—	—	—	—	—	0	10	0
— Holland royal { fine	0	6	5		0	9	6	11	W	—	—	—	—	—	—	—	—	0	14	0
second	0	3	3	12	0	6	3	2	W	—	—	—	—	—	—	—	—	0	10	0
— Ordinary royal	0	3	1	16	0	3	2	11	W	—	—	—	—	—	—	—	—	0	5	0

[200]

INWARDS.

	Duties to be paid on IMPORTATION.		Reference to the several Branches, see Page vi.	Drawbacks to be repaid on EXPORTATION.*		RATES, or supposed value, by 12 Car. II. cap. 4. ‡11 Geo. I cap. 7. from whence the foregoing Duties are computed.
	By BRITISH.	By ALIENS.		If exported to any legal place, except as mentioned in the following column.	If the produce of Europe or the East Indies, and exported to the British Colonies in America.	
	£. s. d. 20ths	£. s. d. 20ths		£. s. d. 20ths	£. s. d. 20ths	£. s. d.
Rochel paper as large as Demy paper, the ream	0 7 1 1	0 7 2 9 10/20	F m			0 9 0
And besides, according to their respective sorts, for which see the acts 10 Ann. cap. 19. and 12 Ann. cap. 9.						
If any of the above Paper is French, and not particularly charged as such, it is to pay more, for every 20s. of the rate	0 9 5 8	0 9 5 8				
In which case the whole duties are to be appropriated to			W c			
Parchment, the dozen, containing 12 sheets	0 4 5 11	0 4 6 13 1/20	O	0 1 9 9	0 1 7 7	0 7 2
the roll, containing six dozen	0 1 6 6	0 1 8 18 4/20	O	0 10 8 14	0 9 8 2	0 2 2
Paste of Jene, the pound	0 1 6 18	0 1 8 1 1/20	A	0 1 4 13	0 1 9 1	0 7 0
Pasteboards. Vide Boards.						
Pearls. Vide Diamonds.						
Pears, the bushel	0 1 3 15	0 1 4 10 1 1/2/20	C	0 1 2 5	0 1 0 15	0 5 0
Pears or Apples dried, the barrel	0 2 1 4	0 2 2 15 1/2/20	A	0 1 10 4	0 1 7 4	‡0 10 0
Pease. Vide Corn.						
‡Pelts. Vide Skins.						

Paper, vacat.

* But if imported by Aliens Drawback more, 1s. 3d. for every 100l. of the Rate or Value.

INWARDS.

	Duties to be paid on IMPORTATION.		Reference to the several Branches, see Page vi.	Drawbacks to be repaid on EXPORTATION.*	
	By BRITISH.	By ALIENS.		If exported to any legal place, except as mentioned in the following column.	If the produce of Europe or the East Indies, and exported to the British Colonies in America.
	£. s. d. 20ths	£. s. d. 20ths		£. s. d. 20ths	£. s. d. 20ths
Pencils of all sorts, the groce, containing 12 dozen	0 2 7 10	0 2 9 1	C	0 2 4 10	0 2 1 10
Penners, the groce, containing 12 dozen	0 8 4 16	0 8 11 2	A	0 7 4 16	0 6 4 16
Pepper. Vide in Grocery.					
Perrer bits, the groce, containing 12 dozen { Guinea } Vide in Drugs. { long }	0 4 2 8	0 4 5 11	A	0 3 8 8	—
And besides, for every Cwt. of iron	0 5 3	0 5 3	D	0 5 3	—
Perry, the ton — Filled	4 14 6	6 6 0	B a	3 14 6	0 4 6 0
Unfilled	4 3	5 10 10 11	B a	5 1 0	0 3 11 10
	1 18		B a	3 3 1 18	5 3 7
			B a	5 10 11	
And besides, for every 20s. of the value on oath:					
if not French	0 12 7 16	0 13 7 16	F p	0 8 7 16	0 8 7 16
Subject also to the Excise duties.	0 4 2 8	0 4 2 8		0 4 2 8	0 4 2 8
But if and from Guernsey, Jersey, Alderney and Sark, may be imported with-					

* But if imported by Aliens Drawback more, 1 s. 2 d. for every 100 l. of the Rate or Value, except Perry.

INWARDS.

	DUTIES to be paid on IMPORTATION.		Reference to the several Branches, see Page vi.	DRAWBACKS to be repaid on EXPORTATION.*	
	By BRITISH.	By ALIENS.		If exported to any legal place, except as mentioned in the following column.	If the produce of Europe or the East Indies, and exported to the British Colonies in America.
	£. s. d. 20ths	£. s. d. 20ths		£. s. d. 20ths	£. s. d. 20ths
out payment of any other duty, than such Excise as is chargeable on the like liquors made in this kingdom.					
Pestles. *Vide* Mortars.					
Petticoats of silk, the piece	0 13 1 10	0 13 9 7	C	0 11 10 10	0 10 7 10
Pewter old, the Cwt.	0 16 9 12	0 17 10 4	A	0 14 9 12	0 12 9 12
Pheasants, the dozen, from Christmas to Midsummer					
———— Pouts, from Midsummer to Christmas	0 10 6	0 11 1 17 ½	A	0 9 3	0 8 0
Pickled Cucumbers. *Vide* in C.					
Pickles of all sorts, not otherwise rated, the gallon	0 7 17 ¼	0 8 5 ⅜	C	0 7 2 ½	0 6 7 ½
Pictures. *The duty thereon was regulated by S Geo. I. cap. 20. and 11 Geo. I. cap. 7. and is as follows:*					
The Picture of 4 feet square (or 16 superficial feet or upwards) or any dimensions, which being reduced will produce such a square,					

* But if imported by Aliens Drawback more, 1 s. 3 d. for every 100 l. of the Rate or Value.

INWARDS.	Duties to be paid on Importation. By British. £.	s.	d.	20ths	By Aliens. £.	s.	d.	20ths	Reference to the several Branches, see Page vi.	Drawbacks to be repaid on Exportation.* If exported to any legal place, except as mentioned in the following column. £.	s.	d.	20ths	If the produce of Europe or the East Indies, and exported to the British Colonies in America. £.	s.	d.	20ths	Rates, or supposed value, by 12 Car. II. cap. 4. ‡ 11 Geo. I. cap. 7. from whence the foregoing Duties are computed. £.	s.	d.
French	3	8	3		3	8	3		K g	—	—	—	—	—	—	—	—			
not French	3	8	3		3	8	3		K f	—	—	—	—	—	—	—	—			
—— of 2 feet square (or 4 superficial feet) and under 4 feet square (or 16 superficial feet)																				
French	2	5	6		2	5	6		K g	—	—	—	—	—	—	—	—			
not French	2	5	6		2	5	6		K f	—	—	—	—	—	—	—	—			
—— under 2 feet square (or 4 superficial feet)																				
French	1	2	9		1	2	9		K g	—	—	—	—	—	—	—	—			
not French	1	2	9		1	2	9		K f	—	—	—	—	—	—	—	—			
Pike-heads, the piece	0	0	1	5 1/5	0	0	1	6 31/40	A	0	0	1	2 1/5	—	—	—	—	0	0	6
And besides, for every Cwt. of Iron	0	5	3		0	5	3		D	0	5	3		—	—	—	—			
Pikes without heads, the piece	0	0	8	16 2/5	0	0	9	7 17/40	A	0	0	7	15 2/5	—	—	—	—	9	3	6
—— with heads, the piece	0	0	10	1 3/5	0	0	10	14 1/5	A	0	0	8	17 3/5	—	—	—	—	0	4	0
And besides, for every Cwt. of Iron	0	5	3		0	5	3		D	0	5	3		—	—	—	—			
Pile weights. *Vide* Brass.																				
Pincers and Pliers, the dozen	0	0	10	1 3/5	0	0	10	14 1/5	A	0	0	8	17 3/5	—	—	—	—	0	4	0
And besides, for every Cwt. of Iron	0	5	3		0	5	3		D	0	5	3		—	—	—	—			
‖ Pins, the dozen thousand	0	10	6		0	11	1	17 1/2	A	0	9	3		0	8	0		2	10	0

‖ If Iron no Drawback to the British Colonies in America.

* But if imported by Aliens Drawback more, 1s. 3d. for every 100l. of the Rate or Value.

INWARDS.

	DUTIES to be paid on IMPORTATION.		Reference to the several Branches, see Page vi.	DRAWBACKS to be repaid on EXPORTATION.*		RATES, or suppos'd value, by 12 Car. II. cap. 4. & 11 Geo I. cap. 7. from whence the foregoing Duties are computed.
	By BRITISH.	By ALIENS.		If exported to any legal place, except as mentioned in the following column.	If the produce of Europe or the East Indies, and exported to the British Colonies in America.	
	£. s. d. 20ths	£. s. d. 20ths		£. s. d. 20ths	£. s. d. 20ths	£. s. d.
And besides, if { Brass, the dozen thousand	0 2 7 10	0 2 7 10	E	0 2 7 10	0 2 7 10	0 6 8
{ Iron, the Cwt.	0 5 3	0 5 3	D	0 5 3		
Pintadoes, or Callico cupboard cloths (not brought from East India or China) the piece	0 1 9	0 1 10	C	0 1 7	0 1 5	
And besides, as manufactures of Cotton, for every 20s. of the gross price at the candle	0 3 1 16	0 3 1 16	Q	0 3 1 16	0 3 1 16	0 6 8
Pipe and Hogshead staves, the hundred, containing six score						
of and directly from any part of America, if regularly entered and landed, free.						
On failure thereof. See in Wood.						
of or from any part of Europe, except Ireland and France	0 2 1 4	0 2 2 5	B	0 1 111 4	0 1 9 4	
of Ireland, Africa, or Asia	0 1 4 16	0 1 5 17	A	0 1 2 16	0 1 0 16	
of France. See in Wood.						
If imported in foreign ships, to pay duty as Aliens.						

* But if imported by Aliens Drawback more, 1s. 3d. for every 100l. of the Rate or Value.

[205]

INWARDS.

	Duties to be paid on IMPORTATION.		Reference to the several Branches, see Page vi.	DRAWBACKS to be repaid on EXPORTATION.*		RATES, or supposed value, by 12 Car.II. cap.4. ‡ 11 Geo.I. cap.7. from whence the foregoing Duties are computed.
	By BRITISH.	By ALIENS.		If exported to any legal place, except as mentioned in the following column.	If the produce of Europe or the East Indies, and exported to the British Colonies in America.	
	£. s. d. 20ths	£. s. d. 20ths		£. s. d. 20ths	£. s. d. 20ths	£. s. d.
Pipes for children, the gross, containing 12 dozen	0 1 8 3 1/5	0 1 9 8 2/5	A	0 1 5 15 1/5	0 1 3 7 1/5	0 8 0
—— for tabors, the dozen	0 0 10 1 3/5	0 0 10 14 1/5	A	0 0 8 17 3/5	0 0 7 13 3/5	0 4 0
—— of glass. *Vide* Glass.						
Pitch, small or great band, the last, containing 12 barrels. And besides, not being of the product of any of the dominions or plantations of the Crown of Great-Britain, the last. If imported in foreign ships, to pay duty as Aliens.	0 10 6	0 11 17 1/2	A	0 9 3	0 8 0	2 10 0
Plaister of Paris, the mount, containing three thousand weight	0 1 3 15	0 1 3 15	E	0 1 3 15	0 1 3 15	—
Planc irons, the dozen	1 9 4 16 4/5	1 9 11 2	F	0 18 4 16	0 17 4 16	2 0 0
And besides, for *every* Cwt.	0 0 5 0	0 0 5 7 1/16	A	0 0 4 8 4/5	—	0 2 0
	0 0 5 3	0 0 5 3	D	0 0 5 3		
Planks of Ireland, the 100 feet, containing five score	0 2 7 10	0 2 9 9 3/4	A	0 2 3 15	0 2 0	0 12 6
Vide in Wood.						

* If imported by Aliens Drawback more, 1s. 3d. for every 100l. of the Rate or Value.

[206]

INWARDS.

	DUTIES to be paid on IMPORTATION.		DRAWBACKS to be repaid on EXPORTATION.*		RATES, or rated value, by 12 Car. II. cap. 4. 11 Geo. I. cap. 7. from whence the foregoing Duties are computed.
Reference to the several Branches, fee Page vi.	By BRITISH. £ s. d/20ths	By ALIENS. £ s. d/20ths	If exported to any legal place, except as mentioned in the following column. £ s. d/20ths	If the produce of Europe, or the East Indies, and exported to the British Colonies in America. £ s. d/20ths	£ s. d
Platting, or other manufactures of Baft, Straw, Chip, Cane, or Horse hair, to be used in, or pro- per for, making of hats or bon- nets, for every pound weight averdupois, by 10 Geo. III. cap. 43. is rated at — } l. s. d. 0 6 8	0 1 9	0 1 10			0 4 0
Platain, for Dyers use, as by 3 and 4 Ann. cap. 4. for every 20s. of the value upon oath	0 3 1 16	0 3 4 19	0 1 7	0 1 5	0 4 6
Plate silver, white, or ungilt, the ounce					0 5 0
of France	0 3 5 11	0 3 6 4			
of India or China	0 2 7 10	0 2 8 2			
of all other places	0 1 6 18	0 1 7 10			
of silver, parcel gilt, the ounce					
of France	0 3 9 19	0 3 10 13			
of India or China	0 2 10 13	0 2 11 7			
of all other places	0 1 8 9	0 1 9 3			
of silver gilt, the ounce					
of France	0 4 2 8	0 4 3 3			
of India or China	0 3 1 16	0 3 2 11			

* But if imported by Aliens Drawback more, 1s. 3d. for every 100l. of the Rate or Value.

INWARDS.

	DUTIES to be paid on IMPORTATION.			Reference to the several Branches, see Page vi.	DRAWBACKS to be repaid on EXPORTATION.*		RATES, or supposed value, by 12 Car. II. cap. 4. †11 Geo. I. cap.7. from whence the foregoing Duties are computed.
	By BRITISH.	By ALIENS.			If exported to any legal place, except as mentioned in the following column.	If the produce of Europe or the East Indies, and exported to the British Colonies in America.	
	£. s. d. 20ths	£. s. d. 20ths			£. s. d. 20ths	£. s. d. 20ths	£. s. d.
Vide Bullion.	0 1 10 1	0 1 10 16 ¾	N a				‡ 4 0 0
wrought of gold, the ounce	1 1 0 4	1 2 0 12	C		0 19 0 4	0 17 0 4	0 13 4
‖ Plates, *vizt.* { single, white, or black, { the hundred plates the barrel, containing three hundred plates	0 7 4 4 1 2 0 12	0 7 6 6 1 2 6 18	B B		0 7 0 4 1 1 0 12	0 6 8 4 1 0 0 12	2 0 0 1 6 8
double, white, or black, { the hundred plates the barrel, containing three hundred plates	0 14 8 8 2 4 1 4	0 15 0 12 2 5 1 16	B B		0 14 8 8 2 2 1 4	0 13 4 8 2 0 1 4	4 0 0
Harrels plates, or Iron doubles, { the plate the bundle, containing ten plates	0 1 7 6 0 16 1 4	0 1 7 9 1½/10 0 16 2 15 1¼	B B		0 1 7 0 0 15 10 4	0 1 10 0 1 16	0 1 0 0 10 0
Platters of wood, the shock, containing sixty	0 1 7 10	0 2 9 1 ½	C		0 2 4 10	0 2 1 10	‡ 0 10 0
Playing tables, of walnut-tree, the pair. *Vide* Tables *in* T.	0 1 4 16	0 1 5 17	A		0 1 2 16	0 1 0 16	0 6 8
Pliers. *Vide* Pincers.							
Points of capiton, the great groce, containing 12 small groce	0 8 4 16	0 8 11 2	A		0 7 4 16	0 6 4 16	2 0 0
— of fine silk, the small groce, containing 12 dozen							1 10 0

* But if imported by Aliens Drawback more, 1s. 3d. for every 100l. of the Rate or Value.

‖ If Iron, no Drawback to the British Colonies in America.

INWARDS.

	DUTIES to be paid on IMPORTATION.		DRAWBACKS to be repaid on EXPORTATION.*		RATES, or supposed value, by 12 Car. II. cap. 4. ‡ 11 Geo. I. cap. 7. from whence the foregoing Duties are computed.
	By BRITISH.	By ALIENS.	Reference to the several Branches, see Page vi.	If exported to any legal place, except as mentioned in the following column.	If the produce of Europe or the East Indies, and exported to the British Colonies in America.
	£. s. d. 20ths	£. s. d. 20ths		£. s. d. 20ths	£. s. d. 20ths	£. s. d.
Points of thread, the great grosse, containing 12 small grosse	0 4 2 8	0 4 5 11	A	0 3 8 8	0 3 2 8	1 0 0
Pomegranates, the thousand	0 8 4 16	0 8 11 2	A	0 7 4 16	0 6 4 16	2 0 0
Pomegranate peels. *Vide in* Drugs.						
Pomice stones, the ton	0 2 9 12	0 2 11 14	A	0 2 5 11	0 2 1 12	0 13 4
Porcelain, or China ware. *Vide* Earthen ware.						
Pork, the side, of Ireland, free						
——— the ton, of Ireland, free						
Potatoes, the Cwt.	0 3 6	0 3 8 12	A	0 3 1 4	0 2 8	0 5 0
Pots of earth or stone covered, the hundred, containing five score	0 5 7 4	0 5 11 8	A	0 4 11 4	0 4 3 4	0 16 8
——— of earth or stone uncovered, the hundred cast, whether in one pot, or more	0 10 6	0 11 17 2	A	0 9 3	0 8 0	1 6 8
——— *vicat*. Galley-pots, the hundred containing five score	0 8 4 16	0 8 11 2	A	0 7 4 16	0 6 4 16	2 0 0
——— of iron, Flemish making, the dozen	0 8 4 4	1 9 13	B	1 6 10 4		2 10 0
——— of iron, French making, the dozen	0 4 1 4	2 4 10 13	F	1 7 7 4		3 0 0
——— *vicat*. Melting-pots for goldsmiths, the hundred	0 0 7 11 ⅕	0 0 8 0 1/20	A²	0 0 6 13 ⅕	0 0 5 15 ⅓	0 3 0

* But if imported by Aliens Drawback more, 1 s. 3 d. for every 100 l. of the Rate or Value.

INWARDS.

	DUTIES to be paid on IMPORTATION.		DRAWBACKs to be repaid on EXPORTATION.*		RATES, or supposed value, by 12 Car. II. cap. 4. †11 Geo. I. cap. 7. from whence the foregoing Duties are computed.
	By BRITISH.	By ALIENS.	Reference to the several Branches, see Page vi.	If exported to any legal place, except as mentioned in the following column.	If the produce of Europe or the East Indies, and exported to the British Colonies in America.	
	£. s. d.|20ths	£. s. d.|20ths		£. s. d.|20ths	£. s. d.|20ths	£. s. d.
Powder of Sago. *Vide Sago-powder under letter S.*						
Powder of brass for japanning, the ounce — Prints of paper (except of India or Chi-na,) the piece *See the Table of India or China.*	0 0 1 11 ½	0 0 1 13 3/40	C	0 0 1 8 ½	0 0 1 5 1½	† 0 0 6
Unrated East India goods.	0 0 1 11 ½	0 0 1 13 3/40	C	0 0 1 8 ½	0 0 1 5 1½	† 0 0 6
Powder, called Hair powder. By 3 Geo. I. cap. 4. it is declared and enacted, "That "after the 27th of May, 1717, Hair pow-"der made of Starch, or other Powder that "will serve for the same use as Starch, "shall, on the importation thereof, be sub-"ject and liable to the same duties as fo-"reign Starch."						

* But if imported by Aliens Drawback more, 1 s. 3 d. for every 100 l. of the Rate or Value.

INWARDS.

	DUTIES to be paid on IMPORTATION.		Reference to the several Branches, &c. Page vi.
	If taken by any of His Majesty's Ships of War.	If taken by any Private Ship of War.	
	£. s. d. 25ths	£. s. d. 20ths	

PRIZE GOODS, legally condemned, (except of the growth, produce, or manufacture of the East Indies, or any British American colony or plantation) may be secured in warehouses under the King's lock, subject to the regulations directed by the 18th of Geo. III. cap. 15. 19th of Geo. III. cap. 5. 20th of Geo. III. cap. 9. and the 21st of Geo. III. cap. 5. on payment of the following duties, which are not to be drawn back on exportation:

Wine and Vinegar, the ton	3 0 0	3 0 0	Me
Glass manufactures, *not rated by* 12 Cha. II. cap. 4. *(except Glass Beads) for every 20 s. of the rate or value*	0 1 9	0 0 9	Md
Toys, *not rated by* 12 Cha. II. cap. 4. *for every 20 s. of the rate or value*	0 1 8	0 0 8	M
All sorts of Woollen, Worsted, Thread, Cotton, Linen and Silk Manufactures, Medicinal Drugs, and Hats, Handkerchiefs, Checks, Knives, Nails, and all kind of Hardware, *for every 20 s. of the value upon oath*	0 1 6	0 0 6	Md
Military and Ships Stores, which are described by the 21st of Geo. III. cap. 5. to be the following articles, and no other, may be delivered			M

P [211] P

INWARDS.

	DUTIES to be paid on IMPORTATION.		Reference to the several Branches, see Page vi.
	If taken by any of His Majesty's Ships of War.	If taken by any Private Ship of War.	
	L. s. d. 20ths	*L. s. d.* 20ths	M d M
duty free, viz. Sails, Cordage, Anchors and Cables, Masts, Yards, Bowsprits, Blocks, Guns, Gunpowder, Shot, Match, Gun Carriages, Cartridges, and other Materials thereto belonging, and all Timber and Iron converted into and made fit for ship-building, or for any of the uses and purposes aforesaid, Beef, Pork, and Butter salted, Biscuit, Small Beer, Pease and Oatmeal, Sailors Clothes, Hammocks, Bedding, and other Apparatus and Instruments of the Surgeons.			
Tobacco. *Vide in* T.	0 1 6	0 0 6	
of all other sorts, except such as are exempt from duty, *for every* } 20 *s. of the rate or value*			

may be taken out of such warehouse for exportation, under the securities required by law, without payment of any further duty whatsoever.

But if taken out of such warehouse to be consumed in this kingdom, are to pay up the remainder of the duties, which would have been due on such goods regularly imported as merchandize.

INWARDS.

	DUTIES to be paid on IMPORTATION.	
	If taken by any of His Majesty's Ships of War.	If taken by any Private Ship of War.
	£. s. d. 20ths	£. s. d. 20ths

Reference to the several Branches, see Page vi.

PRIZE GOODS, of the production or manufacture of the East Indies, *rated by 12 Cha. II. cap. 4.* are liable to the same duties, and subject to the same rules, regulations, and restrictions, as if imported by the United East India Company, except on exportation of such as are taken by any of His Majesty's ships of war, from the drawback of which as calculated in the course of the Rates, a deduction must be made of one shilling for every twenty shillings of the rate.

─── of the production or manufacture of the East Indies, *not rated by 12 Cha. II. cap. 4. See the Table of Unrated East India Prize goods at the end of the Rates Inwards.*

─── of the growth, produce, or manufacture of any British American colony or plantation, or any other of His Majesty's dominions, are liable to the same duties and drawbacks, as in cases of regular importation.

INWARDS.

	DUTIES to be paid on IMPORTATION.		DRAWBACKS to be repaid on EXPORTATION.*		RATES, or supposed value, by 12 Car. II. cap. 4. 11 Geo. I. cap. 7. from whence the foregoing Duties are computed.
	By BRITISH.	By ALIENS.	Reference to the several Branches, see Page vi.	If exported to any legal place, except as mentioned in the following column.	If the produce of Europe or the East Indies, and exported to the British Colonies in America.
	£. s. d. 20ths	£. s. d. 20ths		£. s. d. 20ths	£. s. d. 20ths	£. s. d.
Prunes. *Vide in* Grocery.	0 1 0 12	0 1 1 4 3/5	C	0 0 11 8	0 0 10 4	0 4 0
—— of Brunolia. *Vide in* Drugs.			A			
Puddings. *Vide in* Saulages.						
Pulleys, *vocat.* of brass, the dozen ——	1 1 0	1 2 3 15	D	0 18 6		5 0 0
—— of iron, the groce, containing 12 dozen	0 5 3	0 5 3	A	0 5 3	0 3 2 8	
And besides, for every Cwt. of Iron	0 4 2 8	0 4 5 11		0 3 8 8		
—— of wood, the groce, containing 12 dozen	0 0 2 10 2/5	0 0 2 13 11/20	A	0 0 2 4 2/3		1 0 0
Punsons and Gravers for goldsmiths, the pound						
And besides, for every Cwt. of Iron	0 5 3	0 5 3	D	0 5 3		0 0 1
Puppets. *Vide* Babies.						

* But if imported by Aliens Drawback more, 1s. 3d. for every 100l. of the Rate or Value.

INWARDS.

Q.

	Duties to be paid on Importation.								Reference to the several Branches, see Page vi.	Drawbacks to be repaid on Exportation. *								Rates, or supposed value by 12 Car. II. cap. 4. ‡ 11 Geo. I. cap. 7. from whence the foregoing Duties are computed.		
	By British.				By Aliens.					If exported to any legal place, except as mentioned in the following column.				If the produce of Europe or the East Indies, and exported to the British Colonies in America.						
	£.	s.	d.	20ths	£.	s.	d.	20ths		£.	s.	d.	20ths	£.	s.	d.	20ths	£.	s.	d.
QUAILS, the dozen	0	1	8	3 1/5	0	1	9	8 2/5	A	0	1	5	15 1/5	0	1	3	7 1/5	0	8	0
Quarters. *Vide* Wood.																				
Quills, *vocat.* Goose-quills, the thousand	0	0	5	0 4/5	0	0	5	7 1/10	A	0	0	4	8 4/5	0	0	3	16 4/5	0	2	0
Quilting of all sorts, whether of Linen, Callico, or cotton (not of India or China) the yard	—	—	—		—	—	—			—	—	—		—	—	—		‡ 0	5	0
—— of Linen, the yard	0	1	3	15	0	1	4	10 3/4	C	0	1	2	5	0	1	0	15			
—— of Callico, the yard	0	2	1	4	0	2	1	19 3/4	B	0	1	11	14	0	1	10	4			
—— of Cotton, the yard	0	1	3	15	0	1	4	10 3/4	C	0	1	2	5	0	1	0	15			
And besides, for every 20s. of the gross prices of the Callico and Cotton quilting at the candle	0	3	1	16	0	3	1	16	Q	0	3	1	16	0	3	1	16			
Quilts of callico, the piece	0	16	9	12	0	17	3	18	B	0	15	9	12	0	14	9	12	2	0	0
And besides, for every 20s. of the gross price at the candle	0	3	1	16	0		1	16	Q	0	3	1	16	0	3	1	16			
—— French making, the dozen	3	10	6	14 2/5	3	11	9	16 4/5	F	2	4	1	18 2/5	2	1	9	2 2/5	4	16	0
—— of sattin, or other silk, the piece	—	—	—	—	—	—	—	—		—	—	—	—	—	—	—	—	6	13	4
Quinces, the hundred	0	1	8	3 1/5	0	1	9	8 2/5	A	0	1	5	15 1/5	0	1	3	7 1/5	0	8	0

* But if imported by Aliens Drawback more, 1s. 3d. for every 20s. of the Rate or Value.

[215]

INWARDS.

R.

RACKEE. *Vide* Spirits.
Rackets, the piece ——
Kacket hoops, the dozen ——
Rags old, old Ropes or Junks, or old Fishing nets, fit only for the making of Paper or Pasteboard, are, by 11 Geo. l. cap. 7. if regularly entered and landed, duty free.
Raisins. *Vide in* Grocery.
Rape of grapes, the ton ——
　　　　　　 not French, filled ——
　　　　　　 ———— *unfilled* ——
　　　　　　 French, filled ——
　　　　　　 ———— *unfilled* ——
Rape-seed, the quarter ——

	DUTIES to be paid on IMPORTATION.		DRAWBACKS to be repaid on EXPORTATION.*		RATES, or supposed value, by 12 Car. ii. cap. 4. ‡ 11 Geo. l. cap. 7. from whence the foregoing Duties are computed.
Reference to the several Branches, see Page vi.	By BRITISH.	By ALIENS.	If exported to any legal place, except as mentioned in the following column.	If the produce of Europe or the East Indies, and exported to the British Colonies in America.	
	£. s. d. 20ths	£. s. d. 20ths	£. s. d. 20ths	£. s. d. 20ths	£. s. d.
A	0 0 1 13	0 0 1 15 7/20	0 0 1 9½	0 0 1 5¾	‡ 0 0 8
C	0 0 4 14	0 0 4 19 40/40	0 0 4 5	0 0 3 16½	‡ 0 0 1 6
A	5 3 11 8	6 15 5 8	4 3 11 8⅕	0 13 11 8⅕	3 0 0
A	4 12 7 6	6 0 3 19	5 10 5 6	0 15 5 6	
A	6 15 5 8	6 6 11 8	3 12 7 8½	0 13 4 18	
F	6 4 1 6	8 6 11 8	4 15 5 6⅕	0 14 8 15	
F			5 6 11 8	1 10 5 8	
F			4 9 1 6	1 11 11 11	
F	7 11 9 19	7 11 9 19	5 11 9 19¾	1 9 10 18	
B	0 12 7 4	0 12 10 7	0 12 1 4	0 11 2 15	1 0 0
				0 11 7 4	

* But if imported by Aliens Drawback more, 1s. 3d. for every 100l. of the Rate or Value, except Rape of Grapes.

[216]

INWARDS.

	DUTIES to be paid on IMPORTATION.		Reference to the several Branches, see Page vi.	DRAWBACKS to be repaid on EXPORTATION.*		RATES, or supposed value, by 12 Car. II. cap. 4. 11 Geo. I. cap. 7. from whence the foregoing Duties are computed.
	By BRITISH.	By ALIENS.		If exported to any legal place, except as mentioned in the following column.	If the produce of Europe or the East Indies, and exported to the British Colonies in America.	
	£. s. d. /20ths	£. s. d. /20ths		£. s. d. /20ths	£. s. d. /20ths	£. s. d.
But by 15 Geo. III. cap. 34. *whenever the price of middling British Rape-seed shall be at or above 17l. 10s. per last,* Rape and all other seeds commonly *used for the purpose of extracting oil therefrom, of the growth of Ireland, may be imported from thence paying duty for every last.* And by the above mentioned act, Rape cakes, or Cakes made of Rape feed, commonly *used for manure, may be imported from Ireland duty free.*	0 1 0 12	0 1 0 12	B			
Rapiers. *Vide* Swords.						
Rashes, *vocat.* Bridges or Leyden rashes, the single piece, containing 15 yards — the double piece, containing two single pieces	0 16 9 12	0 17 10 4	A	0 14 9 12	0 12 9 12	4 0 0
	1 9 4 16	1 11 2 17	A	1 5 10 16	1 2 4 16	7 0 0
—— Cloth rashes, the piece	3 15 7 4	4 0 3 18	A	3 6 7 4	2 17 7 4	18 0 0
Rattans. *Vide* Canes.						
Rattles for children, the groce, containing 12 dozen	0 5 7 4	0 5 11 8	A	0 4 11 4	0 4 3 4	1 6 8

* But if imported by Aliens Drawback more, 1s. 3d. for every 100l. of the Rate or Value.

[217]

INWARDS.

	Duties to be paid on IMPORTATION.		Reference to the several Branches, see Page vi.	DRAWBACKS to be repaid on EXPORTATION.*		RATES, or supposed value, by 12 Car. II. cap. 4. 11 Geo. I. cap. 7. from whence the foregoing Duties are computed.
	By BRITISH.	By ALIENS.		If exported to any legal place, except as mentioned in the following column.	If the produce of Europe or the East Indies, and exported to the British Colonies in America.	
	£. s. d. 20ths	£. s. d. 20ths		£. s. d. 20ths	£. s. d. 20ths	£. s. d.
—— with bells, the dozen	0 1 3 2	0 1 4 1 3/10	A	0 1 1 6 2/5	0 0 11 10 2/5	0 6 0
Razors, the dicker, containing ten	0 4 2 8 2/5	0 4 5 11	A	0 3 8 8		1 0 0
And besides, for every Cwt. of Steel						
Recorders, the set or case, containing five recorders	0 5 9 6	0 5 9 6	D	0 5 9 6	0 3 2 8	
Reeds. *Vide* Canes.						
Rennet, the gallon	0 4 2 8	0 4 5 11	A	0 3 8 8	0 1 14	1 0 0
Ribband of cruel. *Vide* Caddas.						
—— of silk of all sorts, the pound	0 0 2 2	0 0 2 4 7/10	C	0 1 18		4 0 8
Rice, the Cwt.						1 6 8
By 5 *Geo. III. cap.* 45. Rice of the growth and produce of *His Majesty's* colonies or plantations in America may be imported into the ports of *Chichester, Exeter, Poole, Plymouth, Sandwich,* and *Southampton,* in *South-Britain,* and *Glasgow* in *North-Britain,* for exportation, under the regulations prescribed by that law, on payment of, for every Cwt.	0 7 0	0 7 4 4	C	0 6 4	0 5 8	
	0 0 8	0 0 8	M			

* But if imported by Aliens Drawback more, 1s. 3d. for every 100l. of the Rate or Value.

[218]

INWARDS.

	DUTIES to be paid on IMPORTATION.		Reference to the several Branches, see Page vi.	DRAWBACKS to be repaid on EXPORTATION.*		RATES, or supposed value, by 12 C.r.II.cap.4. 11 Geo.I.cap.7. from whence the foregoing Duties are computed.
	By BRITISH.	By ALIENS.		If exported to any legal place, except as mentioned in the following column.	If the produce of Europe or the East Indies, and exported to the British Colonies in America.	
	£. s. d. 20ths	£. s. d. 20ths		£. s. d. 20ths	£. s. d. 20ths	£. s. d.
By 12 Geo. III. cap. 60. the same liberty is extended to the ports of Bristol, Lancaster, Liverpoole and Whitehaven, in South-Britain.						
Rims for seives, the groce, containing 12 dozen	0 1 3 2 2/5	0 1 4 1 1/10	A	0 1 1 6 2/5	0 0 11 10 2/5	0 6 0
Rings, vocat. Rings of Brass, Copper, or St. Martin's, gilt, the groce, containing 12 dozen	0 4 2 8	0 4 5 11	A	0 3 8 8	0 3 2 8	1 0 0
And besides, if { Brass, for every 20s. of the rate { Copper, the Cwt.	0 1 0 12 0 18 4 10 0 0 4 4	0 1 0 12 0 18 4 10 0 0 4 8	E E C	0 1 0 12 0 18 4 10 0 0 3 16	0 1 0 12 0 18 4 8 0 0 3 8	
for curtains, the pound						0 14 0
of hair, the groce, containing 12 dozen	0 0 7 11 1/5	0 0 8 0	A	0 0 6 13 1/5	0 0 5 15 1/5	0 3 0
for keys, the groce, containing 12 dozen	0 1 10 13 3/5	0 1 1 19 3/5	D	0 0 7 19 3/5		0 9 0
And besides, for every Cwt. of Iron	0 5 3	0 5 3		0 5 3		
small, the box, containing two groce, 12 dozen to each groce	0 2 1 4	0 2 2 15 1/2	A	0 1 10 4	0 0 7 4	0 10 0

* But if imported by Aliens Drawback more, 1s. 3d. for every 100l. of the Rate or Value.

INWARDS.	Duties to be paid on Importation. By British.				Duties to be paid on Importation. By Aliens.				Reference to the several Branches, see Page vi.	Drawbacks to be repaid on Exportation.* If exported to any legal place, except as mentioned in the following column.				Drawbacks to be repaid on Exportation.* If the produce of Europe or the East Indies, and exported to the British Colonies in America.				Rates, or supposed value, by 12 Car. II. cap. 4. ‡ 11 Geo. I. cap. 7. from whence the foregoing Duties are computed.		
	£.	s.	d.	20ths	£.	s.	d.	20ths		£.	s.	d.	20ths	£.	s.	d.	20ths	£.	s.	d.
—— of wire, the groce, containing 12 dozen	0	0	10	1 3/5	0	0	10	14 1/5	A	0	0	8	17 3/5	0	0	7	13 3/5	0	4	0
Ropes new. *Vide* Cordage.																				
—— old (fit only for making paper or pasteboard). *Vide* Rags.																				
Rosin, the Cwt.	0	1	4	16	0	1	5	17	A	0	1	2	16	0	1	0	16	0	6	8
And besides, of all sorts (except French Rosin) *not being of the product of any of the dominions and plantations belonging to the Crown of Great-Britain, the Cwt.*	0	0	8	8	0	0	8	8	E	0	0	8	8	0	0	8	8			
If imported in foreign ships, to pay duty as Aliens.																				
Rosa solis. *Vide* Spirits.																				
Rubies. *Vide* Diamonds.																				
Rugs, *vocat.* Irish rugs, the piece	0	2	9	12	0	2	11	14	A	0	2	5	12	0	2	1	12	0	13	4
—— Polish rugs, the piece	0	4	2	8	0	4	5	11	A	0	3	8	8	0	3	2	8	1	0	0
Rum. *Vide* Spirits.																				
Rye. *Vide in* Corn.																				
—— meal. *Vide in* Meal.																				

* But if imported by Aliens Drawback more, 1s. 3d. for every 100l. of the Rate or Value.

INWARDS.

	DUTIES to be paid on IMPORTATION.		Reference to the several Branches, see Page vi.	DRAWBACKS to be repaid on EXPORTATION.*		RATES, or supposed value, by 12 Car. II. cap. 4. ‡ 11 Geo. I. cap. 7. from whence the foregoing Duties are computed.
S.	By BRITISH.	By ALIENS.		If exported to any legal place, except as mentioned in the following column.	If the produce of Europe or the East Indies, and exported to the British Colonies in America.	
	£. s. d. 20ths	£. s. d. 20ths		£. s. d. 20ths	£. s. d. 20ths	£. s. d.
Sack-cloth, the hundred ells, containing six score — of single thread, the piece, containing 15 yards —	1 13 7 4	1 15 8 8	A	1 9 7 4	1 5 7	8 0 0
— with white threads, the yard	0 2 1 4	0 2 15 ½	A	0 1 10 4	0 1 7	0 10 0
— with silk, the yard	0 0 2 10 ⅖	0 2 13 1/10	A	0 0 2 4 ⅖	0 0 1 18 ⅖	0 1 6
Saddles of steel, the piece						0 1 6
And besides, for every Cwt. of Steel	0 4 2 8	0 4 5 11	A	0 3 8 8		0 1 0
Saffiore, for Dyers use, as by 3 and 4 Ann. cap. 4. the pound	0 5 9 6	0 5 9 6	D	0 5 9	0 0 4 0	0 0 0
But by 8 Geo. I. cap. 15. if regularly imported, entered, and landed, duty free.						
But on failure thereof, then to pay						
Saffron, the pound	0 0 6 5	0 0 6 8 7/20 ½	Bb	0 0 5 0	0 0 0	0 1 0
Sails. Vide in Linen.	0 0 3 12	0 0 6 6	A	0 0 19	0 0 13	1 10 0
Salt. White or Spanish salt, the bushel, containing 84 pounds weight —	0 1 13 3/5	1 15 7/10	A	0 1 9	0 1 5	0 1 0
And besides (except for such as shall be used in curing of fish) the like bushel	0 0 1 ½	0 1 11 ½	E	0 0 1 11 ½	0 0 1 11 ½	0 0 8

* But if imported by Aliens Drawback more, 1s. 3d. for every 100l. of the Rate or Value.

INWARDS

	DUTIES to be paid on IMPORTATION.		Reference to the several Branches, see Page vi.	DRAWBACKS to be repaid on EXPORTATION.*		RATES, or supposed value, by 12 Car. II. cap. 4. & 11 Geo. I. cap. 7. from whence the foregoing Duties are computed.
	By BRITISH.	By ALIENS.		If exported to any legal place, except as mentioned in the following column.	If the produce of Europe or the East Indies, and exported to the British Colonies in America.	
	£. s. d. 20ths	£. s. d. 20ths		£. s. d. 20ths	£. s. d. 20ths	£. s. d.
—— White or Spanish salt, the wey, containing 40 bushels, each bushel 84 pounds	0 5 7 4	0 5 11 8	A	0 4 11 4	0 4 3 4	1 6 8
And besides (except for such as shall be used in curing of fish) the like wey	0 5 3	0 5 3	E	0 5 3	0 5 3	
—— Bay or French salt, the like bushel	0 2 16 7/10	0 2 18 1½/10	F s	0 1 3 7/10	0 1 0 7/10	0 0 6
And besides (except for such as shall be used in curing of fish) the like bushel	0 1 11 ½	0 1 11 ½	E	0 1 11 ½	0 1 11 ½	
—— Bay or French salt, the wey, containing 40 bushels, each bushel 84 pounds	0 9 5 8	0 9 8 11	F s	0 3 11 8	0 3 5 8	1 0 0
And besides (except for such as shall be used in curing of fish) the like wey — Subject also to the Salt duties.	0 5 3	0 5 3	E	0 5 3	0 5 3	

If imported in foreign ships, to pay duty as Aliens.

By 5 Geo. I. cap. 18. all Salt imported from the iſlands of Jerſey, Guernſey, Sark and Alderney, is liable to the ſame duties as any other foreign Salt whatſoever.

* But if imported by Aliens Drawback more, 1 s. 3 d. for every 100 l. of the Rate or Value.

INWARDS.

INWARDS	DUTIES to be paid on IMPORTATION.		Reference to the several Branches, See Page vi.	DRAWBACKS to be repaid on EXPORTATION.		RATES, or supposed value, by 12 Car.II. cap.4. 11 Geo.I. cap.7. from whence the foregoing Duties are computed.
	By BRITISH.	By ALIENS.		If exported to any legal place, except as mentioned in the following column.	If the produce of Europe or the East Indies, and exported to the British Colonies in America.	
	£ s. d.20ths	£ s. d.20ths		£ s. d.20ths	£ s. d.20ths	£ s. d.
Saltpetre, the Cwt. for dyers use, as by 3 and 4 Ann. cap. 4.	0 2 1 4	0 2 4 7	Bb	0 1 7 4	0 1 1 4	1 1 0
But if of East India, the Cwt.	0 7 4 4	0 7 7	S c	0 6 10 4	0 6 4 4	
if of France	0 12 7 4	0 12 10	F a	0 7 1 4	0 6 7 4	
Sago powder. By 21 Geo. III. cap. 29. may be imported by any person from any of his Majesty's colonies in North America, at any time before the 1st day of December, 1796, duty-free.						
Sapan wood. Vide Wood for dying.						
Saphora. Vide Barillia.						
Sausages or Puddings of Bologna, or any other place, the pound	0 0 3 3	0 0 3 6 1/10	C	0 0 2 17	0 0 2 11	0 0 8
Saws, vacat. Hand saws, the dozen	0 1 4 16	0 1 5 17	A	0 1 2 16	—	0 6 8
Leg saws, the piece	0 1 4 16	0 1 5 17	A	0 1 2 16	—	0 6 8
Tenant saws, the dozen	0 2 9 12	0 2 11 14 3/4	A	0 2 5 12	—	0 13 4
Whip saws, the piece	0 1 0 12	0 1 1 7	A	0 0 11 2	—	0 5 0
And besides, for every Cwt. of Iron contained in any of the aforesaid Saws —	0 5 3	0 5 3	D	0 5 3	—	
Says, vacat. Double say or serge, the yard —	0 2 6 4	0 2 8 3/5	A	0 2 12 4/5	0 1 11 4/5	0 12 0

* If imported by Aliens Drawback more, 1 s. 3 d. for every 100 l. of the Rate or Value.

[223]

INWARDS.

	DUTIES to be paid on IMPORTATION.		DRAWBACKS to be repaid on EXPORTATION.*		RATES, or supposed value, by 12 Car. II. cap. 4. ‡ 11 Geo. I. cap. 7. from whence the foregoing Duties are computed.
	By BRITISH.	By ALIENS.	Reference to the several Branches, see Page vi.	If exported to any legal place, except as mentioned in the following column.	If the produce of Europe or the East Indies, and exported to the British Colonies in America.	
	£. s. d. 1/20ths	£. s. d. 1/20ths		£. s. d. 1/20ths	£. s. d. 1/20ths	£. s. d.
—— Double fays, or Flanders ferges, the piece, containing 15 yards ——	1 17 9 12	2 0 11 9	A	1 13 3 12	1 8 9 12	9 0 0
—— Hounfcot fay, the piece, containing 24 yards ——	1 5 2 8	1 6 9 6	A	1 2 2 8	0 19 2 8	6 0 0
—— Milled fays, the piece ——	1 5 2 8	1 6 9 6	A	1 2 2 8	0 19 2 8	6 0 0
Scale-boards, the Cwt.						0 3 4
of America, if regularly entered and landed, duty free.						
On failure thereof. See in Wood.	0 8 11 2	0 8 11 12	W d	0 8 10 2	0 8 9 2	
—— of or from any part of Europe, except Ireland or France	0 8 9 18	0 9 10 8	Qa	0 8 8 18	0 8 7 18	0 1 0
—— of Ireland, Africa, or Asia ——	0 10 3 18	0 10 4 8	Qd	0 9 4 18	0 9 3 18	0 7 6
—— of France						
If imported in foreign ships, to pay duty as Aliens.						
Scamoty, the yard	0 3 3	0 3 6 1/20ths	C	0 2 17	0 2 11 2	
—— the piece, containing 7 ½ yards ——	0 1 11 12	0 2 0 16	C	0 1 9 7	0 1 7 2	
And besides, if Cotton, for every 20s. of the gross price at the candle						
Scarlet powder. Vide Grain.	0 3 1 16	0 3 1 16	Q	0 3 1 16	0 3 1 16	

* But if imported by Aliens Drawback more, 1s. 3d. for every 100l. of the Rate or Value.

[224]

INWARDS.	DUTIES to be paid on IMPORTATION.		Reference to the several Branches, seu Paguvi.	DRAWBACKS to be repaid on EXPORTATION.*		RATES, or supposed value, by 12 Car. II. cap. 4. 11 Geo. I. cap. 7. from whence the foregoing Duties are computed.
	By BRITISH.	By ALIENS.		If exported to any legal place, except as mentioned in the following column.	If the produce of Europe, or the East Indies, and exported to the British Colonies in America.	
	£. s. d.¹/₂₀ths	£. s. d.¹/₂₀ths		£. s. d.¹/₂₀ths	£. s. d.¹/₂₀ths	£. s. d.
Sciflars, the groce, containing 12 dozen — *And besides, for every Cwt. of Iron*	0 12 7 4	0 13 4 13	A	0 11 1 4	0 0 8 10	3 0 0
Scoops of wood, the dozen	0 0 5 3	0 0 5 3	D	0 0 5 3	0 0 3 2	‡ 0 3 4
Scaholly roots, the Cwt.	0 0 10 10	0 0 11 0	C	0 0 9 10	0 0 5 15 ⅕	‡ 1 0 0
Scamorie teeth, the pound	0 0 4 2 8	0 0 4 5 11	A	0 0 3 8		‡ 0 3 0
{ Agnus castus seed — *Vide in Drugs.*	0 0 7 11 ⅕	0 0 0 8 ¹¹/₂₀		0 0 6 13 ⅕		
Amcos feed						
Amomi feed						
Canary feed. *Vide* Alphisti.						
Caraway feed } *Vide in Drugs.*	0 2 7 10	0 2 9 1 ½	C	0 2 4 10	0 2 1 10	0 0 0
Carthamus feed	0 12 7 4	0 12 10 7	B	0 12 1 4	0 11 7 4	‡ 1 0 0
Clover feed, the Cwt.	0 0 5 3	0 0 5 3	Fx	0 0 0 3	0 0 0 3	0 0 0
Cole feed, the quarter, containing eight bushels						
more, if French						
Coriander feed } *Vide in Drugs.*						
Cummin feed						
Fennel feed						
Hemp feed, the last, containing ten quarters, each quarter containing eight bushels	4 8 2 8	4 8 5 11	B	4 7 8 8	4 7 2 8	‡ 1 0 0

* But if imported by Aliens Drawback more, 1s. 3d. for every 100l. of the Rate or Value.

INWARDS.

	DUTIES to be paid on IMPORTATION. By BRITISH. £. s. d. 20ths	By ALIENS. £. s. d. 20ths	Reference to the feveral Branches, fee Page vi.	DRAWBACKS to be repaid on EXPORTATION.* If exported to any legal place, except as mentioned in the following column. £. s. d. 20ths	If the produce of Europe or the Eaft Indies, and exported to the Britifh Colonies in America. £. s. d. 20ths	RATES, or fuppofed value, by 12 Car. II. cap. 4. ‡ 11 Geo. I. cap. 7. from whence the foregoing Duties are computed. £. s. d.
Seeds, vocat. — more, if French	0 5 3	0 5 3	F x	0 0 3	0 0 3	
Vide alfo under Linfeed, *letter* L.						
Linfeed. *Vide in* L.						
Lucerne feed, the Cwt.	0 2 7 10	0 2 9 1 ½	C	0 2 4 10	0 2 1 10	‡ 0 10 0
Maw feed, the pound	0 0 1 11 ½	0 0 1 13 1/40	C	0 0 1 8 ½	0 0 1 5 1/5	‡ 0 0 6
Millet feed, the Cwt.	0 4 2 8	0 4 4 18 2/5	C	0 3 9 12	0 3 4 16	‡ 0 16 0
Muftard feed. *Vide in* M.						
Onion feed. *Vide in* O.						
Piony feed — Poppy feed — } *Vide in* Drugs.						
Rape feed. *Vide in* R.						
Semen cucumeris, Cucurb, Citrol, or Melon — Thlafpii femen — Seeds for gardens of all other forts — } *Vide in* Drugs.						
Turnip feed. *Vide* Seeds for gardens.						
Serge of Athens, the yard	0 0 5 0 4/5	0 0 5 7 1/10	A	0 0 4 8 4/5	0 0 3 16 4/5	0 2 0
— of Florence, the yard	0 4 2 8	0 4 5 11	A	0 3 8 8	0 3 2 8	1 0 0
— of all other places. *Vide* Stuffs.						
— *Vide* Says.						

* But if imported by Aliens Drawback more, 1 s. 3 d. for every 100 l. of the Rate or Value.

Gg

INWARDS.

	By BRITISH. (£. s. d. 20ths)	By ALIENS. (£. s. d. 20ths)	Reference to the several Branches, see Page vi.	If exported to any legal place, except as mentioned in the following column. (£. s. d. 20ths)	If the produce of Europe or the East Indies, and exported to the British Colonies in America. (£. s. d. 20ths)	RATES, or supposed value, by 12 Car. II. cap. 4. & 11 Geo. I cap. 7. from whence the foregoing Duties are computed. (£. s. d.)
Serpentine. *Vide* Gunpowder.						
Shavings for hats. *Vide* Platting.						
Shears, *vizt.* Forceps, the groce, containing 12 dozen	0 2 9 12	0 2 11 14	A	0 2 5 12	—	0 13 4
—— for glovers, the pair	0 0 2 10	0 0 2 13 1/2	A	0 0 2 4 8	—	0 1 0
—— for sempsters, the dozen	0 0 8 8	0 0 8 18	A	0 0 8 8 2/5	—	0 3 0
—— for shearmen, new, the pair	0 0 4 2	0 0 5 11	A	0 0 3 8	—	1 0 0
—— for shearmen, old, the pair	0 0 2 9 12	0 0 2 11 14	A	0 0 2 5 12	—	0 13 4
—— for taylors, the dozen	0 3 4 6	0 3 6 16 4/5	A	0 2 11 10 2/5	—	0 10 0
And besides, for every Cwt. of Iron contained in any of the aforesaid Shears	0 5 3	0 5 3	D	0 5 3	—	—
Sheep imported from Ireland to Great-Britain, by the score, free						
Sheeps guts dried to make whips, the groce, containing 12 dozen	0 0 5 5	0 0 5 10 1/4	C	0 0 4 15	0 0 4 5	5 0 0
Ships taken as prize, and regularly condemned in the High Court of Admiralty, for every 20 s. value of each ship, her tackle, apparel, furniture, and spare stores, as ascertained upon oath	0 1 0 12		V			0 1 8

* But if imported by Aliens Drawback more, 1 s. 3 d. for every 100 l. of the Rate or Value.

[227]

INWARDS.

	Reference to the several Branches, see Page vi.	DUTIES to be paid on IMPORTATION.		DRAWBACKS to be repaid on EXPORTATION.*		RATES, or supposed value, by 12 Car.II.cap.4. 11 Geo.I.cap.7. from whence the foregoing Duties are computed.
		By BRITISH.	By ALIENS.	If exported to any legal place, except as mentioned in the following column.	If the produce of Europe or the East Indies, and exported to the British Colonies in America.	
		L. s. d. 20ths	*L. s. d.* 20ths	*L. s. d.* 20ths	*L. s. d.* 20ths	*L. s. d.*
Shovels of wood unshod, the dozen	C	0 2 7 10	0 2 9 1	0 2 4 10	0 2 1 10	0 10 0
Shuttles for weavers, the dozen	C	0 2 7 10	0 2 9 1	0 2 4 10	0 2 1 10	0 10 0
Shruff, or old brass, the Cwt.	A	0 12 2 4	0 13 4 13	0 11 1 4	0 7 4	3 0 0
Shubs of Calabar, the piece or shub	C	0 10 7 6	0 11 0 6	0 9 6	0 8 6	2 0 0
Shumack, the Cwt. *for dyers use, as by 3 & 4 Ann. cap. 4. But by 8 Geo. I. cap. 15. § 10. if regularly imported, entered, and landed, duty free. But on failure thereof, then to pay*						0 13 4
Silk, *viret.* — Bridges silk, the pound, containing 16 ounces	Bb	0 1 4 16	0 1 6 18	0 1 0 16	0 1 0 16	2 0 0
Ferret or Floret silk, the pound containing 16 ounces	A	0 8 4 16	0 8 11 2	0 7 4 16	0 6 4 16	1 0 0
Fillozel, or Paris silk, the pound, containing 16 ounces	C	0 4 8 14	0 4 11 17	0 4 2 14	0 3 8 14	0 15 0
Granada silk black, the pound, containing 16 ounces	F	0 11 0 6	0 11 2 13	0 6 10 16	0 6 6	3 0 0
— in colours, the pound, containing 16 ounces	A	0 12 7 4	0 13 4 13	0 11 1 4	0 9 7 4	3 0 0
— containing 16 ounces	A	0 16 9 12	0 17 10 4	0 14 9 12	0 12 9 12	4 0 0

* *But if imported by Aliens, Drawback more, 1s. 3d. for every 1col. of the Rate or Value.*

[228]

INWARDS.

Silk, vizt.

	DUTIES to be paid on IMPORTATION.		DRAWBACKS to be repaid on EXPORTATION.*		RATES, or supposed value, by 12 Car. II. cap. 4. 11 Geo. I. cap. 7. from whence the foregoing Duties are computed.
	By BRITISH.	By ALIENS.	Reference to the several Branches, see Page vi.	If exported to any legal place, except as mentioned in the following column.	If the produce of Europe or the East Indies, and exported to the British Colonies in America.	
	£. s. d. 20ths	£. s. d. 20ths		£. s. d. 20ths	£. s. d. 20ths	£. s. d.
Naples silk black, the pound, containing 16 ounces —	0 8 4 16	0 8 11 2	A	0 7 4 16	0 6 4 16	2 0 0
— in colours, the pound, containing 16 ounces	0 10 6	0 11 1 17	A	0 9 3	0 8 0	2 10 0
Organzine and all Thrown silk in the gum, the pound, containing 16 ounces	0 4 10 16	0 5 1 8	C	0 3 11 16	0 3 6 16	
But if exported to Ireland, the drawback is						
Pole and Spanish silk, the pound, containing 16 ounces —	0 8 4 16	0 8 11 2	A	0 7 4 16	0 6 4 16	0 16 8
Raw Silk. *The former rates and duties on Raw Silk, are, by 5 Geo. III. cap. 29. repealed, and in lieu thereof, a duty is imposed on every pound weight, containing 24 ounces*	0 1 3 15	0 1 3 15	A	0 1 0 15		2 0 0
If exported to Ireland, the drawback is						
But Raw Silk of the growth and culture of any of His Majesty's colonies or plantations in America, may, by						

* But if imported by Aliens Drawback more, 1s. 3d. for every 100 l. of the Rate or Value, except Raw Silk.

[229]

INWARDS.	DUTIES to be paid on IMPORTATION.		Reference to the several Branches, see Page vi.	DRAWBACKS to be repaid on EXPORTATION.*		RATES, or supposed value, by 12 Car. II. cap. 4. 11 Geo. I. cap. 7. from whence the foregoing Duties are computed.
	By BRITISH.	By ALIENS.		If exported to any legal place, except as mentioned in the following column.	If the produce of Europe or the East Indies, and exported to the British Colonies in America.	
	£. s. d. 20ths	£. s. d. 20ths		£. s. d. 20ths	£. s. d. 20ths	£. s. d.
Silk, vocat. 23 Geo. II. cap. 20. be imported directly from thence into the port of London, under the certificates and oaths required by that law, if regularly entered and landed, duty free. On failure thereof, then to pay ——— for every pound weight, containing 24 ounces. If exported to Ireland, the drawback is						
Sattin silk, the pound, containing 16 ounces	0 1 3 15	0 1 3 15	A	0 1 0 15	0 0 6 4$\frac{4}{5}$	2 0 0
Silk nubs, or Husks of silk, the pound, containing 21 ounces	0 8 4 16	0 8 11 2	A	0 7 4 16	0 0 3 16	0 2 0
Sleeve silk, coarse, the pound, containing 16 ounces	0 0 5 0	0 0 5 7$\frac{1}{10}$	A	0 0 4 8	0 0 1 12	0 13 4
——— fire, or Naples sleeve, the pound, containing 16 ounces	0 2 9 12	0 2 11 14	A	0 2 5 12	0 2 8 6	2 13 4
Thrown silk, dyed, the pound, containing 16 ounces	1 1 6 6	1 2 10 1	A	0 18 6 6	0 16 0 6	5 0 0

* But if imported by Aliens Drawback more, 1s. 3d. for every 100l. of the Rate or Value, except Raw Silk.

[230]

INWARDS.

Silk, vizt.

	DUTIES to be paid on IMPORTATION.		Reference to the several Branches, see Page vi.	DRAWBACKS to be repaid on EXPORTATION.*		RATES, or supposed value, by 12 Car. II. cap. 4. 11 Geo. I. cap. 7. from whence the foregoing Duties are computed.
	By BRITISH.	By ALIENS.		If exported to any legal place, except as mentioned in the following column.	If the product of Europe or the East Indies, and exported to the British Colonies in America.	
	£. s. d. 20ths	£. s. d. 20ths		£. s. d. 20ths	£. s. d. 20ths	£. s. d.
But if exported to Ireland, the drawback is						
Thrown Silk Vide Organzine.						
Wrought silk, imported in ships British built directly from the East-Indies, the pound weight, containing 16 ounces	0 4 10	0 6 15	M	0 19 0 6		0 15 0
And besides, for every 20s. of the true and real value, according to the gross price at which the goods are publicly sold at the sales of the East-India company. See the Table of Unrated East-India goods.						
at any other public legal sales						
imported from the East-Indies in other bottoms, the pound weight, containing 16 ounces						
of the manufacture of Italy, imported from thence in British-built ships, the pound, containing 16 ounces	0 1 0	0 1 0	Pc			1 13 4

* But if imported by Aliens Drawback more, 1s. 2d. for every 100l. of the Rate or Value.

INWARDS.

	DUTIES to be paid on IMPORTATION.		DRAWBACKS to be repaid on EXPORTATION.*		RATES, or supposed value, by 12 Car. II. cap. 4. ‡ 11 Geo. I. cap. 7. from whence the foregoing Duties are computed.
	By BRITISH.	By ALIENS.	Reference to the several Branches, see Page vi.	If exported to any legal place, except as mentioned in the following column.	If of the produce of Europe or the East Indies, and exported to the British Colonies in America.	
	£. s. d. 20ths	£. s. d. 20ths		£. s. d. 20ths	£. s. d. 20ths	£. s. d.

Silk, vocat. ⎧ from Italy
⎪ from any other parts of the world, the pound weight, containing 16 ounces
⎨ Wrought silk Crapes or Tiffanies of the manufacture of Italy, imported from thence in British-built ships, the pound, containing 16 ounces — otherwise imported, the pound
⎩

Silver. *Vide* Plate.

Skates of wood for sliding, shod, the dozen

And besides, for every Cwt. of Iron

Skeets for whitsters, the skeet

Skins, vocat. ⎧ Buck, or Deer skins, in the hair; the skin — dressed, the skin
⎨ *And besides, for every pound weight* — Indian, half
⎩ dressed, the pound weight Calve skins in the hair. *Vide* in C.

	£ s d/20ths	£ s d/20ths	ref	£ s d/20ths	£ s d/20ths	£ s d
Silk Italy	1 11 10 4	1 12 3 9	Pd	1 2 6 10 2/3	1 1 5 4	2 0 0
any other						
Wrought silk Italy	1 1 0	1 14 7 16	Pd	1 4 8 10	1 3 4 10	2 0 0
otherwise						
Skates	0 0 3 18 3/4	0 0 4 4 1 16/20	C	0 0 0 3 11 2/5		‡ 0 1 3
Iron	0 0 5 3	0 0 5 3 1 20/	D	0 0 5 3		0 1 0
Skeets	0 0 2 10	0 0 8 3 6/	A	0 0 2 4		0 2 6
Buck/Deer skin	0 0 7 17	0 0 1 4 3/4	C	0 0 7 2	0 0 1 18	0 5 0
dressed	0 1 3 15	0 0 4 10	C	0 1 2 5	0 0 6 7	
Indian	0 0 9 9	0 0 9 9	D	0 0 0 9	0 0 15 9	
Calve hair	0 0 3 18	0 0 4 2 1 12/	C	0 0 3 11	0 0 0 3	‡ 0 1 3

* But if imported by Aliens Drawback more, 1s. 3d. for every 100l. of the Rate or Value.

INWARDS.

Skins, vocat.

	DUTIES to be paid on IMPORTATION.		DRAWBACKS to be repaid on EXPORTATION.*		RATES, or supposed value, by 12 Car. II. cap. 4. 11 Geo. 1. cap. 7. from whence the foregoing Duties are computed.
	By BRITISH.	By ALIENS.	If exported to any legal place, except as mentioned in the following column.	If the produce of Europe or the East Indies, and exported to the British Colonies in America.	
	£. s. d. 20ths	£. s. d. 20ths	£. s. d. 20ths	£. s. d. 20ths	£. s. d.
Calve skins of Ireland, raw, the dozen	0 5 3	0 5 6 3	0 4 9	0 4 3	0 6 8
But if duly enter'd and landed, duty free, as stated page 33.					
——— dress'd in alum, and salt, or meal, or otherwise tawed, for every 20s. of their value upon oath	0 0 3 3	0 0 3 3 1	0 0 2 3 10	0 0 2 3 10	
——— for every pound weight: tanned, the dozen	0 2 7 10	0 2 9 10	0 2 4 10	0 2 1 10	0 10 0
And besides, for every pound weight:					
Slink calve skins, however dress'd, for every 20s. of their value upon oath	0 0 3 13	0 0 3 13	0 0 2 10	0 0 2 10	
——— for every lb. weight { with the hair on / without the hair	0 5 3	0 5 6 3	0 4 9	0 4 3	
Coney skins, the dozen	0 0 2 2	0 0 2 1 1	0 0 0	0 0 0	
Cordivants of Turkey, East-India, or Scotland, the dozen, (and vide in Leather)	0 0 3 3	0 0 3 6	0 0 0	0 0 0	1 6 8
——— of Turkey, the dozen	0 15 4 16	0 15 9	0 6 8 16	0 6 8 16	
——— of East India, the dozen	1 2 4 16	1 2 9	0 13 8 16	0 13 8 16	

* But if imported by Aliens Drawback more, 1s. 3d. for every 100l. of the Rate or Value.

INWARDS.

Skins, vocat.

	DUTIES to be paid on IMPORTATION.				Reference to the several Branches, fee Page vi.	DRAWBACKS to be repaid on EXPORTATION.*				RATES, or fuppofed value, by 12 Car.II.cap.4. 11Geo.I.cap.7. from whence the foregoing Duties are computed.	
	By BRITISH.		By ALIENS.			If exported to any legal place, except as mentioned in the following column.		If the produce of Europe or the East Indies, and exported to the British Colonies in America.			
	£. s. d.20ths		£. s. d.20ths			£. s. d.20ths		£. s. d.20ths		£. s. d.	
Spanish, Sevil, or Cordivant skins; the dozen	1 14 7 16		1 15 11 11		O	1 4 1 16		1 1 7 16		5 0 0	
Dog skins undressed, the piece	0 0 2 2		0 0 2 4		C	0 0 1 18		0 1 1 14		‡ 0 0 8	
— however dressed, *for every* 20s. *of their value upon oath*	0 5 3		0 5 6		C	0 4 9		0 4 3			
for every pound weight											
Dog-fish skins, for fletchers, the dozen	0 0 0 1		0 0 1 1		D	0 0 0 † 8		0 0 0 1		0 0 6	
Elk skins dressed or undressed, the skin	0 1 1 11		0 1 13 7/16		C	0 0 1 8		0 0 1 5 1/2		0 0 6	
And besides, *if dressed in oil, for every pound weight*	0 6 18		0 1 7 16		C	0 0 1 5		0 0 1 6			
Fisher skins, the piece	0 0 7 7		0 0 7 7		D	0 0 5 0		0 0 5 0		0 0 8	
Fox skins dressed, the dozen	0 1 3 15		0 1 4 10		C	0 1 3 2 5		0 0 3 4 16		0 0 5 0	
And besides, *for every* 20s. *of their real value upon oath*	0 4 2 8		0 4 4 18		C	0 3 9 12		0 3 4 16		0 16 0	
Goat skins { of Barbary or the East country, the dozen	0 6 3 12		0 6 3 12		D	0 3 0		0 3 12			
in the hair { of Ireland, the dozen	0 5 3		0 5 6 3		C	0 4 9		0 4 3		1 0 0	
{ not otherwise rated, the dozen	0 1 9		0 1 10 0		C	0 1 7		0 1 5		0 6 8	
	0 5 3		0 5 6 3		C	0 4 9		0 4 3		1 0 0	

* If imported by Aliens Drawback more, 1s. 3d. for every 100l. of the Rate or Value.

S [234] S

INWARDS.		DUTIES to be paid on IMPORTATION.		Reference to the several Branches, see Page vi.	DRAWBACKS to be repaid on EXPORTATION.*		RATES, or suppofed value, by 13 Car. II. cap. 4. 11 Geo. I. ... from which the foregoing Duties are computed
		By BRITISH.	By ALIENS.		If exported to any legal place, except as mentioned in the following column.	If the produce of Europe or the Eaſt Indies, and exported to the British Colonies in America.	
		£. s. d. 20ths	£. s. d. 20ths		£. s. d. 20ths	£. s. d. 20ths	£. s. d.
Skins, viccat.	*Goat skins, raw or undreſſed, the dozen* — *But by 20 Geo. III. cap. 19. any Goat ſkins raw or undreſſed may be imported in British-built ſhips from any port or place whatſoever, if regularly entered and landed, duty free, until the 20th of June, 1785, and from thence to the end of the then next ſeſſions of parliament. And by 21 Geo. III. cap. 29. Goat ſkins raw or undreſſed may be imported duty free from Ireland, or any of the British colonies or plantations in America, if regularly entered and landed, until the 1ſt of June, 1786, and from thence to the end of the then next ſeſſions of parliament.*	0 14 8 8 0 0 6 6	0 15 2 14 0 0 6 6	S a I a	0 9 8 8 0 0 0 6	0 8 8 8 0 0 0 6	2 0 0
	Goat ſkins tanned, the dozen — *And beſides, for every pound weight* —						

* But if imported by Aliens Drawback more, 1s. 3d. for every 100l. of the Rate or Value.

S   [235]   S

Skins, *&c. &c.*

INWARDS.

	DUTIES to be paid on IMPORTATION.		DUTIES to be paid on IMPORTATION.		Reference to the several Branches, see Page vi.	DRAWBACKS to be repaid on EXPORTATION.*		DRAWBACKS to be repaid on EXPORTATION.*		RATES, or supposed value, by 12 Car.II. cap. 4. ‡ 11 Geo.I. cap. 7. from whence the foregoing Duties are computed.
	By BRITISH.		By ALIENS.			If exported to any legal place, except as mentioned in the following column.		If the produce of Europe or the East Indies, and exported to the British Colonies in America.		
	£. s. d. 20ths		£. s. d. 20ths			£. s. d. 20ths		£. s. d. 20ths		£. s. d.
—— of all other sorts, (except Cordivant) however dressed, for every 20s. of their value upon oath	0 5 3		0 5 6 3		C	0 4 9		0 4 3		
—— for every pound weight	0 0 4 2 8		0 0 4 2 8		Rb	0 0 2 8		0 0 2 8		0 0 6
Gold skins, the skin	0 0 6 6 ½		0 0 6 6 ½		Ia	0 0 6 8		0 0 6 8		
And besides, if dressed, for every 20s. of their real value, upon oath	0 0 1 11		0 0 1 13 3/40		C	0 0 1 8		0 0 1 5		
Hare skins, the dozen	0 0 6 3 12		0 0 6 3 12		Dc	0 0 3 12		0 0 3 12		0 0 4 6
Huffe skins, for fletchers, the skin	0 0 1 1		0 0 1 2 ½		C	0 0 1 9		0 0 17		0 0 0
Kid skins in the hair, the hundred, containing five score	0 0 1 11 ½		0 0 1 13 1/40		C	0 0 1 8		0 0 1 5		2 0 0
if French										
if not French —— dressed, the hundred, containing five score	1 17 9 18		1 18 1 1		Fu	0 19 9 18		0 18 3 18		
if French	0 18 4 10		0 18 7 13		O	0 10 4 10		0 9 4 10		
if not French —— not perfectly dressed, for every 20s. of their value upon oath	2 2 6 6		2 3 0 12		Fu	0 0 6		0 0 6		
—— for every dozen	1 3 7 10		1 4 1 16		O	0 10 1 10		0 9 1 10		
	0 5 3		0 5 6 3		C	0 4 9		0 4 3		
	0 1 6 18		0 1 6 18		Dc	0 0 18		0 0 13		

* But if imported by Aliens Drawback more, 1s. 3d. for every 100l. of the Rate or Value.

[236]

INWARDS. — Skins, vacat.

Item	Duties to be paid on Importation — By British £ s. d./20ths	By Aliens £ s. d./20ths	Ref. to the several Branches, see Paguvi	Drawbacks on Exportation — If exported to any legal place, except as mentioned in the following column £ s. d./20ths	If the produce of Europe, or the East Indies, and exported to the British Colonies in America £ s. d./20ths	Rates, or supposed value, by 12 Car. II. cap. 4, 11 Geo. I. cap. 7, from whence the foregoing Duties are computed £ s. d.
Kip skins however tawed, for every 20 s. of their value upon oath	0 5 3	0 5 3 6	C	0 4 9	0 4 3	††
— for every pound weight	0 3 3	0 3 3	D	0 0 3	0 0 3	†† 0 1 0
Lamb skins dressed in alum, the hundred containing five score	0 5 3	0 5 3 6	C	0 4 9	0 4 3	††
And besides, for every dozen	0 1 0 12	0 1 0 12	D	0 4 12	0 0 12	††
— dressed in oil, the hundred, containing five score	0 1 1 0	0 2 0 12 ½	C	0 19 0	0 17 0	†† 0 4 0
And besides, for every dozen	0 2 1 4	0 2 1 4 ½	D	0 9 4	0 9 4	††
— undressed in the wool, the hundred, containing fix score	0 2 7 10	0 2 9 1	C	0 4 10	0 2 1 10	†† 0 10 0
— flink dressed, the hundred, containing five score	0 2 7 10	0 2 9 1 ¼	D	0 4 10	0 2 1 10	††
And besides, for every 20 s. of their real value upon oath	0 6 3 12	0 6 3 12	C	0 3 12	0 3 12	†† 0 10 0
— flink undressed, in the wool, the hundred, containing fix score	0 1 3 15	0 1 4 10	C	0 2 5	0 0 15	††
— tanned, for every 20 s. of their value upon oath	0 5 3	0 5 3 6	C	0 4 9	0 4 3	†† 0 5 0
— for every dozen	0 1 6 18	0 1 6 18	D	0 6 18	0 6 18	††

* But if imported by Aliens Drawback more, 1 s. 3 d. for every 100 l. of the Rate or Value.

[237]

INWARDS.

Skins, vizct.

	DUTIES to be paid on IMPORTATION.		DRAWBACKS to be repaid on EXPORTATION.*		RATES, or supposed value, by 12 Car. II. cap. 4. 11 Geo. I. cap. 7. from whence the foregoing Duties are computed.
	By BRITISH.	By ALIENS.	If exported to any legal place, except as mentioned in the following column.	If the produce of Europe or the East Indies, and exported to the British Colonies in America.	
	£. s. d. 20ths	£. s. d. 20ths	£. s. d. 20ths	£. s. d. 20ths	£. s. d.
Lion skins, the piece	0 2 7 10	0 2 9 1	0 2 4 10	0 2 1 10	0 0 10 ½
Moose skins, the piece	0 2 7 10	0 2 9 1	0 2 4 10	0 2 1 10	0 0 10 ½
Musquash, the skin	0 0 1 11	0 0 1 13 ¾	0 0 1 8	0 0 1 5	0 0 0 6
Panther skins, the piece	0 0 5 3	0 0 6 3 ¼	0 0 4 9	0 0 4 3	0 0 1 0
Pelts of goats, dressed, the dozen	0 0 5 2	0 0 9 1	0 0 4 1	0 0 2 1	0 0 1 0
—— of goats, undressed, the dozen	0 0 1 3 15	0 0 4 10	0 0 2 5	0 0 1 0 15	0 0 0 5
—— of all sorts, (except Goat pelts) the hundred, containing five score——	0 7 10 10	0 8 3	0 7 1 10	0 6 4 10	1 1 10 0
Portugal skins, the dozen	0 0 10 6	0 0 11 0	0 0 9 6	0 0 8 6	2 0 0 0
And besides, if dressed, for every 20 s. of their real value upon oath	D c				
Racoons, the skin	0 0 3 12	0 0 6 3 12	0 0 3 12	0 0 3 12	
Seal skins, the skin	0 0 1 11	0 0 1 1 13 7/10	0 0 1 8	0 0 1 8	0 0 0 6
And besides, if dressed, for every 20 s. of their real value upon oath	D c				
But by 15 Geo. III. cap. 31. raw or undressed Seal skins caught by the crews of vessels, whole owners are of Great Britain, Ireland, Guernsey, Jersey, or Man, may be imported under the oaths and regula—	0 0 5 5	0 0 5 10	0 0 4 15	0 0 4 5	0 0 1 8
	0 0 6 3 12	0 0 6 3 12	0 0 3 12	0 0 3 12	

* But if imported by Aliens Drawback more, 1 s. 3 d. for every 100 l. of the Rate or Value.

S [238] S

INWARDS.	Duties to be paid on IMPORTATION.		Reference to the several Branches, see Page vi.	DRAWBACKS to be repaid on EXPORTATION.*		RATES, or supposed value, by 12 Car. II. cap. 4. †11 Geo. I. cap. 7. from whence the foregoing Duties are computed.
	By BRITISH.	By ALIENS.		If exported to any legal place, except as mentioned in the following column.	If the produce of Europe or the East Indies, and exported to the British Colonies in America.	
	£. s. d. 20ths	£. s. d. 20ths		£. s. d. 20ths	£. s. d. 20ths	£. s. d.
Shagreen skins, the skin — tions prescribed by that act, duty free.						
And besides, for every 20s. of their real value upon oath	0 0 5	0 0 5 10	C	0 0 4 15	0 0 4 5	0 1 8
Shamway skins, the dozen	0 6 3 12	0 6 3 12	D c	0 0 3 12	0 0 3 12	
And besides, if not particularly charged, for every 20s. of their real value upon oath	0 7 0	0 7 4	C	0 6 4	0 5 8	1 6 8
Sheep skins dressed, the dozen	0 6 3 12	0 6 3 12	D c	0 0 3 12	0 0 3 12	
And besides, if {in oil, the dozen {otherwise dressed, the dozen	0 1 3 15 0 3 1 16	0 1 4 10 0 3 1 16	C D c	0 1 2 5 0 1 1 16	0 1 0 15 0 1 1 16	0 5 0
tanned {for every 20s. of their value upon oath {for every dozen	0 1 0 12	0 1 0 12	D c	0 0 4 12	0 0 4 12	
— in the wool, the skin	0 5 3	0 5 6 3	C	0 4 9	0 4 3	
Spruce skins, tawed, the dozen	0 1 6 18 0 0 0 15 0 11 0	0 1 6 18 0 0 0 16 6 0 11 0	D c C	0 0 6 18 0 9 0 14 0 6	0 0 6 18 0 0 0 12 0 8 6	0 0 3 0 2 0 0
And besides, for every 20s. of their real value upon oath	0 6 3 12	0 6 3 12	D c	0 0 3 12	0 0 3 12	

* But if imported by Aliens Drawback more, 1s. 3d. for every 100l. of the Rate or Value.

INWARDS.

	DUTIES to be paid on IMPORTATION.		DRAWBACKS to be repaid on EXPORTATION.*		RATES, or supposed value, by 12 Car. II. cap. 4. ‡ 11 Geo. I. cap. 7. from whence the foregoing Duties are computed.
	By BRITISH.	By ALIENS.	Reference to the several Branches, see Page vi.	If exported to any legal place, except as mentioned in the following column.	If the produce of Europe or the East Indies, and exported to the British Colonies in America.	
	£. s. d. 20ths	£. s. d. 20ths		£. s. d. 20ths	£. s. d. 20ths	£. s. d.
Skins, vocat. { Swan skins, the piece	0 0 10 10	0 0 11 0	C	0 0 9 10	0 0 8 10	‡ 1 0 4 0
Tails, or Tips of sable, the piece	0 0 6 6	0 0 6 12½	C	0 0 5 14	0 0 5 2	‡ 1 3 0
Tyger skins, the piece	0 0 2 10	0 0 2 9 ⁷⁄₁₀	C	0 0 2 4 10	0 0 2 1 10	‡ 0 2 0
Vizer skins, the piece	0 0 1 15	0 0 1 4 ½	C	0 0 1 2 5	0 0 1 0 15	‡ 0 10 0
Woodhocks, the skin	0 0 1 15	0 0 1 4 ¼	C	0 0 1 2 5	0 0 1 0 15	‡ 0 5 0
And besides the aforesaid duties, if any of the aforesaid Skins are tanned, tawed, or dressed, and not particularly charged as such, they are to pay for every 20 s. of their real value upon oath	0 6 3 12	0 6 3 12	D c	0 6 3 12	0 4 3 12	‡ 0 5 0
All other Skins (except those rated amongst Furs and Leather) and pieces of Skins, for every 20 s. of their value upon oath	0 5 3	0 5 6 3	C	0 4 9	0 4 3	
And besides, if tanned, tawed, or dressed, and not particularly charged as such, for every 20 s. of their real value upon oath	0 6 3 12	0 6 3 12	D c	0 6 3 12	0 3 12	
Slates. Vide Stones.						
Slays for weavers, the dozen	0 1 9	0 1 10 1	C	0 1 7	0 1 5	† 0 6 8

* But if imported by Aliens Drawback more, 1 s. 3 d. for every 100 l. of the Rate or Value.

INWARDS.

	Duties to be paid on Importation.		Reference to the several Branches, see Page vi.	Drawbacks to be repaid on Exportation.*		Rates, or supposed value, by 12 Car. II. cap. 4. 11 Geo. I. cap. 7. from whence the foregoing Duties are computed.
	By British.	By Aliens.		If exported to any legal place, except as mentioned in the following column.	If the produce of Europe or the East Indies, and exported to the British Colonies in America.	
	£. s. d. 20ths	£. s. d. 20ths		£. s. d. 20ths	£. s. d. 20ths	£. s. d.
Slip, the barrel	0 8 8	0 8 18 ½	A	0 7 8	0 6 8	0 3 4
Slude. *Vide* Glass for windows.						
Smalts, the pound	0 0 3 ⅗	0 0 4 13/40	A	0 0 3 6 ⅓	0 0	0 1 6
But by 21 Geo. III. cap. 50. after the 1st of June, 1782, Smalts may be imported duty free, during the continuance of certain acts therein mentioned.						
Snaphances. *Vide* Dags.						
Snowting, the Cwt.	0 5 3	0 5 6 3/10	C	0 4 9	0 4 3	0 0 0
Snuff, from any of the British plantations in America, or from any part of the Spanish West-Indies, in British ships, by 26 Geo. I. rated at ⎱ 0 2 6	0 7 17	0 8 5 1/10	C	0 6 7 ½	0 6 7 ½	
⎧ from Italy, Spain, Portugal, and all other foreign parts, except France ⎫ 0 5 0			C	0 0 15 0	0 0 15 0	‡ 1 0 0
from France, for every 20s. of the true and real value upon oath	0 14 8 8	0 14 11 11	F	0 8 8	0 8 8	
Snuffers of all sorts, the dozen	0 1 4 16	0 1 5 17	A	0 1 2 16	0 1 16	0 6 8

* But if imported by Aliens Drawback more, 1s. 3d. for every 100l. of the Rate or Value.

‖ If Iron no Drawback to the British Colonies in America.

S [241] S

INWARDS.

	DUTIES to be paid on IMPORTATION.		DRAWBACKS to be repaid on EXPORTATION.*		RATES, or supposed value, by 12 Car.II. cap.4. 11 Geo.I. cap.7. from whence the foregoing Duties are computed.
	By BRITISH.	By ALIENS.	If exported to any legal place, except as mentioned in the following column.	If the produce of Europe or the East Indies, and exported to the British Colonies in America.	
	£. s. d. 20ths	£. s. d. 20ths	Reference to the several Branches, see Page vi.	£. s. d. 20ths	£. s. d. 20ths	£. s. d.
And besides, if made of { Brass, the dozen	0 0 4 4	0 0 4 4	E	0 0 4 4	0 0 4 4	3 0 0
{ Iron, the Cwt.	0 5 3	0 5 3	D	0 5 3		4 0 0
Sope, viz. Castile or Venice, the Cwt.	2 2 0	2 2 9	A			
Flemish, the barrel	0 16 9½	0 17 10	Qb			
And besides, for every pound weight hard, of all sorts, not otherwise rated, the Cwt.	0 0 3	0 0 3	Ea			3 0 0
And besides, if of France soft, of all sorts, not otherwise rated, the Cwt.	2 2 0	2 2 9	Fb			
	1 11 6	1 11 6	Qb			
Ant besides, if of France	1 15 8	1 16 1	Fb			1 10 0
Sopers waste, the ton, containing 20 Cwt. duty free	0 15 9	0 15 9				
Socks of thread, or of cotton, the dozen pair	0 1 9	0 1 10 1¼	C	0 1 7	0 1 5	0 10 0
And besides, if Cotton, for every 20s. value of the gross price at the candle	0 3 1 16	0 3 1 16	Q	0 3 1 16	0 3 1 16	0 6 8
Spanish wood. Vide Archelia.						
Spangles of copper, the thousand	0 2 10 4 10	0 0 2 13 1 20 4 10	A	0 0 2 4 4 10	0 0 1 18 4 10	0 1 0
And besides, for every Cwt.	0 18	0 18	E	0 18		

* But if imported by Aliens Drawback more, 1s. 3d. for every 100l. of the Rate or Value.

[242]

INWARDS.

	Duties to be paid on IMPORTATION.		Reference to the several Branches, see Page vii.	Drawbacks to be repaid on EXPORTATION.*		RATES, or supposed value, by 12 Car. II. cap. 4. † 11 Geo. I. cap. 7. from whence the foregoing Duties are computed.
	By BRITISH.	By ALIENS.		If exported to any legal place, except as mentioned in the following column.	If the produce of Europe or the East Indies, and exported to the British Colonies in America.	
	£. s. d. 20ths	£. s. d. 20ths		£. s. d. 20ths	£. s. d. 20ths	£. s. d.
Spars boom, the hundred, containing 120 — For the duties, see B, page 21.	0 6 3 12	0 6 6 15	B	0 5 9 12	0 5 3 12	1 13 4
cant, the hundred, containing 120 — For the duties, see C, page 35.	0 4 2 8	0 4 5 11	A	0 3 8 8	0 3 2 8	1 13 4
Spars small, the hundred, containing fix score — of and directly from any part of America, if regularly entered and landed, free.						
On failure thereof. See in Wood.						
— of or from any part of Europe, except Ireland and France — of Ireland, Africa, or Asia — of France. See in Wood.	0 7 4 4	0 7 7 7	B	0 6 10 4	0 6 4 4	1 0 0
If imported in foreign ships, to pay duty as Aliens.						
Spectacles without cases, the groce, containing 12 dozen	0 1 4 16	0 1 4 16	Ze	0 0 16	0 0 16	
And besides, for every pound of Glass (except green Glass)						1 0 0
Spelter of Germany, the Cwt.	0 13 1 10	0 13 9 7 ½	C	0 11 10 10	0 10 7 10	† 2 10 0

* But if imported by Aliens Drawback more, 1s. 3d. for every 100l. of the Rate or Value.

INWARDS.

	Duties to be paid on IMPORTATION.		Drawbacks to be repaid on EXPORTATION.*		Rates, or supposed value, by 12 Car. II. cap. 4. 11 Geo. I. cap. 7. from whence the foregoing Duties are computed.
	By British.	By Aliens.	Reference to the several Branches, see Page vi.	If exported to any legal place, except as mentioned in the following column.	If the produce of Europe or the East Indies, and exported to the British Colonies in America.	
	£. s. d. 20ths	£. s. d. 20ths		£. s. d. 20ths	£. s. d. 20ths	£. s. d.
Spinal, fine, to make gauze, the pound —	0 2 7 10	0 2 9 14½	C	0 2 4 10	0 2 1 10	‡ 0 10 0
Spirits, vocat. Arrack, imported from any of his Majesty's colonies or territories in the East Indies, is, by 7 Geo. II. cap. 14. subject to the same duties and drawbacks as Brandy and Foreign Spirits.						
Brandy of France, the ton, containing 252 gallons	8 18 6	9 6 4 10	Db	8 3 6	7 8 6	‡ 30 0 0
Brandy of Spain, Portugal, or Italy, the ton, containing 252 gallons	4 19 9	5 3 8 5	Db	4 12 3	4 4 9	‡ 15 0 0
Brandy of all other countries, not otherwise rated, the ton, containing 252 gallons	6 6 0	6 11 3	Db	5 16 0	5 6 0	‡ 20 0 0
If imported in foreign ships, to pay duty as Aliens.						
Citron water, the gallon —	0 5 4	0 5 7 3	Db	0 4 10	0 4 4 11/20	‡ 1 0 0
if French Geneva, the gallon —	0 10 7	0 10 10 3	Db	0 5 1	0 4 7 10/20	‡
Hungary water, the gallon —	0 2 8 10	0 2 10 1	Db	0 3 17	0 0 3 11/20	‡‡ 0 1 0
if of France	0 5 4	0 5 5:1	Db	0 2 5 10	0 2 2 4	‡ ‡ 0 10 0

* But if imported by Aliens Drawback more, 1s. 3d. for every 100l. of the Rate or Value.

INWARDS.

	Reference to the several Branches, see Page it.	DUTIES to be paid on IMPORTATION.		DRAWBACKS to be repaid on EXPORTATION.*		RATES, or supposed value, ly 12 C. r. II. cap. 4. 11 Geo. I cap. from whence the foregoing Duties are computed.
		By BRITISH. £. s. d. 20ths	By ALIENS. £. s. d. 20ths	If exported to any legal place, except as mentioned in the following column. £. s. d. 20ths	If the produce of Europe or the E. Indies, and exported to the British Colonies in America. £. s. d. 20ths	£. s. d.
Spirits, *vocat.* Rackee of Turkey, the gallon	D b	0 1 4 15	0 1 5 10 +⅟	0 1 3 5	0 1 1 15	‡ 0 5 0
Rosa folis, and all other Cordial waters, not otherwise rated, the gallon	D b	0 2 8 10	0 2 10 1	0 5 10	0 2 10	‡ 0 10 0
if of France ——— Rum, the gallon	D b D b	0 5 4 0 0 6 5	0 5 11 −¼+ 0 6 10 −¼+	0 2 7 0 5 15	0 2 4 0 5 5	
But if of the produce of the British Sugar plantations in America, and imported directly from thence, accompanied with a certificate, as is directed by 4 Geo. III. cap. 15. or admitted to entry as such by order of the Commissioners of his Majesty's Customs	D a D a	0 5 4	0 5 9 −¼+	0 5 5 +¼−⁹	0 5 5 +⁴−⁹	‡ 0 1 8
——— Viney from Turkey, the gallon	D b	0 2 8 10	0 2 10 1	0 5 10	0 2 10	‡ 0 10 0
if of France	D b D b D b	0 5 4 10 0 2 8 10 0 5 4	0 5 11 −⅓−⁹ 0 2 10 1 0 5 11	0 2 7 0 5 10 0 2 7	0 2 4 0 2 10 0 2 4	‡ 0 10 0

* But if imported by Aliens Drawback more, 1 s. 3 d. for every 100 l. of the Rate or Value, except Rum of the British plantations.

[245]

INWARDS.

	DUTIES to be paid on IMPORTATION.		DRAWBACKS to be repaid on EXPORTATION.*		RATES, or supposed value, by 12 Car. II. cap. 4. 11 Geo. I. cap. 7. from whence the foregoing Duties are computed.
Reference to the several Branches, fee Page vi.	By BRITISH. £ s. d. 20ths	By ALIENS. £ s. d. 20ths	If exported to any legal place, except as mentioned in the following column. £ s. d. 20ths	If the produce of Europe or the East Indies, and exported to the British Colonies in America. £ s. d. 20ths	£ s. d.
And besides, for such of the above Spirits as are imported in glass bottles, for every dozen quarts of glass ——— Subject also to the Excise duties. But by 3 Geo. I. cap. 4. Spirits of all sorts, of the growth, produce, or manufacture of Guernsey, Jersey, Sark and Alderney, may be imported from thence by the inhabitants of the said islands (under the certificates and oaths required by law) on payment of such duties as are chargeable thereon for the time being on the like goods of the growth, produce, or manufacture of Great Britain. Ze	0 4 2 8	0 4 2 8			
Spokes for cart wheels, longs, the thousand of and directly from any part of America, if regularly entered and landed, free. On failure thereof. See in Wood. ——— of or from any part of Europe, except Ireland or France B	1 17 9 12	1 19 4 10	1 14 9 12	1 11 9 12	16 0 0

* But if imported by Aliens Drawback more, 1s. 3d. for every 100l. of the Rate or Value.

[246]

INWARDS.

	DUTIES to be paid on IMPORTATION.		Reference to the several Branches, see Page vi.	DRAWBACKS to be repaid on EXPORTATION.*		RATES, or supposed value, by † 12 C. 2. II. cap. 4. ‡ 11 Geo. I. cap. 7. from whence the foregoing Duties are computed.
	By BRITISH.	By ALIENS.		If exported to any legal place, except as mentioned in the following column.	If the produce of Europe or the East Indies, and exported to the British Colonies in America.	
	£. s. d. 20ths	£. s. d. 20ths		£. s. d. 20ths	£. s. d. 20ths	£. s. d.
Spokes for cart wheels, long, the thousand, of Ireland, Africa, or Asia —— of France. *See in* Wood.	1 11 6	1 13 0.18		1 8 6	1 5 6	1 3 0 0
If imported in foreign ships, to pay duty as Aliens.						
Spokes for cart wheels, short, the thousand of, and directly from, any part of America, if regularly entered and landed, free.			C			
On failure thereof. See in Wood.						
—— of or from any part of Europe, except Ireland or France	0 18 10.16	0 19 8 5	B	0 17 4.16	0 15 10.16	
—— of Ireland, Africa, or Asia	0 15 9	0 16 6 9	C	0 14 3	0 12 9	
—— of France. *See in* Wood.						
If imported in foreign ships, to pay duty as Aliens.						
Spoons of horn, the groce, containing 12 dozen	0 3 4 6 ⅔	0 3 6 16 ⅘	A	0 2 11 10 ⅔	0 2 6 14 ⅔	0 16 0 0
Sports. *Vide* Baskets.						
Spunges. *Vide in* Drugs.						

* But if imported by Aliens Drawback more, 1s. 3d. for every 100l. of the Rate or Value.

[247]

INWARDS.

S	DUTIES to be paid on IMPORTATION.		Reference to the several Brunches, see Page vi.	DRAWBACKS to be repaid on EXPORTATION.*		RATES, or supposed value, by 12 Car.II.cap.4. ‡11 Geo.I.cap.7. from whence the foregoing Duties are computed.
	By BRITISH.	By ALIENS.		If exported to any legal place, except as mentioned in the following column.	If the produce of Europe or the East Indies, and exported to the British Colonies in America.	
	£. s. d. 20ths	£. s. d. 20ths		£. s. d. 20ths	£. s. d. 20ths	£. s. d.
Standishes of brass, the dozen	0 3 1 16	0 3 3 13 4/5	C	0 2 10 4	0 2 6 12	0 12 0
—— covered with leather gilt, the piece	0 1 4 16	0 1 5 17	A	0 1 2 16	0 1 0 16	0 6 8
And besides, if the Leather be the most valuable part, for every 20s. of the real value upon oath.						
—— vocat. Pocket-standishes, the dozen	0 6 3 12	0 6 3 12	Dc	0 0 3 12	0 0 3 12	2 0 0
—— of wood, the dozen	0 8 4 16	0 8 11 2	A	0 7 4 16	0 6 4 16	4 0 0
Starch, white, the Cwt.	0 10 1 1/5	0 10 14 1/5	A	0 8 17	0 7 13 1/3	5 0 0
if French	5 0 9 12	5 2 1 7	Ta	—	—	
	6 12 3 12	6 13 7 7	Tc	—	—	
Barrel staves, the hundred, containing six score						
—— part of America, if regularly entered and landed, free.						
On failure thereof. See in Wood.	0 1 0 12	0 1 2	B	0 0 11 12	0 0 10 12	2 0 0
—— of or from any part of Europe, except Ireland or France —						
—— of Ireland, Africa, or Asia	0 0 8 8	0 0 8 18	A	0 0 7 8	0 0 6 8	0 3 4
—— of France. *See in Wood.*						

Staves, vocat.

* But if imported by Aliens Drawback more, 1s. 3d. for every 100l. of the Rate or Value.

INWARDS.

	Duties to be paid on Importation. By British. £. s. d. 20ths	Duties to be paid on Importation. By Aliens. £. s. d. 20ths	Reference to the several Branches, see Page vi.	Drawbacks to be repaid on Exportation.* If exported to any legal place, except as mentioned in the following column. £. s. d. 20ths	Drawbacks to be repaid on Exportation.* If the produce of Europe or the East Indies, and exported to the British Colonies in America. £. s. d. 20ths	Rates, or supposed value, by 12 Car. II. cap. 4. † 11 Geo. I. cap. 7. from whence the foregoing Duties are computed. £. s. d.
Staves, *viz.* *If imported in foreign ships, to pay duty as Aliens.*						
Bow staves. *Vide in* B.						
Firkin staves, the hundred, containing six score	—	—		—	—	0 2 0
—— of and directly from any part of America, if regularly entered and landed, free. *On failure thereof. See in* Wood.						
—— of or from any part of Europe, except Ireland or France	0 0 7 11 1/5	0 0 7 17 1/2	B	0 0 6 19 1/5	0 0 6 7 1/5	
—— of Ireland, Africa, or Asia	0 0 5 0 4/5	0 0 5 7 1/10	A	0 0 4 8 4/5	0 0 3 16 4/5	
—— of France. *See in* Wood. *If imported in foreign ships, to pay duty as Aliens.*						
Kilderkin staves. *Vide in* Wood.						
Pipe and Hogshead staves. *Vide in* P.						
Steel, *viz.* Gad steel, the half barrel	2 2 0	2 4 7 10	A	1 17 0	—	10 0 0
And besides, for every Cwt.	0 5 9 6	0 5 9 6	D	0 5 9 6	—	•

* But if imported by Aliens Drawback more, 1 s. 3 d. for every 100 l. of the Rate or Value.

INWARDS.

	DUTIES to be paid on IMPORTATION.		DUTIES to be paid on IMPORTATION.		Reference to the several Branches, see Page vi.	DRAWBACKS to be repaid on EXPORTATION.*		DRAWBACKS to be repaid on EXPORTATION.*		RATES, or supposed value, by 12 Car. II. cap. 4. 11 Geo. I. cap. 7. from whence the foregoing Duties are computed.
	By BRITISH.		By ALIENS.			If exported to any legal place, except as mentioned in the following column.		If the produce of Europe or the East Indies, and exported to the British Colonies in America.		
	£. s. d. 20ths		£. s. d. 20ths			£. s. d. 20ths		£. s. d. 20ths		£. s. d.
——— Long steel, Wisp steel, and such like, the Cwt.	0 12 0 18		0 12 5 12 ½		C	0 11 3 18				1 10 0
——— Steel manufactures unrated, for every 20s. of their value upon oath — And for every Cwt.	0 4 2 8		0 4 5 11		A	0 3 8 8				
Note. By the acts of 2 & 3 Ann. cap. 9. and 9 Ann. cap. 6. no drawback is to be allowed upon the exportation of Steel, or of any ware made of Wrought Steel in foreign parts, exported to the British colonies or plantations in America.	0 5 9 6		0 5 9 6		D	0 5 9 6				
Stockings of thread, or of Cotton, the dozen pair	0 9 2 5		0 9 7 15 ½		C	0 8 3 15		0 7 5 5		‡ 1 15 0
And besides, if Cotton, for every 20s. of the stuff price at the caudle	0 3 1 16		0 3 1 16		Q	0 3 1 16		0 3 1 16 2/5		0 1 0
——— of Wadmoll, the pair	0 0 2 10 2/5		0 0 2 13 11/20		A	0 0 2 4		0 0 1 18 3/5		0 4 0
Stone birds, or whistles, the small groce, containing 12 dozen	0 0 10 1 ⅕		0 0 10 14 ⅕		A	0 0 8 17		0 0 7 13		0 15 0
Stones, vocat. Blood-stones, the pound Vide Lapis hæmatitis in Drugs.	0 3 1 16		0 3 4 3 ¾		A	0 2 9 6		0 2 4 16		

* But if imported by Aliens Drawback more, 1s. 3d. for every 100l. of the Rate or Value.

Kk

[250]

INWARDS.

Stones, vocat.

	DUTIES to be paid on IMPORTATION.		References to the several Branches, see Page 1.	DRAWBACKS to be repaid on EXPORTATION.*		RATES, or supposed val e, by 12 Car. II. c. 4. 11 & 12 Gul. I. c. 7. from wh are the foreign Duties are computed.
	By BRITISH.	By ALIENS.		If exported to any legal place, except as mentioned in the following column.	If the produce of Europe, or the East Indies, and exported to the British Colonies in America.	
	L. s. d. 20ths	*L. s. d.* 20ths		*L. s. d.* 20ths	*L. s. d.* 20ths	*L. s. d.*
Cane-stones, the ton	0 3 3	0 3 4 3¼	A	0 2 9 6	0 2 4 16	0 15 0
Dog-stones, the last, containing three pair to the last. *Vide in* E.	8 3 9 12	8 14 0 9	A	7 4 3 12	2 4 9 12	39 0 0
Emery-stones. *Vide in* E.						
Grave stones of marble unpolished, the foot square, superficial measure	0 0 1 1	0 0 1 2 1/10	C	0 0 0 19	0 0 0 17	0 0 4
— of marble polished, the foot square, superficial measure	0 0 2 2	0 0 2 0 1/10	C	0 0 1 18	0 0 1 14	0 0 8
— of other stone, polished or unpolished, the foot square	0 0 0 5	0 0 0 0 4/10	C	0 0 0 4 ¼	0 0 0 4	0 0 1
Marble Basons, Tables, Mortars, and all other polished marble (except Grave stones and Paving stones polished) the foot square	0 0 3 3	0 0 3 6 1/20	C	0 0 2 17	0 0 2 11	0 0 10
Blocks, the solid foot	0 1 0 12	0 1 1 1/5	C	0 0 0 11 8	0 0 10 4	0 0 4
Paving stones rough, the foot, superficial measure	0 0 1 1	0 0 1 1 1/25	C	0 0 0 19	0 0 0 17	0 0 4
Paving stones polished, the foot square, superficial measure	0 0 2 2	0 0 2 4 1/10	C	0 0 1 18	0 0 1 14	0 0 8
Mill stones, the piece	2 0 0	2 4 7/10	A	1 17 0	1 12 0	10 0 0

* But if imported by Aliens Drawback more, 1s. 3d. for every 100l. of the Rate or Value.

[251]

INWARDS. S

	Duties to be paid on Importation.		Reference to the several Branches, see Page vi.	Drawbacks to be repaid on Exportation.*		Rates, or supposed value, by 12 Car. II. cap. 4. ‡ 11 Geo. I. cap. 7. from whence the foregoing Duties are computed.
	By British.	By Aliens.		If exported to any legal place, except as mentioned in the following column.	If the produce of Europe or the East Indies, and exported to the British Colonies in America.	
	£. s. d. 20ths	£. s. d. 20ths		£. s. d. 20ths	£. s. d. 20ths	£. s. d.
Paving stones, not of marble, the foot square	0 0 5 ¼	0 0 5 4¼	C	0 0 4 3¼	0 0 4 4¼	‡ 0 0 1
Pebble stones, the ton	0 5 3	0 5 6 3	C		0 0 4 3	‡ 1 1 0
But by 3 Geo. I. cap. 4. if of the produce of Jersey, Guernsey, Sark, or Alderney, may be imported from thence by the inhabitants of the said islands, under the certificates directed by that law, duty free.						
Pomice stones. Vide in P.						
Quern stones large, the last	0 18 10 16	1 0 0 19	A	0 16 7 16	0 14 4 16	‡ 4 10 0
———— small, the last	0 9 5 8	0 10 0 9	A	0 8 3 18	0 7 2 8	2 5 0
Slates in frames, the dozen	0 0 10 10	0 0 11 0	C	0 0 9 10	0 0 8 10	0 3 4
Slick stones, the hundred, containing five score	0 3 1 16	0 3 4 3	A	0 2 9 6	0 2 4 16	‡ 0 15 0
Tables of slate in frames, the piece	0 1 3 15	0 1 4 10	C	0 1 2 5	0 1 0 15	0 5 0
———— without frames, the piece	0 0 5 5	0 0 5 10	C	0 0 4 15	0 0 4 5	‡ 0 1 5
Whetstones. Vide in W.						
Stores of iron. Vide in Iron.						
Sturgeon, the firkin	0 6 3 12	0 6 8 6	A	0 5 6 12	0 4 9 12	1 10 0

Stones, vacat.

* But if imported by Aliens Drawback more, 1s. 3d. for every 100l. of the Rate or Value.

INWARDS.

	Duties to be paid on Importation. By British. £. s. d. 20ths	Duties to be paid on Importation. By Aliens. £. s. d. 20ths	Reference to the several Branches, see Page vi.	Drawbacks to be repaid on Exportation.* If exported to any legal place, except as mentioned in the following column. £. s. d. 20ths	Drawbacks to be repaid on Exportation.* If the produce of Europe or the East Indies, and exported to the British Colonies in America. £. s. d. 20ths	Rates, or supposed value, by 12 Car. II. cap. 4. & 11 Geo. I. cap. 7. from whence the foregoing Duties are computed. £. s. d.
Sturgeon, the keg	0 3 1 16	0 3 4 3 ¼	A	0 2 9 6	0 2 4 16	0 15 0
Stuffs of all sorts, made of or mixed with wool, per yard	0 5 3	0 5 6 18 ¾	A	0 4 7 10	0 4 0	1 5 0
Succad, wet or dry, the pound	0 0 7 11 ⅕	0 0 8 0 13/20	A	0 0 6 13 ⅕	0 0 5 15 ⅕	0 3 0
Sugar and sugar candy. *Vide in* Grocery.						
Swingles, the groce, containing 12 dozen	0 15 9	0 16 6 9	C	0 14 3	0 12 9	‡ 3 0 0
Sword-blades, coarse, or Flanders making, the dozen	0 4 2 8	0 4 5 11	A	0 3 8 8	—	1 0 0
—— of Venice, Turkey, or fine blades, the dozen	0 6 3 12	0 6 8 6 ½	A	0 5 6 12	—	1 10 0
And besides, for every Cwt. of Iron	0 5 3	0 5 3	D	0 5 3	—	
Syder and Syder Eager, the ton						4 0 0
not French, filled	5 17 7 4		I	4 17 7 4	1 7 7 4	
		7 9 1 4	I	6 4 1 4	1 9 1 4	
—— *unfilled*	5 6 3 2 ⅖		I	4 6 3 2 ⅖	1 7 0 14 ⅖	
		6 13 11 15 ⅕	I	5 8 11 15 ⅕	1 8 4 11 ⅕	
French, filled	7 19 7 4		E d	5 19 7 4	2 9 7 4	
		9 11 1 4	E d	7 6 1 4	2 11 1 4	
—— *unfilled*	7 8 3 2 ⅖		E d	5 8 3 2 ⅖	2 9 0 14 ⅖	
		8 15 11 15 ⅕	E d	6 10 11 15 ⅕	2 10 4 11 ⅕	

Subject also to the Excise duties.

* But if imported by Aliens Drawback more, 1s. 3d. for every 100l. of the Rate or Value, except Syder.

INWARDS.

	DUTIES to be paid on IMPORTATION.		DRAWBACKS to be repaid on EXPORTATION.*		RATES, or supposed value, by 12 Car. II. cap. 4. ‡ 11 Geo. I. cap. 7. from whence the foregoing Duties are computed.
	By BRITISH.	By ALIENS.	If exported to any legal place, except as mentioned in the following column.	If the produce of Europe or the East Indies, and exported to the British Colonies in America.	
	£. s. d. 20ths	£. s. d. 20ths	£. s. d. 20ths	£. s. d. 20ths	£. s. d.

Of and from Guernsey, Jersey, Sark, and Alderney, may be imported from thence by the inhabitants of those islands, on payment of such Excise duty, as is chargeable, for the time being, on Syder made in this kingdom.

T.

TABLE BOOKS coarse, the dozen———	0 2 1 4	0 2 2 15 ½ A	0 1 10 4	0 1 7 4	0 10 0
——— fine, the dozen	0 4 2 8	0 4 5 11 A	0 3 8 8	0 3 2 8	1 0 0
Tables, *vacat.* Playing tables of walnut-tree. *Vide* Playing tables *in* P.					
and all other sorts, coarse, the pair ——— of wainscot,	0 1 0 12	0 1 1 7 ¾ A	0 0 11 2	0 0 9 12	0 5 0
Tables of marble } *Vide* Stones. ——— of slate ——— }					

*But if imported by Aliens Drawback more, 1 s. 3 d. for every 100 l. of the Rate or Value.

INWARDS.

	Duties to be paid on Importation. By British. £. s. d. 20ths	Duties to be paid on Importation. By Aliens. £. s. d. 20ths	Reference to the several Branches, see Page vi.	Drawbacks to be repaid on Exportation.* If exported to any legal place, except as mentioned in the following column. £. s. d. 20ths	Drawbacks to be repaid on Exportation.* If the produce of Europe or the East Indies, and exported to the British Colonies in America. £. s. d. 20ths	Rates, or supposed value, by 12 Car. II. cap. 4. ‡ 11 Geo. I. cap. 7. from whence the foregoing Duties are computed. £. s. d.
Tacks of iron, the thousand	0 1 4 16	0 1 5 17	A	0 1 2 16	——	0 6 8
And besides, for every Cwt.	0 5 3	0 5 3	D	0 5 3	——	
Tails of cows, the hundred, containing five score	0 2 7 10	0 2 9 1 ½	C	0 2 4 10	0 2 1 10	‡ 0 10 0
Tallow, the Cwt.	0 8 9	0 8 11 12 ½	B	0 8 4	0 7 11	0 16 8
But by 19 Geo III. cap. 22. Tallow, if regularly entered and landed, is duty free, *until March* 25, 1782.						
Tannets of cruel, the yard	0 1 3 2 ⅖	0 1 4 1 $\frac{3}{10}$	A	0 1 1 6 ⅖	0 0 11 10 ⅖	0 6 0
Tape open, the dozen pieces	0 0 7 17 ½	0 0 8 5 ⅜	C	0 0 7 2 ½	0 0 6 7 ½	‡ 0 2 6
Tapestry with caddas, the Flemish ell	0 2 6 4 ⅘	0 2 7 10	C	0 2 3 16 ⅘	0 2 1 8 ⅘	0 8 0
—— with gold or silver, the Flemish ell	——	——		——	——	8 0 0
—— with hair, the Flemish ell	0 0 10 1 ⅕	0 0 10 10	C	0 0 9 5 ⅕	0 0 8 9 ⅗	0 2 8
—— with silk, the Flemish ell	——	——		——	——	0 13 4
—— with wool, the Flemish ell	0 1 3 2 ⅖	0 1 3 15	C	0 1 1 18 ⅖	0 1 0 14 ⅖	0 4 0
Tar, small or great band, the last, containing 12 barrels	0 10 6	0 11 1 17 ½	A	0 9 3	0 8 0	2 10 0
And besides, not being of the product of any of the dominions or plantations of the Crown of Great Britain, the last	0 1 3 15	0 1 3 15	E	0 1 3 15	0 1 3 15	

* But if imported by Aliens Drawback more, 1s. 3d. for every 100l. of the Rate or Value.

[255]

INWARDS.	Duties to be paid on IMPORTATION. By BRITISH. £ s. d. 20ths	By ALIENS. £ s. d. 20ths	Reference to the several Branches, see Page vi.	DRAWBACKS to be repaid on EXPORTATION.* if exported to any legal place, except as mentioned in the following column. £ s. d. 20ths	If of the produce of Europe or the East Indies, and exported to the British Colonies in America. £ s. d. 20ths	RATES, or supposed value, by 12 Car. II. cap. 4. 11 Geo. I. cap. 7. from whence the foregoing Duties are computed. £ s. d.
If imported in foreign ships, to pay duty as Aliens.						
Tarras, the barrel	0 1 4 16	0 1 5 17	A	0 1 2 16	0 1 0 16	0 6 8
Tazels, the thousand	0 1 0 12	0 1 1 7 3/4	A	0 0 11 2	0 0 9 12	0 5 0
Tea. *See the Table of* Unrated East-India goods *at the end of the Rates Inwards.*						
Tea tables lacquered, with or without feet (except of India or China) the piece	0 2 7 10	0 2 9 1	C	0 2 4 10	0 2 1 10	0 10 0 ‡
—— unlacquered (except of India or China) the piece	0 0 7 17 1/2	0 0 8 5 3/4	C	0 0 7 2	0 0 6 7	0 2 6 ‡
Teeth scamorse. *Vide* Scamorse teeth.						
Teuterhooks. *Vide* Nails.						
‖ Thimbles, the thousand	0 0 7 4	0 0 13 4 13	A	0 0 11 4 16	0 0 9 7 4	3 0 0
And besides, if { Brass, *the thousand*	0 3 16	0 3 1 16	E	0 3 3	0 0 3 1 16	
{ Iron, *the Cwt*	0 5 3	0 5 3	D	0 5 3		
Thread, vizt. Bridges thread, the dozen pound	0 9 5 8	0 10 0 9	A	0 8 3 18	0 7 2 8	2 5 0
—— Crofsbow thread, the hundred pound, containing five score	0 14 10	0 14 10 10	A	0 12 4	0 10 8	3 6 8
—— Thread of gold and silver. *Vide in* G.						

* But if imported by Aliens Drawback more, 1 s. 3 d. for every 100 l. of the Rate or Value.

‖ If Iron no Drawback to the British Colonies in America.

[256]

INWARDS.

	DUTIES to be paid on IMPORTATION.		Reference to the several Branches, see Page vi.	DRAWBACKS to be repaid on EXPORTATION.*		RATES, or supposed value, by 12 Car. II. cap. 4. 11 Geo. I. cap. 7. from whence the the other Duties are reckoned.
	By BRITISH.	By ALIENS.		If exported to any legal place, except as mentioned in the following column.	If the produce of Europe or the East Indies, and exported to the British Colonies in America.	
	L. s. d. 20ths	*L. s. d. 20ths*		*L. s. d. 20ths*	*L. s. d. 20ths*	*L. s. d.*
Thread, *vacat.* { Lyons or Paris thread, the bale, containing 100 bolts	22 1 0	22 8 10 10	F	13 16 0	13 1 0	30 0 0
Outnal thread, the dozen pound — Packthread. *Vide* in P.	0 16 9 12	0 17 7 1	C	0 15 3 12	0 13 9 12	3 0 0
Piecing thread, the dozen pound	0 16 9 12	0 17 10 4	A	0 14 9 12	0 12 9 12	4 0 0
Sifters thread, the pound	0 2 7 10	0 2 9 17	A a	0 2 2 3	0 1 10 0	0 15 0
But if French mare, if not European — Whited brown thread, the dozen pound	0 7 10 10	0 7 10 10	F b	0 4 2 10	0 4 2 4 16	
But all Thread of the manufacture of Ireland may be imported directly from thence by British or Irish, upon certificate and oath, free of all duties.	0 3 1 16 0 16 9 12	0 3 4 0 17 10	A A	0 4 2 6 0 14 9 12	0 4 2 0 12 9 12	4 0 0
Thrumbs of linen, or fustian, the pound — of woollen, the pound	0 0 0 0 0 0	0 0 0 0 0 0	A C	0 0 0 1 2 0 2 4 18	0 0 0 0 19 0 1 18 0 1 14	0 6 0 0 1 0 0 8 0
Ticking of the East country, the yard — of Germany, or any other country, not otherwise rated, the piece, containing 36 yards	0 7 10 10	0 8 0 0	C	0 7 1 10	0 6 4 10	0 0 0 1 10 0
Tikes, *vacat.* Brizeil tikes, and counterfeit Brizeil, the tike	0 7 10 10	0 8 3 4	C	0 7 1 10	0 6 4 10	1 10 0

* If imported by Aliens Drawback more, 1s. 3d. for every 100l. of the Rate or Value.

[257]

INWARDS.	DUTIES to be paid on IMPORTATION.		Reference to the several Branches, see Page vi.	DRAWBACKS to be repaid on EXPORTATION.*		RATES, or supposed value, by 12 Car.II.cap.4. ‡ 11 Geo.I.cap.7. from whence the foregoing Duties are computed.
	By BRITISH.	By ALIENS.		If exported to any legal place, except as mentioned in the following column.	If the produce of Europe or the East Indies, and exported to the British Colonies in America.	
	£. s. d. 20ths	£. s. d. 20ths		£. s. d. 20ths	£. s. d. 20ths	£. s. d.
—— of Stoad, the tike ——	0 7 10 10	0 8 3 4	C	0 7 1 10	0 6 4 10	1 10 0
—— Turral tikes, the tike ——	0 7 10 10	0 8 3 3	C	0 7 1 10	0 6 4 10	1 10 0
Tiles. *Vide* Earthen ware.						
Timber. *Vide* Balks *and* Wood.						
Tin, for every 20 s. value upon oath	0 4 2 8	0 4 5 11	A	0 3 8 8	0 3 2 8	0 3 0
And besides, for every Cwt.	1 11 6	1 11 6	D	1 11 6	1 11 6	3 0 0
Tincall. *Vide* Borax in Drugs.						
Tinfoil, the groce, containing 12 dozen —	0 0 8 8	0 0 13 8 18	A	0 0 7 8	0 0 6 8	0 5 0
Tinglass, the Cwt. ——	0 12 7 4	0 0 4 13	A	0 11 1 4	0 9 7 4	0 5 0
Tinsel with copper, the yard	0 2 1 7	0 0 2 1 7	A	0 1 11 2	0 1 7 4	0 10 0
—— with right gold and silver, the yard	0 2 1 14	0 0 2 15	A	0 1 10 4 3/5	0 2 17 3 1/5	0 1 6
Tinshore, the groce, containing 12 dozen —	0 0 3 15 3/4	0 0 4 0 3/4	A	0 0 3 6 3/4	0 0 2 17 3/4	
Tinshore, Spanish and Brazeil Tobacco, or any not British plantation, the lb.	0 2 11 8	0 3 1 0	V 2	0 2 8 8	0 2 5 8	0 10 0
Tobacco, vocat. Spanish and Brazeil Tobacco, in pudding or roll	0 5 3	0 5 3	F b	0 2 9	0 2 9	
And besides { if of France if of any French colony or plantation }	0 2 7 10	0 2 7 10	E	0 2 7 10	0 2 7 10	

* But if imported by Aliens Drawback more, 1 s. 3 d. for every 100 l. of the Rate or Value.

INWARDS.	DUTIES to be paid on IMPORTATION.		Reference to the several Branches, see Page vi.	DRAWBACKS to be repaid on EXPORTATION.		RATES, or supposed value, by 12 Car. II. cap. 4. 11 Geo. I. cap. 7. from whence the foregoing Duties are computed.
	By BRITISH.	By ALIENS.		If exported to any legal place, except as mentioned in the following column.	If the produce of Europe or the East Indies, and exported to the British Colonies in America.	
	L. s. d. 20ths	*L. s. d.* 20ths		*L. s. d.* 20ths	*L. s. d.* 20ths	*L. s. d.*
Tobacco, viz. St. Christopher's, Barbadoes, or any of the Carib islands, Virginia, and Summer islands Tobacco, the lb. British plantation ─── imported directly from the place of its growth ─── not directly from the place of its growth, but from such places and under such regulations as are directed by 20 *Geo. III. cap. 39.* † But by 21 *Geo. III. cap. 16.* Tobacco of the British plantations may be warehoused under the King and merchants joint locks, pursuant to 12 Ann. cap. 8. in which case the duties are as follows: ─── imported directly from the place of its growth, to be paid down on entry ─── †This act is to continue in force during the present hostilities.	0 0 0 10 1 2/3	0 0 0 10 6 2/3	Mb	0 0 0 10 1 2/3	0 0 0 10 1 2/3	0 0 8
	0 0 0 11 1 2/3	0 0 0 11 6 2/3	N	0 0 0 11 1 2/3	0 0 0 11 1 2/3	
	0 0 1	0 0 5	M	0 0 1	0 0 1	

[259]

INWARDS.

Tobacco, *vocat.*†

	DUTIES to be paid on IMPORTATION.		Reference to the several Branches, see Page vi.	DRAWBACKS to be repaid on EXPORTATION.*		RATES, or supposed value, by 12 Car. II. cap. 4. ‡ 11 Geo. I. cap. 7. from whence the foregoing Duties are computed.
	By BRITISH.	By ALIENS.		If exported to any legal place, except as mentioned in the following column.	If the produce of Europe or the East Indies, and exported to the British Colonies in America.	
	£. s. d. 20ths	£. s. d. 20ths		£. s. d. 20ths	£. s. d. 20ths	£. s. d.
	0 0 10 1 5/6	0 0 10 2 1/3	H	0 0 10 1 5/6	0 0 10 1 5/6	
	0 0 2	0 0 2		0 0 2	0 0 2	
	0 0 10	0 0 10	Na	0 0 10	0 0 10	
	0 0 10 3 5/6	0 0 10 4 1/3	H	0 0 10 3 5/6	0 0 10 3 5/6	

—— and to be secured by the importer's own bond —— imported not directly from the place of its growth, but from such places and under such regulations as are directed *by 20 Geo. III. cap. 39.*†

to be paid down on entry
to be secured by the importer's own bond

Of the growth, product, or manufacture of Ireland, may be imported directly from thence into Great Britain, under the regulations and restrictions directed *by 19 Geo. III. cap. 35.* subject to the same duties and drawbacks as Tobacco of the growth, product, or manufacture of the British colonies or plantations in America.

† This act is to continue in force during the present hostilities.

* But if imported by Aliens Drawback more, 1s. 3d. for every 100 l. of the Rate or Value, except Tobacco of the British plantations. ‖ If imported by Aliens.

INWARDS.

	DUTIES to be paid on IMPORTATION.		Reference to the several Branches, see Page vi.	DRAWBACKS to be repaid on EXPORTATION.		RATES, or supposed value, by 12 Car. II. cap. 4. 11 Geo. I. cap. 7. from whence the foregoing Duties are computed.
	By BRITISH.	By ALIENS.		If exported to any legal place, except as mentioned in the following column.	If the produce of Europe or the East Indies, and exported to the British Colonies in America.	
	£ s. d. 20ths	£ s. d. 20ths		£ s. d. 20ths	£ s. d. 20ths	£ s. d.
Tobacco, viz¹.	0 0 10 1 2/7	0 0 10 1 2/7	Mb	0 0 8 11 1/3	0 0 8 11 2/3	
	0 0 1 0 5	0 0 1 0 5	MH	0 0 10 1 5	0 0 10 1 5/6	5,0

Prize Tobacco, of the growth of the British plantations, is subject to the same duty and drawback as such Tobacco imported directly from the place of its growth. ——————— foreign, by 20 Geo. III. cap. 9. is subject to the same duty as Tobacco of the produce of the British plantations imported directly from the place of its growth, *but the drawback being regulated by the circumstances of the capture, the duty and drawback on such Tobacco will stand as follows:* ——————— taken by any of his Majesty's ships of war, *if the whole duties are paid down on entry, the pound* —— if the goods are warehoused under the King's lock,
{ *to be paid down on entry, the pound* ——
{ *to be secured by bonds, the pound* ——

INWARDS.

Item	By BRITISH £ s. d. 20ths	By ALIENS £ s. d. 20ths	Branch	Drawbacks: If exported to any legal place, except as mentioned in the following column £ s. d. 20ths	Drawbacks: If of the produce of Europe or the East Indies, and exported to the British Colonies in America £ s. d. 20ths	RATES, or supposed value, by 12 Car. II. cap.4. 11 Geo. I. cap. 7. from whence the foregoing Duties are computed £ s. d.
Tobacco, vacat.						
Prize Tobacco, taken by any private ship of war, if the whole duties are paid down on entry, the pound ——	0 0 10 1	0 0 10 1 2/3	Mb	0 0 9 11 2/3	0 0 9 11 2/3	1 0 0
if the goods are warehoused under the King's lock, { to be paid down on entry, the pound —— { to be secured by bond, the pound ——	0 1 0 1 / 0 0 10 5/6	0 1 0 1 / 0 0 10 5/6		0 0 10 1 / 0 0 10	0 0 10 1 / 0 0 10 5/6	0 4 6
Tongues. *Vide* Neats Tongues.						
Tools, *vacat.* Carving Tools, the groce, containing 12 dozen ——	0 4 2 8	0 4 5 11 1/2	M	0 3 8 8	0 3 2 8	0 10 0
And besides, for every Cwt. of Iron ——	0 5 3 1/2	0 5 3 2 7/40	H	0 5 3 0 16 1/2		
Tortoiſhell, the pound ——	0 1 2 3	0 1 2 17 1/2	A	0 2 4 10		1 0 0
Tow, the Cwt. ——	0 2 7 10	0 2 9 1 2/3	D			
Toys. *Vide after* Babies heads.			C			
Trays of wood, the ſhock containing 60 ——	0 4 2 8 1/5	0 4 5 11 1/5	C	0 3 8 8 1/3		4 0 0
Treacle, *vocat.* Flanders treacle, the barrel ——	0 16 9 12	0 17 10 4	A	0 14 9 12	0 12 9 12	
—— of Jeane, the pound ——	0 0 3 7	0 0 3 11	A	0 0 2 19	0 2 2 11 1/2	0 1 4
—— common } *Vide in* Drugs. —— of Venice }			A			
Trenchers, red or painted, the groce, containing 12 dozen ——	0 2 6 4 4/5	0 2 8 2	A	0 2 2 12 4/5	0 0 1 11 1/5	0 12 0

* But if imported by Aliens Drawback more, 1s. 3d. for every 100l. of the Rate or Value, except Tobacco.

INWARDS.

	Duties to be paid on Importation. By British. £.	s.	d.	20ths	By Aliens. £.	s.	d.	20ths	Reference to the several Branches, see Page vi.	Drawbacks to be repaid on Exportation.* If exported to any legal place, except as mentioned in the following column. £.	s.	d.	20ths	If the produce of Europe or the East Indies, and exported to the British Colonies in America. £.	s.	d.	20ths	Rates, or supposed value, by 12 Car. II. cap. 4. ‡ 11 Geo. I cap. 7. from whence the foregoing Duties are computed. £.	s.	d.
Trenchers white sort, common, the groce, containing 12 dozen	0	0	10	1 3/5	0	0	10	14 1/5	A	0	0	8	17 3/5	0	0	7	13 3/5	0	4	0
Trenails, or Trunnels, the thousand	0	2	1	4	0	2	2	15 1/2	A	0	1	10	4	0	1	7	4	0	10	0
Tripe. *Vide* Fustians.																				
Truffles, the pound	0	2	1	4	0	2	2	9 1/5	C	0	1	10	16	0	1	8	8	‡ 0	8	0
Trumpets. *Vide in* Brass.																				
Tubs wooden. *Vide in* Wood.																				
Turpentine. *Vide in* Drugs.																				
Tweezes of France, the dozen	2	4	1	4	2	4	10	13	F	1	7	7	4	1	6	1	4	3	0	0
Twine of Hamburgh, the pound	0	0	1	5 1/5	0	0	1	6 31/40	A	0	0	1	2 1/5	0	0	0	19 1/5	0	0	6
—— the Cwt.	0	10	6		0	11	1	17 1/2	A	0	9	3		0	8	0		2	10	0
Twists for band-strings, the dozen knots	0	2	1	4	0	2	2	15 1/2	A	0	1	10	4	0	1	7	4	0	10	0

V.

	£.	s.	d.	20ths	£.	s.	d.	20ths		£.	s.	d.	20ths	£.	s.	d.	20ths	£.	s.	d.
VALLANCES of Scotland, the piece, free	—	—	—	—	—	—	—	—		—	—	—	—	—	—	—	—	0	8	0

* But if imported by Aliens Drawback more, 1 s. 3 d. for every 100 l. of the Rate or Value.

V   [263]   V

INWARDS.

	DUTIES to be paid on IMPORTATION.		DRAWBACKS to be repaid on EXPORTATION.*		RATES, or supposed value, by 12 Car.II. cap.4. 11 Geo.I.cap.7. from whence the foregoing Duties are computed.
	By BRITISH.	By ALIENS.	Reference to the several Branches, see Page vi.	If exported to any legal place, except as mentioned in the following column.	If the produce of Europe or the East Indies, and exported to the British Colonies in America.
	£. s. d. 20ths	£. s. d. 20ths		£. s. d. 20ths	£. s. d. 20ths	£. s. d.
Valonia, for dyers use, as by 3 and 4 Ann. cap. 4. the Cwt.	0 1 1 4	0 1 2 6 13/20	B	0 0 11 2 3/5	0 0 9 0	0 1 7 0
But by 8 Geo. I. cap. 15. §. 10. if regularly imported, entered, and landed, duty free.	0 2 11 14	0 3 1 5 1/2	d	0 2 4 14	0 2 1 14 1/2	
But on failure thereof, then to pay —						
Vellum for table-books, the skin						0 0 10 0
Velvet, vocat. Sparta velvet. Vide in Fustians.						
Velure. Vide in Fustians.	0 7 11 3/5	0 7 17 1/2	C	0 6 19 1/5	0 0 6 7 1/5	0 2 0
Verders of tapestry, with hair, the Flemish ell	0 5 7 4	0 5 11 8	A	0 4 11 4 1/2	0 0 4 3 4	1 6 8
Verditor, the Cwt.	0 0 4 11	0 0 1 13 7/10	C	0 0 1 8 1/2	0 0 1 5 1/2	4 0 6
Vermacielli paste, the pound						
But by 21 Geo. III. cap. 29. Vermacelli may be imported from any of his Majesty's colonies in North America, duty free, until the 1st of December, 1796.						
Ufers. Vide in Wood.						
Vice haps, the dozen	0 5 0	0 5 7 1/10	A	0 4 8 4/5		0 2 0
And besides, for every Cwt. of iron	0 0 3	0 0 5 3	D	0 0 5 3		

* But if imported by Aliens Drawback more, 1s. 3d. for every 100l. of the Rate or Value.

INWARDS.

	DUTIES to be paid on IMPORTATION.		Reference to the several Branches, fee Page vi.	DRAWBACKS to be repaid on EXPORTATION.*		RATES, or supposed value, by 12 Car. II. cap. 4. 11 Geo. I. cap. 7. from whence the foregoing Duties are computed.
	By BRITISH.	By ALIENS.		If exported to any legal place, except as mentioned in the following column.	If the produce of Europe or the East Indies, and exported to the British Colonies in America.	
	£. s. d. 20ths	£. s. d. 20ths		£. s. d. 20ths	£. s. d. 20ths	£. s. d.
Vice Tongues, or Hand vices, the dozen	0 2 6 4/5	0 2 8 2/20	A	0 2 2 12 4/5	2 14 11 8	0 12 0
And besides, for every Cwt. of Iron	0 5 3	0 5 3	D	0 5 3	2 16 5 8	5 0 0
Vinegar, the ton						
Filled	31 8 11 6	30 5 8	Hc	6 4 11 8	2 13 5 8	
Unfilled	29 17 5 3	31 5 2 4/5	Hc	7 12 7 16 4/5	2 14 9 8	
			Hc	5 12 4 8	2 14 9 8	
	32 15 2 8	32 15 2	Ic	6 15 4 8	1 11 2	
And besides, if French						
But of and from Guernsey, Jersey, Alderney, and Sark, may be imported without payment of any other duties than such as are chargeable for the like liquor made in this kingdom.						
Vincloes, the pound	0 7 10 10	0 8 3 4	C	0 7 1 10	0 6 4 10	1 10 0 ‡
Viols, the piece	0 2 9 12	0 2 11 14	A	0 2 5 12	0 2 1 12	0 13 4
Visney. *Vide in Spirits.*						
Vizards, the dozen	0 5 0 9 3/5	0 5 4 5	A	0 4 5	0 3 10 1 1/5	1 4 0
Uiquebaugh. *Vide in Spirits.*						

* But if imported by Aliens Drawback more, 1s. 3d. for every 100l. of the Rate or Value, except Vinegar.

INWARDS.
W.

	DUTIES to be paid on IMPORTATION.		Reference to the several Branches, see Page vi.	DRAWBACKS to be repaid on EXPORTATION.*		RATES, or supposed value, by 1° Car. II. cap. 4. † 11 Geo. I. cap. 7. from whence the foregoing Duties are computed.
	By BRITISH.	By ALIENS.		If exported to any legal place, except as mentioned in the following column.	If the produce of Europe, or the East Indies, and exported to the British Colonies in America.	
	L. s. d.	20ths	*L. s. d.*	20ths		*L. s. d.*	20ths	*L. s. d.*	20ths	*L. s. d.*
WADMOLL, the yard	0 1 17	4/5	0 2 0	17/20	A	0 0 1 13	7/10	0 0 1 8	4/5	‡ 0 0 9
Wafers, the pound	0 5 5	1/4	0 5 10	1/4	C	0 0 4 5		0 0 4 5		† 0 1 8
Wainscots, the hundred, containing six score —										
——— of, and directly from, any part of America, if regularly entered and landed, free.										
On failure thereof. See in Wood.										
——— of or from any part of Europe, except Ireland or France	3 3 0		3 5 7	10	B	2 18 0		2 13 0		
——— of Ireland, Africa, or Asia. See in Wood.										
——— of France. See in Wood.	2 2 0		2 4 7	10	A	1 17 0		1 12 0		
If imported in foreign ships, to pay duty as Aliens.										
Wainscot boards. *Vide* in Wood.										
Wafflers. *Vide* Candle-plates.										
Water, *vocat.* Pyrmont waters, and all other Mineral or Natural waters, not otherwise rated, the dozen bottles or flasks, each bottle or flask { not exceeding 3 pints	0 1 9		0 1 10	1	C	0 1 7		0 1 5		‡ 0 0 6 8
{ exceeding 3 pints	0 2 4		0 2 5	15 7/20	C	0 2 1 13		0 1 10 19		‡ 0 0 9 0

* But if imported by Aliens Drawback more, 1s. 3d. for every 100l. of the Rate or Value.

W [266] W

I N W A R D S.

	DUTIES to be paid on IMPORTATION.		Reference to the several Branches, fee Page vi.	DRAWBACKS to be repaid on EXPORTATION.*		RATES, or supposed value, by 12 Car. II. cap. 4. 11 Geo. I. cap. 7. from whence the foregoing Duties are computed.
	By BRITISH.	By ALIENS.		If exported to any legal place, except as mentioned in the following column.	If the produce of Europe or the East Indies, and exported to the British Colonies in America.	
	£. s. d. 20ths	£. s. d. 20ths		£. s. d. 20ths	£. s. d. 20ths	£. s. d.
Water, vizt. Spaw water, the basket, containing 150 flasks, not exceeding 3 pints each	1 1 0	1 2 0 12	C	0 19 0	0 17 0	† 4 0 0
But if imported in glass bottles or flasks, for every dozen quarts of glass	0 4 2 8	0 4 2 8	Ze			
Wax, the Cwt.	0 8 4 16	0 8 11 4	A	0 7 4 16	0 6 4 16	2 0 0
And besides, if Bees wax —— vizt. Hard wax, the pound	0 2 1 4	0 2 1 4	E	0 2 1 4	0 2 1 4	0 3 4
—— Bay, or Myrtle wax, the pound	0 0 8 8 ½	0 0 8 18 3/10	A	0 0 7 8	0 0 6 6	0 0 6
Weld, for dyers ufe, as by 3 & 4 Ann. cap. 4. the Cwt.	0 0 1 11	0 1 13 ¼	C	0 1 1 8	0 0 1 5	0 0 0
of British fishing, imported by British in British shipping, directly from the place, by the ton	0 0 9 9 ½	0 0 10 4	Bd	0 0 7 19	0 0 6 9	0 5 0
Whale-fins of Newfoundland, or any other his Majesty's colonies or plantations, caught in any ships or vessels truly and properly belonging to Great Britain, and imported in such ships, free.						‡ 50 0 0
not of British fishing, the ton						100 0 0

* But if imported by Aliens Drawback more, 1s. 3d. for every 100l. of the Rate or Value.

INWARDS.

	DUTIES to be paid on IMPORTATION.		Reference to the several Branches, see Page vi.	DRAWBACKS to be repaid on EXPORTATION.*		RATES, or supposed value, by 12 Car. II. cap. 4. 11 Geo. I. cap. 7. from whence the foregoing Duties are computed.
	By BRITISH.	By ALIENS.		If exported to any legal place, except as mentioned in the following column.	If the produce of Europe, or the East Indies, and exported to the British Colonies in America.	
	£. s. d./20ths	£. s. d./20ths		£. s. d./20ths	£. s. d./20ths	£. s. d.
Whale-fins — taken by any shipping belonging to any of his Majesty's colonies and plantations, and imported in such shipping, the ton	2 12 6	2 12 6	V	1 7 6	1 7 6	
— taken in shipping belonging to any of his Majesty's colonies or plantations, but imported in shipping belonging to Great Britain, the ton	1 6 3	1 6 3	V	0 13 9	0 13 9	
of foreign fishing, the ton	93 9 0	93 9 0	O b	84 9 0	75 9 0	
By 15 Geo. III. cap. 31. Whale-fins taken in any part of the ocean by, and imported in, any ship belonging to his Majesty's subjects of Great Britain, Ireland, Guernsey, Jersey, or Man, may be imported duty free.						
Wheat. Vide in Corn.						
Wheat meal. Vide Meal.						
Wheels for spinning, the piece	0 0 4 14½	0 0 4 19 8/10	C	0 0 4 5½	0 0 3 16½	0 1 6

* But if imported by Aliens Drawback more, 1s. 3d. for every 100l. of the Rate or Value, except Whale-fins.

I N W A R D S.

	Duties to be paid on IMPORTATION.			Reference to the several Branches, see Page vi.	Drawbacks to be repaid on EXPORTATION.*		RATES, or supposed value, by 12 Car. II. cap. 4. † 11 Geo. I. cap. /. from whence the foregoing Duties are computed.
	By BRITISH.	By ALIENS.			If exported to any legal place, except as mentioned in the following column.	If the produce of Europe or the East Indies, and exported to the British Colonies in America.	
	£. s. d. 20ths	£. s. d. 20ths			£. s. d. 20ths	£. s. d. 20ths	£. s. d.
Whetstones, the hundred, containing five score.	0 3 6	0 3 8 12 ½	A	0 3 1	0 2 8	0 16 8
Whipcord, the pound	0 0 1 13 7/10	0 0 1 15 7/10	A	0 0 1 9	0 0 1 5	0 0 8
Whisk brooms. *Vide* Brooms.							
Whittles, Cocks, or Bellows, the groce — or Birds of stone, the small groce, containing 12 dozen	0 5 0 9 1/5	0 5 4 5 1/5	A	0 4 5	0 3 10	1 4 0
White lead. *Vide* in Drugs.							
Wines. *See after* Rates Inwards.	0 0 10 1 7/5	0 0 10 14 7/5	A	0 0 8 17 3/5	0 0 7 13 3/5	0 4 0
Wine lees, the ton							
But by 1 Geo. II. flat. 2. cap. 17. are to pay duty as Wine; but are not entitled to any drawback on exportation.							
Brass or Copper wire, not otherwise rated, the Cwt.	2 9 10 10	2 11 6 19 ½	G	2 6 7 10	2 3 4 10	4 0 0
Counterfeit Gold and Silver wire, *for every 20s. of the value upon oath*	0 5 3	0 5 6 3	C	0 4 9	0 3 4 3	4 16 10
Dagger and Quartern wire, the pound	0 0 8 8	0 0 8 18 ½	A	0 0 7 8 3/5	0 0 6 8 3/5	0 3 4
Iron wire, the Cwt.	1 11 6	1 13 5 12 ½	A	1 7 9		0 7 10 0

Wire, vacat.

* But if imported by Aliens Drawback more, 1s. 3d. for every 100l. of the Rate or Value.

W [269] W

INWARDS.

Wire, vocat.

	DUTIES to be paid on IMPORTATION.		Reference to the several Branches, see Page vi.	DRAWBACKS to be repaid on EXPORTATION.*		RATES, or supposed value, by 12 Car. II. cap. 4. ‡ 11 Geo. I. cap. 7. from whence the foregoing Duties are computed.
	By BRITISH.	By ALIENS.		If exported to any legal place, except as mentioned in the following column.	If the produce of Europe or the East Indies, and exported to the British Colonies in America.	
	£. s. d. 20ths	£. s. d. 20ths		£. s. d. 20ths	£. s. d. 20ths	£. s. d.
And besides, for all sorts of foreign Iron wire (except Card wire, and all sorts of Iron wire smaller than the sorts commonly known or called by the names of Fine fine and Superfine, and all Wool cards, or any other wares made of Iron wire) the Cwt. ‖	1 3 7 10	1 3 7 10	D	1 3 7 10	—	6 13 4
Latten wire, the Cwt.	2 10 6 18	2 12 3 18	G	2 7 2 18	2 3 0 18	
Silver wire, for every ounce troy	0 0 9 9	0 0 9 9	Rb	0 0 9 9	0 0 9 9	
And for every 20s. value upon oath	0 0 5 3	0 0 5 3	C	0 0 4 3	0 0 4 3	0 3 4
Steel wire, the pound	0 0 9 12	0 0 9 12	B	0 0 8 7/10	—	
‖ Straßburgh wire, the pound	0 0 2 8 7/10	0 0 8 18 3/10	A	0 0 7 8 7/10	0 0 6 8	
And besides, if { Iron, the Cwt. Brass, the Cwt.	1 3 7 10 1 2 6 18	1 3 7 10 1 2 6 18	D Sb	1 3 7 10 0 0 11 2	1 2 6 18 0 0 9 12	
‖ Virginal wire, the pound	0 1 0 12	0 1 1 7 3/4	A	0 1 3 10	—	0 5 0
And besides, if { Iron, the Cwt. Brass, the Cwt.	1 3 7 10 1 2 6 18	1 3 7 10 1 2 6 18	D Sb	1 3 7 10 1 2 6 18	1 2 6 18	
And besides, all Gilt wire, the ounce troy	0 1 0 12	0 1 0 12	Rb	0 0 0 12	0 0 0 12	

* But if imported by Aliens Drawback more, 1s. 3d. for every 100l. of the Rate or Value.

‖ If Iron no Drawback to the British Colonies in America.

INWARDS.

	Duties to be paid on IMPORTATION.		Reference to the several Branches, see Page vi.	Drawbacks to be repaid on EXPORTATION.*		RATES, or supposed value, by 12 Car. II. cap. 4. ‡11 Geo. I. cap. 7. from whence the foregoing Duties are computed.
	By BRITISH.	By ALIENS.		If exported to any legal place, except as mentioned in the following column.	If the produce of Europe or the East Indies, and exported to the British Colonies in America.	
	£. s. d. 20ths	£. s. d. 20ths		£. s. d. 20ths	£. s. d. 20ths	£. s. d.
Woad, *except* Island or Green wood, the ton, containing 20 Cwt. for Dyers use, as by 3 and 4 *Ann. cap.* 4.	1 11 6	1 15 5		1 4 0	0 16 6	15 0 0
‡Thouloufe woad, the Cwt.	0 3 6	0 3 11 5	Bb	0 2 8	0 1 10	1 13 4
for Dyers use, *as by* 3 *and* 4 *Ann. cap.* 4. ── Anchor flocks, the piece ── of and directly from any part of America, if regularly entered and landed, free.			Bb			0 6 8
On failure thereof. *See the rate at the end of* Wood.						
Europe, except Ireland or France	0 2 1 4	0 2 2 5	B	0 1 11 4	0 1 9 4	
of or from any part of Ireland, Africa, or Asia						
of France. *See the note at the end of* Wood.	0 1 9	0 1 10 1	C	0 1 7	0 1 5	
If imported in foreign ships, to pay duty as Aliens.						
Battens, 6½ inches wide, or under, the hundred, containing six score						1 1 5 0

* But if imported by Aliens Drawback more, 1 s. 3 d. for every 100 l. of the Rate or Value.

W [271] W

INWARDS.

Wood, vizt.
Branches, see Page vi.

	DUTIES to be paid on IMPORTATION.		DRAWBACKS to be repaid on EXPORTATION.*		RATES, or supposed value, by 12 Car. II. cap. 4. ‡ 11 Geo. I. cap. 7. from whence the foregoing Duties are computed.
	By BRITISH.	By ALIENS.	If exported to any legal place, except as mentioned in the following column.	If the produce of Europe or the East Indies, and exported to the British Colonies in America.	
	£. s. d. 20ths	£. s. d. 20ths	£. s. d. 20ths	£. s. d. 20ths	£. s. d.
—— of and directly from any part of America, if regularly entered and landed, free. On failure thereof. See the note at the end of Wood.	0 7 10 10	0 8 2 8 B	0 7 3	0 6 7 10	
—— of or from any part of Europe, except Ireland or France —— of Ireland, Africa, or Asia —— of France. See the note at the end of Wood.	0 6 6 15	0 6 10 13 3¾ C	0 5 11 5	0 5 3 15	
If imported in foreign ships, to pay duty as Aliens.					
Beech boards, 2 inches thick, or under, the hundred, containing 120 —— of and directly from any part of America, if regularly entered and landed, free. On failure thereof. See the note at the end of Wood.	1 5 2 8	1 6 3 B	1 3 2 8	1 1 2 8	‡ 4 0 0
—— of or from any part of Europe, except Ireland or France					

* But if imported by Aliens Drawback more, 1 s. 2 d. for every 100 l. of the Rate or Value.

Wood, *uncut.*

INWARDS.

	DUTIES to be paid on IMPORTATION.		Reference to the several Branches, see Page vi.	DRAWBACKS to be repaid on EXPORTATION.*		RATES, or supposed value, by 12 Car. II. cap. 4. 11 Geo. I. cap. — from whence the foregoing Duties are computed.
	By BRITISH. £. s. d. 1/20ths	By ALIENS. £. s. d. 1/20ths		If exported to any legal place, except as mentioned in the following column. £. s. d. 1/20ths	If the produce of Europe or the East Indies, and exported to the British Colonies in America. £. s. d. 1/20ths	£. s. d.
Beech boards of Ireland, Africa, or Asia — of France. *See the note at the end of Wood.*	1 1 0	1 2 0 12	C	0 19 0	0 17 0	
If imported in foreign ships, to pay duty as Aliens.						
Beech planks, above 2 inches thick, — the load, containing 50 feet — of and directly from any part of America, if regularly entered and landed, free. *On failure thereof. See the note at the end of Wood.*			B			‡ 2 0 0
Europe, except Ireland or France — of or from any part of of Ireland, Africa, or Asia of France. *See the note at the end of Wood.*	0 12 7 4 0 10 6	0 13 1 10 0 11 0 6	C	0 11 7 4 0 9 6	0 10 7 4 0 8 6	
If imported in foreign ships, to pay duty as Aliens.						

* If imported by Aliens Drawback more, 1s. 3d. for every 100l. of the Rate or Value.

W [273] W

INWARDS.

Wood, vocat.

		DUTIES to be paid on IMPORTATION.		DRAWBACKS to be repaid on EXPORTATION.*		RATES, or supposed value, by 12 Car. II. cap. 4. 11 Geo. I. cap. 7. from whence the foregoing Duties are computed.
	Reference to the several Branches, see Page vi.	By BRITISH. £. s. d. 20ths	By ALIENS. £. s. d. 20ths	If exported to any legal place, except as mentioned in the following column. £. s. d. 20ths	If the produce of Europe or the East Indies, and exported to the British Colonies in America. £. s. d. 20ths	£. s. d.
Beech quarters, under 5 inches square, the hundred, containing 120 ———— of and directly from any part of America, if regularly entered and landed, free. *On failure thereof. See the note at the end of Wood.*						
Europe, except Ireland or France ———— of or from any part of of Ireland, Africa, or Asia of France. *See the note at the end of Wood.* *If imported in foreign ships, to pay duty as Aliens.*	B	0 12 7 4	0 13 1 10	0 11 7 4	0 10 7 4	‡ 2 0 0
Beech quarters, 5 inches square, and under 8 inches, the hundred, containing 120 ———— of and directly from any part of America, if regularly entered and landed, &c. *On failure thereof. See the note at the end of Wood.*	C	0 10 6	0 11 0 6	0 9 6	0 8 6	‡ 5 0 0

* But if imported by Aliens Drawback more, 1 s. 3 d. for every 100 l. of the Rate or Value.

Wood, except. — INWARDS.

INWARDS.	DUTIES to be paid on IMPORTATION.		Reference to the several Branches, see Page vi.	DRAWBACKS to be repaid on EXPORTATION.*		RATES,
	By BRITISH.	By ALIENS.		If exported to any legal place, except as mentioned in the following column.	If the produce of Europe or the East Indies, and exported to the British Colonies in America.	super ult. value, [ap. 4.] [ap. 7.] in w.. ence the . ng Duties are computed.
	£ s. d. 20ths	£ s. d. 20ths		£ s. d. 20ths	£ s. d. 20ths	£ s. d.
Beech quarters, 5 inches square, and under 8 inches, the hundred, containing 120:						
── of or from any part of Europe, except Ireland or France	1 11 6	1 12 9 15		1 9 0	1 6 6	
── of Ireland, Africa, or Asia. *See the note at the end of Wood.*	1 6 3	1 7 6 15	B	1 3 9	1 1 3	
── of France. *See the note at the end of Wood.*			C			
If imported in foreign ships, to pay duty as Aliens.						
Box wood, the ton, containing 20 Cwt. of and directly from any part of America, if regularly entered and landed, free. *On failure thereof. See the note at the end of Wood.*						
── of or from any part of Europe, except Ireland or France	2 10 4 16	2 12 6		2 6 4 16	2 2 4 16	‡ 8 0 0
── of Ireland, Africa, or Asia. *See the note at the end of Wood.*	2 2 0	2 4	B	1 18 0	1 14 0	
── of France. *See the note at the end of Wood.*			C			

* But if imported by Aliens Drawback more, 1s. 3d. for every 100l. of the Rate or Value.

INWARDS.

Wcod, vizt.	DUTIES to be paid on IMPORTATION.		Reference to the several Branches, see Page vi.	DRAWBACKS to be repaid on EXPORTATION.*		RATES, or supposed value, by 12 Car. II. cap. 4. ‖ 11 Geo. I. cap. 7. from whence the foregoing Duties are computed.
	By BRITISH.	By ALIENS.		If exported to any legal place, except as mentioned in the following column.	If the produce of Europe or the East Indies, and exported to the British Colonies in America.	
	£. s. d. 20ths	£. s. d. 20ths		£. s. d. 20ths	£. s. d. 20ths	£. s. d.
If imported in foreign ships, to pay duty as Aliens.						
Box wood for combs, the 1000 pieces of and directly from any part of America, if regularly entered and landed, free.	0 10 6	0 10 11 5		0 9 8	0 8 10	1 13 4
On failure thereof. See the note at the end of Wood.	0 7 0	0 7 5 5		0 6 2	0 5 4	
—— of or from any part of Europe, except Ireland or France of Ireland, Africa, or Asia of France. See the note at the end of Wood.			B A			
If imported in foreign ships, to pay duty as Aliens.						
Deals from Russia, and all other countries, not particularly rated, exceeding 20 feet in length, the hundred, containing 120 —— of and directly from any						† 15 0 0

* But if imported by Aliens Drawback more, 1 s. 3 d. for every 100 l. of the Rate or Value

Wood, vocat.

INWARDS.

	Duties to be paid on Importation.		Reference to the several Branches, see Page vi.	Drawbacks to be repaid on Exportation.*		RATES, or supposed value.
	By BRITISH.	By ALIENS.		If exported to any legal place, except as mentioned in the following column.	If the produce of Europe or the East Indies, and exported to the British Colonies in America.	12 Car. II. cap. 4. 11 G. I. cap. 7. from whence the foregoing Duties are computed.
	£. s. d. 20ths	£. s. d. 20ths		£. s. d. 20ths	£. s. d. 20ths	£. s. d.
part of America, if regularly entered and landed, free. *On failure thereof, See the note at the end of* Wood.						
Deals, of or from any part of Europe, except Ireland or France ⎯	4 14 6	4 18 5	B	4 7 0	3 19 6	5 0 0
⎯ of Ireland, Africa, or Asia. *See the note at the end of* Wood.						
⎯ of France. *If imported in foreign ships, to pay duty as Aliens.*	3 18 9	4 2 8	C	3 11 3	3 3 9	
Deals from Sweden, or any other country, of 20 feet in length or under, not otherwise rated, the hundred, containing 120 ⎯						
⎯ of and directly from any part of America, if regularly entered and landed, free. *On failure thereof, See the note at the end of* Wood.						

* But if imported by Aliens Drawback more, 1s. 3d. for every 100l. of the Rate or Value.

INWARDS

	Duties to be paid on IMPORTATION.		References to the several Branches, see Page vi.	DRAWBACKS to be repaid on EXPORTATION.*		RATES, or supposed value, by 12 Car. II. cap. 4. 11 Geo. I. cap. 7. from whence the foregoing Duties are computed.
	By BRITISH.	By ALIENS.		If exported to any legal place, except as mentioned in the following column.	If the produce of Europe or the East Indies, and exported to the British Colonies in America.	
	£. s. d. /20ths	£. s. d. /20ths		£. s. d. /20ths	£. s. d. /20ths	£. s. d.
Wood, —— of or from any part of Europe, except Ireland or France of Ireland, Africa, or Asia of France. *See the note at the end of Wood.* *If imported in foreign ships, to pay duty as Aliens.*	1 11 6	1 12 9 15	B	1 9 0	1 6 6	2 0 0
Ebony wood, the Cwt. *Vide also in E.*	1 6 3	1 7 6 15	C	1 3 9	1 1 3	
—— of and directly from any part of America, if regularly entered and landed, free. *On failure thereof. See the note at the end of Wood.*						
—— of or from any part of Europe, except Ireland or France of Ireland, Africa, or Asia of France. *See the note at the end of Wood.* *If imported in foreign ships, to pay duty as Aliens.*	0 12 7 4	0 13 1 10	B	0 11 7	0 10 7 4	
	0 8 4 16	0 8 11 2	A	0 7 4 16	0 6 4 16	

* But if imported by Aliens Drawback more, 1s. 3d. for every 100l. of the Rate or Value.

INWARDS.

	Reference to the several Branches, see Page vi.	DUTIES to be paid on IMPORTATION.		DRAWBACKS to be repaid on EXPORTATION.*		RATES, or supposed value, by 12 Car. II. cap. 4. 11 Geo. I. cap. 7. from whence the foregoing Duties are computed.
		By BRITISH.	By ALIENS.	If exported to any legal place, except as mentioned in the following column.	If the produce of Europe or the East Indies, and exported to the British Colonies in America.	
		£. s. d. 20ths	£. s. d. 20ths	£. s. d. 20ths	£. s. d. 20ths	£. s. d.

Wood, vocat.

Firewood, the fathom —— of and directly from any part of America, if regularly entered and landed, free.
On failure thereof. See the note at the end of Wood.

—— of or from any part of Europe, except Ireland or France ——
—— of Ireland, Africa, or Asia ——
—— of France. *See the note at the end of Wood.*

If imported in foreign ships, to pay duty as Aliens.

Fir quarters, under 5 inches square, the hundred containing 120 ——
—— of and directly from any part of America, if regularly entered and landed, free.
On failure thereof. See the note at the end of Wood.

		By BRITISH	By ALIENS	Drawback col 1	Drawback col 2	RATES
		0 2 6 4 4/5	0 2 7 10	0 2 3 16 4/5	0 2 1 8 4/5	‡ 0 0 8 0
	B	0 2 1 4	0 2 2 9 1/5	0 1 10 16	0 1 8 8	
	C					‡ 2 0 0

* But if imported by Aliens Drawback more, 1s. 3d. for every 100l. of the Rate or Value.

Wood, vizcat.

INWARDS.

		DUTIES to be paid on IMPORTATION.		Reference to the several Branches, see Page vi.	DRAWBACKS to be repaid on EXPORTATION.*		RATES, or supposed value, by 12 Car. II. cap. 4. 11 Geo. I cap. 7. from whence the foregoing Duties are computed.
		By BRITISH.	By ALIENS.		If exported to any legal place, except as mentioned in the following column.	If the produce of Europe or the East Indies, and exported to the British Colonies in America.	
		*L. s. d.*20ths	*L. s. d.*20ths		*L. s. d.*20ths	*L. s. d.*20ths	*L. s. d.*
—— of or from any part of Europe, except Ireland or France — of Ireland, Africa, or Asia — of France. *See the note at the end of Wood.*		0 12 7 4	0 13 1 10	B	0 11 7 4	0 10 7 4	
If imported in foreign ships, to pay duty as Aliens.		0 10 6	0 11 0 6	C	0 9 6	0 8 6	
Fir quarters, of 5 inches square, and under 8 inches, the hundred containing 120 of and directly from any part of America, if regularly entered and landed, free. *On failure thereof. See the note at the end of Wood.*							
—— of or from any part of Europe, except Ireland or France — of Ireland, Africa, or Asia — of France. *See the note at the end of Wood.*		1 11 6	1 12 9 15	B	1 9 0	1 6 6	1 5 0 0
If imported in foreign ships, to pay duty as Aliens.		1 6 3	1 7 6 15	C	1 3 9	1 1 3	

* But if imported by Aliens Drawback more, 1s. 3d. for every 100l. of the Rate or Value.

INWARDS.

Wood, vocat.

	DUTIES to be paid on IMPORTATION.		Reference to the several Branches, see Page vi.	DRAWBACKS to be repaid on EXPORTATION.*		RATES, or supposed value, by 12 Car. II. cap. 4. 11 Geo. I. cap. 7. from whence the foregoing Duties are computed.
	By BRITISH.	By ALIENS.		If exported to any legal place, except as mentioned in the following column.	If the produce of Europe or the East Indies, and exported to the British Colonies in America.	
	£. s. d. 20ths	£. s. d. 20ths		£. s. d. 20ths	£. s. d. 20ths	£. s. d.
Handfcoops, the dozen	0 0 6 6	0 0 6 12 3/10	C	0 0 5 14	0 0 5 2	0 2 0
Handfpikes, the hundred, containing 120 ────── of and directly from any part of America, if regularly entered and landed, free. *On failure thereof. See the note at the end of Wood.*						0 1 0
────── of or from any part of Europe, except Ireland or France — of Ireland, Africa, or Asia of France. *See the note at the end of Wood.*	0 6 3 12	0 6 6 15	B	0 5 9 12	0 5 3 12	
If imported in foreign ships, to pay duty as Aliens.	0 5 3	0 6 6 3	C	0 4 9	0 4 3	
Kilderkin ſtaves, the hundred, containing 120 ────── of and directly from any part of America, if regularly entered and landed, free. *On failure thereof. See the note at the end of Wood.*						0 2 6

* But if imported by Aliens Drawback more, 1s. 7d. for every 100l. of the Rate or Value.

[281]

Wood, vocat.

INWARDS.	Reference to the several Branches, see Page vi.	DUTIES to be paid on IMPORTATION.		DRAWBACKS to be repaid on EXPORTATION.*		RATES, or supposed value, by 12 Car. II. cap. 4. ‡ 11 Geo. I cap. 7. from whence the foregoing Duties are computed.
		By BRITISH.	By ALIENS.	If exported to any legal place, except as mentioned in the following column.	If the produce of Europe or the East Indies, and exported to the British Colonies in America.	
		L. s. d. 20ths	*L. s. d.* 20ths	*L. s. d.* 20ths	*L. s. d.* 20ths	*L. s. d.*
——— of or from any part of Europe, except Ireland or France — of Ireland, Africa, or Asia — of France. *See the note at the end of Wood.*	B	0 0 9 9	0 0 9 16 7/8	0 0 8 14	0 0 7 19	1 5 0 0
If imported in foreign ships, to pay duty as Aliens.		0 0 7 17 ½	0 0 8 5 3/8	0 0 7 2 ½	0 0 6 7 ½	
Knees of oak for shipping, 8 inches square and under, the hundred, containing 120 ——— of and directly from any part of America, if regularly entered and landed, free. *On failure thereof. See the note at the end of Wood.*						
——— of or from any part of Europe, except Ireland or France — of Ireland, Africa, or Asia of France. *See the note at the end of Wood.*	B	1 1 1 6	1 12 9 15	1 9 0	1 6 6	
If imported in foreign ships, to pay duty as aliens.	C	1 6 3	1 7 6 15	1 3 9	1 1 3	

* But if imported by Aliens Drawback more, 1 s. 3 d. for every 100 l. of the Rate or Value.

INWARDS.

Wood, vacat.

		DUTIES to be paid on IMPORTATION.		Reference to the several Branches, see Page vi.	DRAWBACKS to be repaid on EXPORTATION.*	
		By BRITISH.	By ALIENS.		If exported to any legal place, except as mentioned in the following column.	If the produce of Europe or the East Indies, and exported to the British Colonies in America.
		£. s. d. 20ths	£. s. d. 20ths		£. s. d. 20ths	£. s. d. 20ths
Knees of oak for shipping above 8 inches square, the road, to pay as timber —— of and directly from any part of America, if regularly entered and landed, free. *On failure thereof. See the note at the end of Wood.*						
Europe, except Ireland or France —— of Ireland, Africa, or Asia —— of France. *See the note at the end of Wood.*		0 9 5 8	0 9 10 2 ½	B	0 8 8 8	0 7 11 8
If imported in foreign ships, to pay duty as Aliens.						
Knees of oak, small, for wherries, the hundred, containing 120 —— of and directly from any part of America, if regularly entered and landed, free. *On failure thereof. See the note at the end of Wood.*		0 7 10 10	0 8 3 4 ½	C	0 7 1 10	0 6 4 10
					1 1 10 0	0 10 0 0

* But if imported by Aliens Drawback more, 1s. 3d. for every 100l. of the Rate or Value.

W [283] W

INWARDS.

Wood, vocat.

	DUTIES to be paid on IMPORTATION.		Reference to the several Branches, see Page vi.	DRAWBACKS to be repaid on EXPORTATION.*		RATES, or supposed value, by 12 Car. II. cap. 4. 11 Geo. I. cap. 7. from whence the foregoing Duties are computed.
	By BRITISH.	By ALIENS.		If exported to any legal place, except as mentioned in the following column.	If the produce of Europe or the East Indies, and exported to the British Colonies in America.	
	£. s. d. 20ths	£. s. d. 20ths		£. s. d. 20ths	£. s. d. 20ths	£. s. d.
Europe, except Ireland or France of Ireland, Africa, or Asia of France. *See the note at the end of Wood.*	0 3 11 6 0 2 7 10	0 3 3 7 0 2 9 1	B C	0 2 10 16 0 2 4 10	0 2 7 6 0 2 1 10	1 2 0 0
If imported in foreign ships, to pay duty as Aliens.						
Lathwood, the fathom of and directly from any part of America, if regularly entered and landed, free. *On failure thereof. See the note at the end of Wood.*						
Europe, except Ireland or France of Ireland, Africa, or Asia of France. *See the note at the end of Wood.*	0 12 7 4 0 10 6	0 13 1 10 0 11 0 6	B C	0 11 7 4 0 9 6	0 10 7 4 0 8 6	
If imported in foreign ships, to pay duty as Aliens.						
Lignum vitæ. *Vide in Drugs.*						

* But if imported by Aliens Drawback more, 1s. 3d. for every 1col. of the Rate or Value.

INWARDS.

Wood, vocat.

		DUTIES to be paid on IMPORTATION.		Reference to the several Branches, see Page vi.	DRAWBACKS to be repaid on EXPORTATION.*		RATES, or supposed value, by 12 Car. II. cap. 4. 11 Geo. I. cap. 7. from whence the foregoing Duties are computed.
		By BRITISH.	By ALIENS.		If exported to any legal place, except as mentioned in the following column.	If the produce of Europe, the East Indies, and exported to the British Colonies in America.	
		£. s. d. 20ths	£. s. d. 20ths		£. s. d. 20ths	£. s. d. 20ths	£. s. d.
Mahogany timber or plank, the ton, containing 20 Cwt.		2 10 4 16	2 12 6		2 6 4 16	2 2 4 16	
─── of and directly from any part of America, if regularly entered and landed, free. *On failure thereof. See the note at the end of Wood.*							
─── of or from any part of Europe, except Ireland or France─ of Ireland, Africa, or Asia of France. *See the note at the end of Wood.*		2 0	2 4 1 4		1 18 0	1 14 0	‡ 8 0 0
If imported in foreign ships, to pay duty as Aliens.				B			
Oak boards, under 2 inches thick, and under 15 feet long, the hundred, containing 120				C			
─── of and directly from any part of America, if regularly entered and landed, free. *On failure thereof. See the note at the end of Wood.*							‡ 8 0 0

* But if imported by Aliens Drawback more, 1s. 3d. for every 100 l. of the Rate or Value.

W   [285]   W

INWARDS.

Wood, vocat.

	DUTIES to be paid on IMPORTATION.		Reference to the several Branches, see Page vi.	DRAWBACKS to be repaid on EXPORTATION.*		RATES, or supposed value, by 12 Car. II. cap. 4. 11 Geo. 1. cap. 7. from whence the foregoing Duties are computed.
	By BRITISH.	By ALIENS.		If exported to any legal place, except as mentioned in the following column.	If the produce of Europe or the East Indies, and exported to the British Colonies in America.	
	£. s. d. 20ths	£. s. d. 20ths		£. s. d. 20ths	£. s. d. 20ths	£. s. d.
── of or from any part of Europe, except Ireland or France	2 10 4 16	2 12 6	B	2 6 4 16	2 2 4 16	3 0 0
of Ireland, Africa, or Asia	2 0 0	2 4 1 4	C	1 18 0	1 14 0	
of France. *See the note at the end of Wood.*						
If imported in foreign ships, to pay duty as Aliens.						
Oak plank, the load, containing 50 feet solid ── of and directly from any part of America, if regularly entered and landed, free. *On failure thereof. See the note at the end of Wood.*						
── of or from any part of Europe, except Ireland or France	0 18 10 16	0 19 8 5	B	0 17 4 16	0 15 10 16	
of Ireland, Africa, or Asia	0 15 9	0 16 6 9	C	0 14 3	0 12 9	
of France. *See the note at the end of Wood.*						
If imported in foreign ships, to pay duty as Aliens.						

* But if imported by Aliens Drawback more, 1s. 3d. for every 100l. of the Rate or Value.

W [286] W

Wood, vacat.

INWARDS.	DUTIES to be paid on IMPORTATION.		Reference to the several Branches, see Page vi.	DRAWBACKS to be repaid on EXPORTATION.*		RATES, or supposed value, by 12 Car. II. cap. 4. 11 Geo. I. cap. 7. from whence the foregoing Duties are computed.
	By BRITISH.	By ALIENS.		If exported to any of the ships, except as mentioned in the following column.	If the produce of Europe or the East Indies, and exported to the British Colonies in America.	
	L. s. d. 20ths	*L. s. d. 20ths*		*L. s. d. 20ths*	*L. s. d. 20ths*	*L. s. d.*
Oak timber, the load —— of and directly from any part of America, if regularly entered and landed, free. On failure thereof. *See the note at the end of Wood.*	0 9 5 8	0 9 10 2½	B	0 3 8 8	0 7 11 8	1 10 0
—— of or from any part of Europe, except Ireland or France —— of Ireland, Africa, or Asia —— of France. *See the note at the end of Wood.* If imported in foreign ships, to pay duty as Aliens.	0 7 10 10	0 8 3 4	C	0 7 1 10	0 6 4 10	
Olive wood, the ton, containing 20 Cwt. —— of and directly from any part of America, if regularly entered and landed, free. On failure thereof. *See the note at the end of Wood.*						10 0 0

* But if imported by Aliens Drawback more, 1s. 3d. for every 100l. of the Rate or Value.

INWARDS.

Wood, viezt.

	DUTIES to be paid on IMPORTATION.		Reference to the several Branches, see Page vi.	DRAWBACKS to be repaid on EXPORTATION.*		RATES, or supposed value, by 12 Car.II. cap.4. ‡11 Geo.I.cap.7. from whence the foregoing Duties are computed.
	By BRITISH.	By ALIENS.		If exported to any legal place, except as mentioned in the following column.	If the produce of Europe or the East Indies, and exported to the British Colonies in America.	
	£. s. d. 20ths	£. s. d. 20ths		£. s. d. 20ths	£. s. d. 20ths	£. s. d.
Europe, except Ireland or France ⎫ of Ireland, Africa, or Asia ⎬ of France. See the note at ⎭ the end of Wood.	3 3	3 5 7 10 2 15 1 10		2 18 0 2 7 6	2 13 0 2 2 6	
If imported in foreign ships, to pay duty as Aliens.	2 12 6					
Pailing boards, the hundred, containing 120 of and directly from any part of America, if regularly entered and landed, free.			B C			
On failure thereof. See the note at the end of Wood.						‡ 0 6 8
Europe, except Ireland or France ⎫ of Ireland, Africa, or Asia ⎬ of France. See the note at ⎭ the end of Wood.	0 2 1 4 0 1 9	0 2 2 5 0 1 10 1	B C	0 1 11 4 0 1 7	0 1 9 4 0 1 5	
If imported in foreign ships, to pay duty as Aliens.						

* But if imported by Aliens Drawback more, 1s. 3d. for every 100l. of the Rate or Value

[288]

W   W

INWARDS.	DUTIES to be paid on IMPORTATION.		Reference to the several Branches, see Page vi.	DRAWBACKS to be repaid on EXPORTATION.*		RATES, or supposed value, by 12 Car. II. cap. 4. 11 Geo. I. cap. . from whence the foregoing Duties are computed.
Wood, *viz.*	By BRITISH.	By ALIENS.		If exported to any legal place, except as mentioned in the following column.	If the produce of Europe or the East Indies, and exported to the British Colonies in America.	
	£. s. d. 20ths	£. s. d. 20ths		£. s. d. 20ths	£. s. d. 20ths	£. s. d.
Planks of Ireland, the foot ——— *Vide also in* P.	0 0 6 3/10	0 0 6 11/160	A	0 0 5 1/10	0 0 4 4/5	0 0 1 1/4
Round wood, the hundred, containing 120 ——— of and directly from any part of America, if regularly entered and landed, free. *On failure thereof. See the note at the end of* Wood.						
——— of or from any part of Europe, except Ireland or France ——— of Ireland, Africa, or Asia ——— of France. *See the note at the end of* Wood. *If imported in foreign ships, to pay duty as Aliens.*	0 12 7 4 0 10 6	0 13 1 10 0 11 0 6	B C	0 11 7 4 0 9 6	0 10 7 4 0 8 6	+ 2 0 0
Speckled wood, the Cwt. ——— of and directly from any part of America, if regularly entered and landed, free.						+ 0 13 4

* But if imported by Aliens Drawback more, 1 s. 3 d. for every 100 l. of the Rate or Value.

INWARDS.

Wood, &c.

	DUTIES to be paid on IMPORTATION.		DRAWBACKS to be repaid on EXPORTATION.*		RATES, or supposed value, by 12 Car. II. cap. 4. 11 Geo. I. cap. 7. from whence Duties the foregoing Duties are computed.
	By BRITISH.	By ALIENS.	Reference to the several Branches, see Page vi.	If exported to any legal place, except as mentioned in the following column.	If the produce of Europe, or the East Indies, and exported to the British Colonies in America.
	L. s. d./20ths	*L. s. d.*/20ths		*L. s. d.*/20ths	*L. s. d.*/20ths	*L. s. d.*
On failure thereof. *See the note at the end of Wood.*	0 4 2 8	0 4 4 10	B	0 3 10 8	0 3 6 8	1 5 0
——— of or from any part of Europe, except Ireland or France — of Ireland, Africa, or Asia — of France. *See the note at the end of Wood.*	0 2 9 12	0 2 11 14	A	0 2 5 12	0 2 1 12	
If imported in foreign ships, to pay duty as Aliens.						
Sweet wood of West India, the Cwt. — directly from any part of America, if regularly entered and landed, free. On failure thereof. *See the note at the end of Wood.*	0 7 10 10	0 8 2 8	B	0 7 3	0 7 3	0 13 4
——— when legally imported	0 2 9 12	0 2 11 14	A	0 2 5 12	0 2 1 12	
from Europe. Timber of Ireland, the ton or load — *Vide* Balks.						

* But if imported by Aliens Drawback more, 1 s. 3 d. for every 100 l. of the Rate or Value.

W   [290]   W

INWARDS.		DUTIES to be paid on IMPORTATION.		Reference to the several Branches, see Page vi.	DRAWBACKS to be repaid on EXPORTATION.*		RATES, or supposed value, by 12 Car. II. cap. 4. 11 Geo. I. cap. 7. from whence the foregoing Duties are computed.
		By BRITISH.	By ALIENS.		If exported to any legal place, except as mentioned in the following column.	If the produce of Europe or the East Indies, and exported to the British Colonies in America.	
		£. s. d. 20ths	£. s. d. 20ths		£. s. d. 20ths	£. s. d. 20ths	£. s. d.
Wood, vizt.	Wainscot boards of all sorts, the inch, or foot, containing 12 feet in length and 1 inch in thickness, and in proportion in any greater or lesser length or thickness ——— of and directly from any part of America, if regularly entered and landed, free. On failure thereof. See the note at the end of Wood.	0 0 5 13 2/5	0 0 5 18 1/5	B	0 0 5 4 2/5	0 0 4 15 1/2	0 1 6
	Europe, except Ireland or France ——— of Ireland, Africa, or Asia ——— of France. See the note at the end of Wood.	0 0 4 14 1/2	0 0 4 19 9/40	C	0 0 4 5 1/2	0 0 3 16 1/2	0 1 6
	If imported in foreign ships, to pay duty as Aliens.						0 0 0
	Wooden tubs, the dozen ——— Users single, under 24 feet in length, the hundred, containing 120 ———	0 0 4 14 1/2	0 0 4 19 9/40	C	0 0 4 5 1/2	0 0 3 16 1/2	0 1 6
							0 2 0

* If imported by Aliens Drawback more, 1 s. 3 d. for every 100 l. of the Rate or Value.

INWARDS.

Wood, vecat.

	DUTIES to be paid on IMPORTATION.		Reference to the several Branches, see Page vi.	DRAWBACKS to be repaid on EXPORTATION.*		RATES, or supposed value, by 12 Car.II. cap.4. ‡11 Geo.I. cap.7. from whence the foregoing Duties are computed.
	By BRITISH.	By ALIENS.		If exported to any legal place, except as mentioned in the following column.	If the produce of Europe or the East Indies, and exported to the British Colonies in America.	
	£. s. d. 20ths	£. s. d. 20ths		£. s. d. 20ths	£. s. d. 20ths	£. s. d.
— of and directly from any part of America, if regularly entered and landed, free. *On failure thereof. See the note at the end of Wood.*	0 12 7 4	0 13 1 10	B	0 11 7 4	0 10 7 4	
— of or from any part of Europe, except Ireland or France — — of Ireland, Africa, or Asia — — of France. *See the note at the end of Wood.*	0 10 6	0 11 0 6	C	0 9 6	0 8 6	
If imported in foreign ships, to pay duty as Aliens.						
Users double, of 24 feet in length and upwards, the hundred, containing 120						‡ 5 0 0
— of and directly from any part of America, if regularly entered and landed, free. *On failure thereof. See the note at the end of Wood.*						

* But if imported by Aliens Drawback more, 1s. 3d. for every 100l. of the Rate or Value.

W [292] W

Wood, vocat.

INWARDS.

{ Users double of or from any part of
Europe, except Ireland or France
of Ireland, Africa, or Asia
of France. See the note
at the end of Wood.
If imported in foreign ships, to pay
duty as Aliens.
Brazeil or Fernambuck wood, the
Cwt. for Dyers use, as by 3 & 4
Ann. cap. 4.
By 8 Geo. I. cap. 15. if regularly
imported, entered, and landed,
duty free.
But on failure thereof, then to pay
Brazilletto or Jamaica wood, the
Cwt. for Dyers use, as by 3 & 4
Ann. cap. 4.
By 8 Geo. I. cap. 15. if regularly
imported, entered and landed,
duty free.
But on failure thereof, then to pay }

DUTIES to be paid on IMPORTATION.		Reference to the several Branches, see Page vi.	DRAWBACKS to be repaid on EXPORTATION.*		RATES, or (supposed) value, by 12 Car. II. cap. 4. ‡ 11 Geo. I. cap. 7. from whence the foregoing Duties are computed.
By BRITISH.	By ALIENS.		If exported to any legal place, except as mentioned in the following column.	If the produce of Europe or the East Indies, and exported to the British Colonies in America.	
£. s. d. 20ths	£. s. d. 20ths		£. s. d. 20ths	£. s. d. 20ths	£. s. d.
1 11 6	1 12 9 15	B	1 9 0	1 6 6	1 15 0
1 6 3	1 7 6 15	C	1 3 9	1 1 3	
0 5 6 3	0 5 11 13 ½	Bd	0 4 7 13	0 4 7 13	1 1 8
0 3 4 19	0 3 8 7 ½	Bd	0 2 10 9	0 2 10 9	

* But if imported by Aliens Drawback more, 1s. 3d. for every 100l. of the Rate or Value.

[293]

INWARDS.

Wood, vocat.

	DUTIES to be paid on IMPORTATION.		Reference to the several Branches, see Page vi.	DRAWBACKS to be repaid on EXPORTATION.*		RATES, or supposed value, by 12 Car. II. cap. 4. & 11 Geo. I. cap. 7. from whence the foregoing Duties are computed.
	By BRITISH.	By ALIENS.		If exported to any legal place, except as mentioned in the following column.	If the produce of Europe or the East Indies, and exported to the British Colonies in America.	
	£. s. d. 20ths	£. s. d. 20ths		£. s. d. 20ths	£. s. d. 20ths	£. s. d.
Fustick, the Cwt. for Dyers use, as by 3 & 4 Ann. cap. 4.						
By 8 Geo. 1. cap. 15. if regularly imported, entered, and landed, duty free.						
But on failure thereof, then to pay:						
— of or from any part of Europe, except Ireland and France	0 1 0 12	0 1 1 7 ¾	A d	0 0 11 2	0 0 9 12	0 5 0
— of France	0 3 1 16	0 3 2 11 ¾	F a	0 1 9 6	0 1 7 16	
— of any French colony or plantation	0 1 10 1	0 1 10 16 ¾	B d	0 1 8 11	0 1 8 11	
— of any other place	0 0 9 9	0 0 10 4 ¾	B d	0 0 7 19	0 0 6 9	
Red or Guinea wood, the ton, for Dyers use, as by 3 & 4 Ann. cap. 4.						
By 8 Geo. 1. cap. 15. if regularly imported, entered, and landed, duty free.						
But on failure thereof, then to pay	3 3 0	3 10 10 10	B b	2 8 0	2 8 0	30 0 0
Logwood. Vide in L.						

* But if imported by Aliens Drawback more, 1 s. 3 d. for every 100 l. of the Rate or Value.

W [294] W

INWARDS.

	DUTIES to be paid on IMPORTATION.		Reference to the several Branches, see Page vi.	DRAWBACKS to be repaid on EXPORTATION.*		RATES, or (suppos'd value, by 12 Cur. II. cap. 4. § 11 Geo. I. cap. 7. from whence the foregoing Duties are computed.
	By BRITISH.	By ALIENS.		If exported to any legal place, except as mentioned in the following column.	If the produce of Europe or the East Indies, and exported to the British Colonies in America.	
	£. s. d. 20ths	£. s. d. 20ths		£. s. d. 20ths	£. s. d. 20ths	£. s. d.
Wood for dying, viza. Nicorago wood, the Cwt. for Dyers ufe, as by 3 & 4 Ann. cap. 4.	0 1 3 2 ⅔	0 1 4 7 ⅔	Bd	0 1 0 14 ⅔	0 1 0 14 ⅔	0 8 0
By 8 Geo. I. cap. 15. if regularly imported, entered, and landed, duty free.						
But on failure thereof, then to pay						
Wood for dying, of all other forts, not otherwife rated, the Cwt.	0 1 16	0 1 8 9 ½	Bd	0 1 3 18	0 1 0 18	0 10 0
If Sapan wood, for Dyers ufe, as by 3 & 4 Ann. cap. 4. and by 8 Geo. I. cap. 15. if regularly imported, entered, and landed, duty free.						
But on failure thereof, then to pay ——— of all other forts, of or from any part of Europe, except Ireland and France	0 3 7 4	0 3 3 7 ½	B	0 2 10 16	0 2 7 16	
——— of France	0 7 4	0 7 5 15 ½	F	0 4 7 4	0 4 4 4	
——— of Ireland, Afia, or Africa ——— of and directly from any part of America, if regularly imported, entered, and landed, duty free.	0 2 7 10	0 2 9 1 ½	C	0 2 4 10	0 2 1 10	

* But if imported by Aliens Drawback more, 1s. 3d. for every 100 l. of the Rate or Value.

INWARDS.

	DUTIES to be paid on IMPORTATION.		Reference to the several Branches, see Page vi.	DRAWBACKS to be repaid on EXPORTATION:*		RATES, or supposed value, by 12 Car. II. cap. 4. 11 Geo. I. cap. 7. from whence the foregoing Duties are computed.
	By BRITISH.	By ALIENS.		If exported to any legal place, except as mentioned in the following column.	If the produce of Europe or the East Indies, and exported to the British Colonies in America.	
	£. s. d. 20ths	£. s. d. 20ths		£. s. d. 20ths	£. s. d. 20ths	£. s. d.
On failure thereof, then to pay: of any French colony or plantation	0 4 8 14	0 4 10 5	C	0 4 5 14	0 4 5 14	
Wood of and directly from any other part of America, (masts, yards, and bowsprits excepted) under the acts of 8 Geo. I. cap. 12. and 11 Geo. III. cap. 41. if regularly entered and landed, duty free.	0 2 7 10	0 2 9 1 ½	C	0 2 4 10	0 2 1 10	
On failure thereof, then to pay: Deemed for Dyers use. See these Articles under their respective heads.						
Not for Dyers use, rated by 12 Car. II. cap. 4. for every 20 s. of the rate, of the produce of any French colony or plantation	0 9 5 8	0 9 8 11	C	0 8 11 8	0 8 11 8	
of the produce of any other part of America	0 4 2 8	0 4 5 11	A	0 3 8 8	0 3 8 8	

* But if imported by Aliens Drawback more, 1 s. 3 d. for every 100 l. of the Rate or Value.

[296]

INWARDS.

	DUTIES to be paid on IMPORTATION.		Reference to the several Branches, see Page vi.	DRAWBACKs to be repaid on EXPORTATION.*		RATES, or supposed value, by 12 Car. II. cap. 4. † 11 Geo. I. cap. 7. from whence the foregoing Duties are computed.
	By BRITISH.	By ALIENS.		If exported to any legal place, except as mentioned in the following column.	If the produce of Europe or the East Indies, and exported to the British Colonies in America.	
	£. s. d. 20ths	£. s. d. 20ths		£. s. d. 20ths	£. s. d. 20ths	£. s.
Wood, rated by 11 Geo. I. cap. 7. for every 20 s. of the rate:						p
of the produce of any French colony or plantation	0 9 5 8	0 9 8 11	C	0 9 8 11	0 8 11 8	
of the produce of any other part of America	0 5 3 8	0 5 6 3	C	0 4 9	0 4 8	
Wood of France, for every 20 s. of the rate	0 14 8 8	0 14 11 11	F	0 9 2 8	0 8 8	
Wood unrated, for every 20 s. of the value upon oath:						
of or from any part of Europe, except Ireland and France	0 6 3 12	0 6 6 15	B	0 5 9 12	0 5 3 12	
of Ireland, Africa, or Asia	0 5 3 8	0 5 6 3	C	0 4 9 8	0 4 8	
of France	0 14 8 8	0 14 11 11	F	0 9 2 8	0 8 8	
of America, under the acts of 8 Geo. I. cap. 12. and 11 Geo. III. cap. 41. if regularly entered and landed, duty free. On failure thereof, then to pay:						
of the produce of any French colony or plantation	0 9 5 8	0 9 8 11	C	0 8 11 8	0 8 11 8	

* But if imported by Aliens Drawback more, 1 s. 3 d. for every 100 l. of the Rate or Value.

INWARDS.

Wool, vacat.

	Reference to the several Branches, see Page vi.	Duties to be paid on IMPORTATION.		Drawbacks to be repaid on EXPORTATION.*		RATES, or supposed value, by 12 C. II. cap. 4. 11 Geo. I. cap. 7. from whence the foregoing Duties are computed.
		By BRITISH.	By ALIENS.	If exported to any legal place, except as mentioned in the following column.	If the produce of Europe or the East Indies, and exported to the British Colonies in America.	
		£. s. d. 20ths	£. s. d. 20ths	£. s. d. 20ths	£. s. d. 20ths	£. s. d.
——— of the produce of any other part of America	C	0 5 3	0 5 6 3	0 4 9	0 4 9	1 1 0 0 6
Note, Wood imported in foreign ships, is subject to the Aliens duty.						
Bever wool, free.						
But by 2 W. & M. cap. 4. for every pound of Bever wool cut and combed (except combed in Russia, and imported from thence in British ships)	D	0 15 9	0 15 9	0 15 9	0 15 9	1 0 0 0 4
Carmenia wool. *Vide* Goats hair.						
Coney wool, the pound	C	0 1 11	0 1 13 4/40	0 1 8 1/2	0 0 15	
Cotton-wool of the British plantations, free.						
——— not of the growth of the British plantations, the pound	A	0 0 16 4/5	0 0 17 17/20	0 0 14 4/5	0 0 12 4/5	
But by 6 Geo. III. cap. 52. may be imported from any port or place whatsoever in British ships, if regularly entered and landed, duty free.						

* But if imported by Aliens Drawback more, 1s. 3d. for every 100 l. of the Rate or Value.

W [298] W

INWARDS.

Wool, contd.

	Duties to be paid on IMPORTATION.		Reference to the several Branches, see Page vi.	Drawbacks to be repaid on EXPORTATION.*		RATES, or supposed value, by 12 Car. II. cap. 4. 11 Geo. I. cap. 7. from which the foregoing Duties are computed.
	By BRITISH.	By ALIENS.		If exported to any legal place, except as mentioned in the following column.	produce of Europe or the East Indies, and exported to the British Colonies in America.	
	£. s. d. 20ths	£. s. d. 20ths		£. s. d. 20ths	£. s. d. 20ths	£. s. d.
By 21 *Geo. III. cap.* 26. imported in any foreign ship, the pound — This act is to continue in force during the present hostilities with *France, Spain,* and the *States General of the United Provinces,* or either of them.	0 0 1 6 ¼	0 0 1 6 ¼	De			
Estridge wool, imported in British-built ships, the Cwt. free. — imported in foreign-built ships, the Cwt.	0 7 4 4	0 7 8 12 ⅕	C	0 6 7 16	0 5 11 8	1 1 8 0
Hares wool, the pound						
Irish wool combed, the pound — free. — uncombed, the Cwt.	0 0 15 3¼	0 0 16 4 30/50	C	0 0 14 ¼	0 0 10 ¼	0 0 0 3
Lambs wool, the Cwt. — free. Polonia wool, the Cwt. — free. Sheeps wool, from any other place than mentioned in the Book of Rates, the pound Spanish wool for clothing, and Spanish felt wool, the Cwt. free. Red wool, the pound, free.	0 0 15 3¼	0 0 16 4 30/50	C	0 0 14 ¼	0 0 12 1¼	0 0 0 3

* But if imported by Aliens Drawback more, 1 s. 3 d. for every 100 l. of the Rate or Value.

INWARDS.

	DUTIES to be paid on IMPORTATION.		DRAWBACKs to be repaid on EXPORTATION.*		RATES, or supposed value, by 12 Car. II. cap. 4. † 11 Geo. I. cap. 7. from whence the foregoing Duties are computed.
	By BRITISH.	By ALIENS.	Reference to the several Branches, see Page vi.	If exported to any legal place, except as mentioned in the following column.	If the produce of Europe or the East Indies, and exported to the British Colonies in America.
	L. s. d. 20ths	*L. s. d.* 20ths		*L. s. d.* 20ths	*L. s. d.* 20ths	*L. s. d.*
Woollen cloths. *Vide* Cloths.						
—— stuffs. *Vide* Stuffs.						
Worm seed. *Vide in* Drugs.						
Worsted, *vocat.* Rusfiel's worsted, or broad worsted, the piece	0 8 4,16	0 8 11 2	A	0 7 4,16	0 6 4,16	2 0 0
—— St. Omer's narrow or half worsted, the piece	0 14 8	0 14 11 11	F	0 9 2 8	0 8 8 8	1 0 0
Wrefts for virginals, the groce, containing 12 dozen	0 5 0 9	0 5 4 5⅓	A	0 4 5 5⅓	—	1 4 0
And besides, for every Cwt. of Iron	0 5 3	0 5 3	D	0 5 3	—	

Y.

Yarn, *vocat.* { CABLE Yarn, the Cwt.	0 8 0,12	0 8 2,14 7⁄20	B	0 5 11 —	0 4,16 —	0 13 4
Camel or Mohair yarn, the pound	0 0 6 6	0 0 6,13 ⅛	A	0 0 2,17 —	0 0 4,16 —	0 2 6
Cotton yarn, the pound	0 0 3 3	0 0 3 6 11⁄20	C	0 0 5 3⅗	0 0 2,11 —	0 1 0
—— of the East Indies, the pound	0 0 5,13 ⅔	0 0 5,16 11⁄20	B e	0 0 5 7	0 0 5 1 ⅔	

* But if imported by Aliens Drawback more, 1 s. 3 d. for every 100 l. of the Rate or Value.

INWARDS.

Yarn, great.

	DUTIES to be paid on IMPORTATION.		Reference to the several Branches, see Page vi.	DRAWBACKS to be repaid on EXPORTATION.		RATES, suppos'd value, by 12 Car. II. cap. 4. 11 Geo. I. cap. 7. from whence the foregoing Duties are computed.
	By BRITISH.	By ALIENS.		If exported to any legal place, except as mentioned in the following column.	If the produce of Europe on the East Indies, and exported to the British Colonies in America.	
	£. s. d. 20ths	£. s. d. 20ths		£. s. d. 20ths	£. s. d. 20ths	£. s. d.
But by 18 Geo. III. cap. 56. Cotton yarn of the manufacture of Ireland may be imported directly from thence, under the certificates and oaths required by that law, duty free.						
Grogram yarn, the pound	0 0 7 11	0 0 8 0 1/20	A	0 0 6 13 1/5	0 0 5 15 1/5	0 3 0
Irish yarn, the pack, containing 4 Cwt. at 6 score pound to the hundred	1 1 0	1 2 3 15	A	0 18 6	0 16 0	5 0 0
But if imported directly from thence by British or Irish, under proper certificate and oath, duty free.						
Raw linen yarn, Dutch, the pound						0 1 0
—— French, the pound						0 1 0
Sail yarn, the pound	0 0 1 10	0 0 1 13 3/40	C	0 0 1 7 1/2	0 0 1 4 1/2	0 0 6
Spruce, or Muscovia yarn, the Cwt.						2 13 4
By 24 Geo. II. cap. 46. the duties upon Dutch, French, Spruce, or Muscovia yarn, and upon all other foreign Raw linen yarns, are, after						

* But if imported by Aliens Drawback more, 1s. 3d. for every 100l. of the Rate or Value, except Raw Linen Yarn.

[301]

Y

INWARDS.

Yarn, vizvot.

	DUTIES to be paid on IMPORTATION.		Reference to the several Branches, see Page vi.	DRAWBACKS to be repaid on EXPORTATION.*		RATES, or supposed value, by 12 Car. II. cap. 4. † 11 Geo. I. cap. 7. from whence the foregoing Duties are computed.
	By BRITISH. £. s. d. 20ths	By ALIENS. £. s. d. 20ths		If exported to any legal place, except as mentioned in the following column. £. s. d. 20ths	If the produce of Europe or the East Indies, and exported to the British Colonies in America. £. s. d. 20ths	£. s. d.
the 25th day of March, 1752, repealed; and in lieu thereof, the following duty was laid:						
For every pound weight of French, Dutch, Muscovia, or Spruce Raw linen yarn, and all other Raw linen yarn	0 0 1 1	0 0 1 1	W a			
But by 19 Geo. III. cap. 27; if imported in British ships, and regularly entered and landed, duty free, to the 24th of June, 1786, and from thence to the end of the then next session of parliament.						
Scotch yarn, the pound, free						
Wick yarn, the dozen pound	0 2 4 7	0 2 5 15 7/20	A	0 2 1 13	0 1 10 19	† 0 1 0
Woollen or Bay yarn, the Cwt.	0 14 0	0 14 10 10	A	0 12 4	0 10 8	0 9 0
By 12 Geo. II. cap. 21. if regularly imported from Ireland, free.						
Worsted yarn, being two or more threads, twisted or thrown, the pound	0 0 9 9	0 0 9 18 9/20	C	0 0 8 11	0 0 7 13	† 0 3 0

* But if imported by Aliens Drawback more, 1s. 3d. for every 100l. of the Rate or Value, except Raw Linen Yarn.

INWARDS.

	Duties to be paid on IMPORTATION.		Reference to the several Branches, see Page vi.	Drawbacks to be repaid on EXPORTATION.*		RATES, or supposed value, by 12 Car. II. cap. 4. 11 Geo. I. cap. 7. from whence the foregoing Duties are computed.
	By BRITISH.	By ALIENS.		If exported to any legal place, except as mentioned in the following column.	If the produce of Europe or the East Indies, and exported to the British Colonies in America.	
	£. s. d. 20ths	£. s. d. 20ths		£. s. d. 20ths	£. s. d. 20ths	£. s. d.
Yokes for oxen, the pair	0 0 3 3	0 0 3 6 13	C	0 0 2 17	0 0 2 11	0 1 0
All other goods not before particularly rated, for every 20s. of their real value and prices, as ascertained by the oath or affirmation of the merchant, in the presence of the customer, collector, comptroller, and surveyor, or any two of them	0 5 3	0 5 6 3	C	0 4 9	0 4 3	

* But if imported by Aliens Drawback more, 1s. 3d. for every 100l. of the Rate or Value.

[303]

WINES.

FRENCH WINE, imported into the port of LONDON, the ton:

	Duty to be paid on IMPORTATION.		Reference to the several Branches, see Page vi.	DRAWBACK to be repaid on EXPORTATION	
	£. s. d. 20ths			To any British colony, or to any British settlemen. in the East Indies. £. s. d. 20ths	To any other legal place. £. s. d. 20ths
— entered as Unfilled { by British	91 16 7 18	4/5	F y	47 9 8 14	39 1 8 14
{ by Aliens	95 19 9 16		F y	51 7 10 12	42 19 10 12
— Filled { by British	94 18 4 16		F y	50 5 0 16	41 17 0 16
{ by Aliens	99 12 10 16		F y	54 14 6 16	46 6 6 16
And besides, if imported in flasks or bottles, for every dozen quarts of Glass ——	0 4 2 8		Z e		
For Prisage:					
— entered as Unfilled { in British ships	84 7 6 14	2/3	F z	41 0 7 10	32 12 7 10
{ in Foreign ships	87 3 0		F z	43 16 0 16	35 8 0 16
— Filled { in British ships	86 10 4 16		F z	42 17 0 16	34 9 0 16
{ in Foreign ships	89 13 4 16		F z	46 0 0 16	37 2 0 16
And besides, if imported in flasks or bottles, for every dozen quarts of Glass ——	0 4 2 8		Z e		

Note. Wine imported in a foreign ship is subject to the same duty, and entitled to the same drawback as if imported by Aliens.

W I N E S.

	Duty to be paid on Importation. £.	s.	d.	20ths	Reference to the several Branches, see Page vi.	Drawback to be repaid on Exportation: To any British colony in America, or to any British settlement in the East Indies. £.	s.	d.	20ths	To any other legal place. £.	s.	d.	20ths
FRENCH WINE, imported into an OUT-PORT, the ton:													
Entered as Unfilled — By British	87	13	6		F y	43	6	6	16	34	18	6	16
Entered as Unfilled — By Aliens	91	16	7	18 ⅖	F y	47	4	8	14 ⅖	38	16	8	14 ⅖
Filled — By British	90	3	10	16	F y	45	10	6	16	37	2	6	16
Filled — By Aliens	94	[illegible]	4	16	F y	50	0	0	16	41	12	0	16
And besides, if imported in flasks or bottles, for every dozen quarts of Glass	0	4	2	8	Z e	—	—	—	—	—	—	—	—
For Prisage:													
Entered as Unfilled — In British ships	81	12	1	8 ⅘	F z	38	5	2	4 ⅘	29	17	2	4 ⅘
Entered as Unfilled — In Foreign ships	84	7	6	14 ⅘	F z	41	0	7	10 ⅖	32	12	7	10 ⅖
Filled — In British ships	83	7	4	16	F z	39	14	0	16	31	6	0	16
Filled — In Foreign ships	86	10	4	16	F z	42	17	0	16	34	9	0	16
And besides, if imported in flasks or bottles, for every dozen quarts of Glass	0	4	2	8	Z e	—	—	—	—	—	—	—	—

Note, Wine *imported in a foreign ship is subject to the same duty, and entitled to the same drawback, as if imported by Aliens.*

W I N E S.

RHENISH, GERMANY, and HUNGARY Wine, imported into LONDON, or any OUT-PORT, the ton:

		Duty to be paid on IMPORTATION		Reference to the several Branches, see Page vi.	DRAWBACK to be repaid on EXPORTATION		
		L. s. d./20ths			To any British colony in America. *L. s. d.*/20ths	To any British settlement in the East Indies. *L. s. d.*/20ths	To any other legal place. *L. s. d.*/20ths
entered as Unfilled	by British	48 0 6 9 3/5		N b	44 10 6 9 3/5	35 10 1 13 3/5	31 6 1 13 3/5
	by Aliens	52 3 8 8		N b	44 14 6 8 8	39 8 3 12	35 4 3 12
Filled	by British	52 3 8 8		N b	48 13 8 8	39 3 8 8	34 19 8 8
	by Aliens	56 18 2 8		N b	43 18 2 8	43 13 2 8	39 9 2 8
For Prisage:		0 4		N e			
entered as Unfilled	in British ships	39 3 8 12 4/5		N d	35 13 8 12 4/5	27 13 3 16 4/5	23 9 3 16 4/5
	in Foreign ships	41 19 1 18		N d	35 16 4 6	30 8 9 2	26 4 9 2
Filled	in British ships	42 4 2 8		N d	38 14 2 8	30 4 2 8	26 0 2 8
	in Foreign ships	45 7 2 8		N d	38 17 2 2	33 7 2 8	29 3 2 8
		0 4		N e			

And besides, if imported in flasks or bottles, for every dozen quarts of Glass ——

And bottles, if imported in flasks or bottles, for every dozen quarts of Glass ——

Note. Wine imported in a foreign ship is subject to the same duty, and entitled to the same drawback, as if imported by Aliens.

W I N E S.

PORTUGAL and MADERA WINE, imported into the port of LONDON, the ton:

		Duty to be paid on IMPORTATION			Reference to th several Brandies, &c. Page vi.	DRAWBACK to be repaid on EXPORTATION		
		£	s.	d./20ths		To any British colony in America. £ s. d./20ths	To any British settlement in the East Ind. £ s. d./20ths	£ s. d./20ths
Entered as Unfilled	by British	43	17	4 11	Zb	40 7 4 11	31 6 11 5	27 2 11 5
	by Aliens	48	1	6 9	Zb	40 11 4 1	35 5 1 13	31 1 1 13
Filled	by British	47	9	2 8	Zb	43 19 2 8	34 9 2 8	30 5 2 8
	by Aliens	52	3	8 8	Zb	44 3 0	30 18 8 8	34 14 8 8
And besides, if imported in flasks or bottles, for every dozen quarts of Glass		0	4	2	Ze			
For Trissage: entered as Unfilled	in British ships	36	8	3 7	Zd	32 19 3 7 0	27 17 10 11	23 9 3 16
	in Foreign ships	39	3	8 12	Zd	33 0 0	27 13 3 16	22 17 2 8
Filled	in British ships	39	4	2 2	Zd	35 11 3 0	27 4 2 8	26 0 2 8
	in Foreign ships	42	4	8 8	Zd	35 14 2 8	30 4 2 8	
And besides, if imported in flasks or bottles, for every dozen quarts of Glass		0	4	2	Ze			

Note. Wine imported in a foreign ship is subject to the same duty, and entitled to the same drawback, as if imported by Aliens.

WINES.

PORTUGAL and MADEIRA Wine, imported into an Out-Port, the ton:

	Duty to be paid on Importation	Reference to the several Branches, see Page vi.	Drawback to be repaid on Exportation — To any British colony in America	Drawback — To any British settlement in the East Indies	Drawback — To any other legal place
	£. s. d. 20ths		£. s. d. 20ths	£. s. d. 20ths	£. s. d. 20ths
entered as Unfilled — by British	39 14 2 12 4/5	Z b	36 4 2 12 4/5	27 3 9 16 4/5	22 19 9 16 4/5
— by Aliens	43 17 4 11 1/5	Z b	36 8 2 3 1/5	31 1 11 15 1/5	26 17 11 15 1/5
Filled — by British	42 14 8 8	Z b	39 4 8 8	29 14 8 8	25 10 8 8
— by Aliens	47 9 2 8	Z b	39 9 2 8	34 4 2 8	30 0 2 8
And besides, if imported in flasks or bottles, for every dozen quarts of Glass	0 4 2 8	Z e			
For Prisage:					
entered as Unfilled — in British ships	33 12 10 1 3/5	Z d	20 10 1 3/5	22 2 5 3/5	17 18 5 3/5
— in Foreign ships	36 8 3 7 1/5	Z d	30 5 5 15 1/5	24 10 11 1/5	20 3 10 11 1/5
Filled — in British ships	35 18 2 2	Z d	32 8 2 8	23 18 2 8	19 14 2 8
— in Foreign ships	39 1 2 8	Z d	32 11 2 8	27 1 2 8	22 17 2 8
And besides, if imported in flasks or bottles, for every dozen quarts of Glass	0 4 2 8	Z e			

Note. Wine imported in a foreign ship is subject to the same duty, and entitled to the same drawback, as if imported by Aliens.

[308]

WINES.

SPANISH, LEVANT, and all other Wines, not contained in the preceding Tables, imported into the port of LONDON, the ton:

		Duty to be paid on IMPORTATION.		References to the several Branches, See Page vi.	DRAWBACK to be repaid on EXPORTATION		
					To any British colony in America.	To any British settlement in the East Indies.	To any other foreign place.
		l. s. d. 20ths			*l. s. d.* 20ths	*l. s. d.* 20ths	*l. s. d.* 20ths
In ships qualified, entered as Unfilled	by British	44 15 10 6 4/5		Z b	41 5 10 6 4/5	32 5 10 8	28 5 10 9 4/5
	by Aliens	48 19 0 4		Z b	41 9 0 8	36 3 7 8	31 19 7 8
Filled	by British	48 10 2 8		Z b	45 0 2 8	35 10 2 8	31 6 2 8
	by Aliens	53 4 8		Z b	45 4 8	39 19 8 8	35 15 3 8
And besides, if imported in flasks or bottles, for every dozen quarts of Glass		0 4 2		Z c			
In ships unqualified, entered as Unfilled	by British	46 7 3 6 2/5 4/5		Z c	42 17 3 6 2/5 4/5	32 6 11 9 2/5 4/5	28 2 11 9 2/5 4/5
	by Aliens	50 15 11 15		Z c	43 1 6	36 5 4 11	32 1 4 11
Filled	by British	50 5 10 16		Z c	46 15 10 16	35 11 10 16	31 7 10 16
	by Aliens	55 6 8 8		Z c	47 0 8 8	40 1 8 8	35 17 8 8
And besides, if imported in flasks or bottles, for every dozen quarts of Glass		0 4 2 8		Z e			

[309]

WINES.

		DUTY to be paid on IMPORTATION.		Reference to the several Branches, see Page vi.	DRAWBACK to be repaid on EXPORTATION		
					To any British colony in America.	To any British settlement in the East Indies.	To any other legal place.
		L. s. d. 20ths			*L. s. d.* 20ths	*L. s. d.* 20ths	*L. s. d.* 20ths
For Prisage: entered as Unfilled	in British ships	36 8 3 7		N² d	32 18 3 7	24 17 10 11	20 13 10 11
	in Foreign ships	39 3 8 12		N² d	33 0 11 0	27 13 3 16	23 9 3 15
Filled	in British ships	39 1 2 8		N² d	35 11 2 8	27 1 2 8	22 17 2 8
	in Foreign ships	42 4 2 8		N² d	35 13 2 8	30 4 2 8	26 0 2 8
Glass		0 4 2 8		c			

And besides, if imported in flasks or bottles, for every dozen quarts of

Note. Wine imported in a foreign ship is subject to the same duty, and entitled to the same drawback, as if imported by Aliens.

[310]

W I N E S.

SPANISH, LEVANT, and all other Wines, not contained in the preceding Tables, imported into an OUT-PORT (LEVANT Wines into the ports of Bristol or Southampton excepted) the ton:

	Duty to be paid on IMPORTATION.	Reference to the several Branches, see Page vi.	DRAWBACK to be repaid on EXPORTATION.		
			To any British colony in America.	To any British settlemen{t} in the East Indies.	To any other legal place.
	£. s. d. 20ths		£. s. d. 20ths	£. s. d. 20ths	£. s. d. 20ths
In ships qualified, { by British	40 12 8	Zb	37 2 8	28 2 3 12	23 18 3 12
by Aliens	44 15 10 6 2/5	Zb	37 6 7 18 2/5	32 0 5 10 2/5	27 16 5 10 2/5
——— entered as Unfilled { by British	43 15 8	Zb	40 5 8 8	30 15 8 8	26 11 8 8
by Aliens	48 10 2	Zb	40 10 10 2	35 5 2 8	31 1 2 8
——— Filled { by British	0 4 2 8	Zc			
by Aliens					
And besides, if imported in flasks or bottles, for every dozen quarts of Glass					
In ships unqualified, { by British	41 18 6 17 7 2/5	Zc	38 8 6 17 7 2/5	28 3 7 17 7 2/5	23 19 6 7 7 2/5
by Aliens	46 7 3 6 2/5	Zc	38 12 9 11 6 2/5	32 1 11 9 11 6 2/5	27 17 9 11 6 2/5
——— entered as Unfilled { by British	45 5 1 4	Zc	41 15 1 4	30 17 1 4	26 13 1 4
by Aliens	50 5 10 16	Zc	41 19 10 16	35 6 10 16	31 2 10 16
——— Filled { by British					
by Aliens					

[311]

WINES.

		Duty to be paid on IMPORTATION.		Reference to the several Branches, see Page vi.	Drawback to be repaid on EXPORTATION		
		£. s. d. 20ths			To any British colony in America. £. s. d. 20ths	To any British settlement in the East Indies. £. s. d. 20ths	To any other legal place. £. s. d. 20ths
And besides, if imported in flasks or bottles, for every dozen quarts of Glass		0 4 2 8		N c			
For Prisage:							
——— entered as Unfilled	{ in British ships	33 12 10 1		N d	30 2 10 1	22 2 5 5	17 18 5 5
	in Foreign ships	36 8 3 7 3/5		N d	30 5 5 15	24 17 10 11 3/5	20 13 10 11 3/5
——— Filled	{ in British ships	35 18 2 8		N d	35 8 8 8	23 19 2 8	19 14 2 8
	in Foreign ships	39 1 2 8		N d	37 11 2 8	27 1 2 8	22 17 2 8
And besides, if imported in flasks or bottles, for every dozen quarts of Glass		0 4 2 8		N c			

Note. Wine imported in a foreign ship is subject to the same duty, and entitled to the same drawback, as if imported by Aliens.

[312]

W I N E S.

LEVANT Wine, imported into the ports of Bristol or Southampton, the ton:

	Duty to be paid on IMPORTATION	Reference to the several Customs, see Page vi.	DRAWBACK to be repaid on EXPORTATION		
			To any British colony in America.	To any British settlement in the East Indies.	To any other Place.
	$l.$ $s.$ $d.|20^{ths}$		$l.$ $s.$ $d.|20^{ths}$	$l.$ $s.$ $d.|20^{ths}$	$l.$ $s.$ $d.|20^{ths}$
In ships qualified, entered as Unfilled { by British	42 0 5 0 $\frac{4\cdot3}{5\cdot5}$	Z b	38 10 5 0 $\frac{4\cdot3}{5\cdot5}$	29 10 0 4 $\frac{4\cdot3}{5\cdot5}$	25 6 0 4 $\frac{4\cdot3}{5\cdot5}$
by Aliens	46 3 6 19	Z b	38 14 4 11	33 3 2 3	29 4 2 3
Filled { by British	45 7 7 2	Z b	41 17 7 8	32 7 2 8	28 3 2 8
by Aliens	50 1 3 8	Z b	42 1 1 8	36 16 8 8	32 12 8 8
And besides, if imported in flasks or bottles, for every dozen quarts of Glass	0 4 2 8	Z c			
In ships unqualified, entered as Unfilled { by British	43 11 10 0 $\frac{16}{25\cdot3}$	Z c	40 1 10 0 $\frac{16}{25\cdot3}$	29 11 3 0 $\frac{12}{25\cdot3}$	25 7 3 0 $\frac{12}{25\cdot3}$
by Aliens	48 0 6 9	Z c	40 6 0 14	33 9 11 5	29 5 11 5
Filled { by British	47 2 10 16	Z c	43 12 10 16	32 8 10 16	28 4 10 16
by Aliens	52 3 8 8	Z c	43 17 8 8	36 18 8 8	32 14 8 8
And besides, if imported in flasks or bottles, for every dozen quarts of Glass	0 4 2 8	Z e			

WINES.

	Duty to be paid on IMPORTATION.	Reference to the several Branches, see Page vi.	DRAWBACK to be repaid on EXPORTATION		
			To any British colony in America.	To any British settlement in the East Indies.	To any other legal place.
	£. s. d. 20ths		£. s. d. 20ths	£. s. d. 20ths	£. s. d. 20ths
For Prisage:					
Entered as Unfilled { in British ships	33 12 10 1	N d	30 2.10 1	22 2 5 3-5	17 18 5 3-5
{ in Foreign ships	36 8 3 7	N d	30 5 5 15	24 17 10 11 1-5	20 13 10 11 1-5
Filled { in British ships	35 18 2 8	N d	32 8 2 8	23 18 2 8	19 14 2 8
{ in Foreign ships	39 1 2 8	N d	32 11 2 8	27 1 2 8	22 17 2 8
All besides, if imported in flasks or bottles, for every dozen quarts of Glass	0 4 2 8	N e			

Note. Wine imported in a foreign ship is subject to the same duty, and intitled to the same drawback, as if imported by Aliens.

[314]

W I N E S.

LONDON DUTY.

DUTY.	Reference to the several Branches, &c. Pa. xi.
L. s. d. 20ths	
	Oa
	Pb
4 14 6	
3 3 0	

WINES having been entered and landed in an OUT-PORT, and afterwards brought to LONDON, or within 20 miles of the Royal Exchange, the difference of the duties must be first paid to the Collector of the Customs nearest the place from whence the Wines are to be removed; this is usually called the LONDON DUTY, and is as follows:

RHENISH, GERMANY, and HUNGARY Wines, *Nothing*; the duties thereon being the same in all ports.

FRENCH, PORTUGAL, LEVANT, SPANISH, and all other Wines (except LEVANT Wines from Bristol or Southampton,) the ton ——————

LEVANT Wines having been imported into Bristol or Southampton, the ton ——————

A TABLE of the DUTIES and DRAWBACKS on UNRATED EAST INDIA GOODS,

Imported by the UNITED EAST INDIA COMPANY:

For every 100 l. of the gross price at the sales of the said Company.

	Duties to be paid on IMPORTATION.	Reference to the several Branches, see Page vi.	DRAWBACKS to be repaid on EXPORTATION.	
			To any legal place, except the British colonies in America.	To the British colonies in America.
	£. s. d. 20ths		£. s. d. 20ths	£. s. d. 20ths
Candles of wax, supposing the quantity to be 1000 pounds in weight	60 4 10 17 ⅔	G b	40 15 8 3 ⅔	38 13 2 14 ⁷⁸⁄₉₁
China ware	42 18 2 3 ¹⁰⁄₁₁	K d	44 12 10 4 ⁴⁄₅	43 6 0 4 ⁴⁄₅
Cotton manufactures	45 19 8 13	K d	27 2 6	25 7 6
Cowries	28 17 6	C c	34 14 0 19 ¹¹⁄₂₁	33 2 7 ⁵⁄₂₁
Drugs manufactured	36 5 6 13 ¹¹⁄₃₁	K d	26 10 4 7 ³⁷⁄₃₁	24 15 0 19 ⁵⁄₃₁
unmanufactured	28 5 7 14 ³⁷⁄₄₁	D f		
Goods manufactured, deemed for Dyers use, as by 3 and 4 Ann. cap. 4. and not free by 8 Geo. I. cap. 15.	28 17 6	S c	27 2 6	25 7 6
unmanufactured, deemed for Dyers use, as by 3 and 4 Ann. cap. 4. an' not free by 8 Geo. I. cap. 15.	18 17 0 10 ¹⁹⁄₂₁	S d	16 17 3 5 ⁵⁄₁₄	14 17 6
Goods of the manufacture of East India, China, or Persia, prohibited to be worn or used in Great Britain, as Bengals and Stuffs mixed with silk or herba, and manufactures of Cotton printed, painted, stained or dyed, or furniture or apparel made thereof	6 6 0 3 ³⁷⁄₄₁	M f		

For the drawback on such of the above goods as are exported to Africa, see the Table at the end of Unrated East India goods.

[317]

	DUTIES to be paid on IMPORTATION.		DRAWBACKS to be repaid on EXPORTATION	
		Reference to the several Branches, see Page vi.	To any legal place, except the British colonies in America.	To the British colonies in America.
	£. s. d. 20ths		£. s. d. 25ths	£. s. d. 20ths
Japanned or lacquered wares ———	47 5 0	B c	44 15 0	42 5 0
Muslins or white Callicoes, flowered, stitched, &c.	47 0 2 14 6 1/4	Ld † Kh ‡	43 13 10 7 3/4	42 18 10 7 3/4
if exported to Africa, the drawback is ———			45 13 10 7 1/4	
if printed, stained, painted, or dyed in this kingdom, the drawback is			45 13 10 7 1/4	
Tea ———	25 16 3	C e	‖25 16 3	42 18 10 7 1/4
All other East India manufactures, not particularly charged ———	34 6 4 13 3	B e	32 13 11 15 5/5	25 16 3
All other East India unmanufactured goods, not particularly charged ———	25 16 3	C e	23 19 9 10	31 1 6 17 2/5
				22 3 4

† If Callicoes.   ‡ If Muslins.   ‖ To Ireland only.

UNRATED EAST INDIA GOODS,

Taken as PRIZE, and legally condemned.

For every 100 l. of the gross price at the public sales thereof, as regulated by 20 Geo. III. cap. 9. and 21 Geo. III. cap. 5.

	Duties to be paid on IMPORTATION.	Reference to the several Branches, see Page vi.	DRAWBACKS to be repaid on EXPORTATION.	
			To any legal place, except the British colonies in America.	To the British colonies in America.
	l. s. d./20ths		*l. s. d.*/20ths	*l. s. d.*/20ths
Candles of wax, supposing the quantity to be 1000 pounds in weight	61 17 —	G b	42 17 —	40 11 10 3 9/10
China ware	45 2 7 10 30/—	K d	46 3 15 5/6	44 14 2 17 —
Cotton manufactures	47 12 4 13 3	K d	28 5 3 12 —	26 7 10 16 —
Cowries	30 2 8 8 —	C c	36 7 3 6 66/—	34 13 7 14 7 10/—
Drugs manufactured	38 0 10 18 5 8/—	K d	27 12 3 19 11/31	25 14 7 10 30/31
— unmanufactured	29 10 0 7 —	D f		
Goods manufactured, deemed for Dyers use, as by 3 and 4 Ann. cap. 4. and not free by 8 Geo. I. cap. 15;	30 2 8 8 —	S c	28 5 3 12 —	26 7 10 16 —
— unmanufactured, deemed for Dyers use, as by 3 and 4 Ann. cap. 4. and not free by 8 Geo. I. cap. 15.	19 8 6 — —	S d	17 6 0 — —	15 3 6 — —
Goods of the manufacture of East India, China, or Persia, prohibited to be worn or used in Great Britain, as Bengals, and Stuffs mixed with silk or herba, and manufactures of Cotton, printed, painted, stained, or dyed, or furniture or apparel made thereof	6 14 — 7 17 32/41	M f		

For the drawback on such of the above goods as are exported to Africa, see the Table at the end of Unrated East India goods.

[319]

	Duties to be paid on IMPORTATION.	Reference to the several Branches, see p'ge vi.	DRAWBACKS to be repaid on EXPORTATION.	
			To any legal place, except the British colonies in America.	To the British colonies in America.
	L. s. d. 20ths		L. s. d. 20ths	L. s. d. 20ths
Japanned or lacquered wares	47 5 0		44 15 0	42 5 0
Muslins or white Callicoes, flowered, stitched, &c.	48 14 7 1/9	Be Kd† Kh†	45 6 0 10 1/11	42 11 0 10 1/11
if exported to Africa, the drawback is			47 6 0 10 1/11	
if printed, stained, painted, or dyed in this kingdom, the drawback is			47 6 0 10 1/11	
Tea				
All other East India manufactures, not particularly charged	26 17 3	Ce	26 17 3	26 17 3
	35 19 0 13	Be	34 4 5 2	32 9 9 11
All other East India unmanufactured goods, not particularly charged	26 17 3	Ce	24 18 3 10	22 19 4

[320]

PROHIBITED EAST INDIA GOODS.

By 6 Geo. III. cap. 57. upon the exportation to Africa* of the undermentioned goods having been sold at the East-India Company's sales, (or taken as prize, and sold under the regulations directed by 20 Geo. III. cap. 9. and 21 Geo. III. cap. 5.) the following Drawbacks are to be allowed:

	DRAWBACK.	Reference to the several Branches, see Page vi.	RATE, by 6 Geo. III. cap. 52. from which the foregoing Drawbacks are computed.
	£. s. d. 20ths		£. s. d.
Alejars, the piece	0 0 7 4	R.i	0 12 0
Bejutapants, the piece	0 1 0	R.i	1 0 0
Byrampants, the piece	0 0 9	R.i	0 15 0
Blue Long Cloth, the piece	0 2 0	R.i	2 0 0
Brawles, the piece	0 0 2 8	R.i	0 4 0
Callaway Pores, the piece	0 0 9	R.i	0 15 0
Cushtaes, the piece	0 0 7 4	R.i	0 12 0
Coopes, the piece	0 0 7 4	R.i	0 12 0
Chints, the piece	0 0 9	R.i	0 15 0
Chelloes, the piece	0 0 9 12	R.i	0 16 0
Cotton Romalls, the piece	0 0 6	R.i	0 10 0
Guinea Stuffs, the piece	0 0 2 8	R.i	0 4 0
Nicanees small, the piece	0 0 7 4	R.i	0 12 0
Nicanees large, the piece	0 0 9 12	R.i	0 16 0
Neganepants, the piece	0 0 1 0	R.i	0 1 0
Photaes, the piece	0 0 9	R.i	0 15 0
Sastra Cundies, the piece	0 1 0	R.i	1 1 0
Tapseils, the piece	0 0 9 12	R.i	0 16 0

* By 13 Geo. III. cap. 74. this Drawback is not allowed to the Madeira, Canary, Azores or Western Islands.

RATES of GOODS and MERCHANDIZE

OUTWARDS,

As fettled by the ACTS of

12 CAR. II. cap. 4. and 8 GEO. I. cap. 15. &c.

A [322] A

OUTWARDS.

A.

	DUTY		RATES, or supposed value, by 12 Car. II. cap. 4. 1 Geo. I cap. 15. from whence the foregoing Duties are computed.	
	l. s. d. 20ths	Reference to the several Branches, see Page 11.	*l. s. d.*	
ADZES. *Vide* Iron wrought.				
Agarick, trimmed or pared, foreign, the pound	0 0 2 2	Tb	+0 6 8	*Free.
—— rough or untrimmed, foreign, the pound	0 0 0 10 ½	Tb	+0 1 8	
Alabaster, the load	0 1 0 12	Tb	+2 1 0	
Alum, British, the Cwt.				
Ale. *Vide* Beer.				
Annotto, foreign, the pound	0 0 0 6 7/10	Tb	+0 1 0	*Free.
Antimonium crudum, foreign, the Cwt.	0 0 2 2	Tb	+0 6 8	
Anvils, the Cwt.		Tb	0 10 0	
Apothecary and Confectionary wares of all sorts, the Cwt.			2 0 0	
Apples, the bushel			0 0 1	
—— *viz.* Pippins, the bushel	0 1 2 ½	Tb	+2 5 0	*Free.
Aqua fortis, foreign, the bottle, containing four gallons	0 0 2 3	Tb	+2 0 0	
Aqua vitæ, the hogshead	0 0 7 7	Tb	+1 3 4	
Argol, foreign, the Cwt.				
Armour. *Vide* Iron wrought.				
Arsinick, foreign, the pound weight	0 0 0 7/10	Tb	+0 0 1 ½	*Free.
Ashes of British wood, the last, containing 12 barrels			1 13 4	
Axes. *Vide* Iron wrought.				

* See the Note at the end of the Rates Outwards.

OUTWARDS.

B.

	Reference to the several Branches, see Page vi.	DUTY. $L.\ s.\ d.\ 20^{\text{ths}}$	RATES, or supposed value, by 12 Car. II. cap. 4. 18 Geo. I. cap. 15. from whence the foregoing Duties are computed. $L.\ s.\ d.$	
BACON, the flitch	T b	0 0 1 8	0 10 0	Free.
Bags, the dozen			0 10 0	} * Free.
Bandaliers, the hundred collars			0 10 0	
Bayberries, foreign, the Cwt.			0 4 5⅓	
Barnstaple, coarse, of 20 pounds weight and under, the bay			0 12 6	
Manchester, or Barnstaple, fine, and all other single bays, not exceeding 34 pounds weight, the piece			1 0 0	} Free.
Double bays, the piece, in weight from 34 pounds weight to 60 pounds weight			2 0 0	
Minikin bays, containing in weight from 60 pounds weight to 90 pounds weight, to pay as three single bays			3 0 0	Free.
And if they do contain above 90 pounds in weight, and not above 112 pounds, to pay all duties, as for four single bays, and no more			4 0 0	
Beef, the barrel			3 0 0	
Beer, the ton. *See after Rates Outwards.*				
Beer eager, the ton			1 0 0	} ⸗ Free.
Bell-metal, the Cwt.			4 0 0	
Beaver skins — *Vide under letter S.*				
— wool or wombs, the dozen			0 6 0	} * Free.
Bellows, the dozen			0 6 0	
Billets, the thousand			2 0 0	

Bays, *vacat.*

* See the note at the end of the Rates Outwards.

B [324] B

OUTWARDS.

	DUTY.	Reference to the several Branches, see Page vi.	RATES, or supposed value, by 12 Car. II. cap. 4. 18 Geo. I. cap. 15. from whence the foregoing Duties are computed.	
	£. s. d. 20ths		£. s. d.	
Birding-pieces, the piece. *Vide* Iron wrought.			1 10 0	* Free.
Bird-lime, the Cwt.				
Biscuit. *Vide* Bread.				
Bits. *Vide* Iron wrought.				
Boxes, *vocat*. Tobacco boxes. *Vide* Haberdashery.			0 6 8	⎫
Bodies, *vocat*. Stitched bodies with silk, the pair			0 5 0	⎬ * Free.
of whalebone, the pair			0 16 8	⎭
Bones, *vocat*. Ox-hones, the thousand				Free.
Books printed, unbound or bound, the Cwt.	0 0 11 0	T b	‡ 1 15 0	Free.
Bottles. *Vide* Glass.	0 0 6 16 ½	T b	‡ 1 1 8	
Brass manufactures of all sorts, the Cwt.				
Brass wire made in Great Britain				
Brazeil, or Fernambuck wood, foreign, the Cwt.			0 1 8	⎫ * Free.
Braziletto, or Jamaica wood, foreign, the Cwt.			0 10 0	⎭
Bread				
Bricks. *Vide* Earthen ware.				
Bridles, the dozen				
Brushes, British, of heath, the dozen				
Buck-weed, the quarter, *Vide* Corn.				
Bullion. *Vide* Coin,				

* See the note at the end of the Rates Outwards.

OUTWARDS.

	DUTY.	Reference to the several Branches, see Page vi.	RATES, or supposed value, by 12 Car. II. cap. 4. 18 Geo. I. cap. 15. from whence the foregoing Duties are computed.
	£ s. d. 20ths		£ s. d.
Buttons of hair, the small groce, containing 12 dozen —— Vide also Haberdashery ware.			0 0 6 * Free.
Butter, good or bad, the barrel ——			3 0 0 Free.

C.

CALVE skins, the dozen, of 36 pounds weight, undressed and dressed —— By strangers			2 10 0
No one skin in any dozen, dressed or undressed, to exceed 4 pounds in weight. But by 20 Car. II. cap. 5. and 9 Ann. cap. 6. Calve skins tanned, tawed, or dressed, are, on exportation, to pay, the Cwt.	0 1 0 12	T b	5 0 0
Cambodium, the pound ——			0 1 6 * Free.
Cambricks. Vide Linen.			
Candles, the dozen pound ——			0 5 0 } Free.
—— the barrel, containing ten dozen pound ——			2 10 0
Canvas, British, tufted, the piece, containing 30 yards. Vide Linen.			
—— Shropshire making, the hundred ells, containing five score, Vide Linen.			

* See the note at the end of the Rates Outwards.

OUTWARDS.

	DUTY.	Reference to the several Branches, see Page vi.	RATES, or supposed value, by 12 Car. II. cap. 4. 18 Geo. I. cap. 15. from whence the foregoing Duties are computed.	
	£. s. d. 20ths		£. s. d.	
Caps, vizt. Monmouth caps { plain, the dozen			0 6 0	* Free.
———— trimmed, the dozen			0 12 0	
———— buttoned, British making, the dozen			0 8 4	
———— of wool, black, the dozen			0 10 0	Piece.
Cards, vocat. Stock cards, the dozen			1 4 0	* Free.
———— Tow cards, new, the dozen			0 5 0	
Wool cards, vocat. { new, the dozen			0 10 0	* Free.
———— { old, the dozen			0 6 0	* Free.
Playing cards, the Cwt.	0 0 6 6	Tb	0 5 0	
Card boards, the small groce, containing 12 dozen			1 0 0	* Free.
Carpets, Northern, the piece			0 11 8	
Catlings, or British hat-makers strings, the groce, containing 12 dozen			0 16 0	Free.
Chariots. *Vide* Coaches.				
Chairs, vocat. Sedan. *Vide* Horse litters.				
Cheese, the Cwt.	0 0 3 15 ¾	Tb	1 0 0	
Cloaks old, the piece. *Vide* Garments.				
Cloak bags, the dozen			0 15 0	* Free.
Clock work. *Vide* Iron wrought.				
Cloth shreds. *Vide* Shreds.				
Cloths. *Vide after Rates Outwards.*				
Coaches and Chariots of all sorts, the piece			5 0 0	* Free.

* See the note at the end of the Rates Outwards.

OUTWARDS.

	RATES, or supposed value, by 12 Car. II. cap. 4. 1 & Geo. I. cap. 15. from whence the foregoing Duties are computed.	
	L. s. d.	
Coin of gold or silver, or bullion, foreign, upon entry		Free
Coals, *vocat.* { Sea coals, the chalder, Newcastle measure, exported by British, in British-built bottoms	8 0 0	
Sea coals, the chalder, London measure, exported by British, in British-built bottoms	5 0 0	
Sea coals of Wales, or the West-country, which shall be transported into Ireland, the Isle of Man, or Scotland, to pay twelve-pence the chalder, water measure.		
The officers of the ports to take good security for the landing of the said Coals respectively.		
The merchant-stranger to pay double Custom, if he carry out Coals in a foreign bottom; but if in any British bottoms, then fourteen shillings the chalder.		
That if any British transport Coals in strange-built bottoms, to pay strangers Custom.		

Reference to the several Branches, see Page vi.

DUTY. *L. s. d.* 20ths

OUTWARDS.

But by the acts of 9 Ann. cap. 6. § 9. and 9 Ann. cap. 23; § 90. the rates and duties payable on Coals exported from and after the 8th day of March, 1710, were regulated and settled as follows:

	DUTY.				Reference to the several Branches, see Page vi.	RATES, or supposed value, by 12 Car. II. cap. 4. 18 Geo. I. cap. 15. from whence the foregoing Duties are computed.
	£.	s.	d.	20ths		£. s. d.

Coals of Wales, or the West of England, or the West of Scotland:

	£	s	d	20ths	
For every chalder, consisting of 36 bushels, Winchester measure, — To Ireland	0	1	0	12	Tb
— To the Isle of Man	0	1	0	12	Tb
— To any of his Majesty's plantations in Foreign-built bottoms	0	2	1	4	Tb
— beyond the seas, in British-built bottoms	0	12	7	4	Tb
For every chalder, New-castle measure, For such Coals, in case they are usually sold by weight:	0	3	1	16	Tb
— To Ireland	0	0	8	8	Tb
— To the Isle of Man	0	0	8	8	Tb
— To any of his Majesty's plantations in Foreign-built bottoms	0	0	1	4	16	Tb
— beyond the seas, in British-built bottoms	0	0	4	2	8	Tb
For every ton, reckoning it to be 20 Cwt.	0	4	1	4	Tb
And more,	0	1	0	12	Tb

By 12 Ann. stat. 2. cap. 9. 30 Geo. II. cap. 19. and 5 Geo. III. cap. 35. to any part beyond the sea (except to Ireland, the Isle of Man, or his Majesty's plantations) the chalder, Newcastle measure:

	£	s	d	20ths	
in Foreign ships	0	13	7	16	S
in British ships	0	11	6	12	S

[329]

O U T W A R D S.

	DUTY.	Reference to the several Branches, see Page vi.	RATES, or supposed value, by 12 Car. II. cap. 4. 18 Geo. I. cap. 15. from whence the foregoing Duties are computed.	
	*L. s. d.*20ths		*L. s. d.*	
Exit by 6 Geo. III. cap. 40. the inhabitants of Jersey, Guernsey and Alderney, are allowed to export annually from the ports of Newcastle and Swansea certain quantities of Coals, without payment of the sum of 4s. 2d. 8/20 per chalder, a part of the above duty.				
Cobweb lawns, the yard			0 0 8	*Free.
Cochineal foreign, the pound weight			0 0 6	
Coals of wood, bone, or horn, or any other sort. *Vide* Haberdashery.				
Comfits, the pound. *Vide* Apothecary and Confectionary wares.				
Concy-hair, or wool, black or white, the pound	0 0 2 2	Tb	0 6 0	
Copper of the produce of Great Britain				*Free.
Copper manufactures of all sorts, the Cwt.	0 0 3 15 1/5	Tb	0 16 8	
Copperas (as excepted by 8 Geo. I. cap. 15.) for every 20s. value upon oath	0 1 0 12	Tb	0 10 0	*Free.
Cordage, tarred or untarred, the Cwt.			0 10 0	
⎧ Barley, the quarter, containing eight bushels			0 10 0	
⎪ Beans, the like quarter			0 6 0	
Corn, *viz.* ⎪ Malt, the like quarter			0 10 0	
By 1 *W.* & *M.* ⎨ Oats, the like quarter			0 10 0	
cap. 12. & 11 ⎪ Pease, the like quarter			1 0 0	
& 12 *W.* III. ⎪ Rye, the like quarter			0 10 0	
cap. 23. free. ⎩ Wheat, the like quarter				
Buckwheat, the like quarter				

U u

* See the note at the end of the Rates Outwards.

OUTWARDS.

	DUTY.	Reference to the several Branches, see Page xi.	RATES, or supposed value, by 12 Car. II. cap. 4. ‡ 8 Geo. I. cap. 15. from whence the foregoing Duties are computed.
	£. s. d. 20ths		£. s. d.
Cottons, Northern, Manchester, Taunton, and Welsh cottons, the hundred goods, called Welsh plains, the hundred goads	—		2 0 0 } Free.
	—		2 10 0 }
Coverlets of wool and hair, the piece	—		0 1 8 } Free.
of caldas, the piece	—		0 1 3 }
Cream of tartar, foreign, the Cwt.	0 1 0 12	T b	2 0 0 ‡
Culm to the city of Lisbon, under the regulations and securities required by 31 Geo. II. cap. 15. and 13 Geo. III. cap. 70. for every chalder, in any British ship or vessel	0 1 0 12	T b	
in any Foreign ship or vessel	0 1 6 18	T b	1 0 0 } * Free.
Curry-combs. *Vide* Iron wrought.			
Cushions of Yorkshire, the dozen			

	l. s. d.
Cyder, exported, by 1 *W. & M.* cap. 22. the ton	0 1 0
Cows or Heifers, by 22 *Car.* II. cap. 13. each	0 1 0

* See the note at the end of the Rates Outwards

OUTWARDS.

D.

	Reference to the several Branches, see Page vi.	RATES, or supposed value, by 12 Car. II. cap. 4. & 8 Geo. I. cap. 15. from whence the foregoing Duties are computed.	
		L. s. d.	
DARNIX, *weat.* of British making, the yard		0 0 9	} Free.
—— Coverlets, British, the piece		0 3 4	
Dice. *Vide* Haberdashery ware.			
Dimity, the yard			
Doublets of leather, the piece. *Vide* Garments.		0 0 4	* Free.
Dust of Cloves, of Ginger, of Lignum vitæ, of Mace, of Nutmeg, of Pepper, of all Spices, and the like, are to be exported Custom-free, having paid at the importation.			

E.

EARTHEN ware, *weat.* Bricks and Tiles of all sorts, the thousand		0 3 4	
All other sorts of Earthen and Stone ware made in Great-Britain (not rated) the hundred parcels		0 3 4	} Free.
Entry Monies, the Cwt.		0 3 4	

* See the note at the end of the Rates Outwards.

OUTWARDS.

F.

	DUTY.		Reference to the several Branches, &c. Pa. cxxi.	RATES, or supposed value, by 12 Car. II. cap. 4. 18 Geo. I. cap. 15. from whence the foregoing Duties are computed.	
	£. s. d. 20ths			£. s. d.	
FENNEL-SEED, the Cwt.				1 10 0	* Free.
Figurettes with silk or copper. *Vide* Silks.				0 15 0	} * Free.
—— narrow, the piece				1 10 0	
—— broad, the piece					
Filleting. *Vide* Haberdashery ware.					
Filozelloes broad, of silk, the yard. *Vide* Silks.					
Fire-locks, the piece. *Vide* Iron wrought.					
Fish. *Vide* Herrings.					
Fitches, the timber, containing 40 skins	0 1 9	Tb		1 13 4½	Free.
Flannel, the yard				0 0 4½	* Free.
Flasks of horn. *Vide* Haberdashery ware.					
Flax, the Cwt.				1 0 0	Free.
Flocks of horn. *Vide* Iron wrought.				0 0 6	Free.
Fowling-pieces. *Vide* Iron wrought.					
Freezes, the yard	0 0 1 11/12	Tb			
Frames for stockings. *Vide* Stocking-frames.					
Italian-making of all sorts, to go out free.					
Fustick, foreign, the Cwt.				† 5 0	

* See the note at the end of the Rates Outwards.

[333]

G.

OUTWARDS.

	Reference to the several Branches, see Page vi.	DUTY			RATES, or supposed value, by 12 Car. II. cap. 4. & 8 Geo. I. cap. 15. from whence the foregoing Duties are computed.	
		l. s. d. 20ths			*l. s. d.*	
GALLS, foreign, the Cwt.		0 1 0 12			2 0 0	} Free.
Garments, or wearing apparel, of all sorts, ready made, to go out free.						
Garterings of cruel, the groce, containing 12 dozen					0 8 4	
Garters of worsted, the groce, containing 12 dozen					0 2 6	
Geldings, or Nags, the piece. *Vide* Horses.						
Girdles of leather, for men, the groce, containing 12 dozen	Tb				0 16 8	
—— for children, the groce, containing 12 dozen					0 10 8	
—— of Norwich, the dozen					0 6 8	
Glass broken, the barrel					0 3 4	} *Free.
—— for windows, the chest					0 10 4	
Glasses to drink in, Bottles, and all other sorts of Glasses, the hundred		0 0 10 10			0 3 4	
Glue, British, the Cwt.					0 16 8	
Gloves of buck leather, the dozen	Tb				1 0 0	} *Free.
—— plain, of sheep, kid, or lambs leather, the dozen pair					0 4 8	
—— fringed and stitched with silk, the dozen pair					0 6 8	
—— furred with coney-wool, the dozen pair					0 6 8	
Glovers clippings, the fat or maund					2 0 0	
Goose-quills, the thousand					0 2 0	
Grindle-stones, the chalder					0 13 4	

* See the note at the end of the Rates Outwards.

OUTWARDS.

	DUTY.	Reference to the several Branches, see Page vi.	RATES, or supposed value, by 12 Car. II. cap. 4. 18 Geo. I. cap. 15. from whence the foregoing Duties are computed.	
	£. s. d. 1/20ths		£. s. d.	
Gum-Arabick foreign, the Cwt.	1 11 9 3	Hd	‡ 0 10 0	
Gum-Senega foreign, the Cwt.	0 5 6 3	Hd	‡ 0 10 0	
N. B. I'y 6 Geo. III. cap. 46. §. 5. any quantity of Gum-Senega, *or* Gum-Arabick, *not exceeding 30 tons averdupois weight of both the said Gums, may be exported to Ireland by any of his majesty's subjects (being natives of Great-Britain or Ireland, in any one year, for the use of the Linen manufactures of Ireland, duty free, under the restrictions by that law laid down and established.*				
Gunpowder, the Cwt.			2 0 0	} * Free.
Guts, *vocat.* Ox guts, the barrel			1 0 0	

H.

HABERDASHERY ware, *vocat.* Packthread, Incle, Tape, Filletting, Buttons of all sorts, Hooks and Eyes, and other Haberdashery, British making, not particularly rated, by the Cwt.	0 1 8 3	Tb	1 0 0	} * Free.
Hair, *vocat.* Harts-hair, the Cwt.	0 6 3 12⁄5	Tb	1 12 0	
———— Horse-hair, the Cwt.	0 2 1 4	Tb	6 0 0	
———— Ox or Cow-hair, the Cwt.	0 1 0 12	Tb	2 0 0	
———— Hair of all other sorts, *for every* 20 s. *value upon oath*				

* See the note at the end of the Rates Outwards.

OUTWARDS.

	Reference to the several Branches, see Page vi.	RATES, or supposed value, by 12 Car. II. cap. 4. † 8 Geo. I. cap. 15. from whence the foregoing Duties are computed.			DUTY.		
		L.	*s.*	*d.*	*L.*	*s.*	*d.* 20ths
Hair-cloth, the piece		0	13	4	0	1	0 12
Hares wool, *for every* 20s. *value upon oath*		0	3	4			
Hake-fish, the hundred, containing six score	} * Free.	1	0	0			
Harnefs, *vocat.* Coach-harnefs, the pair, with bridles		1	12	0			
Hartfhorn, the Cwt.		0	5	0			
Hatbands of cruel, the groce, containing 12 dozen	} * Free.	2	0	0			
Hatchets, the dozen. *Vide* Iron wrought.							
Hats, *vocat.* Bevers and Demicasters, of British making, the dozen		0	10	0			
Felts, and all other Hats, the dozen		0	2	0			
Hat-makers firings. *Vide* Catlings.		2	0	0			
Hawks hoods, the dozen		8	13	4			
Hempfeed, the quarter, containing eight bufhels		8	0	0			
Herrings, *vocat.* Winter- herrings	white, full { packed, the barrel	} * Free.	0	6	8			
	packed, the laft, containing 12 barrels						
	unpacked, or fea flicks, the laft, containing 18 barrels						
	white, fhotten { packed, the barrel		4	0	0			
	packed, the laft, containing 12 barrels						
	unpacked, or fea flicks, the laft, containing 18 barrels		4	0	0			

* See the note at the end of the Rates Outwards.

OUTWARDS.

			DUTY.	RATES, or supposed value, by 12 Car. II. cap. 4. 18 Geo. I. cap. 13. from whence the freezing Duties are computed.
			L. s. d. 20ths	*L. s. d.*
Herrings, *weat.*	red, full	the cads, containing five hundred		0 6 0
		the last, containing 20 cades, or ten thousand		6 0 0
Winter-herrings	red, shotten	the cade, containing five hundred		0 3 0
		the last, containing 20 cades, or ten thousand		3 0 0
		the last, containing the barrel		0 8 0
Herring, *weat.*	shotten, white	packed, the last, containing 12 barrels		0 6 0
		unpacked, or sea-sticks, the last, containing 18 barrels		4 0 0
Summer-herrings	shotten, red	the cade, containing five hundred		0 3 0
		the last, containing 20 cades, or ten thousand		3 0 0
And other Sea-fish taken by the subjects of this realm.				* Free.
Hoes. *Vide* Iron wrought.				
Hogs. *Vide* Swine.				
Holsters, the dozen pair				0 10 0
Hoops for barrels, the thousand				0 13 4
Hops, the Cwt.				1 10 0
Hooks and Eyes. *Vide* Haberdashery wares.				
Horns, *weat.* Blowing horns, small, the dozen				0 4 0
of bucks, the hundred				0 4 0
weat. Inkhorns, the dozen. *Vide* Haberdashery ware.				
for lanthorns, the thousand leaves				1 0 0

* See the Note at the end of the Rates Outwards.

[337]

OUTWARDS.

DUTY.	Reference to the several Branches, see Page vi.	RATES, or supposed value, by 12 Car. II. cap. 4. †18 Geo. I. cap. 15. from whence the foregoing Duties are computed.
£. s. d. /20ths		£. s. d.
———— *vocat.* Ox-horns, the thousand ————		2 10 0 } Free.
———— *vocat.* Powder-horns, the dozen ————		0 4 0
———— of rams, the thousand ————		1 0 0
———— of sheep, the thousand ————		0 3 4
———— *vocat.* shoeing-horns, the dozen ————		0 0 8
———— *vocat.* Stags horns, the hundred ————		1 12 0
———— *vocat.* Tips of horns, the thousand ————		0 15 0
Horse-litters, and Sedans, the piece ————		2 10 0
Horses, *vocat.* Stone-horses, the piece ————		66 13 4
———— Geldings, or Nags, the piece ————		20 0 0
———— Geldings, or Nags, to the British plantations ————	Tb	10 0 0
———— Mares, the mare ————		126 13 4

But by 22 Ca. II. cap. 13. § 8. it is declared and enacted, for the further encouragement of the breed of Horses, That, from and after the 24th day of June, 1670, any person or persons, native or foreigners, may, at any time or times, ship, lade, and transport, by way of merchandize, Horses or Mares, into any parts beyond the seas in amity with his Majesty, paying for each Horse, Mare, or Gelding, the sum of

Horse-collars, the hundred, containing five score	0 5 3	2 0 0 } * Free.
Horse-tails with hair, the hundred, containing five score		4 0 0

* See the note at the end of the Rates Outwards.

[338]

OUTWARDS.

	DUTY.	Reference to the several Branches, see Pag. &c.	RATES, or supposed value, by 12 Car. II. cap. 4. & 8 Geo. I. cap. 15. from whence the foregoing Duties are computed.	
	£. s. d. 20ths		£. s. d.	
JEWELS, Precious stones, and Pearls, free.				
Inckle. *Vide* Haberdashery ware.				
Indigo of all sorts, foreign, the pound weight	0 0 1 1	Ib	0 3 4	Free.
Irish mantles, the mantle	—	—	0 3 4	
Iron, the ton	—	—	16 0 0	} * Free.
Old iron, the ton	—	—	16 0 0	
Iron ordnance, the Cwt.	—	—	2 0 0	
Iron wrought, *viz.* Adzes, Armour, Axes, Bits, Fowling-pieces, Hoes, Knives, Locks, Muskets, Pistols, Scissars, Stirrops, and all Carpenters and Gravers Tools, Jack-work, Clock-work, and all Ironmongers Wares, perfectly manufactured, the Cwt.	0 0 10 10	Ib	0 10 0	* Free.
Isinglass, foreign, the Cwt.	—	—	1 13 4	

OUTWARDS.

	DUTY.
	£. s. d. 20ths

K.

KNIVES, *vacat.* Shoemakers Paring knives, the dozen ⎫
Cutting knives, the dozen ⎬ *Vide*
Sheffield knives, the small groce, con- ⎬ Iron wrought.
taining 12 dozen ⎭
——— London knives, ordinary, the dozen ———

L.

LACE of gold and silver, the pound ——— ⎫
——— of velvet, the pound ——— ⎬ *Vide* Silk.
Statute-lace, the groce, containing 12 dozen ⎭
Lamperns, the thousand ——————————————— 0 0 1 12
Lawns, French. *Vide* Linen.
Lapis calaminaris, *for every* 20 s. *value upon oath* 0 2 1 4
And besides, by 7 *and* 8 *W. III. cap.* 10. *and* 8 *and* 9 *IV. III. cap.* 20. ⎱ 1 1 0
ditto ⎰
Lead, cast and uncast, the fodder, containing 20 Cwt. 0 1 0
Lead ore, *for every* 20 s. *value upon oath* 0 1 0'12

* See the note at the end of the Rates Outwards.

OUTWARDS.

	DUTY.	Reference to the several Branches, see Page vi.	RATES, or supposed value, from whence the former Duties are computed.	
	£ s. d.		12 Car. II. cap. 4. 18 Geo. I. cap. 15.	
			£ s. d.	
Letharge of lead, the Cwt.	0 0 20 2/5		0 4 0	
Leather of all sorts, tanned, tawed, or dressed, the Cwt.	0 2 10	T b	0 0 10	} * Free.
Leather manufactures of any sorts, not particularly rated, the pound	0 1 0 2	T b	0 13 4	* Free.
Lime, the chalder			0 10 0	
Linen, viz. all sorts of cloth made of hemp or flax, fine or coarse, of				
British manufacture, the piece, not exceeding 40 ells	0 3 1 16	V c	2 0 0	} *Free.
Cambricks, foreign, the piece, containing 13 ells, to any of his Majesty's colonies in America	0 3 1 16	V c	3 0 0	Free.
French Lawns, the like piece, to such colonies				
Linen shreds, the maund or fat				
Linseed, the quarter, containing eight bushels	0 0 6 6	T b	1 10 0	
Linsey-wolfey. *Vide* Stuff.			1 0 0	
Lists of cloth, the thousand yards	0 1 0 12	T b	2 0 0	
Litmus, foreign, the Cwt.				
Locks. *Vide* Iron wrought.				
Logwood, foreign, the Cwt.				

But by 7 Geo. III. cap. 47. this duty is repealed upon Logwood exported, provided that due entries be made at the Custom-house, in the same manner and form, expressing the quantities and qualities, as was used before making the said act; and to be shipped outwards in the presence of the proper

* See the note at the end of the Rates Outwards.

OUTWARDS.

	DUTY.	Branches, see Page vi.	RATES, or supposed value, by 12 Car. II. cap. 4. & 1 S Geo. I. cap. 15. from whence the foregoing Duties are computed.	
	L. s. d. 20ths		*L. s. d.*	
officers of the Customs, and in British-built ships, navigated according to law: on failure of which, it is to be liable to the same duty as if this act had not been made.				
Loom work, the yard			0 0 6	* Free.

M.

MADDER of all sorts, foreign, the Cwt.	0 0 9 9	T b	1 10 0	‡‡
Madder roots, foreign, the pound weight	0 0 0 2 1/10	T b	0 0 4	‡‡
Malt ——— } *Vide* Corn.				
Meal ———				
Maps and Sea-cards of all sorts, the Cwt.			0 5 0	
Melasses, or Rameales, the ton			10 0 0	} * Free.
Muskets. *Vide* Iron wrought.				
Mustard-feed, the Cwt.			0 10 0	

	l. s. d.
Mum, by 5 *W. & M. cap.* 22. the ton, to pay	0 1 0

* See the note at the end of the Rates Outwards.

OUTWARDS.

N.

	DUTY.	Reference to the Branches, &c.	12 Car. II. cap. 4. 18 Geo. I. cap. 15. from whence the foregoing Duties are computed.	
	L. s. d. 20ths		*L. s. d.*	
NAILS of all sorts, the Cwt.	0 4 2 8		0 5 0	* Free.
Nicaragua wood, foreign, the ton weight		Tb	8 0 0	
Nuts small, the barrel, containing three bushels			0 6 8	* Free.

O.

OATS. *Vide* Corn.				
Oat-meal, the bushel			0 0 3	
— the barrel, containing three bushels			0 0 10	
Oker, yellow or red, the Cwt.	0 1 0 12	Tb	1 0 0	⎱ Free. ⎰ * Free.
Orchal, foreign, the Cwt.	0 0 6 6	Tb	2 0 0	
Orchelia, foreign, the Cwt.				
Oil, *vocat.* Train-oil, made in Great-Britain, the ton			10 0 0	⎫ ⎬ * Free. ⎭
Oysters, the small barrel, in pickle			0 1 4	
Oxen, the ox			6 13 4	

l. s. d.
But by 22 Car. II. cap. 13. the Ox, Steer, Cow, or Heifer, each to pay 0 1 0

* See the note at the end of the Rates Outwards.

OUTWARDS.

P.

	DUTY.				RATES, or supposed value, by 12 Car. II. cap. 4. ‡8 Geo. I. cap. 15. from whence the foregoing Duties are computed.		
	L.	s.	d.	20ths	L.	s.	d.
PACKTHREAD. *Vide* Haberdashery ware.							
Parchment, the roll					0	13	4
Paste-boards, the groce, containing 12 dozen					0	12	0
Pearls, or Precious stones. *Vide* Jewels.							
Pease. *Vide* Corn.							
Perpetuanas. *Vide* Stuffs.							
Pewter. *Vide* Tin.							
Pictures of British making, the Cwt. printed or painted							} *Free.
Pilchers, *vel* Pilchard, the ton, by strangers					0	5	0
					20	0	0
Pistols. *Vide* Iron wrought.							
Points of Leather, the small groce, containing 12 dozen					0	0	6
Pomegranate peels, foreign, the Cwt.	0	0	4	4	‡ 0	13	4
Pork, the barrel					4	0	0
Purls of broad cloth, the piece					0	0	2 } Free.

* See the Note at the end of the Rates Outwards.

[344]

OUTWARDS.

R.

	DUTY. $L.\ s.\ d.\ 20^{ths}$	Reference to the several Branches, see Page vi.	RATES, or supposed value, by 12 Car. II. cap. 4. 18 Geo. I. cap. 15. from whence the foregoing Duties are computed. $L.\ s.\ d.$	
RAPE-CAKES, the thousand			0 10 0	
Rape-feed, the quarter, containing eight bushels			3 0 0	
Rameeles. *Vide* Melasses.				
Rashes, *vocat.* Silk rashes, broad or narrow, the yard. *Vide* Silk ware.				
Red, or Guinea wood, foreign, the Cwt.	0 0 9 ‡	Tb	1 10 0	} * Free.
Ribbon. *Vide* Silk manufactures.				
Rugs, *vocat.* Irish rug, the yard			0 0 4	} Free.
—— Irish rugs for beds, the rug			0 0 8	} * Free.
Rusleting for painters, the Cwt.			0 5 0	

S.

SACKCLOTH to make facks, the bolt or piece. *Vide* Linen.				
Saddles, *vocat.* Great faddles, the piece			0 5 0	
—— All other faddles of all forts, the piece			0 3 0	} * Free.
Saddle-trees, the dozen	0 0 0 6 $\frac{13}{10}$ ‡	Tb	0 3 4	
Safflore, foreign, the pound weight			0 1 0	
Saffron, the pound			1 10 0	* Free.

* See the note at the end of Rates Outwards.

OUTWARDS.

	DUTY.		Reference to the several Branches, see Page vi.	RATES, or supposed value, by 12 Car. II. cap. 4. 13 Geo. I cap. 15. from whence the foregoing Duties are computed.	
	£	s	d 20ths		£ s d	
Sal-armoniack, foreign, the pound weight	0	0	0 3 ⅓	Tb	0 0 6	
Sal-gem, foreign, the pound weight	0	0	0 1 ⅖	Tb	0 0 2	
Salt-petre, the Cwt.					0 4 0	
Sapan wood, foreign, the Cwt.					4 0 0	* Free.
Saunders red, foreign, the Cwt.	0	0	3 3	Tb	0 10 8	
Scabbards for swords, the dozen	0	0	8 8	Tb	1 1 8	
Sciffars. *Vide* Iron wrought.						
Seamorse teeth, the pound					0 3 4	
Sedans. *Vide* Horse-litters.						
Shag with thread, the yard ⎫ *Vide* Linen.						⎫ * Free.
——— the piece ⎭						⎭
Shoes old, the hundred dozen pair					4 0 0	
All new Shoes, Boots, and Slippers, the pound weight					0 0 10	Free.
Shovels shod, the dozen					0 4 0	
——— unshod, the dozen					0 3 6	
Shreds and pieces of Broad-cloth, the pound	0	0	4 4	Tb	0 13 4	* Free.
Shoemack, foreign, the Cwt.					0 3 4	
Silk raw. *See the note at the end of this letter S.*					1 8	
West. British Thrown Silk, the pound, containing 16 ounces						
All other Silk manufactures made of silk only, or of silk and worsted, or of silk and thread, or hair, the pound weight						

* See the note at the end of the Rates Outwards.

[346]

OUTWARDS.

Skins, *vocat.*	DUTY. $l.\ s.\ d.\ 20^{lbs}$	Reference to the several Branches, see Page vi.	RATES, or supposed value, by 12 Car. II. cap. 4. & 8 Geo. I. cap. 15. from whence the foregoing Duties are computed. $l.\ s.\ d.$
Badger skins, the piece ———	0 0 0 12	Tb	0 1 0
Beaver skins, for every skin, or piece of skin ———	0 0 7 7⅕	Kb	1 6 8
—— wool, or wombs, the pound weight averdupois ———	0 1 6 18	Kb	4 13 4
Cat skins, the hundred ———	0 1 4 16	Tb	0 10 0
Coney skins black, with silver hairs or without, the hundred, containing six score	0 2 9 12	Tb	2 13 4
—— grey flag, the hundred, containing six score ———	0 1 6 6	Tb	0 10 0
—— grey, seasoned, the hundred, containing six score ———	0 1 0 12	Tb	1 0 0
—— grey, tawed, the hundred, containing six score ———	0 0 8 8	Tb	0 13 4
—— tawed and dyed into colours, the hundred, containing 120 ———	0 1 0 12	Tb	1 0 0
Dog skins, the dozen ———	0 1 0 12	Tb	0 2 0
Elk skins, the piece, raw ———	0 0 8 8	Tb	0 0 8
Fitches. *Vide under letter F.*	0 0 3 6	Tb	0 0 3
Fox skins, the piece ———	0 0 6 8	Tb	0 10 0
Hare skins, in the hair, the hundred, containing five score ———	0 0 8 8	Tb	0 13 4
Kid skins in the hair, the hundred, containing five score ———	0 0 10 10	Tb	0 16 8
—— dressed, the hundred, containing five score tawed with the wool, the hundred, containing six score	0 0 10 10	Tb	0 16 8
Lamb skins, *vocat.* Morckins { untawed, the hundred, containing six score			

OUTWARDS.

Skins, vocat.		DUTY.	Reference to the several Branches, see Page vi.	RATES, or supposed value, by 12 Car. II. cap. 4. 18 Geo. I. cap. 15. from whence the foregoing Duties are computed.
		£ s. d. 20ths		£ s. d.
——— white or black	{ tawed with the wool, the hundred, containing six score	0 1 6 18	T b	1 10 0
	untawed, the hundred, containing six score	0 1 4 16	T b	1 6 0
Otter skins, raw, the piece		0 0 0 12	T b	0 1 4
——— tawed, the piece		0 0 0 16	T b	0 1 0
——— wombs, the mantle		0 0 0 6	T b	0 1 0
Rabbit skins, black, the hundred		0 0 0 9	T b	0 15 0
Sheep and Lamb skins	{ tawed with the wool, the hundred, containing six score	0 3 1 16	T b	3 0 0
	dressed without wool, the hundred, containing six score	0 2 7 10	T b	2 10 0
	pelts, the hundred, containing five score	0 5 ⸺	T b	3 6 8
But by 20 Car. II. cap. 5. and 9 Ann. cap. 6. Sheep skins tanned, tawed, or dressed, are to pay, the Cwt.		0 1 0 12	T b	
See Calve skins in C.				
Squirrel skins, the thousand		0 2 7 10	T b	2 10 0
Swan skins, the piece		0 0 1 11	T b	0 2 6
Wolf skins, tawed, the piece		0 0 3 15	T b	0 6 0
All other Skins (except Deer skins, native or foreign, dressed in oil in Great Britain) for every 20s. value upon oath		0 1 0 12	T b	

Slate. *Vide* Stones.

Sleeves of leather. *Vide* Garments.

OUTWARDS.

	Reference to the several Branches, see Page vi.	DUTY.	RATES, or supposed value, by 1 Geo. II. cp. 4. § Sch. I. cy. 15. from whence the foregoing Duties are computed.	
		£. s. d. 20ths	£. s. d.	
Soap hard, British make, the Cwt.			0 10 0	} * Free.
—— the barrel			1 0 0	
Spanish Suttup, British making, the single piece, containing 15 yards } Vide Silk.			0 1 8	} Free.
—— the double piece, containing 30 yards			1 0 0	
Sprats, the cade, containing a thousand			0 1 0	} * Free.
Starch, the Cwt.			0 0 4	
Steel, vocat. Gad steel, the Cwt.			0 5 0	
Stock lock, foreign, the pound weight	Tb	0 0 0 2 1/10	0 1 3	
Stirrops. Vide Iron wrought.			0 3 9	
Stockings, Irish, the dozen				
—— Kersey long, the pair			0 1 8	} Free.
—— Kersey short, the dozen pair			0 3 4	
—— Leather, the dozen. Vide Garments.			0 5 0	
—— Silk. Vide Silk manufactures.			0 12 6	
—— Woollen for children, the dozen			0 6 8	
—— Worsted for children, the dozen				
—— Woollen for men, the dozen			0 3 4	} * Free.
—— Worsted for men, the dozen			0 15 0	
—— Lower ends of worsted stockings, the dozen				
Stones, vocat. Hilling stones, the thousand				
—— Slate, the thousand				

* See the note at the end of the Rates Outwards.

OUTWARDS.

	Reference to the several Branches, fee Page vi.	RATES, or supposed value, by 12 Car. II. cap. 4. 18 Geo. I. cap. 15. from whence the foregoing Duties are computed.	DUTY.
		£. s. d.	£. s. d. 20ths
Stone ware. *Vide* Earthen ware.			
Stuff, *vozat.* Perpetuanas and Serges, in regard of their coarseness, the pound weight		0 1 3	} Free.
All other Stuffs made of wool, or mixed with hair or thread, the pound weight		0 1 4	
Sugar of all sorts, formerly brought into this kingdom, and after refined and made into loaves, and exported by way of merchandize, the Cwt.		0:10 0	} * Free.
Swine, or Hogs, by 22 *Car. II. cap.* 13. to pay each ——— 0 0 2½			

N. B. Silk Raw, *imported from his Majesty's colonies and plantations in America into the port of London, and bounty granted thereon, by 9 Geo. III. cap.* 38 *cannot, by said act, be exported without repaying such bounty to the chief officer of the Customs at the port of exportation, on forfeiture of the said Silk, and double the value thereof.*

* See the note at the end of the Rates Outwards.

OUTWARDS.

T.

	DUTY.		RATES, or supposed value, by 12 Car. II. cap. 4. 1 & Geo. I. cap. 15. from whence the foregoing Duties are computed.	
	£. s. d. 20ths		£. s. d.	
TALLOW, British, the Cwt.			2 0 0	* Free.
Tapestry, or Dornix hangings, of what foever, made in Great-Britain, whereof any part of wool, the pound weight			0 0 10	Free.
Thread black, the pound — *Vide* Haberdashery ware.				
—— brown, the pound				
—— blue, *vocat.* Coventry blue, the pound			0 13 4	* Free.
Thrums, the hundred, containing five score pounds				
Ticking, British, the piece. *Vide* Linen.				
Tiffany made of thread. *Vide* Linen.				
Tiles. *Vide* Earthen ware.				
Tin unwrought, the Cwt.	0 3 1 16	Tb	7 6 8	* Free.
But by 8 and 9 W. III. cap. 34. § 1. Tin unwrought, the Cwt.				
—— wrought, *vocat.* Pewter, the Cwt.			5 0 0	* Free.
By said act of 8 and 9 W. III. cap. 34. § 1. Tin wrought was to pay 2 s. 1 d. ¼ 1/1, Cwt. duty on exportation, and no more.				
Tobacco-pipes, the small groce, containing 12 dozen			0 1 0	
Tuftaffataes, British, broad, the yard — ⎱ *Vide* Silk.				
—— British, narrow, the yard ⎰				
—— with thread, the yard				
Turnsole, foreign, the pound weight	0 0 0 1 ⅔	Tb	0 0 2 ⅔	* Free.

* See the note at the end of Rates Outwards.

[351]

OUTWARDS.

V.

	DUTY.		RATES, or supposed value, by 12 Car.II.cap.4. 18 Geo.I.cap.15. from whence the foregoing Duties are computed.	
	L. s. d. 20ths	Reference to the several Branches, see Page vi.	*L. s. d.*	
VALONIA, foreign, the ton weight	0 3 8 2		1 7 0 0	} * Free.
Velures, British, the single piece, containing seven yards — the double piece, containing fifteen yards			0 10 0 0 1 0 0 0	
Verdigrease, foreign, the pound weight	0 0 0 3 ½	Tb	0 0 6 0 2 6 0 1 0 0	} * Free.
Vinegar of wine, the ton		Tb		
Virginals, the pair				

W.

WADMOLL, the yard			0 0 4	* Free.
Waistcoats of wadmol, the dozen — of cotton, the dozen — of kerseys, of flannel, the piece — of worsted, knit, the piece — of woollen, knit, the piece				} *Vide* Garments.
Watches of all sorts, the piece			0 10 0 0 6 0 0 0 2 0	} * Free.
Wax, British, the Cwt. — British hard, the pound				

* See the note at the end of the Rates Outwards.

OUTWARDS.

	DUTY.	Reference to the several Branches, see Page vi.	RATES, or supposed value, by 12 Car. II. cap. 4. †8 Geo. I. cap. 15. from whence the foregoing Duties are computed.	
	£. s. d. 20ths		£. s. d.	
Weld, the Cwt.			1 5 0	
Whale-bone, cut or wrought. *Vide* Haberdashery ware.				
Whale-fins, the groce, containing 12 dozen			0 2 0	
Wine-lees, the but			1 0 0	} *Free.
Wire. *Vide* Brass and Copper.				
Woad, British, the ton			15 0 0	
Woadnets, the hundred, containing five score			0 10 0	
Wood, *sccat*. Box wood, the ton			4 0 0	
Gambray wood, the Cwt.			1 4 6	
Red wood, the Cwt.			1 10 0	
Red wood foreign. *Vide under* R.				
Wool, Spanish, free.		Tb		
Beaver-wool, or wombs. *Vide under* Skins.				
Coney-wool. *Vide in* C.				
Cotton-wool of the British plantations, *for every* 20 s. *value upon oath*	0 1 0 12			* Free.
But if exported in British-built ships				
Hares-wool. *Vide in* H.				
Wool cards. *Vide under letter* C.			0 15 0	} Free.
Worsteds narrow, British, the piece			1 0 0	
broad, British, the piece				

* See the note at the end of the Rates Outwards.

OUTWARDS.

Y.

Y ARN, *vocat.* Grogram yarn, the pound

			RATES, or supposed value, by 12 Car. II. cap. 4. 18 Geo. I. cap. 15. from whence the foregoing Duties are computed.	
	DUTY		£. s. d.	
	£. s. d. 20ths		0 4 0	* Free.
				* Free.

Reference to the several Branches, see Page vi.

Z Beer
{
    12 Car. II. cap. 4.
    For every ton of Beer, to be exported in shipping ⎫
    British-built, in money   ⎬ 0 2 0
    For every ton of Beer exported in any other ship- ⎭
    ping, in money   0 6 0
    By 1 *W. & M. cap.* 22. Beer and Ale exported, to pay one shilling per ton.
    But by 8 *Geo. I. cap.* 15.

And if there shall happen to be brought in, or carried out of this realm, any Goods-liable to the payment of Custom and Subsidy, which either are omitted in this Book, or are not now used to be brought in, or carried out; or, by reason of the great diversity of the value of some Goods, could not be rated; that in such case every Customer or Collector, for the time being, shall levy the said Custom and Subsidy of Poundage, according to the value and price of such Goods, to be affirmed upon the oath of the Merchant, in the presence of the Customer, Collector, Comptroller, and Surveyor, or any two of them.

* See the note at the end of the Rates Outwards.

OUTWARDS.	DUTY.	Reference to the several Branches, see Page vi.	RATES, or supposed value, by 12 Car. II. cap. 4. 8 Geo. I. cap. 15. from whence the foregoing Duties are computed.
	L. s. d. 20ths		*L.* | *s.* | *d.*
	0 1 0 12	T b	

NOTE. *By* 8 *Geo. I. cap.* 15. All Goods and Merchandize of the product or manufacture of Great-Britain, (not particularly excepted by law) may be exported duty free, provided the same are regularly entered and shipped; otherwise they will be liable to such duties as would have been due if this act had not been made; which duties are, for such goods as are not particularly charged in the course of the Rates Outwards, for every twenty shillings of the rate, or, if not rated, for every twenty shillings of the value upon oath ——

Directions for the Payment of the Subsidy upon Woollen Cloths, or Old Drapery.

EVERY *British* man shall pay for every SHORT CLOTH, containing in length not above 28 yards, and in weight not above 64 pounds, white or coloured, by him to be shipped, and carried out of this kingdom — *l.* 0 *s.* 3 *d.* 4

Being after the rate of two farthings and half a farthing the pound weight.

And so after that rate for all other sorts of Cloths of greater length and weight, allowing not above 28 yards and 64 pounds to a short Cloth; that is to say, for every pound weight over and above 64 pounds, two farthings and half a farthing; and for all other sorts of lesser Cloths to be allowed to a short Cloth, as hereafter is expressed.

Every Stranger shall pay for every SHORT CLOTH, containing in length not above 28 yards, and in weight not above 64 pounds, white or coloured, by him to be shipped and carried out of this kingdom — 0 6 8

Beside the old — 0 1 2

And so after that rate for all other sorts of Cloth of greater length and weight, and for all sorts of lesser Cloths to be allowed to a short Cloth, as hereafter is expressed.

But by 11 and 12 W. III. cap. 20. may be exported free.

What and how many Sorts of the Lesser Woollen Cloths, hereafter specified, shall be allowed to a SHORT CLOTH.

Seven {
- Dorset and Somerset dozen rudge washed
- Cardinals
- Pin-whites
- Straits
- Statutes
- Stockbridges
- Tavistocks
} shall go and be accounted for a short Cloth, and shall pay after the rate of the short Cloth before rated, and for over-weight 2 farthings and half the pound.

[356]

			But by 11 *and* 12 *W.* III. *cap.* 20. *may be exported free.*
Four Five	⎧ Tauntons, Bridgewaters, and Dunsters, the five not exceeding 64 pounds in weight ⎫		⎫ shall go and be accounted for a short Cloth, and shall pay after the rate of the short Cloth before rated, and for over-weight 2 farthings and half the pound.
	⎨ Devon dozen, containing 12 or 13 yards, in weight 13 pounds ⎬		
	⎩ Ordinary Penistones or Forest Whites, containing between 12 and 13 yards, and in weight 28 pounds ⎭		
Three	⎧ Sorting Penistones, containing 13 or 14 yards, and in weight 35 pounds unfrized ⎫		
	⎨ Narrow Yorkshire Kerseys, white and red, containing not above 17 or 18 yards, and in weight 22 pounds ⎬		
	⎩ Hampshire ordinary Kerseys ⎭		
Two	⎧ Newbury Whites, and other Kerseys of like making, containing 24 yards, and in weight 28 pounds ⎫		
	⎨ Sorting Hampshire Kerseys, containing 28 yards, and in weight 32 pounds ⎬		
	⎩ Northern dozens single sorting Penistones, containing between 14 and 15 yards, and in weight 35 pounds frized ⎭		
	One Northern dozen double		

The new sort of Cloth, called Spanish Cloth, otherwise Narrow List; Western Broad Cloth, not exceeding 25 yards in length, and 43 pounds in weight, to be accounted two thirds of the short Cloth before rated.
And for every pound weight exceeding 43 pounds, two farthings and half a farthing the pound weight.
Cloth Rashes, alias Cloth Serges, containing 30 yards, weighing 40 pounds, to be accounted two thirds of the short Cloth before rated.
And for every pound weight exceeding 40 pounds weight, two farthings and half a farthing the pound weight.
And for any other sort of Woollen Cloth of the old or new Drapery, and not mentioned in this Book, to pay two farthings and half a farthing for the Subsidy of every pound weight thereof.

But by 6 *Ann. cap.* 8. *a new duty was laid on* WHITE WOOLLEN CLOTH *exported, being*

For every piece of WHITE WOOLLEN CLOTH, commonly called BROAD CLOTH ———— £.0 5 3 | T b | *See page* 6.

A TABLE of the NEAT DUTIES payable upon all Goods brought Coastwise from Port to Port in Great-Britain, together with the DRAWBACKS thereof on Exportation.

COASTWISE INWARDS.

Goods		DUTY			References to the several Branches, see Page vi.	DRAWBACK		
		L.	s.	d. 20ths		L.	s.	d. 20ths
COALS, except Char-coals made of wood — { In case they are such as are most usually sold by weight, for every ton, consisting of 20 Cwt.		0	3	4·19	H a	0	3	4·19
In case they are most usually sold by the chalder, or by any other measure whatsoever reducible to the chalder, for every chalder, consisting of 36 bushels, Winchester measure —		0	5	1 8½	H a	0	5	1 8½
Culm, for every chalder, consisting of 36 bushels, Winchester measure		0	1 0	5 7/2	H a	0	1 0	5 7/2
Cynders made of Pit-coal, for every such chalder		0	5	1 8½	H a	0	5	1 8½

And so, after the above rates, for any greater or lesser quantity.

But such of the above goods as are carried from the Bridge of Stirling to the town of Dunbar, or to Redhead, in North-Britain, or to any part betwixt them; or from Ellen-Foot to Bank-End, in the county of Cumberland in South-Britain, or from any creek or place to any other creek or place betwixt them, are not, by reason of such carriage, liable to the above duties.

And besides, if brought into the port of London, the following duties are payable:

Coals and Culm, the chalder or ton ——— 0 3 0·17 10½ V

But any quantity of Coals may be brought into the port of London from Newcastle upon Tyne, or any other place, free of this duty, not exceeding 100 chalders by the year, for the only use and service of the ROYAL HOSPITAL at Chelsea.

A TABLE of the NEAT DUTIES payable upon all Goods sent Coastwise from Port to Port in Great-Britain.

COASTWISE OUTWARDS.

	DUTY.	Reference to the several Branches, see p. &c. vii.
	£. s. d. 20ths	
Culm to be used for the burning of lime, in any ships, vessels, or boats, not exceeding 30 tons burthen, from any place within the limits of the port of Milford, in the county of Pembroke, to any other place within the counties of Pembroke, Carmarthen, Cardigan, or Merioneth, or any of them, for every chalder	0 1 0	0 5 10 H a

Hemp and Flax,

4 Geo. III. cap. 26.

	l.	*s.*	*d.*
Hemp water rotted, bright and clean, or rough and undressed Flax, imported directly from his Majesty's plantations in America, under the regulations required by law — until June 24, 1785, the ton —	4	0	0

Hemp,

19 Geo. III. cap. 37.

—— water rotted, bright and clean, of the growth of Ireland, imported directly from thence, under the regulations required by law

	l.	*s.*	*d.*
from June 24, 1779, to June 24, 1786, the ton —	8	0	0
from June 24, 1786, to June 24, 1793, the ton —	6	0	0
from June 24, 1793, to June 24, 1800, the ton —	4	0	0

Indigo,

* *21 Geo. II. cap. 30.*
17 Geo. III. cap. 44.

—— imported directly from any of the British colonies or plantations in America, under the regulations required by law, being the growth or produce of the plantation from whence imported, and of the quality described in the act * —— to March 25, 1781, and from thence to the end of the then next sessions of parliament —— the pound 0 0 4

Naval Stores,

* 2 Geo. II. cap. 35.
14 Geo. III. cap. 86.

		l. s. d.
Imported directly from the British Plantations in America, under the regulations required by law, viz.		
Masts, Yards, and Bowsprights, the ton, allowing 40 feet to each ton, girt measure, according to the customary way of measuring round bodies	{ to June 24, 1781, and from thence to the end of the then next sessions of parliament —	1 0 0
Tar clean, good, merchantable, well conditioned, clear of dross or water, and fit in every respect for making of cordage, the ton, containing eight barrels, and each barrel to gauge 31½ gallons, to be well hooped and filled up	{ to June 24, 1781, and from thence to the end of the then next sessions of parliament —	2 4 0
—— clean, good, merchantable, well conditioned, clear of dross or water, and fit in every respect for making of cordage, made from trees prepared according to the directions mentioned in the "Act, the ton, containing eight barrels, and each barrel to gauge 31½ gallons, to be well hooped and filled up on the importation thereof	{ to June 24, 1781, and from thence to the end of the then next sessions of parliament —	4 0 0
But no premium is to be paid on any Tar, unless each barrel contains 31½ gallons, and the Officers not to survey the Tar till the water is all drawn off, and every barrel filled up with Tar.		
Pitch, clean, good, merchantable, and well conditioned, not mixed with dirt or dross, the ton, containing 20 gross hundreds, neat pitch, to be brought in eight barrels of equal size	{ to June 24, 1781, and from thence to the end of the then next sessions of parliament —	1 0 0
Turpentine, clean, good, and merchantable, clear of dross and water, the ton, containing 20 gross hundreds, neat Turpentine, to be brought in eight barrels of equal size	{ to June 24, 1781, and from thence to the end of the then next sessions of parliament —	1 10 0
Brought from Scotland into any part of South Britain.		
Trees of twelve inches diameter and upwards, fit for Masts, Yards, and Bowsprights, regularly converted and hewed at least into eight squares, found, fresh, and in good merchantable condition, the ton, allowing 40 feet to each ton, girt measure, according to the customary way of measuring round bodies	{ to June 24, 1781, and from thence to the end of the then next sessions of parliament —	1 0 0

Portage,

Is a bounty given by the Commissioners of the Customs, by virtue of their patent, to masters of ships inwards, for making true reports of their ships and cargoes, and otherwise demeaning themselves according to law and custom, and is granted on the net amount of the undermentioned branches, paid or secured for the goods imported in their respective ships, certified by the proper officers of the port (damages and over-entries first to be deducted) and is as follows :

	l.	*s.*	*d.*
Wines, for every 100*l.* of the net amount of the Customs and Impost	0	6	8
Currants, for every 100*l.* of the net amount of the Branch of Customs	0	6	8
Norway goods, for every 100*l.* of the net amount of the Branch of Customs	0	0	0
Other goods, for every 100*l.* of the net amount of the Branch of Customs	2	0	0
But no Portage is granted when it doth not amount to ten shillings, except for Norway goods.	0	10	0

Raw Silk,

9 *Geo.* III. *cap.* 38.

Of the growth of the British Colonies in America, imported directly from thence into the port of London, under the regulations required by law, for every 100*l.* value
{ to January 1, 1784 —— 20 0 0
from January 1, 1784, to January 1, 1791 —— 15 0 0 }

Tobacco,

9 *Geo.* I. *cap.* 21.

—— damaged, for every pound weight cut off —————— 0 0 0¼'s

A a a

Damaged, corrupt, or unmerchantable; if the importer shall refuse to pay the duties thereon, the Commissioners of the Customs may cause such Wines to be received into the custody of the proper officers, and to be publicly sold, in order to be distilled into Brandy or made into Vinegar, and shall cause the produce of such sale to be paid to the importer, but not to exceed the following Allowances:

	l.	*s.*	*d.*
of the growth of Germany, or which pay duty as such, the ton ———	4	0	0
of the growth of France, the ton ———	4	0	0
of the growth of Spain, Portugal, or elsewhere, the ton ———	3	0	0

* But no Allowance to be made for any Wines, unless imported in casks on board a merchant's ship directly from the place of the growth, or the usual place of first shipping, (except as to ships stranded).

Allowance or Drawback of the Duties on COALS used in melting Copper or Tin ores within the counties of Cornwall and Devon, or in Fire-engines for drawing Tin or Copper mines in Cornwall.

9 *Ann. cap.* 6.
14 *Geo.* II. *cap.* 41.

All Coals used in either of the above works, and for which the duties have been first answered, upon proof, by oath made before the Customer and Collector of the said duties, that they have been so used, shall have a drawback of all the duties, to be repaid by the Collector of the duties to the person making such proof.

Cordage,

6 *Geo. III. cap.* 45. after July 1, 1766, for five years, and to the end of the then next sessions of parliament.
12 *Geo. III. cap.* 60. continued for three years.
13 *Geo. III. cap.* 74.
14 *Geo. III. cap.* 86. further continued for three years.
17 *Geo. III. cap.* 44. further continued for four years, and to the end of the then next sessions of parliament.

British made from foreign hemp (except of the produce of the British American colonies) or from hemp of the growth of Great Britain, exported, under the regulations required by law, to any part of Europe (except the Isle of Man, the islands of Faro or Ferro, Madeira, the Canaries, or the Azores or Western islands) the Cwt. — $\left.\begin{array}{c}\\ \\ \\ \end{array}\right\}$ *l. s. d.* 0 2 4¾

Corn,

‖ 13 *Geo. III. cap.* 43.
* 20 *Geo. III. cap.* 31.
* 21 *Geo. III. cap.* 29.

Of the growth and produce of this kingdom, when the price of middling British Corn or Grain at the port of exportation shall appear to be under the following prices, then the bounty affixed thereto is to be allowed on exportation in British shipping, under the regulations directed by law.

	Price.			Bounty.	
	l.	*s.*	*d.*	*s.*	*d.*
Wheat, the quarter	2	4	0	5	0
Malt made therefrom				5	0
Rye, the quarter	1	8	0	3	6
Barley, Beer, or Bigg, the quarter	1	2	0	2	6
Malt made therefrom				2	6
Oats, the quarter				2	0
Oat meal, the quarter, containing 276 pound weight	0	14	0	2	6

* But if exported in foreign ships, one moiety only of the above Bounty is to be allowed, until March 25, 1782.

Of the manufacture of Great Britain, exported by way of merchandize, under the regula- ⎫ until Sept. 29, 1785, and from ⎫ *l. s. d.*
tions required by law, for every barrel, containing 100 pounds net weight ⎬ thence to the end of the then ⎬ 0 4 6
⎭ next sessions of parliament — ⎭

Linen,

29 *Geo. II. cap.* 15.
5 *Geo. III. cap.* 43.
10 *Geo. III. cap.* 38.
19 *Geo. III. cap.* 27.

Made of Hemp or Flax in Great-Britain, Ireland, or the Isle of Man, exported (under the regulations required by law) to Africa,
America, Spain, Portugal, Gibraltar, the island of Minorca, or the East Indies, until June 24, 1786, and from thence to the end of
the then next sessions of parliament:

For every yard of the breadth of 25 inches or more, under the value of 5*d.* the yard ——————————— 0 0 0½
For every yard of the breadth of 25 inches or more, value 5*d.* and under the value of 6*d.* the yard ——— 0 0 1
For every yard of the breadth of 25 inches or more, value 6*d.* and not exceeding 1*s.* 6*d.* the yard ——— 0 1 1½
For every yard of British checked or striped linen, of the breadth of 25 inches or more, and not exceeding ⎫ 0 0 0¼
1*s.* 6*d.* and not under 7*d.* in value per yard ⎬
For every square yard of Diaper, Huckaback, Sheeting, and other species of linen, upwards of one yard English ⎫ 0 0 1½
in breadth, and not exceeding 1*s.* 6*d.* the square yard in value ⎬

[365]

	l.	*s.*	*d.*
For every yard of British and Irish Buckrams and Tillettings	0	0	0¼
For every yard of British and Irish Linen, and of British Callicoes and Cottons, or Cotton mixed with Linen, printed, painted, or stained in Great Britain, of the breadth of 25 inches or more, which before the printing, painting, or staining thereof, shall be under the value of 5*d.* per yard	0	0	0¼
For every yard of the value of 5*d.* and under the value of 6*d.* per yard	0	0	1
For every yard of the value of 6*d.* and not exceeding 1*s.* 6*d.* per yard	0	0	1½

The bounties granted by the * act above mentioned are to be paid during the continuance of an act passed in the 20th year of his present Majesty's reign in the kingdom of Ireland, by which certain bounties were granted on the exportation of Linens, Buckrams, and Tillettings of the manufacture of that kingdom.

* 21 *Geo. III. cap.* 40.

Sail-cloth,

12 *Ann. cap.* 16.
4 *Geo. II. cap.* 27.
18 *Geo. III. cap.* 45.

British made Sail-cloth exported under the regulations required by law, for every ell — until Sept. 29, 1785, and from thence to the end of the then next sessions of parliament — 0 0 2

British manufactures of Silk,

8 *Geo. I. cap.* 15.
14 *Geo. III. cap.* 86.

	l.	s.	d.
Silk Stockings, Silk Gloves, Silk Fringes, Silk Laces, Stitching or Sewing Silk, the pound avoirdupoise weight	0	1	3
Stuffs of Silk and Grogram Yarn, the pound avoirdupoise weight	0	0	8
Stuffs of Silk mixed with Incle or Cotton, the pound avoirdupoise weight	0	1	0
Stuffs of Silk and Worsted, the pound avoirdupoise weight	0	0	6

Sugar refined in Great Britain.

5 Geo. III. cap. 45.

Refined from Sugar of the produce of the British plantations, under the directions and regulations required by law, and exported after the 1st day of June, 1765:

In loaves complicat and whole, and in lumps duly refined, for every Cwt. — 0 14 6
Called Baffards, ground or powdered Sugar, and Sugar broken in pieces, and Candy properly refined, for every Cwt. 0 6 4

* 21 Geo. III. cap. 16.

Refined from Sugar imported into Great Britain after the 5th day of April, 1781, and which shall have paid the duty imposed by this * act, and exported on or after the 5th day of July, 1781,

In the Loaf, and whole, the Cwt. — 0 11 6
Called Baftards and ground or powdered Sugar, and refined Loaf Sugar broken in pieces, and all Sugar called Candy, the Cwt. 0 5 4

These two laft mentioned allowances are to be paid over and above all other allowances or drawbacks allowed by law for the fame, and are alfo fubject to the fame rules, regulations and reſtrictions.

White Herring Fishery.

Granted by 11 *Geo. III. cap.* 31. { for seven years, from October 22, 1771, and from thence to the end of the then next sessions of parliament.

Continued by 19 *Geo. III. cap.* 26. { for seven years, and from thence to the end of the then next sessions of parliament.

The following Bounty is annually allowed, provided the limitations, restrictions, and directions relating thereto, in the acts above-mentioned, are complied with, viz.

l. s. d.

For every decked vessel, from twenty to eighty tons burthen, which shall be fitted out and employed in the above Fishery, the sum of ———— } 1 10 0 per ton.

Whale Fishery in the Greenland Seas, Davis's Streights, or the adjacent Seas.

11 *Geo. III. cap.* 38.
15 *Geo. III. cap.* 31.
18 *Geo. III. cap.* 55.

For every ship which shall proceed on the said Fishery (the several provisions and directions relating thereto in the acts above-mentioned being complied with) from December 25, 1781, to December 25, 1786, the sum of ———— } 1 0 0 per ton.

[367]

15 Geo. III. cap. 31.
18 Geo. III. cap. 55.

The several Bounties hereafter mentioned are allowed annually for eleven years, for a certain number of vessels employed in this Fishery, provided the limitations, restrictions, and directions relating thereto, in the acts above-mentioned, are complied with,

viz. Such British-built vessels, fitted and cleared out after the 1st of June, 1776, and, after that day in each succeeding year, which shall proceed to the Banks of Newfoundland, and having catched a cargo of fish upon those Banks, consisting of not less than ten thousand fish by tale, shall land the same at one of the ports on the southern or eastern side of the island of Newfoundland, between Cape Ray and Cape de Grat, on or before the 15th of July in each year; and shall make one more trip at least to the said Banks, and return with another cargo of fish catched there, to the same port; in which case,

	l.	s.	d.	
The twenty-five vessels first arriving at the said island of Newfoundland from the Banks thereof, with a cargo of fish catched there, consisting of ten thousand fish by tale at the least, and after landing the same at one of the ports within the limits before-mentioned in Newfoundland, shall proceed again to the said Banks, and return to the said island with another cargo of fish, shall be entitled to ――	40	0	0	each
One hundred vessels, which shall so arrive the next in order of time, on or before the 15th of July in each year, at the said island, with a like cargo, and shall proceed again to the said Banks, and return from thence in the manner herein before mentioned, shall be entitled to ――	20	0	0	each
One hundred other vessels, which shall so arrive the next in order of time, on or before the 15th of July in each year, at the said island, with a like cargo, and shall proceed again to the said Banks, and return from thence in the manner herein before mentioned, shall be entitled to ――	10	0	0	each

15 Geo. III. cap. 31.
16 Geo. III. cap. 47.
18 Geo. III. cap. 55.
20 Geo. III. cap. &c.

The several Bounties hereafter mentioned are allowed annually for eleven years for five vessels employed in this Fishery, provided the limitations, restrictions, and directions relating thereto in the acts above mentioned, are complied with, viz. Such British-built vessels fitted and cleared out after the 1st day of January, 1776, and after that day in each succeeding year, which shall take and kill one whale at least in the seas above mentioned, and shall return within the time limited by law with the oil of such whale or whales:

	l.	s.	d.
For the vessel which shall so arrive in each year with the greatest quantity of oil so taken as aforesaid	500	0	0
For the vessel which shall in like manner arrive with the next greatest quantity of oil so taken as aforesaid	400	0	0
For the vessel which shall in like manner arrive with the next greatest quantity of oil so taken as aforesaid	300	0	0
For the vessel which shall in like manner arrive with the next greatest quantity of oil so taken as aforesaid	200	0	0
For the vessel which shall in like manner arrive with the next greatest quantity of oil so taken as aforesaid	100	0	0

Whale Fishery in the Seas to the Southward of the Latitude of Forty-four Degrees North.

16 *Geo. III. cap.* 47.
18 *Geo. III. cap.* 55.
20 *Geo. III. cap.* 60.

The several Bounties hereafter mentioned are allowed annually for eleven years for five vessels employed in this Fishery, provided the limitations, restrictions, and directions relating thereto in the acts above mentioned, are complied with, viz. Such British-built vessels fitted and cleared out after the 1st day of August, and before the 1st day of November, 1776, and between the 1st day of August and the 1st day of November in each succeeding year, which shall take and kill one whale at least in the seas above mentioned, and shall return within the time limited by law with the oil of such whale or whales:

	l.	*s.*	*d.*
For the vessel which shall so arrive in each year with the greatest quantity of oil so taken as aforesaid	500	0	0
For the vessel which shall in like manner arrive with the next greatest quantity of oil so taken as aforesaid	400	0	0
For the vessel which shall in like manner arrive with the next greatest quantity of oil so taken as aforesaid	300	0	0
For the vessel which shall in like manner arrive with the next greatest quantity of oil so taken as aforesaid	200	0	0
For the vessel which shall in like manner arrive with the next greatest quantity of oil so taken as aforesaid	100	0	0

[371]

Goods prohibited to be Imported.

Bandstrings.
Books, Lug'ish, reprinted abroad.
Buttons, of all sorts.
Callicoes, Muslins, or Stuffs, made of linen yarn, or cotton wool only, or linen yarn and cotton wool mixed, wherein shall be wove in the warp, in the selvage only, through any part of the length of the piece, one or more blue stripes of one or more threads.
Chocolate, ready made.
Cocoa Paste.
Coin (current) false or counterfeit, to be uttered.
Cutwork.
Embroidery.
Fringes of thread or silk.
Wire, Card wire or Iron wire for making of Wool Cards.

Goods prohibited to be Imported AND USED in Great Britain.

Bone Lace of silk or thread, except Thread Lace made in Flanders.
Brass, work made thereof. See Gold.
Brocade of gold or silver.
Cambricks and French Lawns.
Copper, work made thereof. See Gold.
East India wrought silks, Bengalls, and stuffs mixed with silk or herba, of the manufacture of Persia, China, or East-India; and Callicoes printed, painted, or dyed there.
Embroidery. See Gold.
Fringe, Gold, &c. See Gold.
Gloves and Mits of leather or silk.
Gold or Silver Thread Lace, Fringe, or work made of copper, brass, or any inferior metal; or gold or silver wire or plate, embroidery, or gold or silver brocade.
Lace of gold. See Gold.
—— of thread or silk. See Bone Lace.
Mits of leather or silk.
Needlework of silk or thread, except East-India.

Bbb 2

Goods prohibited to be *Imported* FOR SALE.

Bits.
Cards *for wooll*.
Cattle, *great Sheep, Swine, Beef, Pork,* (*except Bacon*) *Mutton or Lamb, except six hundred head yearly from the isle of Man into Chester, Liverpoole, or Wircwater.*
But *Cattle and Salted Provisions of and from Ireland may be imported duty free.*
Cauls *made of silk*.
Chapes.
Cheese *from Ireland*.
Coin, *false or counterfeit*.

Daggers.
Dagger blades.
Girdles.
Handles *for knives*.
Harness, Girdles, *and* Horse Harness.
Hilts.
Knives.
Locks.
Mutton. *See* Cattle.
Pins.
Points.
Pork. *See* Cattle.
Provisions. *See* Cattle.
Pummels.

Rapiers.
Ribbands *of silk only, or mixed with other materials*.
Saddles.
Scabbards *and* Sheaths *for knives*.
Silk, *wrought by itself, or with any other stuff, in Ribbands, Laces, Girdles, Corses, Cauls, Corses of Tissue, or Points*.
Stirrups.
Swine. *See* Cattle.
Wire, *Card Wire or Iron Wire for making of Wooll Cards*.

Goods prohibited to be *Imported* FOR SALE, *without Licence from His Majesty*.

Ammunition.
Arms.

Gunpowder.

War, *Utensils of*.

Goods prohibited to be Imported FOR SALE by any Persons, except made and wrought in Ireland, or taken upon the Seas, or wrecked.

Andirons.
Balls, *Tennis*.
Basans, *Counterfeit*.
Bells, viz. *Sacring Bells*.
Blanch Iron Thread, vocat. *White Wire*.
Bodkins.
Bosses for *Bridles*.
Brushes.
Buskins.
Candlesticks, *hanging*.
Caps, *Woollen*.
Cards, *Playing*.
Cards, *for Wool*.
Caskets.
Chafing Balls or Dishes.
Chelsea.
Cloths, *Woollen*.
Combs.
Corses.
Daggers.
Dice.
Dripping-pans.
Ewers.
Fringes of *silk and thread*.

Furs, *Tawed*.
Galley Tiles. *See* Painted Wares.
Girdles.
Goloches, or Corks.
Gridirons.
Hammers.
Harness, pertaining to *saddles*.
—— for girdles of *iron, latten, steel, tin, or alkmine*.
Hats.
Iron Thread, vocat. *White Wire*.
Knives, vocat. *Wood Knives*.
Laces.
—— of *Thread or Gold*.
Ladles.
Leather, any thing wrought of *Tawed Leather*.
Locks.
Needles, vocat. Pack Needles.
Painted Wares, except Paper and Pictures, and Earthen Ware, the manufacture of Europe, other than Galley Tiles.
Pattens.
Pinsons.
Points.

Purses.
Rapiers.
Razors.
Ribbands.
Rings of *copper or latten gilt for curtains*.
Saddles.
Scissars.
Scumners.
Sheaths
Sheers, *for Taylors*.
Shoes.
Silk Embroidered *and* Silk Twined.
Spurs.
Stirrups.
Tires of *silk or gold*.
Tongs, viz. *Fire Tongs*.
White Wire.
Wire of Iron, v.z. Card Wire, and all sorts of iron wire smaller than fine fine; and superfine and wool cards, or any other wares made of iron wire.
Woollen Caps.
Woollen Cloths, or Old Drapery.

Goods prohibited to be Imported FOR SALE, by Strangers or Aliens.

Andirons.
Balls of any forts, except Hawk's Balls.
Bits.
Blacksmiths, } any wares pertaining to them
Blacksmiths, }
Boots.
Broaches or Spits.
Bottle-makers, any wares pertaining to them.
Buckles, for shoes.
Candlesticks, hanging.
— Iron, standing.
Card-makers, any wares pertaining to them.
Chafing-dishes.
Chains.
Clasps for gowns.
Cloths, painted.
Copper-smiths, any wares pertaining to them.
Cupboards.
Cutlers, any wares pertaining to them.
Forcers.
Forks, called Fire-Forks.
Founders, any wares pertaining to them.
Girdlers, any wares pertaining to them.
Girdles.
Glass, painted.
Glovers, any wares pertaining to them.

Gold beaten, in papers for painters.
Gold-beaters, any wares pertaining to them.
Grates.
Gridirons.
Hangers.
Harness, wrought for girdles.
— vocat. Horse-Harness.
Hinges and Garnets.
Horners, any wares pertaining to them.
Horns, for lanthorns.
Hurers, any wares pertaining to them.
Images, painted.
Joiners, any wares pertaining to them.
Iron, Ware.
Keys.
Knives.
Laces.
Latten, Ware.
Lavers, hanging.
Locks, called Stock-locks.
Lorimers, any wares pertaining to them.
Nails of latten, with iron shanks.
Painters,
Pinners,   } any wares pertaining to
Point-makers, } them.
Purlers,

Pins.
Points.
Pouches.
Purses.
Rings, for curtains.
Sadlers, any wares pertaining to them.
Saddles.
Saddle Trees.
Scissars.
Sheers, for Taylors.
Silver, (beaten) in papers for painters.
Spits.
Spoons of tin or lead.
Spurriers, any wares pertaining to them.
Spurs.
Stirrups.
Stock-locks.
Stops, vocat. Holy Water Stops.
Taylors Sheers.
Tongs.
Turnets.
Weavers and   } any wares pertaining to
Wire-mongers   } them.
Wool Cards, except Roan Cards.

Goods prohibited to be *Imported*, except in particular WEIGHTS, PACKAGES, &c.' or under some other RESTRICTIONS.

Aqua Vitæ, *except in ships belonging to Great Britain or Ireland, or of the same country with the goods.*

Ashes, Pot, *from the Netherlands or Germany.*

—— *from any other place, except in ships belonging to Great Britain or Ireland, or of the same country with the goods.*

Beef, *except from the isle of Man into Chester; and Irish Beef into any part of Great Britain.*

Boards, *except in ships belonging to Great Britain or Ireland, or of the same country with the goods.*

Brandy, *in casks containing less than 60 gallons.*

—— *in any cask, except in ships belonging to Great Britain or Ireland, or of the same country with the goods. See Spirits.*

Cambricks and French Lawns, *except into the port of London by licence from the Commissioners, and in bales, &c. covered with sackcloth or canvas, containing 100 whole pieces or 200 demy pieces.*

—— *or Lawn from Ireland, until the importation there shall be prohibited.*

Candles, Soap, and Starch, *in any package less than 224 lb. wt.*

Coffee, *but in packages of 112 lb. net.*

Coin, *viz. light or base silver coin, exceeding 5 l.*

Corn or Grain, *except in ships belonging to Great Britain or Ireland, or of the same country with the goods.*

Currants (Turky) *except in British-built ships, or ships of the same country with the goods, &c.*

Deal Boards *from the Netherlands or Germany, except Deal Boards of the growth of Germany, imported from thence by British in British-built ships, &c.*

Figs, *except in ships belonging to Great Britain or Ireland, or of the same country with the goods.*

Fir Timber, *from the Netherlands or Germany, except of the growth of Ger-* *many, imported from thence by British in British-built ships owned by British.*

Fish, Flat or Fresh, *in foreign ships, taken by or bought of foreigners, except eels, stockfish, anchovies, sturgeon, botargo, caveare, lobsters, and turbots.*

Flax, *except in ships of Great Britain or Ireland, or of the same country with the goods.*

Geneva *in casks containing less than 60 gallons, except 2 gallons for each Seaman. See Spirits.*

Grocery *from the Netherlands or Germany.*

Hats or Bonnets *of bast, straw, chip, cane, or horse-hair, to be imported in bales containing 75 dozen.*

—— Plaiting, *or other materials for making such hats, to be imported in packages not less than 224 lb. wt.*

Isle of Man, Brandy, Rum, Strong Waters or Spirits, *not to be imported from thence.*

Masts, *from the Netherlands or Germany, except of the growth of Germany, imported from thence by British, in British-built ships owned by British.*

——— to be imported from any other place only in ships belonging to Great Britain or Ireland, or of the same country with the goods.

Oak Bark, not to be imported when the price is under 10l. per load, &c.

Oil (Olive) from the Netherlands or Germany.

——— to be imported from any other place only in ships belonging to Great Britain or Ireland, or of the same country with the goods.

Packet Boats, any goods or merchandize therein, without Commissioners licence.

Pepper, to be imported into the port of London only.

Pitch, from the Netherlands or Germany.

——— to be imported from any other place only in ships belonging to Great Britain or Ireland, or of the same country with the goods.

Plaiting for hats. See Hats.

Pot-ashes. See Ashes.

Prunes, may be imported only in ships belonging to Great Britain or Ireland, or of the same country with the goods.

Raisins, ditto.

Rosin, from the Netherlands or Germany.

——— from any other place, to be imported only in ships belonging to Great Britain or Ireland, or of the same country with the goods.

Rum, in casks under 60 gallons, but if imported from the British dominions in America in small casks, without fraud, &c. for private use, &c. the Commissioners may admit it to entry. See Spirits.

Sail Cloth or Canvas from Ireland, only in intire bolts or pieces.

Salt, in ships under 40 tons or otherwise than in bulk, except for the ship's provision.

——— of Great Britain or Ireland, or other Salt coming from Ireland, or the Isle of Man, except for the ship's provisions, or taken in to cure fish at sea from the Netherlands or Germany.

——— from any other place but in ships belonging to Great Britain or Ireland, or ships of the country of which it is the produce.

Silk, Thrown, of the growth or product of Turky, Persia, East India, China, or any other country, except Italy, Sicily and Naples, brought directly from those places respectively by sea, in ships legally navigated) may not be imported.

Soap, in any package less than 224 lb. weight.

Spicery imported by licence; the package must be, Cinnamon in bales of 70 lb. Nutmegs, Cloves, or Mace, in casks of 300 lb. or upwards.

——— except by licence, may not be imported from the Netherlands.

Spirits of any kind, in casks under 60 gallons, not to be imported from Europe in ships of any burthen, nor from other parts in ships under 100 tons, on forfeiture of ship and goods.

Starch, in any package less than 224 lb. weight.

Sugar, only in ships of Great Britain on Ireland, or of the built of the country of which it is the growth, &c.

Tar, from the Netherlands or Germany.

——— from any other place but in ships of Great Britain or Ireland, or of the built of the country of which it is the produce.

Tea, only from the place of its growth, though formerly exported from hence.

——— except by licence, in case the India Company do not supply the market in British-built ships.

Timber, to be imported only in ships of Great Britain or Ireland, or of the built of the country of which it is the growth.

Tobacco, of the British plantations in America, only in casks, &c. of 450 lb. weight.

[377]

—— from the Netherlands or Germany.

Turky goods, to be imported only in British-built ships, or ships of the country of which they are of the growth, &c.

Vinegar, to be imported only in ships of the built of Great-Britain or Ireland, or of the country of which it is the produce, &c.

Whalebone cut, (except in Fins.)

Wines, to be imported only in ships belonging to Great Britain or Ireland, or of the country of which the goods are the produce, &c.

—— no Wines, other than Rhenish from the Netherlands or Germany, except Hungary Wines, which may be imported from Hambro', paying duty as Rhenish.

—— Spanish, Portugal, and French Wines, in any smaller cask than an hogshead (except for private use).

—— in flasks, or bottles, or vessels containing less than 25 gallons, except French Wine in bottles and for private use; and Wines of the dominions of the Great Duke of Tuscany, in open flasks, or of Turkey or any other part of the Levant sea, in the manner as heretofore usually imported.

Goods prohibited to be Exported.

Ashes, white.
Bell, Metal.
Boxes, for Clocks or Watches, without the movements, &c.
Brass, Metal.
Bullion, unless a certificate is produced to the Commissioners that it is foreign, and not molten from Coin of this realm, or clippings thereof; nor plate wrought in this kingdom.
Cases, for Clocks and Watches of any metal without the movements, &c.
Clocks, without the movements, made fit for use, with the maker's name.
Coin of Gold and Silver without the King's licence, except foreign Coin upon entry. Repealed as to Ireland.
Copper, except made of British ore.
—— in shots or bars, not to be exported or carried coastwise, when restrained by order in Council or Proclamation.
Dial Plates for Clocks or Watches, without the movements, &c.
Frames or Engines for knitting of Stockings.
Fullers Earth, or Scouring Clay.
Gunpowder, when the price exceeds 5l. per barrel.
Hides of Ox, Steer, Cow, Bull, or Calf, except Calf Skins dressed without the hair, unless for the ship's use, not exceeding 6 lives.
Horns, British, unwrought.
Isle of Man, Wrought Silks, Bengals, and Stuffs mixed with Silk or Herba, of the manufacture of Persia, China, or East-India; Callicoes painted, dyed, printed, or stained there, Cambricks or French Lawn, may not be exported to the Isle of Man.
Lambs, alive.
Latten.
Metal, Brass, Copper, Latten, Bell-metal, Pan-metal, Gun-metal, Shruff-metal, (except Lead and Tin and Copper,

and Mundick, Metal made of British ores) and foreign Copper in bars.	Tea, to Ireland, or the British plantations, except in the original package.	per pair, and Spinners Cards not exceeding 1 s. per pair, exported to any British Colony in America.
Money. See Coin.	Thrumbs.	Watches without the movement, or fit for use
Mortlings.	Tobacco-pipe Clay, except to the British Sugar Colonies in the West Indies, for a limited time.	with the maker's name.
Mundick Metal. See Metal.		Wool, Sheep, Woolfells, Mortlings, Shortlings, Yarn made of Wool, Woolflocks, Fullers Earth, Fulling Clay, and Tobacco-pipe Clay
Packet-boats, any goods or merchandize therein without licence.	Tools or Utensils, Machines, Engines, Press Paper, Implements, or any Model or Plan thereof, in the Cotton, Linen, Woollen, or Silk manufactures, may not be shipped, unless to be directly landed again in Great Britain or Ireland.	
Pan Metal See Metal.		
Rams, alive.		
Scowering Clay.		— Coverlids, Waddings, or other manufactures of Wool slightly woven or put up together, so as they may be reduced to Wool and used as Wool again, or Mattresses or Beds stuffed with combed Wool, or Wool fit for combing.
Sheep, alive.		
Shortlings.	not to be collected together to be conveyed by open sea to any place, except to Great Britain.	
Shruff Metal. See Metal.		
Silver melten, except marked at Goldsmiths hall, and by certificate, &c. See Bullion.	but not to extend to Wool Cards or Stock Cards, not exceeding in value 5 s.	Woollen Yarn.
Tallow.		Worsted.

N. B. Goods of Muscovy, Russia, or the dominions of the Emperor or Empress thereof, are not to be imported, except in ships belonging to Great Britain or Ireland, or of the same country with the goods.

—— of Asia, Africa, or America, must be brought only in British ships legally navigated from the place of their growth, &c. or from such ports where they are, usually have been, or can only be, first shipped for transportation, except Oil of Cloves, Oil of Cinnamon, Oil of Mace, and Oil of Nutmegs.

the usual places of Lading in British ships, except Raw Silk and Mohair Yarn, which can be brought only from the Dominions of the Grand Seignior.

—— but not to extend to Goods of the Streights or Levant seas, and East India Goods, from

Spain, Portugal, or the Western islands called the Azores, or Madeira, or Canaries, respectively, in British ships.

nor to Goods of the Spanish or Portugueze Plantations, which may be brought from

nor to Bullion, or Gold taken as prize.

nor to Persian Goods brought through Russia by the Russia Company.

nor to Gum Senega imported from Europe by British.

──────── nor to Cochineal or Indigo.
──────── nor to Spice by licence.
──────── nor to coarse printed Callicoes, and other prohibited East India Goods, Cowries and Arrangoes imported by licence.
──────── may not be put on board *ships or vessels of war*, upon forfeiture of the value, or £500, to be paid by the Commander, or other officer receiving or permitting the Goods to be received on board, besides being cashiered, &c.
──────── but not to extend to Goods for the *sole* use of the ship.
──────── nor to Gold, Silver, or Jewels.
──────── nor to Goods wrecked, or in imminent danger thereof.
──────── nor to what shall be ordered on board by the Lords of the Admiralty.
──────── imported or exported in the *Packet-boats* (unless by the Allowance of the managers or chief officers of the Customs) are forfeited, with £100 penalty on the Master, besides loss of place.

But during the present hostilities with France, Spain, or the United Provinces, Goods of Muscovy, Russia, or the dominions thereof, or any Masts, Timber or Boards, Salt, Pitch, Tar, Rosin, Hemp, Flax, Raisins, Figs, Prunes, Olive Oils, Corn or Grain, Sugar, Pot Ashes, Wines, Vinegar, or Spirits called Aqua Vitæ, or Brandy-Wine, Currants, and Goods of the Ottoman or Turkish empire, may be imported in ships built in Great Britain, or in any of his Majesty's dominions, and sold to Foreigners, so as the Master and three-fourths of the mariners are of the country of which the Goods are the growth, &c.

The above Goods (or any other) being the produce of the Streights or Levant seas, may be imported in neutral ships from any place.

Flax, or Flax Seed, may be imported in neutral ships navigated with foreign mariners.

Naval Stores, laden in neutral vessels, may be purchased for his Majesty's service by the Commissioners of the Navy, and landed in Great Britain.

Goods of the growth, &c. of any place under the dominion of the Crown of Portugal may be imported by any persons in Portugueze vessels from Portugal, or the Western islands called the Azores, or Madeiras.

Any sort of Wool, Barilla, Jesuits Bark, and Linen Yarn, may be imported by any person in neutral ships from any place.

Orchella Weed and Cobalt may be imported by any person from any place in British ships legally navigated, or in neutral ships navigated by foreign mariners, free of duty, on entry, &c.

For a limited time { trading vessels may be navigated with three-fourths foreign seamen and one-fourth British.
                   { Italian fine organzined thrown Silk may be imported from any place in any ship.

F I N I S.

ERRATA.

In Page 46—omit the Note.
48—add to the Note " except Coffee."
52—omit the Note.
53—omit the Second Note.
54—omit the Note.
55 & 56—omit the second Note.
115—in the column of References, *for* F h *read* F q, *and for* C d *read* C g.
128, 142, 149, 165—in the Note, *for* 20*s*. *read* 100 *l*.
130—omit the words " except Fish" in the Note.
172—omit the Note.
178—in the column of References, *for* V *read* V c, and omit the Note.
179—in the column of References, *for* V *read* V f.
316—in the column of References, *for* K d *read* L d.
346—in the column of References, *for* E b *read* I b.
357—in the column of References, *for* V *read* V b.

www.ingramcontent.com/pod-product-compliance
Lightning Source LLC
Chambersburg PA
CBHW032019220426
43664CB00006B/299